Copyright's Paradox

NEIL
WEINSTOCK
NETANEL

Copyright's Paradox

UNIVERSITY PRESS

2008

OXFORD
UNIVERSITY PRESS

Oxford University Press, Inc., publishes works that further
Oxford University's objective of excellence
in research, scholarship, and education.

Oxford   New York
Auckland   Cape Town   Dar es Salaam   Hong Kong   Karachi
Kuala Lumpur   Madrid   Melbourne   Mexico City   Nairobi
New Delhi   Shanghai   Taipei   Toronto

With offices in
Argentina   Austria   Brazil   Chile   Czech Republic   France   Greece
Guatemala   Hungary   Italy   Japan   Poland   Portugal   Singapore
South Korea   Switzerland   Thailand   Turkey   Ukraine   Vietnam

Copyright © 2008 by Neil Weinstock Netanel

Published by Oxford University Press, Inc.
198 Madison Avenue, New York, NY 10016

www.oup.com

Oxford is a registered trademark of Oxford University Press

Library of Congress Cataloging-in-Publication Data
Netanel, Neil.
Copyright's paradox / Neil Weinstock Netanel.
   p. cm.
ISBN 978-0-19-513762-0
1. Copyright—United States.   2. Freedom of speech—United States.
3. Freedom of expression—United States.   I. Title.
KF2994.N46 2008
346.7304'82—dc22   2007022685

9 8 7 6 5 4 3 2

Printed in the United States of America
on acid-free paper

For Niki, Shalev, and Adam

———

And in memory of our dear friend,
Yemima Paz, ז״ל,
whose zest for life overflowed life's bounds

COPYRIGHT AND FREEDOM OF SPEECH have intertwined since John Milton's eloquent call in *Areopagitica* to repeal the Licensing Act that gave the London Stationers' an exclusive charter to publish books.[1] The nascent copyright law and free speech jurisprudence that arose in the Licensing Act's wake came to promote a shared understanding that public liberty is guaranteed only when knowledge is widely diffused, when "the plain citizen and planter reads and judges for himself."[2]

Yet the copyright–free speech embrace has unraveled in recent decades. In many ways, copyright now stands for private censorship, not public liberty. Copyright once helped to free authors and the press from servile dependency on royal and church patronage; it now gives behemoth media conglomerates control over the images, sounds, and texts that are the very language of our culture. Copyright once made it possible for authors to disseminate their message to a broad audience; it now makes outlaws of millions of individuals who post their creative digital remixes and mashups of copyrighted expression on MySpace and YouTube. Copyright once underwrote new contributions to our store of knowledge; it now places archival material out of reach for documentary filmmakers and online libraries. Copyright once supported Thomas Paine and Charles Dickens; it now provides corporations, churches, and authors' estates a tool to silence critics.

Those changes, both real and perceived, flow from a myriad of social, technological, economic, and legal developments. Primary among them, copyright has metamorphosed from a narrow, short-term exclusive right to print books to a broad bundle of rights lasting for upwards of a century. To the extent copyright owners' permission must be obtained even for quite minimal, ethereal borrowings from existing works and copyrights endure for a time that economists tell us is "functionally perpetual," copyright will increasingly stand at odds with the speech of critics, satirists, archivists, virtual street corner pamphleteers, and, indeed, any writer, artist, filmmaker, or musician who would draw upon existing expression in conveying his or her own message.

In this book I trace the growing tension between freedom of expression and copyright law's grant of property rights in expression. That tension cannot be eradicated: by giving authors exclusive rights, copyright *both* encourages the creation of new works *and* necessarily prevents some speakers from copying from existing expression to convey their message effectively. But while that tension is inevitable, it is not wholly irremediable. As I argue, copyright can and should be redrawn to better serve free speech goals in both traditional and digital media.

I have two caveats about my project. First, due to space limitations, I focus almost entirely on the law and system of free expression in the United States. Copyright and free speech simultaneously face and embrace each other in other countries as well, and while copyright's paradox has received first, most intensive attention in the United States, non-American scholars, lawmakers, and judges have also joined the fray, yielding much insight.[3] I hope that my foreign colleagues will draw parallels to my exploration of the U.S. experience.

Second, especially as applied to digital networks, copyright is a highly fluid area of law and policy with new, noteworthy developments taking place almost every day. Unfortunately for readers, but perhaps thankfully for tired authors, there comes a time when texts published in hard copy are put to bed and can no longer reflect ongoing developments. With isolated exceptions, this book reflects developments only through April 1, 2007. I trust that its thesis and argument will remain relevant for a good time after that, even as some of its detail is overtaken by subsequent events.

This book has been more than a decade in the making. My study of copyright and free speech originated in my doctoral studies and dissertation at Stanford Law School, which I began in 1993. Not surprisingly, my work has undergone considerable transformation in the ensuing years, reflecting new technological and legal developments and picking up themes from several articles I have since written and presented at various fora.

I owe tremendous gratitude to the many colleagues and friends who have inspired, taught, and debated with me along the way. First and foremost, Ed Baker, Terry Fisher, Jessica Litman, David Nimmer, Tony Reese, and Tim Wu read my entire manuscript and gave me invaluable comments. This book reflects many of their suggestions and, indeed, much that I have learned from their writing and conversation over the years. The remaining flaws are, of course, my own. I also owe a special debt to Peggy Radin, Paul Goldstein, and Tom Grey, my mentors at Stanford, who so generously took me under their wing, introduced me to new intellectual horizons, challenged my thinking, and supported me in the early stages of this project and my academic career. My special thanks to Paul Goldstein for his support and generosity of spirit even as I have disagreed with him in print (including in parts of this book). I am deeply thankful as well to those who have reviewed, engaged, and encouraged me to write portions of this book or precursor articles. They include, most prominently, Larry Lessig, Mark Lemley, Niva Elkin-Koren, Mike Abramowicz, Yochai Benkler, Pam Samuelson, Howard Shelanski, Bernt Hugenholtz, Jonathan Griffiths, Fiona Macmillan, Christopher Yoo, Eli Noam, Kim Treiger, Eugene Volokh, Willy Forbath, Jack Balkin, Wendy Gordon, and Diane Zimmerman. My thinking and knowledge have also benefited greatly from conversations with David Ginsburg and fellow members of the Los Angeles Copyright Society, as well as from online discussion with academic colleagues on Cyberprof and musicians, technologists, and lawyers on Pho. A further thanks to my research assistant Lisa Kohn, who edited my entire manuscript in addition to providing crucial research. Without her thorough work, my manuscript would not now be a book. Finally, I greatly appreciate the encouragement, direction, and corrections of my editors at Oxford University Press, Dedi Feldman, James Cook, and Keith Faivre.

My most profound debt is to my family. Of particular relevance to this book, to Moshe for sharing experiences of teaching and scholarship; to Phil for our discussions of cutting-edge issues in telecommunications; to Peter and Paula for lively conversation about everything from democratic politics to philosophy of the mind; to Mom and Dad for endless support and encouragement—and tirelessly asking me, "So when will you finish the book?"; to my sons, Shalev and Adam, for introducing me to wonderful new music and letting me tell you some of the copyright stories behind it; and most of all, to Niki, עיניים שלי, for sharing your life with me . . . and, for over half our marriage, with this book.

CONTENTS

Copyright's Paradox

CHAPTER ONE

Introduction

A *"Largely Ignored Paradox"*

THE U.S. SUPREME COURT has famously labeled copyright "the engine of free expression."[1] Copyright law, the Court tells us, provides a vital economic incentive for the creation and distribution of much of the literature, commentary, music, art, and film that makes up our public discourse.

Yet copyright also burdens speech. We often copy or build upon another's words, images, or music to convey our own ideas effectively. We cannot do that if a copyright holder withholds permission or insists upon a license fee that is beyond our means. And copyright does not extend merely to literal copying. It can also prevent parodying, remolding, critically dissecting, or incorporating portions of existing expression into a new, independently created work.

Consider *The Wind Done Gone,* a recent, best-selling novel by African American writer Alice Randall. Randall's novel revisits the setting and characters of Margaret Mitchell's classic Civil War saga, *Gone with the Wind,* from the viewpoint of a slave. In marked contrast to Mitchell's romantic portrait of antebellum plantation life, Randall's story is laced with miscegenation and slaves' calculated manipulation of their masters. As Randall explained, she wrote her novel to "explode" the racist stereotypes that she believes are perpetuated by Mitchell's mythic tale.[2] Perhaps Randall could have vented her rage in an op-ed piece, street corner protest, or scholarly article instead. But what more poignant way to drive her point home than to write a sequel that turns Mitchell's iconic story on its head?

Mitchell's heirs did not suffer Randall's adulterations gladly. They brought a copyright infringement action against Randall's publisher, and a Georgia district court preliminarily enjoined the novel's publication, castigating Randall's upending of Mitchell's classic as "unabated piracy."[3] Yet the Eleventh Circuit Court of Appeals soon vacated the preliminary injunction. It held that by barring public access to Randall's "viewpoint in the form of expression that she chose," the trial court's order acted "as a prior restraint on speech," standing sharply "at odds with the shared principles of the First Amendment and copyright law."

Copyright is thus a potential impediment to free expression no less than an "engine of free expression." Copyright does provide an economic incentive for speech. But it may also prevent speakers from effectively conveying their message and challenging prevailing views. Indeed, while Randall eventually emerged victorious, not all courts have proven as solicitous of First Amendment values as the Eleventh Circuit panel that lifted the ban on her novel.

In a seminal article from 1970, Melville Nimmer, the leading copyright and First Amendment scholar of his day, aptly termed the copyright–free speech conflict a "largely ignored paradox."[4] At that time, those who valued creative expression happily favored both strong copyright protection and rigorous judicial enforcement of First Amendment rights without perceiving any potential tension between the two.

That sanguine view, first questioned by Professor Nimmer, has now been shattered by a spate of widely debated lawsuits. The battle over *The Wind Done Gone* led op-ed pieces across the nation to ponder whether copyright unduly chills minority voices. When the Supreme Court rejected Web publisher Eric Eldred's constitutional challenge to the Sonny Bono Copyright Term Extension Act—which gave copyright holders another twenty years of protection for existing books, movies, songs, and other works—the *New York Times* headlines proclaimed a "corporate victory, but one that raises public consciousness."[5] The American Civil Liberties Union stepped in to defend artist Tom Forsythe against Mattel's copyright and trademark infringement action over Forsythe's photographs of naked Barbie dolls attacked by household appliances—photographs, the artist stated, that were designed to lay bare the "objectification of women" and "perfection-obsessed consumer culture" that the Barbie character embodies. Princeton University computer science professor Edward Felten petitioned a court to affirm his First Amendment right to present his research at an academic conference after a recording industry trade association threatened that the presentation would subject him to liability under the Digital

Millennium Copyright Act (DMCA). Martin Luther King's heirs provoked concerted media protest when they sued CBS for copyright infringement over the network's documentary on the civil rights movement that included some of its original 1963 footage of King delivering his seminal "I Have a Dream" speech. Diebold Election Systems, a leading producer of electronic voting machines, sent copyright infringement cease-and-desist letters to three college students and their Internet service providers in a vain attempt to quash the Internet posting of internal company e-mails revealing technical problems with the machines' performance and integrity. Publishers and authors sued to prevent Google and several major research libraries from making vast repositories of books and other printed material available to Internet users for online search. Millions of users of peer-to-peer file-trading networks, like Grokster, Kazaa, and the original Napster, have been given cause to consider whether assembling and exchanging a personalized mix of one's favorite music recordings (or a creative "remix" of segments of various recordings) is an exercise of expressive autonomy or the deplorable theft of another's intellectual property. The *New York Times Magazine* ran a cover story on this emerging "copyright war," encapsulating the tumultuous crosscurrents both in the article's perplexed, interrogatory title, "The Tyranny of Copyright?" and in its unmistakably declarative notice, "Copyright 2004 The New York Times Company."[6]

Why has the conflict between copyright and free speech come so virulently to the fore? What values and practices does it put at stake? How should the conflict be resolved? These are the principal questions this book seeks to answer.

At its core, copyright has indeed served as an engine of free expression. In line with First Amendment goals, the Constitution empowers Congress to enact a copyright law in order to "Promote the Progress of Science," meaning to "advance learning." Copyright law accomplishes this objective most obviously by providing an economic incentive for the creation and dissemination of numerous works of authorship. Yet copyright promotes free speech in other ways as well. As it spurs creative production, copyright underwrites a community of authors and publishers who are not beholden to government officials for financial support. Copyright's support for authorship may also underscore the value of fresh ideas and individual contributions to our public discourse.

But copyright has strayed from its traditional, speech-enhancing core, so much so that in its present configuration and under present conditions, copyright imposes an unacceptable burden on the values that underlie First

Amendment guarantees of free speech. As the Supreme Court has emphasized, the First Amendment aspires to the "widest possible dissemination of
information from diverse and antagonistic sources."[7] Yet copyright too often
stifles criticism, encumbers individual self-expression, and ossifies highly
skewed distributions of expressive power. Copyright's speech burdens cut a
wide swath, chilling core political speech such as news reporting and political commentary, as well as church dissent, historical scholarship, cultural
critique, artistic expression, and quotidian entertainment. And copyright
imposes those speech burdens to a far greater extent than can be justified by
applauding its "engine of free expression" role.

The primary, immediate cause for copyright's untoward chilling of speech
is that copyright has come increasingly to resemble and be thought of as a
full-fledged property right rather than a limited federal grant designed
to further a particular public purpose. As traditionally conceived, copyright
law strikes a careful balance. To encourage authors to create and disseminate
original expression, it accords them a bundle of exclusive rights in their works.
But to promote public education and creative exchange, it both sharply cir-
cumscribes the scope of those exclusive rights and invites audiences and
subsequent authors freely to use existing works in every conceivable manner
that falls outside the copyright owner's domain. Accordingly, through most
of the some 300 years since the first modern copyright statute was enacted,
copyright has been narrowly tailored to advance learning and the wide circulation of information and ideas, ends that are very much in line with those
of the First Amendment. Copyright holders' rights have been quite limited
in scope and duration and have been perforated by significant exceptions
designed to support robust debate and a vibrant public domain. Indeed, as
courts have repeatedly suggested, it is copyright's traditional free speech
safety valves—principally the fair use privilege, copyrights' limited duration,
and the rule that copyright protection extends only to literal form, not idea
or fact—that have enabled copyright law to pass First Amendment muster.

In recent decades, however, the copyright bundle has grown exponentially. It now comprises more rights, according control over more uses of an
author's work, and lasting for a longer time, than ever before. If copyright
law remained as it was in 1936, the year Margaret Mitchell wrote *Gone with
the Wind,* Mitchell's copyright would have already expired, and Randall
could have written her sequel without having to defend a copyright infringement lawsuit.[8] Under copyright law as it stood when Martin Luther
King delivered "I Have a Dream," King would have likely been held to
dedicate his speech to the public domain, leaving CBS and anyone else free to
incorporate King's words in historical accounts of the civil rights era.[9] Prior

to the Digital Millennium Copyright Act of 1998, Professor Felten's paper on digital music encryption would have fallen entirely outside the reach of copyright law. Had he presented his findings before the DMCA took effect, he would have had no need to invoke the First Amendment to protect his right to speak.

There are a number of interrelated causes for copyright's ungainly distension, including relentless copyright industry lobbying, judges' inconstant application of copyright's traditional free speech safeguards, and the prevalence of a "clearance culture" in which distributors regularly require that authors obtain copyright licenses even for uses of others' expression that are likely noninfringing.[10] Whatever the cause, as copyright expands, its fundamental character changes. As "engine of free expression," copyright law's traditional aim has been to provide sufficient remuneration so that authors and publishers will create and distribute original expression. Copyright holders have enjoyed exclusive rights in their works, but those rights have been narrowly tailored in line with the understanding that they serve primarily to provide a public benefit. In concert with copyright's expansion, however, copyright is increasingly treated more akin to conventional property than a finely honed instrument of expressive diversity.

The preeminent eighteenth-century English jurist, Sir William Blackstone, depicted property as an individual's "sole and despotic dominion . . . over the external things in the world, in total exclusion of the right of any other individual in the universe."[11] In actual fact, property rights come in varied shapes and sizes and are subject to policy-laden limitations. Nonetheless, Blackstone's hyperbolic, individual-as-sovereign formulation reverberates within the libertarian ethos of American culture to heavily influence the way we think about "property." As such, it sets the default assumption for demarcating property rights.

So it is with copyright. Property rhetoric, whether invoked reflexively or strategically, has tended to support a vision of copyright as a foundational entitlement, a broad "sole and despotic dominion" over each and every possible use of a work rather than a limited government grant narrowly tailored to serve a public purpose. Examples begin with Blackstone himself, who argued that copyrights are common-law "property" and should thus last in perpetuity. In similar fashion, today's motion picture industry lobbyists insist that Congress must mandate technological controls that would override fair use in order to "protect private property from being pillaged." And courts brand as "theft" any unauthorized use of a copyright holder's work, including even uses like Alice Randall's that contain considerable independent creative expression and critique.

The more copyright embraces the features and rhetoric of conventional property, the more it serves not just to spur Margaret Mitchell's creation of *Gone with the Wind* but to bolster her heirs' efforts to control how that work is presented and perceived well over half a century later. The result is a sharpening conflict between copyright and free speech.

———

The copyright–free speech conflict cuts across traditional and emerging electronic media alike. Yet digital technology adds a vast new dimension. Armed with personal computers, digital recording devices, and the Internet, millions of people the world over can cut, paste, and recombine segments of existing sound recordings, movies, photographs, and video games to create new works and distribute them to a global audience. Such creative appropriation has given birth to entire new art forms: remixes, mashups, fan videos, machinima, and more. It has also spawned an acrimonious debate about copyright's place in the digital age, pitting entertainment media bent on stamping out massive "digital piracy" against individuals who increasingly perceive copyright as an undue and unworthy impingement on their liberty and expressive autonomy.

Copyright law was designed to create order in the publishing trade, to prevent ruinous competition when unscrupulous firms engage in wholesale commercial piracy. So how does copyright law apply in an age in which millions of individuals are both authors and publishers? How is copyright to respond when anyone can easily make perfect copies of existing works, as well as cut, paste, edit, remix, and post them on YouTube, MySpace, FanFiction.net, Machinima.com, and a multitude of other Web sites online? The incumbent copyright industries understandably view these ubiquitous acts as a mortal threat, worse even than the commercial piracy of old. They argue that more extensive copyright protection and enforcement mechanisms are required to combat the nefarious "culture of contempt for intellectual property" that courses through the Internet.[12]

The industries have met a receptive ear in Congress and the courts. And evoking Blackstone, the industries insist that if they are to serve the digital marketplace, they must enjoy the effective and enforceable right to assert hermetic control—even greater control than was previously imaginable—over their movies, music recordings, and books. They must have the legal entitlement, if they wish to exercise it, to seal their content in tamper-proof containers and charge every time an Internet user reads, views, or hears a work online. To that end, the motion picture, recording, and publishing industries have begun to use digital encryption to control and meter access and uses of their content, and have successfully lobbied Congress to prohibit the circumvention of those technological controls even to engage in fair use.[13]

The industries have looked to traditional copyright to tame the Internet beast as well. They have sued thousands of individual file traders, as well as companies that facilitate peer-to-peer file trading. And motion picture studios and record labels are now taking on the remix culture of YouTube and MySpace. As I write these words, those sites are targets of lawsuits brought, respectively, by Viacom and Universal Music, characterizing them as iniquitous dens of "user-stolen" intellectual property.

At the other end of this Kulturkampf are scholars, bloggers, archivists, and activists who view the Internet as a precious opportunity to remake our public discourse. These commentators celebrate digital technology's capacity to unleash the power of individuals' speech and drastically reduce our dependence on the mass media for information, opinion, and entertainment. And—much to copyright industries' consternation—they tolerate file trading and herald individuals' creative appropriation and remixing as "the art through which free culture is built."[14] Some activists suggest, indeed, that the Internet will realize its full free speech potential only if copyright is banished from its realm. In this view, at its very best, copyright is irrelevant to the profuse and richly diverse array of expression that individuals regularly post on the Internet without any intention of preventing others from copying and borrowing as they wish. At worst, copyright and technology controls threaten to reshape the Internet into something like an expanded multichannel cable television or celestial jukebox, a platform for the one-way transmission of content from mass media conglomerates to passive consumers.

Real-world developments are rapidly overtaking some of the extreme positions that have been staked out. First and foremost, the sheer magnitude and global reach of peer-to-peer file trading, the explosive growth of Web sites featuring user-created content, and the freely copying and remixing mind-set of a generation of Internet users have thus far surpassed the copyright industries' ability to curtail, much less control. As a result, we are starting to see some cracks in the industries' opposition to freewheeling Internet culture. Warner Music, for instance, broke ranks with other major labels to license YouTube to show both Warner Music videos and user-created clips that incorporate Warner music. And after threatening to sue YouTube for "tens of millions of dollars," Universal Music followed in Warner's footsteps (but shortly thereafter sued MySpace). The YouTube deals reflect a growing blurring of Internet culture and traditional media: Rupert Murdoch bought MySpace, Simon & Schuster has signed book deals with fan fiction writers, newspaper Web sites feature numerous blogs and online reader discussion groups, and NewsCorp and NBC Universal announced plans to make TV and movie clips available for user sharing and remixing on their online video site.[15]

It is too soon to tell whether these moves will culminate in the copyright industries' acquiescent embrace of remix culture or an industry campaign to clip its wings. Much may depend on the outcome of the pending YouTube and MySpace litigation. Certainly, though, the battles that have raged in the space between digital anarchy and digital lockup will continue in new contexts, new media, and new uses of copyrighted expression.

———

This book takes First Amendment values as its lodestar for navigating that contested space. Copyright, I argue, should be delimited primarily by how it can truly serve as an "engine of free expression." Copyright's scope, duration, and character should be shaped to best further the First Amendment goals of robust debate and expressive diversity. Copyright law and policy can rightly accommodate other goals as well, including maximizing economic efficiency, securing authors' interest in creative control, and providing incentives for technological innovation. But overall, it is First Amendment values that should dominate and inform copyright.

My claim for employing free speech as the dominant metric to assess copyright law rests on two principal pillars. First, as a matter of normative principle, free speech concerns *should* play a central role in shaping copyright doctrine. Copyright law has the capacity to both promote and burden speech and thus implicates values that lie at the heart of our liberal democratic society. It behooves us to give those values considerable, if not overriding, weight in copyright law and policy.

Second, viewing copyright through a free speech lens makes clear, where other approaches do not, that determining copyright's character and reach *necessarily* rests on questions of speech and media policy. How broad and enduring should copyright holders' exclusive rights be? When should copyrights give way to fair use? In what circumstances should copyright holders' proprietary veto over unlicensed uses be replaced by a right of reasonable compensation? Our answers to such questions heavily impact the types of speech and speakers who will have a voice in our public discourse. They tip the scales between market and nonmarket expression and, often, between mainstream and dissident speakers. The free speech lens lays bare those trade-offs.

The First Amendment lodestar can helpfully guide us not only in assessing current copyright doctrine, but also in adapting copyright law to the rapidly changing conditions wrought by digital technology. Copyright can continue to serve as an engine of free expression in the digital arena. But to do so, copyright must be narrowly tailored to further its speech-enhancing objectives, no less than in traditional, off-line media. Contrary to what some entertainment industry lobbyists would have us believe, copyright is not ultimately about securing strong property rights. Rather, copyright's fundamental ends, like those of the First Amendment, are to "Promote the Progress of Science" by spurring the creation and widespread dissemination of diverse expression. To the extent exclusive rights in original expression best serve those ends, copyright doctrine should provide for proprietary rights. But to the extent property rights in expression unnecessarily stand as an obstacle to free speech, they should be limited in scope and duration or even jettisoned in favor of less constraining and less censorial mechanisms for securing authorship credit and remunerating producers and purveyors of original expression.[16]

My argument and analysis unfold in three parts. The first grounds my claim that our current bloated copyright imposes unacceptable burdens on speech. I begin in chapter 2 by providing concrete illustrations of why we should care, of how copyright often prevents speakers from effectively conveying their message. In chapter 3, I turn, more analytically, to our basic understandings of "free speech" and "First Amendment values." Given those understandings, copyright is properly said to burden "free speech" in some ways but does not truly implicate free speech concerns in some others. Finally, in chapter 4, I document the most troublesome areas of copyright expansion that fuel the copyright–free speech conflict.

The second part juxtaposes copyright's conflicting roles as engine of free expression and impediment to free expression. In chapter 5, I elucidate copyright's traditional "engine of free expression" role and consider whether copyright still serves that function given the profusion of nonmarket expression on the Internet. In chapter 6, I identify several distinct, if interrelated, ways in which copyright burdens speech. Those speech burdens include copyright holders' deliberate silencing of certain expressive uses of their works, speaker and distributor self-censorship in the face of copyright holder overreaching, prohibitively costly copyright license fees and transaction costs, and copyright law's buttressing of media concentration. Along the way, I show that even the influential school of economic analysis of copyright—which purports to consider only economic efficiency—must, by its very terms, ultimately devolve to making value judgments of speech policy. Chapter 7 then counters arguments that a proprietary, Blackstonian copyright would actually foster expressive diversity.

The third part presents a blueprint for addressing the copyright–free speech conflict. I argue in chapter 8 that a correct and consistent reading of the First Amendment would impose certain external constraints on copyright holder prerogatives, at the very least to ensure that copyright law's internal free speech safety valves live up to their task. Finally, in chapter 9, I present some proposals for modifying copyright law to better protect and promote First Amendment values beyond what is required as a matter of First Amendment doctrine. Copyright and free speech will always stand in some tension. But there are ways in which the copyright–free speech conflict can be ameliorated, in which copyright can continue to serve as an engine of free expression while maintaining ample room for speakers to build on copyrighted works to convey their message, express their personal commitments, and fashion new art.

CHAPTER TWO | From *Mein Kampf* to Google

FOR SOME, COPYRIGHT'S SPEECH burdens are painfully obvious. But many others do not perceive that copyright poses any serious conflict with freedom of speech. They view copyright infringers as merely making "other people's speeches."[1] Or they say that, after all, the underlying ideas and information presented in authors' works are free for anyone to use, that copyright merely prevents others from copying the unique way in which a particular author presents ideas. Or they view copyright as basically just about trivial entertainment products, nothing with any real import for expressive autonomy and diversity.

This chapter presents some illustrative examples that ought to at least give doubters some pause; we leave for later discussion whether, when, and how copyright's speech burdens should be ameliorated. The examples range from speech that is overtly political to purely artistic, from fantasy to documentary, from discrete cases to entire expressive genres, from religious tracts to counterculture comics, from analog to digital, from out-and-out copying to highly creative recasting, and from copyright holders' calculated suppression of unwanted expression to speakers' inability to pay the copyright license fee that was offered. Like the battle over Alice Randall's *The Wind Done Gone,* they demonstrate that copyright may indeed prevent us from effectively conveying a message, pursuing deeply held beliefs, expressing artistic inspiration, participating in a cultural tradition, or, for that matter, promoting "the progress of science."

Alan Cranston's Unauthorized Mein Kampf

Alan Cranston served in the U.S. Senate for more than two decades, beginning in January 1969. As a young man, in the late 1930s, Cranston worked as a journalist for the International News Service, covering England, Germany, and Italy. While stationed in Europe, Cranston, a fluent speaker of German, read Adolf Hitler's *Mein Kampf* and reacted with horror. But when Cranston later came across the Nazi blueprint's official English translation in Macy's bookstore in New York, he was doubly disturbed. The official translation was a heavily edited, bowdlerized version designed to make Hitler more palatable for British and American readers. Cranston was so incensed that he set out to produce his own, unauthorized translation. Published just months before Germany's blitzkrieg invasion of Poland, Cranston's translation also heavily abridged Hitler's two-volume original but highlighted the ominous passages that Hitler's licensed translator had strategically expurgated. To further sound the alarm, Cranston added critical commentary unmasking Hitler's propaganda and distortions and featured a lurid, red cover depicting Hitler carving up the world. Cranston's edition pledged, "Not 1 cent of royalty to Hitler," and promised that any profits would go to help refugees from the Nazi Reich. Cranston's thirty-two-page newsprint pamphlet, priced at only ten cents a copy, sold half a million copies in ten days.

Hitler's U.S. publisher was Houghton Mifflin. Years later that firm championed freedom of speech in its defense against the Margaret Mitchell estate lawsuit over *The Wind Done Gone*. But, in 1939, Houghton Mifflin was the aggrieved copyright owner. It sued Cranston for copyright infringement, and upon Houghton Mifflin's motion, the court enjoined further publication of Cranston's avowedly anti-Hitler translation.[2] With that, Cranston ceased further distribution and, at this critical time in history, the American public was left without his pointed corrective to the whitewashed translation.[3]

Worldwide Church of God Dissidents

Herbert Armstrong was the founder and pastor general of the Worldwide Church of God. Shortly before his death in 1986, Armstrong completed a book, *Mystery of the Ages,* in which Armstrong pontificated on a variety of issues, including divorce, remarriage, divine healing, and race relations. The Worldwide Church of God distributed more than 9 million free copies of *Mystery of the Ages.* But some two years after Armstrong's death, the church's

Advisory Council of Elders disclaimed a number of Armstrong's positions. The church then ceased distribution of the book and destroyed all remaining inventory copies, expressing particular concern that Armstrong had "conveyed outdated views that were racist in nature" and would perpetuate "ecclesiastical error."[4]

Unable to abide the church's new dogma, two former church ministers founded the Philadelphia Church of God, a breakaway sect that preached strict adherence to the teachings of Herbert Armstrong. It viewed *Mystery of the Ages* as central to its religious practice and made the book required reading for all new members. When the Philadelphia Church began making and distributing copies of the book, the Worldwide Church did not rest at renunciation to suppress this heresy. It sued the offshoot church for copyright infringement.

The district court found in favor of the defendants, but the Ninth Circuit reversed. It found that, as a matter of law, the Philadelphia Church was not entitled to claim fair use. "Even an author who ha[s] disavowed any intention to publish his work during his lifetime [is] entitled to protection of his copyright," the court opined.[5] "The public interest in the free flow of information is assured by the law's refusal to recognize a valid copyright in facts."[6] (If someone held a copyright in the Bible and sued to prevent its distribution, would the court be so sanguine that the law's refusal to recognize copyright in facts is sufficient to protect free speech?) So holding, the Ninth Circuit remanded for entry of a preliminary injunction against the Philadelphia Church, pending a trial on damages.

The Ninth Circuit's ruling is typical of a number of cases involving the publication of religious tracts, sometimes for use by adherents and sometimes in order to criticize the mainstream church. In case after case, courts have applied copyright, denied fair use, and enjoined publication.

Jon Else's Stagehands' Ring Cycle

Jon Else is a widely acclaimed documentary filmmaker and a journalism professor at the University of California at Berkeley. In 1990, Else filmed a documentary entitled *Sing Faster: The Stagehands' Ring Cycle.* The film portrays a San Francisco Opera production of Richard Wagner's *Ring Cycle* from the perspective of the union stagehands working behind the scenes.[7] As seen in the interwoven shots of foreground and background action, both onstage and off, Else adroitly juxtaposed two sharply contrasting realms, each an integral component of the production: the stylized, fantastical heights of

German Romantic opera and the sometimes frenetic, sometimes tedious workaday world of the stagehands.

At one point, Else focused on stagehands playing checkers in a backstage room while the opera was being performed onstage. In a corner of the room was a television set, and at the instant Else filmed the stagehands, a scene from an episode of *The Simpsons* featuring Homer Simpson happened to be playing. The checkers scene in Else's film contained a 4.5-second serendipitous shot of Homer Simpson, out of focus and with no sound, on the television in the background.

It took Else nine years to obtain funding to complete the editing and production of his one-hour-long film. When the Public Broadcasting Service agreed to air *The Stagehands' Ring Cycle* in 2000, Else was required to complete a visual cue sheet and obtain copyright releases for any copyrighted material appearing in any scene, as is typical for broadcasters' errors and omissions insurance. Else assumed that obtaining release for *The Simpsons* background shot would be a trivial matter, and so it seemed at first. The assistant to *The Simpsons* creator Matt Groening told Else that including the shot in Else's film was no problem at all, but that Else would have to check with Groening's production company's corporate parent. The parent told Else the same: "As far as we're concerned, you're most welcome to use the shot, but you need to check with our parent company." That led Else to Twentieth Century Fox Film Corporation, holder of the copyright in *The Simpsons.* Fox insisted on a licensing fee of $10,000, a fee—for a 4.5-second out-of-focus, no-sound background shot—several orders of magnitude higher than the licensing fees that Else paid to clear other copyrights for his film.

Else pleaded that his film was a PBS documentary, not a commercial venture, and that *The Simpsons* shot had been entirely unplanned. Fox explained that the $10,000 fee was the company's minimum rate for non-commercial documentary films. Else told Fox that he would have to cut the scene from his film rather than pay anything more than a fraction of Fox's demanded fee. To no avail.[8]

Else consulted with copyright counsel. He was advised, absolutely correctly: "Your shot is most probably a fair use, but, given the unpredictability and inconsistencies of fair use case law, you can't be certain. And they will drive you into the ground in litigation." Even if Else had been willing to defend his fair use in court, he would have been lucky to find a broadcaster and distributor willing to take that risk.

Else kept the checkers scene in his film, but he digitally removed *The Simpsons* from the television screen and replaced it with an excerpt from another of his films. As a result, Else's audience has been deprived of a shot poignantly showing Homer Simpson, perhaps the quintessential popular culture foil to Wagnerian high art, as part of the stagehands' background to an opera about Teutonic gods. And, no less to Else's dismay, a film that is supposed to be a documentary contains a bit of calculated untruth.

A recent study, *Untold Stories: Creative Consequences of the Rights Clearance Culture for Documentary Filmmakers,* makes abundantly clear that Else's experience is anything but atypical.[9] Documentary filmmakers regularly edit out background footage and music to avoid the increasing costs, delays, difficulties, and barriers of obtaining copyright clearances. Moreover, filmmakers typically face broadcasters, distributors, and errors and omission insurance carriers who insist on such clearances even for uses of public domain material and for incorporation of copyrighted images and music that should fit comfortably within the realm of fair use. As a result, the documentary films we see have often been stripped of clips, background shots, music, and archival footage that would have greatly enhanced poignancy, artistic quality, and historical elucidation.

Journalist Declan McCullagh

Declan McCullagh is a reporter for CNET News. While researching a story on airport security measures, McCullagh came upon four documents on the Transportation Security Administration Web site that, according to a brief description on the site, covered "airport security procedures, the relationship between federal and local police, and a 'liability information sheet.' "[10] The documents were encrypted; the Web site permitted McCullagh to download the files but required a password to open and read them. A confidential source gave McCullagh what the reporter believed to be the correct secret password to the documents.

Like any journalist worth his salt, McCullagh's first impulse must have been to enter the password, read the documents, and report on any newsworthy contents. That has been the soul of investigative newsgathering since long before the *New York Times* published the Pentagon Papers. But McCullagh, who often reports on technology and intellectual property issues, feared that, by using a purloined password to de-encrypt the document, he could face civil and criminal liability under the Digital Millennium Copyright Act. The DMCA forbids circumventing a technological protection measure—for example, encryption—that effectively controls access to copyrighted material, and courts have held that there is no fair use exception to that prohibition. McCullagh chose the better part of valor. He declined to use the password to view the documents but reported on his own dilemma with the hope that, perhaps, some reporter in a country not shackled by the DMCA would uncover the contents of the mysterious documents.

Ironically, a couple courts have since held that circumventing means only hacking a technology protection measure not using a password that the content provider issued to an authorized user.[11] But, even if that interpretation continues to prevail, the DMCA still threatens journalists, muckrakers, and whistleblowers who, without a password, can view encrypted documents only by using computer technology or know-how to circumvent the encryption.

Free Republic Web Site

Free Republic is a Web site described by its operators as an "online gathering place for independent, grassroots conservatism."[12] Part of the Web site is devoted to criticizing the way the mainstream media cover current events and politics. In doing so, Free Republic Web site visitors regularly posted verbatim copies of various *Los Angeles Times* and *Washington Post* news articles and then added remarks and commentary critical of the articles. Visitors also discussed the underlying news events covered in the articles.

The *Times* and *Post* sued to stop the copying and posting of their articles. In response, Free Republic's operators asserted a fair use and First Amendment defense. They contended that copying was necessary to enable Free Republic Web site visitors effectively to express their views concerning media coverage of current events. They emphasized that the omissions and biases in newspaper articles would be difficult to convey unless Free Republic visitors could post the full text of each article.

The court rejected Free Republic's claims.[13] The Free Republic defendants, the court held, failed to show that copying news articles verbatim was essential to communicating Web site visitors' opinions and criticisms. Even where media coverage was the subject of the critique, the court held, the gist of the comments usually could be communicated without full-text copying of the article. Finally, the court found that rather than copying news articles, defendants could post links to plaintiffs' Web sites, even if Internet users following links to noncurrent articles have to pay a fee to access *L.A. Times* and *Washington Post* Web site archives.

Faced with a $1 million damages award, the Free Republic operators settled the case rather than bring an appeal. For months thereafter, the site contained no discussion of *L.A. Times* or *Washington Post* articles. Now, apparently having revamped its Web site technology, Free Republic includes just the first paragraph of the article being discussed, followed by a link that sends discussants to newspapers' own Web sites to read the entire article. That change, while not costless, seems like a relatively minor burden on the discussants' speech. But the current procedure relies on the newspapers' provision of free access to their sites, thus precluding stories, op-eds, and entire Web sites that are open only to paid subscribers. In addition, as we will shortly see, a copyright infringement action against Google's news story aggregation service, Google News, has questioned the legality even of Free Republic's quotation of just the first paragraph of the mainstream media news articles that its discussants regularly lambaste.

The Air Pirates

The Air Pirates were a group of underground cartoonists who worked in San Francisco at the height of Haight-Ashbury hippie counterculture. In the early 1970s, the group created a counterculture comic book that depicted Mickey Mouse and other Disney cartoon characters engaged in various sexual acts and illicit drug taking. Through that flagrantly outrageous parody, they sought to contest Disney's all-American "world of scrubbed faces, bright smiles and happy endings."[14] Not surprisingly, Disney strenuously objected to the perverse variant of Mickey Mouse's "innocent pleasure." Disney obtained a court order enjoining publication, bringing an end to the Air Pirates' effort at social critique. In an often-criticized ruling, the court emphatically denied that the Air Pirates' parody was fair use. (Ironically, the first commercially successful Mickey Mouse cartoon, the 1928 animated short *Steamboat Willie,* was itself a loose parody of Buster Keaton's silent film classic *Steamboat Bill Jr.* One wonders how Walt Disney would have fared in today's copyright environment if forced to defend his "piracy" of Keaton's story.)

As the Air Pirates case underscores, copyright's regulation even of low-culture entertainment might implicate concerns about free speech. There are, of course, many ways to challenge romanticized imaginings of American life. But the humorous denigration of a cultural icon can be a particularly potent way to do so.

Hip-Hop Music

Our next example concerns an entire genre of music. Hip-hop music is composed of speech voiced in cadence over urban funk, rock, and disco beats.

Hip-hop emerged from a rich African and African diaspora tradition of rhythmic verbal jousting, ranging from West African griot storytelling to Jamaican dub music.[15] It owes its immediate origins to South Bronx DJ and Jamaican immigrant Kool Herc, who, in the 1970s, regaled neighborhood parties by using two turntables to meld percussive and melodic fragments from an array of sound recordings while joking and boasting over a microphone. Herc's turntable "cuttings" were often recorded on cassette tapes. Copies rapidly spread through New York City, inspiring other DJs to engage in similar performances. As the practice caught on, hip-hop music, the interplay of rhythmic speech over prerecorded beats, vocal segments, and melody lines, grew to become a significant—and highly commercially successful—expression of African American urban culture and experience.

Most important for our purposes, the mixing and sampling of sounds from existing sound recordings were central to hip-hop's origins and emergence as a popular art form. By the mid-1980s, hip-hop artists regularly used digital synthesizers to copy, incorporate, alter, and rearrange myriad short segments from existing recordings. For these artists, the combination of digital technology and vintage, primarily vinyl record albums became their musical instruments. Significantly, hip-hop samplers called themselves "producers" rather than "composers" or "musicians" and viewed themselves as bearers of the DJ turntable tradition. Their aesthetic acumen lay in their vast collections and knowledge of vintage record albums, their ability to mine those recordings for break beats and for textures resonant in the distinct production values of earlier record labels and producers, and their melding and modification of numerous and varied samples.[16] Their intricate, digitally manipulated montages, weaving disparate prerecorded riffs, beats, and production qualities, created a unique sound, far more complex, sharp, and hard-hitting than any attempted re-creation of similar sounds by studio musicians.[17]

Beyond that aural aesthetic, sampling was also a vehicle to recover, reclaim, and pay homage to earlier DJs, recording engineers, and African American performers. As hip-hop chronicler Greg Tate described it, "Hip-hop is ancestor worship."[18] In other instances, artists directed their sampling to parody, social criticism, reinterpretation, or simply the ironic juxtaposition of sounds from sources as incongruous as Israeli folk music, bebop jazz, and television news broadcasts. Those myriad creative and expressive uses of sampling pervaded and defined the new musical genre. As one commentator notes, "[S]ampling . . . [is] an inherent part of what makes hip-hop music identifiably hip-hop."[19]

Copyright changed all that. In the late 1980s, record producers, music publishers, and songwriters brought a handful of copyright infringement actions against hip-hop artists whose recordings sampled prior works. The early cases were inconclusive. Nevertheless, the credible threat of successful copyright infringement litigation induced risk-averse record labels to refuse to produce and distribute hip-hop recordings without clearing rights for each sample. Then in a 1991 decision that began with the biblical admonition "Thou shall not steal," a New York district court enjoined the distribution of a Biz Markie album containing a song that sampled three words and looped a background music fragment from a recording of Gilbert O'Sullivan's composition "Alone Again (Naturally)." That sampling also led the court to refer Markie to the district attorney for criminal prosecution. Courts and industry practice have steadily and severely constrained unlicensed sampling since that decision. Most recently, in perhaps the ultimate culmination of that trend, the Sixth Circuit Court of Appeals ruled that any sampling what-soever from a sound recording, presumably even a single note, infringes the copyright in the sampled recording.[20]

The Sixth Circuit blithely assumed that its bright line rule of "[g]et a license or do not sample" would not "stifl[e] creativity in any significant way."[21] Like other courts and commentators, the Sixth Circuit expressed an unbridled faith in the efficacy of the copyright licensing market (in addition to failing utterly to grasp that for hip-hop producers live instrumentation cannot replace earlier sound recordings): "[T]he market will control the license price and keep it within bounds. The sound recording copyright holder cannot exact a license fee greater than what it would cost the person seeking the license to just duplicate the sample in the course of making the new recording."[22]

But as Jon Else and numerous documentary filmmakers have discovered, the copyright market does not operate like many courts and commentators naively assume. With few exceptions, clearing rights to multiple samples on a single recording has become prohibitively time-consuming and expensive. Recorded music consists of at least two separate copyrighted works, the recorded musical composition and the sound recording of the composition as performed in the studio or onstage. Thus, each sample of recorded music requires clearances from the owners of copyrights in both the sampled music composition, typically a music publisher, and the sound recording, typically a record label.

The publishers and labels do not generally issue sampling licenses with-out first hearing the entire track in which the sample appears, and clearance invariably requires the consent of a substantial number of people, including lawyers, artists, and various other copyright-holder representatives. That means that the hip-hop artist must take the risk that, after investing the time and expense of recording the track, some publisher or label representative will refuse to license or will hold up the artist's release unless paid an exorbitant license fee or given a large share of ownership in the album. Even aside from such holdouts, each publisher and label typically sets its sampling license fee or demand for ownership share without discounting for what others might be demanding. Consequently, the sum total of the demanded license fees and ownership shares in the hip-hop artist's recording often renders the recording commercially infeasible, sometimes even exceeding what the artist can hope to receive.[23]

The result of this market failure, as hip-hop artist Chuck D laments, is that the "whole collage element is out the window."[24] Today's hip-hop recordings typically feature only one primary sample, rely on vanilla-wrap samples from sample libraries rather than judiciously selected vintage recordings, or incorporate prerecorded mini-segments that are buried so deeply in the mix as to be wholly unrecognizable (and the Sixth Circuit's any-sampling-is-infringement ruling threatens even that practice).[25] Those artists who do include recognizable samples must carefully select and limit their source material in accordance with lawyers' advice, or simply throw caution to the wind and hope that they do not get sued. Although hip-hop albums still garner considerable commercial success and critical acclaim, the copious remixing and brazen sampling that once defined the genre and gave hip-hop music its distinctive artistic edge are no more: this, the principal consequence of neither artistic choice nor cultural evolution, but the chilling effect of the law.

While classic hip-hop's flagrant celebration of copying and focus on sound recordings as raw material for artistic inspiration might have been unique, its practice of incorporating strands of preexisting music was not. Copying is endemic to music. As Olufunmilayo Arewa has recently limned in rich detail, classical composers from Beethoven to Mozart to Bartok to Charles Ives have regularly recycled themes, motifs, and segments of prior works.[26] Handel borrowed so extensively that he was even accused of plagiarism. Contemporary popular musicians also commonly mine existing music for riffs, melodies, and rhythms. For that matter, our classical literary tradition is no different. Shakespeare borrowed heavily from Plutarch; Milton from the Bible; Coleridge from Kent, Schelling, and Schlegel; Yeats from Shelly; Kafka from Kleist and Dickens; Joyce from Homer; and T. S. Eliot from Shakespeare, Whitman, and Baudelaire, all in ways that would infringe today's bloated copyright. In literature and music, as in other forms of expression, such "patterns of influence—cribbing, tweaking, transforming— [are] at the very heart of the creative process."[27] And, for all, the line between permissible and infringing expression twists elusively with the vagaries of copyright law and enforcement.

Google

Google, a multibillion-dollar Internet search engine company, will no doubt strike some readers as an unlikely hero for illustrating the conflict between copyright and free speech. But First Amendment protagonists are not limited to individuals and media entities that produce new speech. Our First Amendment–inspired commitment to the "widest possible dissemination of information from diverse and antagonistic sources" also embraces institutions that make the existing store of knowledge and culture, ranging from ancient Greek plays to vintage sound recordings, widely available in useful form. Such speech disseminators have traditionally included libraries, schools, universities, and even the postal service, through its preferential rates for printed material. Together, these institutions collect vast inventories of recorded expression, organize the store of knowledge so that patrons can actually make use of it, and make information widely available to the public. That collection, organization, and diffusion of knowledge plays a vital role in our system of free expression.

Yet important as these traditional institutions have been, their capacity as repositories, catalogers, and disseminators of information has been limited by storage space, transport capability, geography, and, indeed, the relative imperviousness of the physical media of print. As a result, they are now increasingly supplanted by the Internet, which puts information from diverse sources at our fingertips to an extent exceeding the wildest dreams of previous generations. Digital communication and storage hold the promise of making virtually the entire store of the world's recorded knowledge and expression available online. Digitized collections can also be organized in ways that dramatically improve our ability to find and use the information we need. Indeed, the technologies of search engines, hyperlinking, and bookmarks can transform library collections—which traditionally have been composed of vast numbers of distinct books—into an integral part of the World Wide Web. It can enable us seamlessly to discover information within books and follow connections among books and other materials. As *Wired* magazine cofounder Kevin Kelly graphically puts it, "Once text is digital, books seep out of their bindings and weave themselves together."[28]

Enter Google. Google's search engine provides Internet users access to billions of Web pages, responding to users' keyword search requests with a high degree of precision and recall in a fraction of a second.[29] The company earns several billion dollars per year selling twelve-word "sponsored links," unobtrusive yet highly effective advertising snippets targeted to users' search queries. That vehicle has made it financially feasible—indeed presumably highly profitable—for the company to advance the Internet's speech-enhancing promise, first, by scanning into searchable, digital format vast amounts of information and expression that have thus far not been available on the Internet and, second, by applying its search engine algorithm to text, pictures, music, and video.

Google has incurred copyright holders' wrath on a number of fronts. I focus here on two particularly noteworthy Google initiatives, the Google Book Search Project and Google News.

The Google Book Search Project aspires to make all of the world's printed books available for digital search, without charge, for anyone with access to the Internet.[30] To that end, Google has thus far contracted to scan, at its cost, significant portions of the print collections of the libraries of several elite universities (as of this writing: Harvard, Stanford, Oxford, Michigan, Wisconsin, all campuses of the University of California, and the Universidad Complutense Madrid), as well as the New York Public Library. Those libraries contain some 15 million unique titles, which represent about one-half of all titles contained in the collections of the world's libraries.[31] Google's costs for scanning the books have been estimated at between $10 and $25 per book.[32] Its investment in this initial stage of its project would thus amount to between $150 million and $375 million (and possibly more if Google finds it necessary to scan some titles from more than one source).

Because of copyright, the Google Book Search Project will be something far less than a universal, fully accessible and searchable digital library of the world's printed books. Google will maintain a digital copy of each book on its searchable database and will give a copy to the library from whose collection the book was scanned. And by entering a search query in the Google search engine, users will be able to browse the full text of public domain materials. But for books that were first published after 1922 and thus might still be under U.S. copyright, users will be able to see only a three-sentence "snippet," comprising the sentence that contains the search term and the sentence before and after that sentence, together with the book's bibliographic information.[33] When a search term appears more than three times in a book, only the first three snippets will appear. Hence, Google will display no more than nine sentences of a potentially in-copyright book in response to a book search query. (Under Google's Partner Program, a publisher or author controlling the applicable copyrights can license Google to scan books and display a couple pages or more of a book's text in response to a user search query. But I focus here only on unlicensed scanning and displays, which, as we will see, would necessarily make up the lion's share of Google's project.)

Even with those significant constraints for displaying unlicensed post-1922 books, Google's Book Search is a highly useful research tool. Its users will be able to identify which books are likely most germane to a specific inquiry, to locate the pages on which the search term appears, and to get a limited sense of what the book might say with regard to the subject of the user's search. Google will also list local libraries where the book might be found and post links to third-party sites, like Amazon.com, where users may purchase the book or view or download portions of it for a price. For the Internet user, then, Google's Book Search Project is roughly akin to having ready access to a virtual card catalog for a significant portion of the world's books, with the huge added value of being able to apply search engine queries to the entire text of every book, view the full text of public domain materials, and receive information about where to locate or buy copyright-protected materials.

Google's Book Search Project comes on the heels of a number of nascent nonprofit efforts to digitize portions of university and public library archives. Yet the Google project dwarfs these nonprofit efforts in commitment of resources and scope. The nonprofit campaigns generally scan books published prior to 1923 only, but Google plans to scan and display millions of post-1922 books (at least those in collections in the United States), including those that are still in copyright. That will make a significant difference in the scope and comprehensiveness of Google's database. More than 80 percent of the research libraries' collections that Google has already agreed to scan are potentially in copyright.

Google plans to include millions of potentially in-copyright books in its database for two reasons. First, it believes that there is significant consumer demand for being able to search post-1922 books despite the constraint of viewing only a few lines of text for a given search query. Consequently, advertisers will pay good money for sponsored links targeted at such queries. Second, Google believes that because it displays only a few lines of text, the project avoids copyright infringement.

A number of publishers and authors vehemently disagree with Google's reading of copyright law. In response to those objections, Google announced that it would honor all copyright holders' requests to exclude books from the project. Upon receipt of a copyright holder's request, Google will refrain from scanning the identified book or, if it has already scanned the book, will delete it from the Book Search database. Yet a number of copyright holders insist that Google's project infringes their rights nonetheless. In their view, Google's proffered opt-out procedure turns "every principle of copyright on its ear" by shifting "responsibility for preventing infringement to the copyright owner rather than the user."[34] The Authors Guild and the five major members of the Association of American Publishers have accordingly brought copyright infringement lawsuits against Google seeking a court order forbidding Google from scanning their books without the copyright holder's express prior authorization.

Make no mistake. If the authors and publishers succeed in their lawsuits, the dream of creating and making available on the Internet a value-added virtual "card catalog" for the complete collections of the world's greatest research libraries, let alone all of the world's printed books, will lie dormant for the foreseeable future. To seek and obtain explicit copyright holder permission for each of millions of titles would render the project excessively expensive and unwieldy, even for Google.[35] For millions of titles, indeed, it would simply be impossible to clear rights.

Tellingly, Google's primary cost might not even be the license fees it would have to pay to copyright owners; those fees could well pale in comparison to the overwhelming burden of administering and negotiating permissions, including locating the parties who controls the copyrights needed to grant the permission. Only some 25 percent of all post-1922 books, and less than 2 percent of all in-copyright books published in the United States prior to 1950, remain in print.[36] The original publishers of many such books no longer exist. And given that neither copyright assignments nor testamentary dispositions need be recorded with the Copyright Office, the current copyright holders, whether they be successors to the publisher or the author's heirs, can often be located only with great difficulty if at all.

In many cases, moreover, finding the publisher or author's heirs will not be enough because no one knows who holds the electronic rights that Google needs to license to include the book in its Book Search Project. Book publishing contracts more than a few years old generally leave unclear whether the author or publisher would have the right to license scanning a digital copy of the book into an electronic database and publicly displaying portions of the contents over the Internet. As a result, even when the publisher or the author's heirs can be found, clearing rights to include a book in Google's project would require a legal opinion regarding which party has the authority to grant those rights under the original book publishing contract (or, barring that, obtaining a new agreement among all relevant parties).

Nonprofit digital archives estimate that the copyright clearance process consumes approximately a dozen man-hours per work even when the copyright owner is easy to find. The cost of locating the copyright owner of the print book and determining whether that party has the authority to license the book to Google's Book Search Project, let alone negotiating and paying royalties, would be prohibitively expensive for millions of books. The result would be a database of far less comprehensiveness and utility for researchers.

Google's primary legal defense of its Book Search Project is that its scanning of complete copyrighted texts and display of three-sentence snippets surrounding a user's search term are both fair use. Most observers assume that, under prevailing fair use doctrine, Google's most difficult legal hurdle will be to defend its scanning of entire books. Google's display of three-sentence snippets responding to a user's search inquiry would seem to fall more comfortably within traditional fair use. Displaying short excerpts of others' texts also comports with search engines' typically accepted practice, at least when the material that the search calls up has already been made available on the Internet by the copyright owner. But a recently settled lawsuit against Google News threatens to make even that practice subject to the copyright owner's exclusive, proprietary control.

The Google News Web site uses Google's search engine algorithms to gather news stories from some 4,500 English-language sources and arrange them in order of importance. For each leading news story, Google News displays the headline, less than two sentences of the story lead, and a miniature thumbnail version of a photograph from a press Web site (smaller even than the thumbnails displayed on any Google image search). Each headline and photograph is hyperlinked to lead the reader to the newspaper's or news agency's own Web site. Google News also displays numerous links—often thousands—to related stories from other sources immediately below each story lead. Readers may conduct word searches within the Google News material and may customize the Google News page to highlight stories on topics of personal interest or from certain regions of the world. As such, Google News is an invaluable tool for anyone wanting to assess and compare how a wide variety of press outlets from around the world cover a given story or to find news coverage of topics of general or personal import without having to go to the multiple Web sites of individual newspapers.

In March 2005, Agence France Presse (AFP), which claims to be the world's oldest news agency, sued Google for including headlines, story leads, and thumbnail versions of photographs from the agency's stories on Google News. The agency claimed that its headlines and story leads are each "original copyrightable text and qualitatively one of the most important aspects of AFP's news stories" and that Google's reproduction and display of that short text, as well as thumbnails of AFP news photos, constituted a willful infringement of AFP's copyrights, even if readers who sought to read the AFP story or see a full-size photograph had to click on a link leading to either the AFP Web page or the page of the news outlet that posted the material under license with AFP. Google settled the AFP lawsuit in part by agreeing to link AFP material only to the AFP Web site, thus bypassing the news outlets that are AFP customers. But AFP's legal arguments remain for others to assert, and the World Association of Newspapers has announced on behalf of its 18,000 member newspapers that it, too, intends to challenge the "exploitation of content" by Google and other search engines.[37]

The Google initiatives and the lawsuits against them raise a difficult question: Should Google be required to share with copyright holders a portion of the revenue that it earns from compiling and organizing (and thus adding substantial value to) copyright-protected material? We will revisit that question later. More important here, the Google cases illustrate the potential conflict between our free speech aspirations and proprietary copyright. In line with traditional rules applicable to tangible property, advocates of a proprietary copyright contend that, at the very least, Google's projects are subject to a copyright holder's entitlement to withhold permission and, more broadly, to Google's obligation to seek out and obtain copyright holder consent. Even honoring copyright holders' requests to opt-out, the procedure that Google assiduously follows, creates holes in Google's information repositories, rendering them less valuable for users. To require, beyond that, that Google cannot include any texts unless it has received prior express consent from the appropriate copyright holder, would sound the death knell for Google's projects (and, if applied to search engines generally, for Google itself).

At its core, copyright shares our First Amendment commitment both to increasing the store of knowledge and to making it widely available for learning, inspiration, enjoyment, and further expression. Yet, as the Google cases make clear, today's proprietary copyright threatens to stand as an obstacle to the Internet's realization of our First Amendment ideals.

———

As with Alice Randall, copyright does not completely suppress the speakers I have just described. With the exception of Google, all these speakers could present their ideas without copying or incorporating copyrighted expression. Yet in each instance, that speech would be significantly diminished. Alan Cranston, for example, might have merely drafted a critical review of the original *Mein Kampf* or the official English translation. More broadly, he could have simply spoken out against the Nazi regime and warned of the dangers of appeasement. But Cranston's translation reached a much wider audience and conveyed Cranston's message in a far more pointed and accessible manner. As was no doubt Cranston's aim, his translation also likely reached a portion of the public that would have otherwise been duped by reading the official, expurgated version.

Likewise, to one degree or another, with the Philadelphia Church of God, Jon Else, Free Republic, the Air Pirates, and countless other speakers. Some credibility, some understanding, some communicative force is lost when a speaker is deprived of the use of particular words, images, or sounds. Whatever might be its benefits, copyright stifles, muffles, or, at the very least, imposes costs on speech. And today's bloated copyright does so to a far greater extent than ever before.

There are, of course, counternarratives of writers, artists, and musicians devoted to creative endeavor and dependent on copyright for sustenance. I do not mean to be dismissive of that viewpoint; as I will discuss, copyright has traditionally played an important role in underwriting creative work and supporting professional authorship. But stories about "[s]acrificial days devoted to . . . creative activities" have dominated copyright discourse for some three centuries—and have often been used by copyright industries to gain support for new entitlements that only indirectly benefit actual creators, if at all.[38] Lost in that discourse is any recognition that speakers who use existing copyrighted works in conveying their message are often no less deserving and, indeed, no less creative than the author of the prior work. Nor does the reward-for-authors rhetoric capture the complexities and tremendous potential for disseminating knowledge embodied in new technological media, of which the Google projects are but two of many examples.

CHAPTER THREE | # What Is Freedom of Speech?
(And How Does It Bear on Copyright)?

I N JULY 1939, when the United States faced momentous choices re-garding whether to prepare for conflict with Nazi Germany, a court banned Alan Cranston's pointed translation of *Mein Kampf*'s most offensive passages. Most readers, I presume, share the intuition that enjoining Cranston's clarion call chilled free speech, a consequence that, at the very least, the court should have weighed heavily in considering Hitler's publisher's claim. But can the same be said regarding Air Pirates' depiction of Mickey Mouse taking drugs and having sex? Or hip-hop artist Biz Markie's sampling of Gilbert O'Sullivan? Or a teenager's amassing of a personal collection of thousands of music recordings downloaded from unlicensed peer-to-peer file-trading networks? For that matter, what is at stake in the publishers' lawsuit against Google Book Search? Is it really "freedom of speech" or is it just a business dispute?

To begin to answer these questions, we must first parse what we mean by "freedom of speech" and how it might apply to copyright. What counts as "speech" for purposes of "freedom of speech"? What free speech principles can guide us in determining when copyright unduly burdens speech and when, in contrast, we should readily countenance the restraints that copyright imposes?

Freedom of Speech Encompasses Copyright-Impacted Expression

The question of what counts as "speech" for "freedom of speech" has two distinct facets. First, not all self-expression constitutes "speech." Say I like to drive at 150 miles per hour on a remote desert highway. That act is self-expressive in the sense that it manifests my intention and personal identity. But, as I discuss later, not every self-expressive act comes within the realm of freedom of speech. A person's use of words, images, or symbols to communicate, whether it be Alan Cranston's translation or Biz Markie's song, fits quite comfortably with what theorists define as "speech." Amassing a personal collection of TV shows that I have downloaded from an unlicensed peer-to-peer network might be more like driving at high speed—self-expressive but not "speech."

Second, not all "speech" implicates "freedom of speech." By most accounts, words used to engage in criminal fraud or conspiracy, even if nominally "speech," fall entirely outside the realm of "freedom of speech." For some theorists, so do advertising, deliberate falsehood, securities filings, abstract art, and quotidian entertainment. Where does that leave Alan Cranston's translation, Alice Randall's sequel, the Air Pirates'cartoon, and hip-hop music? For that matter, is copyright truly "the engine of free expression" when it provides an incentive for creating *Gone with the Wind,* Mickey Mouse cartoons, and bubblegum pop songs? Even if we recognize that such copyright-impacted expression is "speech," is it the sort of speech we mean when we invoke the principle of "freedom of speech"?

The response to such questions turns upon our best understandings of what "freedom of speech" means and why speech should enjoy greater freedom than other human activity.[1] Yet commentators differ sharply in this respect. Some view free speech as instrumental to collective self-government and democratic deliberation. For others, free speech is, rather, an essential element of individual autonomy and self-realization. Still others emphasize free speech's importance for the search for truth. And for some, free speech's central meaning lies in nurturing dissent, fostering tolerance, or checking government abuse.

I do not intend to present a normative argument in favor of one theory or another. Suffice to say that, at least as a descriptive matter, each theory contributes to our free speech jurisprudence, yet none can single-handedly explain it. The principle of "freedom of speech" flows, rather, from a loose constellation of reasons, axioms, and theories. No theory standing alone comfortably embraces all types and instances of expression. But, taken together, the theories combine to cover the broad range of expression that most would agree has come to constitute the realm of free speech, including most copyright-impacted expression.

Having expressed my general agnosticism, however, I do want to take on the free speech theory that poses the most difficulty for bringing abstract art and popular culture—the subject matter of much copyright law—under the free speech umbrella. That is the venerable claim that only patently political expression implicates freedom of speech. In this view, free speech is all about a well-functioning democracy, and the sole purpose of free speech is to produce an alert and informed electorate. Alexander Meiklejohn, the leading proponent of this view, put it thus: "As the self-governing community seeks, by the method of voting, to gain wisdom in action, it can find it only in the minds of its individual citizens. If they fail, it fails. That is why freedom of discussion for those minds may not be abridged."[2]

On this understanding of free speech, only speech that assists voters in understanding the issues they must decide merits First Amendment protection. Some scholars argue, accordingly, that artistic works should receive little or no First Amendment recognition unless they contain political speech or address important public issues.[3] In that vein, some commentators are dismissive of copyright's speech burdens (and speech benefits) because of the explicit or implicit notion that copyright-impacted speech is, after all, just art and idle entertainment, much the opposite of speech that serves deliberative democracy. Perhaps Alan Cranston's critical translation of *Mein Kampf* deserves free speech solicitude, but not Air Pirates' comics, hip-hop music, or even Alice Randall's novel.

First, a reality check: the view that artistic expression is less deserving than political speech has not won the day in First Amendment case law. Under current First Amendment doctrine, abstract art enjoys the same constitutional protection as political discourse. As the Supreme Court has emphasized, the "painting of Jackson Pollock, music of Arnold Schoenberg, or Jabberwocky verse of Lewis Carroll" is "unquestionably shielded."[4]

Nor do the dismissive views of copyright make sense even if we accept, for the purposes of argument, that the sole purpose of free speech is collective self-governance. For one, like Alan Cranston's critical translation, much copyright-impacted expression involves core political speech. It includes investigative journalism, political memoirs, partisan tracts, news reporting, and documentary film. Moreover, even artistic expression and entertainment that lack an explicit political message may have a constitutive role for collective self-governance. Meiklejohn himself came to recognize that artistic works should enjoy First Amendment protection; he posited that art helps people make political decisions through sharpening intelligence and developing sensitivity to human values.[5] Meiklejohn might have been too optimistic in believing that art—especially commercial entertainment—makes better voters. Nevertheless, commercial entertainment and popular culture play a primary role in collective self-governance: they profoundly color our attitudes, beliefs, and perceptions of the world around us.

Mass-media products are central features of daily life. In addition to serving as common reference points for imagination and conversation, they shape the agenda for public discourse and reinforce or redirect widely held assumptions about our social and political universe. Our public discourse comprises a rambunctious, effervescent brew of spectacle, prurient appeal, social commentary, and political punditry. As it entertains, it often reveals contested issues and deep fissures within our society, just as it may reinforce widely held beliefs and values. To be understood by their audiences, films, songs, and television programs must deal in the currency of prevailing practices, ideologies, and stereotypes, and in so doing must either challenge or reinforce them. Even seemingly innocuous cartoon characters, like Homer Simpson and Mickey Mouse, may be used to subvert (or buttress) prevailing cultural values and assumptions—and with greater social impact than the most carefully considered Habermasian dialogue. For that reason, speakers, ranging from the Air Pirates to amateur creators of YouTube videos, often appropriate mass-media images, stories, and characters to challenge, trumpet, or make sense of the prevailing understandings those icons carry.

Indeed, many creative works have broad political and social implications even if they do not convey a rationally apprehensible ideological message. Abstract, "pure" artistic expression may challenge accepted modes of thought and belie the efforts of governments or cultural majorities to standardize individual sensitivities and perceptions. Like early hip-hop music, creative genres can also give voice to dissident and minority group culture, identity, and attitudes. For that reason, totalitarian regimes have prohibited styles of art and music that might be seen as politically innocuous in other contexts— notably the Soviet Union banned all abstract art, and the Central Intelligence Agency responded by surreptitiously promoting American abstract expressionism in post–World War II Europe.[6]

At bottom, then, even if collective self-governance were our sole First Amendment lodestar, freedom of speech would encompass not just speech that delivers a clear political message but also creative expression that is neither overtly political nor rationally apprehensible. A vast swath of copyright-impacted expression fits well within the free speech domain.

Free Speech Principles and How They Apply to Copyright

Yet to conclude that the Air Pirates' comics implicate "free speech" tells us little about how, given free speech principles, we should regard Disney's use of copyright law to ban their publication. Copyright supports some "speech" and abridges other "speech." When and in what way does copyright thus involve and, possibly, violate free speech principles?

FREE SPEECH AND THE FIRST AMENDMENT

I begin that inquiry with an important definitional point: to say that copyright abridges or burdens free speech does not necessarily mean that copyright law runs afoul of the First Amendment. Free speech principles extend far beyond First Amendment speech protections. I mean this in two senses. First, First Amendment law, by its very nature, falls short of free speech principles. The First Amendment provides that "Congress shall make no law . . . abridging the freedom of speech, or of the press." As courts have construed that injunction, the First Amendment broadly limits the legal authority of government (not just Congress) to burden speech. But it does not necessarily compel government to adopt policies that produce an optimal environment for speech. One could plausibly argue, for example, that free speech principles or, if you will, First Amendment "values" strongly support enabling Alan Cranston to publish his unauthorized translation, but that First Amendment law imposes no duty on Congress to accord Cranston that privilege. The argument based on principles or values is that Congress really ought to provide an exception to copyright holders' rights for cases like Cranston's. The argument based on First Amendment law is that Congress *must* provide the exception, that a statute or particular application of a statute that abridges Cranston's speech is constitutionally infirm. The former argument goes to the question of what is the best policy for protecting and promoting speech. The latter interprets and applies a constitutional mandate.

Second, even if First Amendment law is ideally coextensive with free speech principles and policy, First Amendment law as enforced by judges is not. Like most constitutional case law, First Amendment doctrine reflects normative and practical constraints on judicial power as much as it does the substance of the underlying constitutional rights. In particular, federal courts, as an unelected coequal branch of government, accord some degree of deference to legislative judgment in considering First Amendment challenges to speech regulation (with the degree of deference depending on the category of speech regulation and the type of speech that is burdened). So even if Alan Cranston might be said in the abstract to have a First Amendment right to publish his translation, he does not necessarily have a justiciable claim to enforce that right. A judge might believe in some ideal sense that the Copyright Act as applied to Cranston abridges Cranston's freedom of speech, but nevertheless feel constrained to follow First Amendment precedent that, implicitly or explicitly, recognizes the limits of judicial competency and thus leaves the First Amendment norm "underenforced."[7]

Constitutional scholars differ on the nature and extent of the distinction, if any, among constitutional law as enforced by judges, constitutional law beyond case law, and constitutional principle. For our purposes, it will suffice to distinguish between free speech principles (or First Amendment values), on the one hand, and First Amendment doctrine, on the other. Judges' reasoned application of First Amendment doctrine can often tell us something about the principles and values that underlie the First Amendment. But First Amendment doctrine is not exhaustive of free speech principles in scope or application.

So when I say that a broad, proprietary copyright impairs freedom of expression, I do not *necessarily* mean that copyright is constitutionally infirm or that judges should impose First Amendment constraints. I do argue in chapter 8 that some provisions of the Copyright Act run afoul of First Amendment law and that the First Amendment should be brought to bear upon copyright law to limit copyright holders' prerogatives in certain ways. But those constitutionally mandated First Amendment strictures are narrower than the free speech concerns that should generally be given weight as a matter of copyright policy.

FREE SPEECH IS MORE THAN FREEDOM FROM GOVERNMENT CENSORSHIP

Freedom of expression is secured most basically by constitutional constraints on the state's censorial power. First Amendment jurisprudence posits that, with some exceptions, government may not suppress speech because it disfavors certain viewpoints or subject matter. Nor may government censor speakers for fear that audiences will take offense, be swept up in emotional appeals, or respond by committing socially undesirable acts. Seen in that light, freedom of expression is fundamentally a "negative liberty" right. It is a right to an absence of government interference in what individuals might choose to say or hear, or, somewhat more narrowly, to be free from government interference when government sets out to target a given speaker or message.

But while that right to be free from government censorship is central to freedom of expression, it constitutes but a part of what Thomas Emerson has described as an intricate, broadly based "system of freedom of expression." A system of freedom of expression encompasses, in addition to the negative liberty right of free speech, an elaborate matrix of speech-related entitlements, institutions, types of speakers, and regulatory regimes.[8] Most important, it entails government policies to further expressive diversity and underwrite a vibrant, independent press, not just limitations on the state's power to abridge speech rights.

Liberal democratic states commonly provide affirmative support for expression and seek to shape the contours of public discourse in line with their constitutional vision. Governments fund and manage communications channels such as the Internet and broadcast spectrum. They also subsidize particular speakers, ranging from artists to mass media. Alongside that financial support, governments additionally pursue regulatory policies designed to promote (within various bounds) expressive diversity and the free flow of information. Such policies range from media ownership restrictions aimed at fostering a plurality of voices in the institutional press to requirements that media entities serve minority communities and provide a platform for non-media speakers.

The negative liberty component of freedom of speech looms larger in the United States than in other Western democracies. Yet the United States is certainly no stranger to state intervention to promote First Amendment values. Congress subsidized the press from the beginning of the Republic through preferential postal rates, free newspaper delivery among printers, maintaining postal roads for printers' private use, and awarding newspaper publishers lucrative government printing contracts.[9] In our time, commercial television, public broadcasting, and the Internet have all received substantial support from the public fisc. Over the years, Congress and the Federal Communications Commission have also implemented a broad range of regulations designed to foster expressive diversity, a multiplicity of media sources, coverage of matters of public importance, and public access to mass media for both speakers and audiences. Those regulations have, for example, supported the emergence of multichannel cable and satellite television, while maintaining free off-air broadcasting by requiring cable and satellite to carry broadcast channels. They have required cable television operators to dedicate channels for education and public access and television networks to cover opposing viewpoints on issues of public importance. They have sought to prevent undue media concentration by prohibiting or restricting cable/broadcaster, newspaper/broadcaster, and radio/television cross-ownership, imposing various ceilings on broadcasters' station ownership and audience share, and requiring national television networks to license most of their prime-time programming from independent producers.[10] They have required that proprietors of communications networks, including the various components of the Internet, act as common carriers, conveying information without discrimination as to source, use, or content. Many of these rules have fallen in a wave of deregulation begun in the Reagan administration in the 1980s. Nevertheless, as the U.S. Supreme Court has repeatedly emphasized, it remains a fundamental goal of U.S. telecommunications policy and, for that matter, of the First Amendment to actively promote—through a combination of regulation, subsidy, and market forces—the "widest possible dissemination of information from diverse and antagonistic sources."[11]

Copyright is an integral part of our system of freedom of expression. The Copyright Act contains numerous, detailed provisions that implement various aspects of speech and telecommunications policy.[12] These primarily entail statutory licenses for various institutional speakers and distributors to use copyrighted material without permission from the copyright holder, generally upon payment of a set fee but sometimes for free. Beneficiaries include public broadcasters, cable and satellite television operators, webcasters, commercial radio and television broadcasters, libraries, educational institutions, and record labels. Like the structural media and telecommunications regulations they complement, these statutory copyright licenses serve to foster a multiplicity and diversity of sources for information and opinion.

Moreover, copyright law aims to serve First Amendment values not just through these discrete, media-specific provisions but from copyright's basic core as well. As the Supreme Court has reminded us, the framers viewed copyright as an "engine of free expression." And as I discuss in chapter 5, copyright's limited exclusive rights have historically fostered a broad range of original expression, subsidized a robust sector of authors and media enterprises independent from government subsidy, and highlighted the value of individual's creative expression in our public discourse.

Yet copyright law inevitably favors some media and potential speakers, and some types of expression, over others. Copyright both fosters original expression and impedes uses of existing expression. It underwrites independent authors and publishers. But, depending on how copyright law is configured, it can also entrench media conglomerate incumbents and burden creative appropriators and new media.

Copyright, in short, plays a significant yet highly complex role in shaping our system of free expression. Copyright law accords exclusive rights that in many ways operate like property rights in tangible objects. Yet it is a mistake to view copyright as just another property right. Unlike most property rights, copyright law is fundamentally an instrument of media and communications policy and an integral part of our system of free expression.[13] Copyright's fabric of incentives and restraints, exclusive entitlements and statutory licenses, capacious rights and exceptions to those rights, does far more than allocate private interests and regulate trade. It fundamentally benefits and burdens speech.

EXPRESSIVE DIVERSITY

The central importance of robust exchange among diverse views has long stood as a defining pillar of free speech jurisprudence and liberal democratic governance.[14] Yet observers disagree not only about how best to attain expressive diversity but also about what expressive diversity really means. As we will see in later chapters, that dispute has, in turn, spilled over into debates over copyright's proper character and scope.

Expressive diversity serves a number of constitutive ends. A public discourse that gives play to a broad array of information and opinion poses a constant challenge to prevailing assumptions, attitudes, political institutions, and social norms. As such, expressive diversity supports political and social change. It gives voice and power to minorities and dissidents who wish to overturn official dogma or simply to resist the hegemony of the majority by developing their own distinct discourse and culture.

More broadly, "uninhibited, robust, and wide-open" debate among opposing views helps to engender a vibrant democratic culture, one whose citizens possess the independent spirit, discursive skill, political awareness, and mutual recognition required for collective self-governance.[15] A state whose citizenry has not internalized these skills and values will rule through fiat and obedience rather than the commitments of a self-governing polity. An inert polity is also more susceptible to the sweeping force of demagoguery and the domination of powerful elites. Additionally, there is evidence to suggest that a broad exchange of views from a multiplicity of sources, in which each position is tested against the others, enables a clearer elucidation of issues and values and yields objectively better decisions at all levels of government and civil society.[16]

Finally, policies that promote expressive diversity provide opportunities for individuals both to speak and to gain exposure to a wide spectrum of expression and information. That rich and variegated expressive stew nurtures individual autonomy and self-realization. It fosters our individual, as well as collective, capacity to speak and think for ourselves.

That is the ideal, the ample reasons for why our system of free expression—including our copyright law—should foster expressive diversity. To what extent does our current system adequately serve and aspire to that ideal? That question is the subject of a bitter debate raging in the context of large media conglomerates' overwhelming domination of cultural production and public discourse. Critics argue that, given media conglomerate dominance and the resulting juggernaut of insipid, mainstream content, our current system of free expression falls far too short of the ideal of expressive diversity—or at least would far short if media and telecommunications conglomerates are ever able to tame remix culture and control the Internet. Defenders point to the multiplicity of genres and wealth of expressive output that characterize our commercial mass media and insist that our current regime serves expressive diversity well enough after all.

A vast scholarly literature is available on the causal relation between industry concentration, on the one hand, and diversity of output and innovation, on the other. Scholars present conflicting views and empirical results on this issue, regarding both industry generally and media and telecommunications firms in particular.[17] Some studies find that concentrated, commercial media underserve minority tastes, and, as noted earlier, some scholars decry media conglomerates' production of what they characterize as bland, uncontroversial content for the lowest common denominator.[18] Other commentators insist that large media firms in highly concentrated markets in fact produce expressive works of diverse genres, ranging from reality TV to animated sitcoms.[19] Still others survey the literature and conclude that empirical and theoretic studies of the relation between media concentration and diversity of output remain inconclusive.[20]

I suspect that today's media conglomerates in fact produce more homogeneous fare than would obtain in less concentrated markets. The economic models predicting that concentrated media markets will yield more diverse output than competitive ones apply only when there are very few competitors. They suggest conversely that public discourse in media markets consisting of numerous speakers and speech outlets will be the most diverse. Certainly, the totality of user-generated content on the Internet reflects a far broader spectrum of expression than found on mass-media outlets. Accordingly, to the extent copyright law fuels media concentration, an issue I will examine later, copyright may operate to diminish expressive diversity.

More fundamentally, the focus on diversity of output is largely beside the point. From a free speech perspective, expressive diversity requires much more than product differentiation, the production of a variety of genres and formats. Expressive diversity must also entail a dispersal of communicative power. As Ed Baker perceptively states, "Democratic values mean that it makes a huge difference whether any lack of a particular type of diversity is imposed by a few powerful actors or reflects the independent judgments of many different people ... with the ultimate power to determine content."[21] Our free speech jurisprudence posits that a broad range of speakers and constituencies should have the opportunity to impact public discourse. Robust debate requires distinct and disparate voices in the fray, even if they might ultimately coalesce around a common statement. A dispersal of communicative power also serves to counter the danger of the potential "Berlusconi" effect, where, like the Italian media magnate who became prime minister, the owners of media conglomerates use their power to assert inordinate influence on political decision making. The Supreme Court thus wisely characterizes expressive diversity not in terms of expressive output per se, but rather as the "widest possible dissemination of information from diverse and antagonistic sources."[22]

Of particular importance to copyright, expressive diversity in the sense of dispersal of communicative power requires ample opportunity for the creation and dissemination of what we might call "oppositional expression," speech that directly challenges mainstream culture and popular works. Like Alice Randall, oppositional speakers recast or appropriate seminal works of popular culture in order to subvert prevailing understandings, make an unpopular political statement, or present an iconoclastic artistic conception. As Steven Shiffrin and others have emphasized, our First Amendment tradition seeks, among its central aims, to protect and foster expressions of dissent—"speech that criticizes existing customs, habits, traditions, institutions, or authorities" and that "communicates the fears, hopes, and aspirations of the less powerful to those in power."[23] Oppositional speakers, those who build on popular works in order to subvert and criticize the views and assumptions those works reinforce, make up a vital part of that dissenting voice. A public discourse comprising multitudinous genres and formats but that, because of copyright, lacks sufficient opportunities for effective, oppositional expression would fail to meet the goal of expressive diversity.

Indeed, a truly diverse expressive arena must encompass speakers with a range of motivations, concerns, practices, and institutional arrangements for speaking. Of particular note, the speech of nonmarket participants in the give-and-take of online fora has a very different tenor than speech created and distributed by commercial media or, for that matter, public-funded broadcasters.[24] Contributors to blog discussion, volunteers who post new Wikipedia entries or modify existing ones, and *Star Trek* fans who post their short stories and videos incorporating series' characters, settings, and plot elements speak because something bothers them or piques their interest, or because they want to impart information or exchange ideas, parody, commentary, and creativity with others. They are typically not motivated to reach a broad audience or produce a marketable product. Their acts of speech, in fact, are more like participating in an ongoing conversation than producing a fixed, mass-distributed product. Such digital network speech is firmly embedded in a social context of give-and-take. Each contribution joins an ever-changing series of additional posts, comments, modifications, and links. It thus has a fundamentally different import for individual autonomy and engagement in the making of culture than do mass-media products. The nonmarket and commercial media speech practices are qualitatively distinct in ways that matter for First Amendment values even in those instances in which content converges as a result of digital network participants' creative appropriation and remixing of mass-media expression.

Over and above whatever impact it may have on media concentration and differentiated output, proprietary copyright control tends to stifle nonmarket appropriation and oppositional expression. Nonmarket speakers are often unable to pay copyright license fees or to litigate to assert fair use rights when faced with a cease-and-desist letter from a copyright holder. Even oppositional speakers with financial backing are far less able to acquire copyright permissions than are speakers who fall within the mainstream. Oppositional expression often targets iconic copyrighted works or uses such works in ways that run counter to copyright holders' views or, more likely, inventory management and marketing plans. The Margaret Mitchell estate insisted, for example, that no *Gone with the Wind* sequel contain miscegenation or homosexuality.[25] Alice Randall's novel pointedly flouted both conditions, taking aim at the oppressive stereotypes that sustain Mitchell's idealized portrait. Nonmarket speech and oppositional expression like Randall's are crucial elements of expressive diversity; they are certainly no less valuable for individual autonomy, bottom-up participation in the making of culture, and a robust democratic polity than is the production of a wide spectrum of expressive genres.

Yet the other side of that coin is that our concern for copyright's chilling of oppositional and nonmarket speech should not lead to calls to erase the commercial mass media and replace it with a universe of yeomen bloggers and amateur YouTube video creators. Copyright-supported media enterprises constitute a vital component of our system of free expression. An institutional press that possesses the political and financial independence to reach a mass audience, galvanize public opinion, and engage in sustained investigative reporting and critique is critical to democratic governance.

A free and vibrant press can also provide a rich field for individual elucidation and self-definition. Digital technology creates unprecedented opportunities for geographically dispersed individuals to collaborate in investigative reporting, conveying opinion, and producing artistic expression. But First Amendment values and the goal of expressive diversity are best served by a lively interplay between the blogosphere and traditional press, and between commercial and nonmarket expression, rather than either supplanting the other.

Some Implications for Copyright Policy

APPROPRIATION LIES AT THE HEART OF FREE SPEECH

Some commentators insist that speakers who draw upon the original expression of another have a materially weaker speech interest than those whose speech does not appropriate existing expression.[26] That perception has even found its way into First Amendment case law. As the Supreme Court opined in rejecting Eric Eldred's constitutional challenge to the Copyright Term Extension Act: "The First Amendment securely protects the freedom to make—or decline to make—one's own speech; it bears less heavily when speakers assert the right to make other people's speeches."[27]

To so diminish speakers' appropriation of existing expression reduces free speech to an exceedingly narrow realm. It is also flat-out wrong as a matter of First Amendment law (as I discuss in chapter 8) and runs contrary to our common experience. Speakers regularly express themselves most fully and effectively imparting words others have written. Consider the Lysistrata Project, when hundreds of simultaneous readings of Aristophanes' play were held nationwide to protest the Bush administration's plans to go to war in Iraq; the public renderings of the Gettysburg Address to commemorate the first anniversary of September 11; street corner preachers who hand out copies of the Bible; the countless protesters, electoral candidates, and commencement speakers who have quoted liberally from Martin Luther King's ringing "I Have a Dream" speech; those who sing the national anthem—or "The Internationale"—at public events; and the schismatic traditionalists who adopted the church founder's tract that had been repudiated by mainstream church leaders. And, of course, not all who impart others' words limit themselves to just that existing expression. Numerous speakers, like Alan Cranston, Jon Else, Alice Randall, and the Air Pirates, most powerfully convey their message and artistic vision by combining their own original expression with what they have appropriated from others.

Appropriation lies at the heart, not the margins, of freedom of speech. As Jack Balkin perceptively underscores, freedom of speech is precisely our ability to "participate in culture through building on what [we] find in culture and innovating with it, modifying it, and turning it to [our] purposes."[28] In a robust and democratic system of free expression, dissenters, artists, commentators, and everyday discussants "are free to appropriate elements of culture that lay to hand, criticize them, build upon them, and create something new that is added to the mix of culture and its resources."[29] This ability to formulate speech by relaying or incorporating elements of existing expression that resonate with oneself and one's audience is critical to a broad array of free speech theories, ranging from those that emphasize self-realization and expressive autonomy to those grounded in the participatory character of a democratic polity. Our speech does not arise from a tabula rasa. Rather, we are born into an expressive universe brimming with texts, songs, and images that others have created. We cannot make sense of our world, find our own voice, communicate to others, or seek to affect others' perceptions and understandings without appropriating, recoding, referring to, and imparting the expressive works that constitute our common language.

The fundamentally appropriative character of freedom of speech does much to explain the heightened tension between copyright and free speech in the digital arena. The Internet has spawned a vast universe of decentralized creativity and communication. Yet, at the same time, mass-media-produced expression continues to dominate our cultural landscape (and will most probably continue to do so for the foreseeable future). As a result, those who wish to criticize mainstream culture, document historical events, or even just express themselves through widely understood cultural referents often have little choice but to invoke mass-media images, symbols, characters, stories, and icons. The Air Pirates could hardly target the mainstream, all-American aura of Disney's cartoon characters without invoking those particular characters in their counterculture romp. Jon Else's forced deletion of Homer Simpson left his scene bereft of a sharply ironic juxtaposition of popular culture with high art. *Eyes on the Prize,* a landmark documentary about the American civil rights movement, lay on the shelf for years, until recently being rescued by a major Ford Foundation grant, because clearances for period music and archival television footage had expired.

The appropriative recasting of culturally salient images, music, and characters has been a cornerstone of art, politics, and social critique at least since the ancient Greeks. It has also long populated daily conversation, humor, and folk culture. Even U.S. presidential candidates have a venerable tradition of wholesale adoption of popular songs—the Clinton-Gore campaign's use of Fleetwood Mac's "Don't Stop (Thinking about Tomorrow)" is one example—that resonate with voters and capture the essence of the campaign theme.[30] But the Internet and digital technology greatly magnify cultural appropriation's extent and global reach. Today, anyone with access to a computer, moderately priced software, and the Internet can appropriate, edit, remix, and transform mass-media products and then make creative appropriations available all over the world. That individual empowerment, and the ensuing remix culture, has brought delight to millions of Internet users and grave concern to many copyright holders.

PERSONAL COPYING AND FILE SHARING

A person's creative transformation or even literal rendering of existing expression to convey a message or artistic statement fits quite comfortably within what we would generally call "speech," even if some have questioned whether it is the type of speech we should be concerned to protect and promote. But what of another use of existing expression that digital technology makes startlingly easy: copying thousands of songs, TV shows, movies, pictures, and texts for one's own enjoyment and making one's personal collection available to others for them to enjoy? Are burning CDs, recording an entire season of a TV show on TiVo, and downloading movies and music over the Internet forms of "speech" or merely consumption? What about making one's collection available for others, say by allowing other peer-to-peer network participants to partake of whatever they wish from the shared folder of one's hard drive?

In principle, neither First Amendment law nor First Amendment values should accord any solicitude to these activities unless they constitute or, at least, directly bear upon "speech." A commercial enterprise that illicitly copies thousands of CDs for sale in underground flea markets aims entirely to make money, not convey a message. Something similar might be said of those who download music for free rather than paying a price they could readily afford simply to have more expendable income for buying consumer goods. Free speech policy, it seems self-evident, does not extend to a person who acts entirely from market interest (the desire to make or save money) rather than, at least in part, a speech interest (the desire to convey or receive a message).[31]

Moreover, the absence of a purely market interest is a necessary, but not sufficient, condition for individuals' copying, collecting, and sharing of existing works to constitute "speech." To fall within the rubric of "speech," those activities must also be expressive in a manner distinct from the self-expression that inures in any voluntary conduct. Virtually all voluntary conduct, ranging from eating a gourmet meal to riding a motorcycle, is self-expressive in the sense that it reflects the will of the actor. But the right and principle of free speech cannot simply cover all such "self-expressive" conduct. If we define speech that broadly, we conflate the right of free speech with an amorphous right to liberty of voluntary action. As Frederick Schauer observes, to support a distinct right of free speech, "the definition of 'speech' must serve to delimit an area smaller than the universe of intentional actions, and thus smaller than the universe of actions that in some way manifest the inner feelings of the actor."[32]

Defining what does and what does not constitute "speech" is not merely an exercise in semantics or scholarly classification. Rather, our special solicitude for free speech depends upon a sound, defensible distinction between "speech" and generic willful conduct. The power of the free speech principle, our understanding that "free speech" often trumps countervailing interests, lies in carving out a realm of "speech" that is both narrower and more deserving of protection and promotion than the universe of voluntary action of which speech is but a part. Much human activity, of course, is a mixture of speech and nonspeech conduct, and the right to free speech may well encompass such mixed activity in some circumstances. Nevertheless, as Kent Greenawalt emphasizes, in order to be significant, the principle of freedom of speech must be something more than the "minimal principle of liberty" that government should not constrain individuals' behavior except to prevent harm that the behavior may cause.[33]

For that reason, free speech theorists attempt in various ways to differentiate activity that constitutes "speech" from that which is simply voluntary conduct. Or, put another way, they distinguish activity that is self-expressive in a strong sense from activity that is self-expressive only in a diluted and, for our purposes, fairly meaningless sense of manifesting the actor's will or inner feelings. The most successful attempts define "speech" as activity that is meant and understood to be communicative.[34] Speech, in that view, must constitute an effort to convey thought or imagination or, at the very least, to represent thought or imagination in words or other symbols that are capable of being apprehended by another person even if the speaker, like the keeper of a private diary, has no intention of actually revealing that manifestation of thought to another. Communication need not be rationally apprehensible to constitute speech. It may consist of an abstract collocation of colors, forms, sounds, or movements that is intended to convey a sense of inchoate emotion or aesthetic sentiment. But its purpose must be to communicate (or, again, at least to render thought in some communicable form).

A number of commentators have suggested that personal copying, assembly, and sharing constitute speech.[35] Indeed, at least one court has posited that peer-to-peer file sharing deserves a measure of First Amendment protection because "the file sharer may be expressing himself or herself through the music selected and made available to others."[36] Is that right? Does file sharing truly constitute "speech" in the communicative sense I have described? Or is it merely "self-expressive" in the generic, nonspeech personal liberty sense?

The answer, I think, is that the lion's share of such activity does not qualify as speech. Amassing a collection of music recordings or television programs on one's computer is overwhelmingly consumptive. File sharers may be more actively engaged in selecting which particular items they consume than are traditional consumers of prepackaged media bundles like record albums and TV network schedules. But file sharers' active consumerism no more manifests an intent to render thought or imagination in communicative form than does collecting coins or buying shoes. In fact, while we sometimes publicly tout our choice of clothes, car, or other consumer goods in order to communicate something of our worldview, the same cannot generally be said of file sharing. Peer-to-peer file-sharing programs typically involve anonymous searches for specified items without regard to whose computer might house the item that the searcher wants to obtain. By the same token, when a file sharer makes his movie and music files available for others to download, he merely makes it possible for individual files to appear in others' searches for those items; he does not make public the list of works residing on his computer and hence conveys nothing of his interests and cultural taste.

File sharers thus stand far apart, certainly from those who modify and remix popular works, but also from creators of personal Web pages like MySpace, featuring copies of the creator's favorite photos, poems, videos, and music recordings. To fill a MySpace page with myriad content of one's choosing is a self-expressive act much like that of editors of poetry anthologies, makers of quilts, and creators of collages. Personal page creators' choice and arrangement of others' preexisting works manifest their own thought and imagination. Unlike file sharers, they display their personal selection to express something of who they are.

That does not end our analysis, however: even though file sharing is not itself "speech," unlicensed peer-to-peer file-sharing networks might still further First Amendment values in two principal ways. First, the music, video, and other works that are available on such networks are "speech," and *access* to speech, to the expression and information that others have rendered in communicable form, is no less central to our system of free expression than is the making of speech. As the Supreme Court has repeatedly iterated, First Amendment law and free speech policy serve listeners as well as speakers.[37] It, accordingly, has long been a part of U.S. telecommunications policy to ensure cheap access to information and opinion through such vehicles as public libraries and free over-the-air television.[38]

In that light, unlicensed file trading provides access to a great deal of expression that would not otherwise be available. Undoubtedly, only a small percentage of a typical teenager's 10,000-song collection, downloaded through unlicensed peer-to-peer networks, actually displaces music that the teenager could or would otherwise have bought. To the extent unlicensed peer-to-peer file sharing enhances access to speech, it serves First Amendment goals. That most certainly does not mean that untrammeled file sharing's free speech benefits outweigh its evisceration of copyright incentives to create new work. But in fashioning copyright doctrine for the digital age, we need be mindful that copyright and the First Amendment share the goal of promoting the widespread dissemination of original expression as well as its creation.

Second, unlicensed copying, assembly, and recirculation of copyrighted works may have *instrumental* value for our system of free expression. As I discuss in later chapters, peer-to-peer file trading networks, YouTube, and other sites for digital distribution of expression help to lessen copyright-supported commercial media's dominance of content distribution. As such, those sites create openings for authors and artists who are not affiliated with major labels, publishers, and studios to reach a sizeable audience. They also afford an outlet for the creative appropriations, remixes, and mashups that, in digitally intertwining elements of disparate well-known works, have emerged as a potent art form and sometime vehicle for social critique and political commentary.

So even though individual file traders are not themselves engaged in "speech," peer-to-peer file trading networks and other sites where individuals post copyrighted works might, on balance, provide a salutary structural contribution to our system of free expression by enhancing expressive diversity. Like many new media throughout copyright history, including early radio and cable television, today's nascent digital distribution sites might have great difficulty getting off the ground—and thus might never be developed in the first place—if unable to feature popular expression. Often, it is only by first attracting a critical mass of audience for familiar, mainstream expression that new media can provide meaningful outlets for independent artists as well. That is not to say that copyright holders should go uncompensated.

But, as we will see, it does suggest that First Amendment values might best be served if incumbent studios, record labels, and publishers are unable to impose a bottleneck on new media by exercising a veto over the noncommercial copying, distribution, and remixing of their works.

AUTHORS' INTEREST IN CONTROLLING THE FORM AND CONTEXT IN WHICH THEIR CREATION APPEARS

Many authors care deeply about how their work is conveyed to the public even years after a work's creation. Former Doors drummer, John Densmore, is one example.[39] Densmore recently rebuffed Cadillac's $15 million offer to license the Doors song "Break on Through (to the Other Side)" for a commercial selling the company's luxury SUVs. Densmore has steadfastly refused to license Doors songs for advertising, viewing that use as contrary to the meaning of the band's music. As Densmore put it: "I've had people say kids died in Vietnam listening to this music, other people say they know someone who didn't commit suicide because of this music. . . . On stage, when we played these songs, they felt mysterious and magic. That's not for rent." Regarding Cadillac in particular, Densmore reportedly insisted that "he just couldn't sell a song to a company that was polluting the world." Other popular artists who consistently refuse to license their songs for use in commercials include Bruce Springsteen, Neil Young, Carlos Santana, and Tom Waits.

Authors might also object to the use of their work to express an explicit political message with which they do not agree. The Who guitarist Pete Townshend refused Michael Moore permission to end the film *Farenheit 9-11,* Moore's searing pre–2004 election dismembering of George W. Bush, with the Who's rock anthem "Won't Get Fooled Again."[40] That song, Townshend stated, was meant to question "the heart of democracy," to ask why "we vote heartily for leaders who we subsequently always seem to find wanting," not to take sides for or against any particular politician or cause. Decades ago, at the height of the cold war, Dmitri Shostakovich and three fellow Soviet composers sued Twentieth Century Fox to prevent the use of their music in the score of an anti-Soviet spy thriller.[41] The composers decried the "false imputation of disloyalty to their country" that, in their view, the use of their work in that context cast upon them. And, of course, the Margaret Mitchell estate's insistence that no *Gone with the Wind* sequel contain miscegenation or homosexuality may well reflect Mitchell's own views.

In all these instances, authors view their work as an ongoing communication to the public. As such, they would like to control the form and context in which their work is communicated. Like all speakers, authors can often influence the way their expression is initially apprehended by choosing the precise locution, media, timing, and circumstances to present their thoughts. And, as David McGowan puts it, many authors would like to "keep on trying to manage the meaning of a work" even long after the work is published.[42]

I have no doubt that for many authors it is painful and humiliating to see their work distorted or otherwise deployed to convey a meaning that they oppose. But the key question for us is whether authors' understandable desire for continuing control over their creative expression falls within the province of "freedom of speech." Would Michael Moore's use of "Won't Get Fooled Again" without Pete Townshend's permission be an affront to First Amendment values? Should an author's interest in preventing others from using a decades-old work in a manner that the author believes distorts the work's original meaning or runs contrary to the message that the author now wishes to propound be given weight in designing free speech policy, particularly in tailoring copyright law to promote speech?

For Professor McGowan, it is "obvious" that an author's desire to influence his work's meaning by controlling the form and context in which the work is perceived over time, not just upon its first dissemination to the public, constitutes a cognizable speech interest. Justin Hughes agrees: "[F]reedom of expression is meaningless without assurances that the expression will remain unadulterated. Free speech requires that speech be guaranteed some integrity. It follows that if intellectual property is expression, it merits the same guarantee."[43]

Professors McGowan and Hughes correctly identify a speech interest in authors' continuing control, but that interest is far narrower and thus translates to a far more limited scope of control than they assume. Authors do have a speech interest in presenting their work to the public in the precise formulation, context, and media that they believe will best convey their message and aesthetic sensitivities. Some right to communicate one's words without distortion is central to speech's value for individual autonomy and self-realization, and might also further expressive diversity. Granted, no one who puts pen to paper can control how distant, or, for that matter, even immediate, audiences will interpret and respond to his expression. But the importance of expression for self-definition and autonomy lies largely in our Sisyphean attempts to formulate and transmit our thoughts in the manner that we believe will most likely lead to an understanding of what matters most to us in each expression.

However, an author's speech interest in presenting his work in unadulterated form and context does not extend per se to an exclusive right to control each and every instantiation of his work. Margaret Mitchell's speech interest in communicating *Gone with the Wind* is fully realized by the distribution of her novel in the iteration she conceived. Having communicated her expression, she has no cognizable speech interest in controlling others' creative appropriation of parts of the novel in their own speech, any more than she has a speech interest in preventing others from applying her ideas or criticizing or interpreting the novel in ways she does not like.

The reiteration and reformulation of Mitchell's written work are "non-rivalrous" in both an economic and a free speech sense. Alice Randall's sardonic recasting of Mitchell's characters and scenes does not in any way preclude Mitchell's heirs from conveying their and Mitchell's message in a formulation of their choosing. If Mitchell's heirs wish to perpetuate Mitchell's voice in unadulterated form, free from any distortion of her chosen locution, they need only to continue to distribute *Gone with the Wind.* In that way, Mitchell speaks *and* Randall speaks (and, by adopting Mitchell's words as their own, her heirs speak as well).[44]

Of course, if Randall has her way, *The Wind Done Gone* will so devastatingly subvert *Gone with the Wind* that no one will ever view Mitchell's Civil War saga the same way again. But that does not mean that Mitchell or her heirs have a speech interest in preventing Randall from recasting the saga from the viewpoint of a slave. They have no more speech interest in barring Randall's use of Mitchell's original characters, scenes, and dialogue than in preventing Randall from deploying any other words to make people think differently of *Gone with the Wind.* Mitchell's heirs are free to respond to Randall's speech with their own. They can repel Randall's charge by directly countering her criticism, savaging Randall's reformulation, writing their own *Gone with the Wind* sequel, or simply continuing to market Mitchell's novel with the hope that Mitchell's original words will be sufficiently powerful to continue to convey something of Mitchell's (and now her heirs') intended message and aesthetic sensitivity. If, to borrow from Justice Brandeis, Randall's novel propagates "falsehood and fallacies, . . . the remedy to be applied is more speech, not enforced silence."[45]

There are but two discrete circumstances in which authors' desire for continuing creative control might implicate First Amendment values. First, another's use of an author's work is sometimes perceived as originating from the author or otherwise disseminated with the author's approval. Authors do have a cognizable speech interest in refraining from appearing to convey or endorse a message that is not their own. As the Supreme Court has emphasized, "One important manifestation of the principle of free speech is that one who chooses to speak may also decide 'what not to say.' "[46] In *Hurley v. Irish-American Gay, Lesbian and Bisexual Group of Boston, Inc.,* the Court unanimously held that the Commonwealth of Massachusetts could not require organizers of Boston's Saint Patrick's Day parade to allow a group supporting gay rights to march, since that group's message might be understood to have originated with or be shared by the parade organizers. In other cases, the Court has similarly held that the government may not compel speech that suggests affirmance of a belief with which the speaker disagrees.[47]

Unlike government-compelled speech, a private party's unlicensed use of another's expression in a way that falsely implies endorsement would not normally give rise to a First Amendment claim. Nonetheless, an author's interest in avoiding such compelled speech does implicate free speech values. It thus deserves serious consideration in shaping an author's legal entitlements.[48]

But an author's speech interest in avoiding false endorsement does not translate to an across-the-board exclusive right to control her work, at least after she has already released her work to the public. If Pete Townshend has a speech interest in preventing Michael Moore's use of "Won't Get Fooled Again," it is that Moore's audiences are likely to associate that song with Townshend and thus will likely believe that Townshend endorses (or at least does not oppose) Moore's message. Townshend's speech interest does not lie in the song itself but in the fact that people identify the song with him and thus might view Moore's use of the song as Townshend's speech, much as parade watchers might have seen the gay rights group's participation in the St. Patrick's Day parade as the parade organizer's speech. Conversely, where no one would reasonably attribute a use of an author's work to the author— Alice Randall's biting reversal of Margaret Mitchell's *Gone with the Wind* is an obvious example—the author has no speech interest in preventing the use. She is, after all, free to press her own interpretation of her work through her own speech. As the Supreme Court has recently reiterated in rejecting law schools' compelled-speech First Amendment challenge to a law requiring them to allow military recruiters on campus, "Nothing about recruiting suggests that law schools agree with any speech by recruiters, and nothing in the [statute] restricts what the law schools may say about the military's policies."[49]

Note that, like the law schools, the author's speech interest in preventing forced speech derives from the audience's reasonable perception. If filmmakers like Michael Moore were generally free to use songs without the copyright holders' permission and most film audiences knew that, few would regard Moore's use of Townshend's song as saying one thing or another about Townshend's own beliefs. Certainly, given the ubiquity of cover recordings of popular songs, which may be produced and distributed under statutory license without the copyright holder's permission, a cover of "Won't Get Fooled Again" by the Nazi punk band White Pride would hardly be understood to mean that Townshend is a Nazi. Thus, at bottom, an author's speech interest in preventing false endorsement rests on a self-feeding circle. The author's speech interest is contingent on social practices and perceptions that are themselves contingent on whether authors enjoy exclusive rights.

The second circumstance in which an author might have a speech interest in creative control is when another person's use could drown out the author's voice. Ted Turner acquired the copyrights in a library of hundreds of old films, including John Huston's film noir classic *The Asphalt Jungle* (1950). As fitting with his artistic vision, Huston had shot his film in high-contrast black-and-white, but Turner colorized it for showing to television audiences. To the extent that black-and-white copies are unavailable or, perhaps, just if Turner's mass-marketed colorized version overwhelms audience consciousness of Huston's original, Huston's speech is effectively silenced.

The wave of product placement advertising in television and film presents another possible example. The Writers Guild of America has called for an end to studios and advertisers forcing writers to shoehorn products into their work regardless of whether product placement fits the story line. When writers must modify story lines to incorporate shots of advertisers' products in contexts that place those products in a positive light, the writer's own creative vision does not reach the screen.

These scenarios present a conflict between a work's creator and the publisher or studio that finances and distributes the work. It presents a conflict, in other words, between individuals who are often (though not always) driven to convey a message or artistic vision and a commercial entity that has significant incentives to modify and distribute the work in a manner calculated to maximize a firm's overall profits. And ironically in the present context, it is the commercial entity, not the creator, that typically owns the copyright.

The conflict between authors and publishers (including studios) over creative control is as old as copyright itself. Authors have traditionally relied on publishers to communicate to the public, yet market dictates (as well as other factors) can lead publishers to be unfaithful conveyors of an author's expression. Especially in capital-intensive, scale-economy mass-media markets, publishers have an incentive to modify expressive products to cater to advertisers and meet the lowest common denominator of consumer taste.[50]

Commentators have long viewed publishers' market-driven infidelities as an obstacle to the expressive autonomy of authors. Indeed, none other than Immanuel Kant, writing in the eighteenth century, insisted that in order for an author's speech to constitute an autonomous exercise of the author's free will, the publisher must act solely as the author's agent and thus may not obtain title to the author's work.[51] Kant's writing about authorship served as a theoretical foundation for the continental European doctrine of moral rights, which accord authors with the inalienable personal right to claim authorship credit and prevent gross distortions of their work, even at the hands of persons who hold the economic copyright.

We should look to something like moral rights, not proprietary copyright, if we want to further authors' expressive autonomy in the face of commercial publishers' and studios' drive to produce conventional, advertiser-friendly product. John Huston and his heirs had no claim against Ted Turner in the United States because Turner had acquired the copyright. But when Turner licensed his colorized version of *Asphalt Jungle* to a French broadcaster, the French Supreme Court found the colorization to infringe Huston's moral rights. In the absence of such moral rights under U.S. copyright law, the Writers Guild and Directors Guild have sought to obtain similar protection through collective bargaining agreements that require the copyright holder studios to grant writers and directors greater creative control and thus give more play to individuals' artistic vision. Those rights of creative control *diminish* the copyright holder's prerogatives, much like inalienable moral rights. They certainly do not serve to justify Blackstonian copyright as an instrument of furthering authors' speech rights.

Conclusion

Free speech theory and policy intertwine with copyright at multiple points. Copyright profoundly shapes the mix of speech and speakers that populate our public discourse. Both the speech and speakers that copyright impacts stand at the heart of free speech policy and the First Amendment. A copyright of narrow scope and duration serves First Amendment goals by fostering market-based expression while leaving ample room for creative appropriation and other types of speech and speakers for whom copyright may be more of a hindrance than needed incentive. Regrettably, as we will now explore in some detail, today's copyright has ballooned well beyond these modest proportions and, in so doing, has strayed from its salutary speech-enhancing core.

CHAPTER FOUR | Copyright's Ungainly Expansion

COPYRIGHT, JAMES MADISON WROTE in *The Federalist Papers,* is an instance in which the "public good fully coincides ... with the claims of individuals."[1] Few of Madison's contemporaries would have disagreed. The nascent republic, they believed, required an educated, independent-minded citizenry, and they viewed authors as educators and literary works as instruments of pedagogy and patriotism. The Constitution thus empowers Congress to "to promote the progress of science" by according authors exclusive rights for limited times. Likewise, the first federal copyright statute, the Act of May 1790, was entitled "An Act for the encouragement of learning."[2]

The federal copyright that the Framers enacted was a narrow, short-term right in printed matter.[3] The Act of May 31, 1790, granted to U.S. citizens and residents who authored maps, navigational charts, or books the exclusive right to "print, reprint, publish, or vend" for a once-renewable fourteen-year term. That decidedly limited grant left others free to use copyrighted works in a myriad of ways, including reciting books in public, making copies by hand, and making and publishing translations and abridgments. It also pointedly circumscribed the universe of expression that could be subject to an author's exclusive rights. Under the 1790 Act, works authored by foreigners were ineligible for copyright. Nor did copyright extend to graphics, sheet music, newspapers, or other types of creative works that were not enumerated in the statute.

Moreover, the 1790 Act conditioned copyright protection on compliance with several nontrivial procedural requirements. A prospective copyright owner had to obtain a copyright registration prior to the work's publication by depositing a printed copy with the local district court. The owner was then required to publish a notice of that registration in a U.S. newspaper for at least four weeks and, within six months of publication, to deposit another printed copy with the secretary of state.[4] Those prerequisites seem to have greatly curtailed copyright's effective reach. Only a small fraction of the books published in the United States in the decade following enactment of the federal statute were registered for copyright.[5] Nonetheless, a U.S. book trade grew and flourished, based largely on publishing British and public domain works.

Today's copyright law bears scant resemblance to its original formulation. Compared with their early American counterparts, current copyright holders enjoy a capacious bundle of rights in many more uses of many more types of published works for a far greater time and with fewer preconditions. The sharply delineated boundaries within which the Framers cabined copyright began slowly to give way early in the nineteenth century. In 1802, Congress extended copyright protection to etched and engraved prints.[6] In 1831, it added musical compositions and lengthened the copyright term.[7] Copyright's expansion gained momentum in the late nineteenth and early twentieth centuries with the addition of new copyrightable subject matter, a still longer duration, and new rights, such as the exclusive right to make translations.

Yet, until recent decades, copyright law's basic contours still evinced an understanding of copyright as a decidedly limited grant. It has been largely since Congress enacted the Copyright Act revision of 1976 that copyright's scope and duration have burst from their moorings, growing with unwonted precipitousness and force. That expansion, in turn, has spawned a vicious cycle. Over time, as copyright law provides for ever greater exclusive rights, it both fuels and increasingly comports with a naive notion of absolute property right. It reinforces the view that copyright owners are intrinsically entitled to control and reap the full value of each and every use of copyright-protected expression, thus smoothing the way to still further expansion.

To be certain, one could hardly expect copyright law to remain unchanged since 1790. Among other factors, the more than two centuries since the first U.S. copyright statute was enacted have seen the emergence of new forms of expression (such as photographs, movies, and sound recordings) and new means of dissemination (including cinema, broadcasting, and Internet transmission). Congress has rightly recognized that securing authors' limited exclusive rights in those forms of expression and means of dissemination, no less than the exclusive right to reproduce printed material, can provide an important incentive for making valuable contributions to the store of knowledge and culture.

But other areas of copyright expansion are far more troublesome. They give today's copyright holders an unprecedented right to constrain speakers' ability to build on existing works to convey ideas and create new expression. Copyright's recent expansion in these areas raises concern particularly because it far exceeds what can be justified or explained by any need to provide an incentive for the creation and dissemination of creative expression.

Nor does copyright's conceptual metamorphosis from limited grant to robust property right bode well for applying copyright's traditional delicate balance in the digital arena. The Internet and other digital technology demand that we adapt and reformulate copyright doctrine to radically different markets, incentives, and possibilities for bottom-up speech that challenge large media firms' domination of public discourse. We need to determine whether copyright owners will be entitled to prevent individuals from creating and disseminating their digital remixes and mashups, writing fan fiction, posting copyrighted works on personal Web pages, and seeking out and trading copyrighted songs, video, text, and graphics on peer-to-peer networks, including "bootleg" and other versions of works that copyright owners do not make publicly available. We must also ask whether inventors of new technological means of disseminating, experiencing, and organizing expression, like Google, YouTube, TiVo, Bit Torrent, and Clean Flicks, should be subject to copyright holders' veto over applying their innovative technologies to copyrighted works.

I do not pretend that these are easy questions; the Internet and other digital technologies empower individuals to copy, share, parse, manipulate, and access expression in ways that significantly erode if not completely supplant the traditional markets upon which authors, publishers, and commercial media have long relied. To properly address these issues we need to translate copyright's fundamental principles to circumstances that traditional copyright doctrine did not anticipate. Our understanding of those fundamental principles will heavily color our approach and will thus shape copyright doctrine in the coming years. And, regrettably, the ascending view of copyright as Blackstonian property, rather than a grant narrowly tailored to promote the shared goals of "progress of science" and free speech, has already skewed legislative initiatives and judicial decisions in applying copyright to the digital arena.

This chapter outlines some of the most troublesome areas of copyright's untoward expansion. I canvass copyright duration, creative appropriation, the constriction of fair use, "paracopyright," personal uses, and new technological means of dissemination.

Duration

The Constitution's Copyright Clause empowers Congress to secure authors' exclusive rights for "limited times." Copyright's finite duration is central to its speech-enhancing purpose. If copyright's object is to promote learning and discourse, then at some point the public must be able freely to copy, modify, and reformulate the creative expression that has become an integral part of our cultural matrix. Under copyright's traditional schema, as David Nimmer has aptly noted, creative "works are relegated to the public domain to become the heritage of all humanity and copyright is simply a temporary way station to reward authors on the road to that greater good."[8]

The Framers' copyright grant was fully in keeping with this injunction. When Congress enacted the Act of May 31, 1790, it limited copyright to a fourteen-year term, which the copyright owner could renew for one additional fourteen-year term only if the author was still living and still a U.S. citizen or resident at the expiry of the initial term.[9] Congress subsequently lengthened copyright's duration. But until the last quarter of the twentieth century, it did so quite haltingly and modestly. In 1831, Congress doubled the initial term to twenty-eight years.[10] Then, as part of the general copyright revision of 1909, it doubled the renewal term as well.[11] The Copyright Act of 1909 thus resulted in an overall maximum fifty-six-year term. But since the vast majority of copyrights were never renewed for a second term, copyright's effective duration for most works remained only twenty-eight years from publication.[12]

That quite sparing term of protection remained in force until the enactment of the Copyright Act of 1976.[13] With that general revision, Congress abolished the renewal requirement for newly created works and extended the standard duration of the copyright owner's exclusive rights to the life of the author plus 50 years, with the term for works for hire (for which the employer is deemed to be the author) 75 years from publication or 100 years from creation, whichever expires first.[14] In 1998, following concerted copyright industry lobbying, Congress extended the copyright term yet again. The Sonny Bono Copyright Term Extension Act gives copyright owners another 20 years of protection and applies that extension retrospectively to subsisting copyrights, as well as prospectively to works yet to be created.[15]

Congressional amendment of the copyright term has not been entirely one-sided. Unpublished works fell outside the ambit of federal copyright law until the Copyright Act of 1976, and under applicable state common law, such works, at least in theory, enjoyed perpetual protection. Since the effective date of the 1976 Act, works of authorship are subject to the specified finite copyright terms even if they remain unpublished. Nevertheless, for published and unpublished works alike, copyright owner control may now commonly endure for more than a century before a work enters the public domain. That term, leading economists agree, is "functionally perpetual." The two decades that the Sonny Bono Act tacked on at the end of an already lengthy copyright term provide no additional economic incentive for authors to create new expression.[16] Nor, as we will see later, does an extended copyright term even enhance the continued dissemination and availability of old works.

As a result, it is increasingly difficult to see copyright's limited term as a means for securing First Amendment values. The Framers' plain intent was to sharply restrict the duration even of what was then a very limited monopoly over speech. But today's copyright law has forsaken that original understanding. Except for works of a bygone era, much of the literature, art, film, and music that serves as the wellspring for further creative expression, or simply the most resonant vehicle for a speaker to convey her message, is subject to copyright holders' proprietary control.

Creative Appropriation

Good artists borrow; great artists steal.
—Pablo Picasso

A good composer does not imitate; he steals.
—Igor Stravinsky

Immature poets imitate; mature poets steal.
—T. S. Eliot

He just steals from me, but I steal from everybody.
—Woody Guthrie

All authorship builds upon preexisting expression. Authors—not just the greats, but all of us who share our thoughts and creative impulses through traditional media or the Internet—regularly take from existing art, literature, music, and film. At the very least, our work reflects the information and inspiration we draw from existing speech. Yet much of our expressive creation is also populated with explicit references to the works of others. We commonly build upon, reference, translate, critique, comment upon, parody, excerpt, and otherwise creatively reformulate existing works. The speech of our predecessors constitutes our raw material; our refinements nourish those that follow.

However, copyright expansion has sharply constricted authors' liberty to take from others' expression in creating their own. Throughout most of the nineteenth century, authors were free to build upon existing works as long as they made their own substantial contribution and did not displace demand for the original work in its original form. In one landmark case, for example, an unauthorized German translator of *Uncle Tom's Cabin* defeated Harriet Beecher Stowe's copyright infringement action against him; the court held that the translation was a new work and not merely a reproduction of the original.[17] The principle that copyright is delimited by what the defendant has contributed began to erode in the late nineteenth century, however, and has continued steadily to crumble into the twenty-first century.[18]

Today, copyright law's governing premise, far from being solicitous to secondary, transformative authorship, is that "no plagiarist can excuse the wrong by showing how much of his work he did not pirate."[19] That unitary focus on what the defendant appropriated is broadly applied even to highly creative secondary authors who engage in little or no verbatim copying of the copyrighted work. For a novelist or screenwriter to infringe under current law, it is often enough to draw upon an earlier work's basic themes, bare storyline, or characters, no matter that the author has copied not a single sentence or line of dialogue. Given these loose standards, a leading copyright commentator concludes—with good reason—that if Shakespeare's *Romeo and Juliet* were protected by copyright today, the Broadway musical *West Side Story* might well be found to infringe.[20] Likewise with music. Under current case law, a songwriter can unwittingly infringe even if she did not consciously copy from a prior song and, indeed, even if her melody bears no resemblance to the original. She can be held liable if a musicologist convinces the court that her chord progression, key, tempo, rhythm, and genre create an "impression of similarity" with the prior song.[21] Indeed, across all types of expression, infringement has been held to lie in nothing more than a similar combination of uncopyrightable ideas and generic, stock elements that are entirely standard for works of that genre.[22]

Forced to grapple with copyright's loose standards for nonliteral infringement, Judge Learned Hand lamented some fifty years ago, "The test for infringement of copyright is necessarily vague" and "[d]ecisions . . . must therefore inevitably be ad hoc."[23] That is even more true under our current regime. Today's artists, writers, and musicians build upon the works of their predecessors at their peril.

The move from solicitude to general intolerance for a secondary author's creative appropriation is manifested in both statute and case law. The Copyright Act of 1976 now accords copyright owners a broad, exclusive right to prepare derivative works based on the original.[24] These include translations, arrangements, versions in other media, and "any other form in which a work may be recast, transformed, or adapted." At the same time, courts have liberally construed the exclusive right to reproduce copies, holding that a secondary author may infringe that right by evoking an existing work's "total concept and feel," without literally copying or even paraphrasing any of the original's expression.[25]

Because of these developments, speech that copies from an existing work at a high level of abstraction, containing no identity or even close similarity of words or specific elements of design, but only a resemblance of style, mood, and overall aesthetic appeal, may well run afoul of the copyright holder's rights. Courts apply a dizzying array of tests to determine when the defendant's work is "substantially similar" to the plaintiff's and thus infringing. In some, courts purport to apply the total concept and feel test in a "more discerning manner," with a greater focus on specific copyrightable elements.[26] But given the inconsistent application of these tests—the Ninth Circuit has repeatedly referred to the "turbid waters" of what is supposed to be its objective, analytic test for substantial similarity—many cases go the jury with the amorphous instruction to make a subjective, even emotional assessment of "whether defendant took from plaintiff's works so much of what is pleasing to [the lay audience] that defendant wrongfully appropriated something which belongs to the plaintiff."[27]

Moreover, as we have seen with hip-hop, a defendant who has copied verbatim only a minuscule portion of a preexisting work and incorporated it as a minuscule portion of his own work may likewise run afoul of the reproduction right in the original. Under today's rule of "fragmented literal similarity," the fact that the defendant's contribution far outweighs what he copied is irrelevant to the prima facie case of copyright infringement.[28] In short, like the producers of *West Side Story,* T. S. Eliot might today run afoul of copyright were not *The Waste Land* a pastiche of centuries-old material.

Copyright doctrine does contain limits on copyright holders' rights, designed largely to mitigate copyright's burden on creative appropriation. These primarily include the idea/expression dichotomy, the rule that de minimis copying will not infringe, and the fair use doctrine. The problem is that as copyright holders' rights have expanded, these purported free speech safeguards have atrophied. First, consider the idea/expression dichotomy.

THE IDEA/EXPRESSION DICHOTOMY

Copyright law prevents speakers from copying only the copyright holder's particular literary form or "expression," not the ideas or facts that are expressed. As the Supreme Court has underscored, in order to serve both First Amendment goals and the Copyright Clause's stated objective of "promot[ing] the progress of science and the useful arts," copyright doctrine "assures authors the right to their original expression, but encourages others to build freely upon the ideas and information conveyed by a work."[29] Speakers, in other words, are invited to convey the ideas and facts contained within the copyright holder's work so long as they do so in words, graphics, or other expressive components that are not "substantially similar" to those that constitute the copyright holder's work.

The idea/expression dichotomy came into being when copyright holders' rights expanded to encompass creative adaptations and reformulations of existing expression. Once copyright holders' exclusive rights extended beyond mere verbatim and near-verbatim copying, it became necessary to define some outer limit to those rights, lest copyright holders' proprietary control over existing expression unduly burden new speech. But the idea/expression dichotomy is a highly uncertain and undependable vehicle for safeguarding transformative speech. Under the total-concept-and-feel and audience tests for substantial similarity, what might once have been considered the permissible, indeed laudable, reformulation of an unprotected "idea" may now purportedly constitute infringing copying of "expression." Indeed, even a shared sequencing of plot ideas and generic elements has been held to be an unlawful copying of "expression."[30] The result, as Nimmer pointedly laments, is that the law of substantial similarity as applied in our courts repeatedly runs counter to the Supreme Court's injunction in *Feist Publications, Inc. v. Rural Telephone Service Co.* that copyright infringement may lie only in copying copyrightable expression.[31]

At bottom, the problem is not simply that expression has steadily gobbled up idea, but that there is no clear line between idea and expression. The idea/expression dichotomy is notoriously malleable and indeterminate, far more useful as a shorthand for justifying judges' case-by-case conclusions regarding when a defendant has prima facie inappropriately copied than as a mechanism for predicting what sorts of copying and borrowing are permissible. As Judge Learned Hand conceded, the line between idea and expression, "wherever it is drawn, will seem arbitrary."[32]

As a result, even though courts sometimes hold that the defendant has only copied an idea, the idea/expression dichotomy's very vagueness induces considerable self-censorship among speakers. Copyright supposedly encourages speakers to incorporate and build upon existing ideas. But how are speakers to know in advance whether their transformative speech is infringing reproduction or permissible reformulation of existing "idea"? Given the indeterminate character of the idea/expression dichotomy and the broad reach of what constitutes "substantial similarity," speakers who seek to build upon existing ideas often risk finding themselves on the receiving end of a copyright infringement action.

DE MINIMIS COPYING

The same can be said with respect to the doctrine of de minimis copying. Under that doctrine, trivial copying of minute portions of existing works is deemed noninfringing despite nominally constituting fragmented literal similarity. But the doctrine of de minimis copying is applied inconsistently at best. One court held that a television program's cropped and out-of-focus background shots of the plaintiff's artwork, totaling twenty-seven seconds, were not de minimis and were thus infringing.[33] On other occasions, courts have blocked the release of entire films because copyrighted objects, such as a courtyard or chair, appeared fleetingly in the background of a single scene.[34] As Jon Else's experience demonstrates, the pervasive uncertainty over whether a court would find a background shot to be infringing or a permissible de minimis use (or fair use) has a chilling effect on speech. As noted earlier, moreover, the Sixth Circuit has recently responded to that uncertainty by simply abolishing the de minimis defense for sampling a sound recording. Under such circumstances, neither the idea/expression dichotomy nor the doctrine of de minimis use adequately safeguards transformative expression.

FAIR USE

The fair use doctrine affords a privilege to make what would otherwise be an infringing use of copyrighted expression. Ironically, what is now the fair use privilege—a limitation on copyright holders' rights—began as copyright's first tentative step in pushing beyond the exclusive right to make literal or near-literal copies. Supreme Court justice Joseph Story sketched out what later became the fair use doctrine in *Folsom v. Marsh,* an 1841 decision involving a compilation of George Washington's letters.[35] As Justice Story recognized, under the law of the time, a "fair and bona fide abridgment," consisting of a "real, substantial condensation of the materials, and intellectual labor and judgment bestowed thereon," did not infringe the copyright in the original. Justice Story held, however, that while a secondary author is generally entitled to rework an existing book into a new one, it is not a fair and bona fide abridgment to copy verbatim so many key passages that the defendant's work would usurp the market for the original.

Today, the fair use privilege operates against a default rule that holds infringing even nonliteral reworkings and minimal copying that pose no threat to the market for the original. As codified in the Copyright Act of 1976, the fair use doctrine requires courts to undertake a case-by-case analysis, employing as a general guide for decision four statutory factors plus any other factor the court deems appropriate.[36] Fair use is meant to give free rein to uses of existing expression where that would serve copyright's broad goal of promoting "the creation and publication of edifying matter."[37] The fair use doctrine is said to embody copyright law's recognition that "[e]very book in literature, science, and art, borrows and must necessarily borrow, and use much which was well known and used before."[38] It crystallizes the understanding that copyright stands in tension with this need to borrow and build upon prior work. While copyrights should generally be protected, "one must not put manacles upon science."[39]

With those salutary purposes in mind, courts and commentators often state that fair use, like the idea/expression dichotomy, ameliorates the tension between copyright and free speech. Indeed, courts consistently hold that fair use provides a free speech safety valve within copyright law that obviates any need for external, First Amendment constraint on copyright holders' entitlements. But that faith in fair use's power to protect speech mistakes flowery rhetoric about the privilege's philosophical underpinnings for how the doctrine actually operates in practice. In fact, fair use suffers from much the same infirmities as the idea/expression dichotomy. Far from serving as the robust free speech safeguard that courts often imagine, fair use has come to be an exceedingly feeble, inconstant check on copyright holders' proprietary control.

Like the idea/expression dichotomy, fair use's protection of First Amendment interests has become increasingly sporadic in recent decades. The watershed in fair use's debilitation came in the Supreme Court's 1985 decision in *Harper & Row Publishers, Inc. v. Nation Enterprises.*[40] In that case, the *Nation* had scooped copyright licensee *Time* magazine by obtaining former president Gerald Ford's unpublished memoirs and running a story that revealed Ford's reasons for pardoning Richard Nixon. The *Nation*'s story quoted some 300 words from Ford's over 200,000-word manuscript. When Harper & Row, Ford's publisher, sued the *Nation* for copyright infringement, the *Nation* argued fair use. The district court held for Harper & Row, but on appeal, the

Second Circuit reversed. It held that the *Nation*'s minimal borrowing of Ford's actual words was vital to lending authenticity and understanding to its news story. As the court emphasized, free speech concerns must color our interpretation of fair use. The Copyright Act, it stated, "was not meant to obstruct the citizens' access to vital facts and historical observations about our nation's life."[41]

The Supreme Court then reversed the Second Circuit in a 6-to-3 decision (with the Nixon, Ford, and Reagan appointees outvoting Justices Brennan, Marshall, and White). The case is admittedly a close one, given that *Time* was poised to publish key portions of the manuscript and then killed its story as a result of the *Nation*'s scoop. But my concern here is with the Court's reasoning, not its result. In rejecting the *Nation*'s fair use argument, the Court adopted a crabbed, decidedly property-centered view of fair use. It labeled the privilege as an "exception" to the copyright holder's exclusive rights available only in isolated cases when market failure prevents copyright licensing.

Fair use, the Court stated, is inappropriate unless a " 'reasonable copyright owner [would] have consented to the use' " given the " 'importance of the material copied or performed *from the point of view of the reasonable copyright owner.*' " Applying that standard, the Court posited that fair use rightly applies only in cases where the copyright owner and user would have likely agreed on a license but were prevented from doing so because of the high costs of negotiation. Even in those cases, moreover, the Court restricted fair use to instances in which neither the use in question nor similar uses by other persons would adversely affect the potential market for the copyrighted work. Finally, further undermining fair use's First Amendment potency, the Court defined the privilege as an "affirmative defense," placing the burden of proof on the party claiming fair use.[42] In short, following *Harper & Row*, it is the user who must demonstrate the absence of harm to potential markets, including harm that might be caused by other users and harm even to potential markets for derivative works that the copyright holder might never wish to exploit.[43] As Justice Brennan rightly decried in his *Harper & Row* dissent, "The progress of arts and science and the robust debate essential to an enlightened citizenry are ill served by this constricted reading of the fair use doctrine."

Since *Harper & Row*, the Blackstonian property-centered view of fair use has steadily gained ground. Courts have repeatedly invoked the bare possibility of licensing in potential markets for the copyright holder's work to deny fair use and have insisted that while evidence of market harm generally dooms a fair use claim, the absence of such evidence in no way guarantees that the use will be deemed fair.[44] In some cases, courts have denied fair use even where the copyright holder's avowed purpose is to suppress publication of material that might show the copyright holder in an unfavorable light.[45] The Supreme Court has also reiterated, and Congress has insisted, that fair use is indeed an affirmative defense, with the latter expressly criticizing the few post–*Harper & Row* courts that have dared to hold otherwise.[46] Commentators and government officials have even suggested that fair use will be largely unnecessary when digital technology and electronic communication sharply reduce licensing transaction costs and thus remedy the market failures that, they posit, provide the sole justification for fair use.[47] And a Second Circuit panel suggested that Congress could eliminate fair use without running afoul of the Copyright Clause or the First Amendment.[48]

Happily, there is a contrary strand of cases that stress the need to interpret fair use in line with First Amendment values. The Eleventh Circuit's reversal of the preliminary injunction against *The Wind Done Gone* is one of them. In so ruling the Court referred to fair use's "constitutional significance as a guarantor to access and use for First Amendment purposes."[49] Another is the Ninth Circuit's ruling that Tom Forsythe's "Food Chain Barbie" photographs qualified as fair use. Forsythe depicted naked Barbie dolls attacked by vintage household appliances in order to "lambast . . . the conventional beauty myth and social acceptance of women as objects [that] Barbie embodies" qualified as fair use. As the Court stated: "By developing and transforming associations with Mattel's Barbie doll, Forsythe has created the sort of social criticism and parodic speech protected by the First Amendment and promoted by the Copyright Act."[50]

Yet another counterweight to the property-centered view of fair use is the Second Circuit's recent rejection of a copyright holder's claim that fair use should be unavailable for a publisher that could have purchased a copyright license to incorporate reduced-size reproductions of rock concert posters in its illustrated history of the Grateful Dead. The Court characterized the publisher's book as a biographical work that serves a different expressive purpose from the plaintiff's posters. Such transformative speech, the Court held, can qualify for fair use even given an actual licensing market. For this Second Circuit panel, First Amendment values outweigh the market rationale trumpeted in cases following *Harper & Row*. A copyright holder, the Second Circuit held, "cannot prevent others from entering fair use markets merely 'by developing or licensing a market for parody, news reporting, educational or other transformative uses of its own creative work.'"[51]

The fate of numerous cases, including the pending lawsuit against Google's Book Search Project, hinges largely on whether the courts will follow a

Blackstonian or First Amendment approach to fair use. In the meantime, with some courts denying fair use whenever the defendant could have obtained a license or the use might harm a potential market that the copyright holder might conceivably wish to enter, and other courts proving highly solicitous of what they define as "transformative uses," fair use provides a highly unreliable defense of First Amendment values. Given the doctrine's open-ended, case-specific cast and inconsistent application, it is exceedingly difficult to predict whether a given use in a given case will qualify as the sort of transformative self-expression that enjoys the privilege.[52] That means, as Larry Lessig curtly puts it, that fair use boils down to "the right to hire a lawyer," to engage in protracted, costly, and time-consuming litigation to defend one's right to speak.[53]

Given the vagaries of fair use doctrine, fair use thus provides a highly permeable, often merely theoretical, defense of First Amendment interests. This is certainly so for individuals and nonmarket speakers who can ill afford to risk being sued or fight a lawsuit if they are. But it also holds true for the risk-averse publishers, studios, broadcasters, and record labels that serve as speakers' gateways to a mass audience. Copyright's inconstant, unpredictable free speech safety valves, coupled with the high cost of litigation, have engendered a "clear it or delete it" culture in which these gateway intermediaries—and their errors and omissions insurance carriers—regularly insist that speakers obtain permissions for all potentially actionable uses, even those that likely do not infringe.[54]

Paracopyright

Recent years have seen copyright industries' widespread (though not entirely successful) use of digital encryption and other "technological protection measures" designed to control access and use of digital content. At the same time, the industries have increasingly deployed Web site terms of use and other mass-market contracts to impose further restrictions on access and use of content. If such technological measures and contractual restrictions are enforceable and widely applied, they have the potential to expand copyright holders' control far beyond traditional copyright. Indeed, they could effectively render fair use, the idea/expression dichotomy, and copyright's limited duration—even in their current much reduced form—little more than a quaint relic of copyright's bygone safety net for free speech. Nevertheless, we now face a nascent "paracopyright" regime that would give those controls the full imprimatur of the law.

TECHNOLOGICAL PROTECTION MEASURES

Adobe Systems' early ebook version of Lewis Carroll's public domain classic, *Alice's Adventures in Wonderland,* bore the following restrictions on its copyright page:

> Copy: No text selections can be copied from this book to the clipboard.
> Print: No printing is permitted of this book.
> Lend: This book cannot be lent or given to someone else.
> Give: This book cannot be given to someone else.
> Read Aloud: This book cannot be read aloud.[55]

Adobe's *Alice's Adventures* ebook restrictions referred to technological controls, not contractual prohibitions on conduct: The "No text selections can be copied" restriction meant that the ebook was encrypted to make copying and pasting physically impossible, not that users faced a legal obligation requiring that they resist the temptation to copy. Likewise, "This book cannot be read aloud" meant that Adobe's Read Aloud feature would not work with the book, not that parents were forbidden from reading it to their children. Yet Adobe's technological controls were quite far-reaching just the same. They made it impossible to print or "copy" from (in the sense of using computer copy-and-paste commands) what is, after all, an edition of a public domain book.

Moreover, while unrestricted editions of the 140-year-old *Alice's Adventures* are widely available, both in print and on the Internet, new movies, sound recordings, and, of course, video games are increasingly distributed only in digital format. In the not-too-distant future, the same will be true of television programs, books, and, possibly, newspapers. If motion picture studios, record labels, video game manufacturers, and publishers have their way, technological controls embedded in digital copies, Web site gateways, personal computers, DVD players, ebook readers, game consoles, cell phones, and even television sets will seamlessly govern all access and uses of those works from their initial release, through the long duration of their copyright, and beyond. Given those technological controls, it will not be possible to cut and paste images and sounds from culturally salient expression to create artistic collage, video mix, machinima, political commentary, fan fiction, or even grade school research projects.

It will not be possible, that is, unless someone hacks the encryption and releases unprotected copies onto the Internet. That is where a 1998 amendment to the Copyright Act steps in. The Digital Millennium Copyright Act

(DMCA) forbids circumventing technology that controls access to copyrighted works.[56] The DMCA does not prohibit circumventing technological measures that prevent unlicensed copying. Congress deemed that unnecessary because unlicensed copying is itself a copyright infringement (or fair use). But a number of courts have apparently viewed every act of rendering protected content as gaining "access," such that virtually all copy controls are also access controls.[57] Moreover, the DMCA also proscribes the manufacture and distribution of any device, including software, that is marketed or primarily designed to circumvent a copy or access control. As a result, most people will be unable to obtain the tools they need to circumvent technological protection measures in order to engage in fair use or other noninfringing copying.

The DMCA dramatically expands copyright holders' control on a number of fronts. To begin with, by protecting access control measures from circumvention, the DMCA moves toward providing copyright holders with a right over access to their works. Traditional copyright law provides no such right. Once a book appears on bookstore shelves or a sculpture in a public place, anyone may view the work without needing the copyright holder's permission. Similarly, once I buy a CD, I can listen to it as often as I like. Reading, viewing, and listening, unlike copying, modifying, public display, and public performance, do not fall within the ambit of the copyright holder's exclusive rights.[58]

But when a copyright holder employs encryption or some other technological measure to control access to a work, for example, by including the work in an online database that cannot be entered without a password or distributing freestanding copies that cannot be viewed or played except on equipment containing the access "key," it is a violation of the DMCA to circumvent that access control or supply a device that others can use to circumvent it. In effect, then, by employing access control technology, the copyright holder enjoys the DMCA-supported ability to prevent, limit, or set the conditions for access, even if the act of gaining access would not infringe traditional copyright per se. Thus armed, the copyright holder might bar access to certain works, require a payment each time a reader "opens" an ebook or views a text online, or condition a music lover's continued access to songs he downloaded from a subscription service on his ongoing payment of monthly fees to the service.

Now, it is by no means certain that the emerging access right in and of itself radically expands copyright holder prerogatives; that right might merely shift copyright laterally to account for new means of distributing original expression. At some point, the "celestial jukebox," from which users may gain immediate access to texts, movies, and music of their choosing, may increasingly supplant downloading and owning hard-copy books, news-papers, DVDs, and CDs as the favored means for reading, viewing, and lis-tening to expression. It often already makes more sense to experience a work online without making or acquiring a copy. Ubiquitous portable communi-cations devices and wireless broadband networks fuel this trend. Selling access will not likely replace distributing copies entirely: among other things, given the free-falling cost of digital storage, bringing iPods that can easily hold every song ever recorded, owning digital copies might rival network access in convenience and affordability. But to the extent digital technology makes access on demand a desirable substitute for owning copies (or, for that matter, over-the-air broadcast) even some of the time, copy-right's goal of promoting the creation and dissemination of original expres-sion would be ill served by failing to accord a right to control access. To afford an access right in those circumstances is simply to translate copyright's principles—and traditional balance—to new technologies and conditions.

So if Congress merely added an access right narrowly tailored to this new means of distribution but still subject to copyright's traditional exceptions and limitations, I would hesitate to label it a dramatic expansion of copyright holder control. But the DMCA does more than that. It also lays the legal groundwork for copyright holder control—over copying as well as access—untrammeled by the exceptions and limitations that are supposed to apply to the copyright holder's rights.

For one, the DMCA's circumvention and device prohibitions apply even when users seek to circumvent technological protection measures to use copyrighted works in ways that would otherwise be permitted under copy-right law. The students who posted Diebold Election Systems internal e-mails describing potential flaws in the company's electronic voting ma-chines successfully argued fair use, with the court stressing the need to ac-commodate First Amendment values. But had Diebold encrypted its e-mails, anyone who circumvented to discover their contents, or provided software needed to circumvent, would violate the DMCA. As courts have interpreted the Act, the students' fair use privilege to post the e-mails on the Web would provide no defense to that cause of action.[59] Not surprisingly, as we saw with Declan McCullagh, the threat of civil or criminal sanctions under the DMCA has already blocked journalists from uncovering encrypted documents. In the absence of a fair use or First Amendment privilege to circumvent, it will present a significant obstacle to future whistleblower revelations and inves-tigative reporting.

In addition to trumping fair use, the DMCA effectively enables content providers to prevent circumvention even when the encrypted work is in the public domain. The Act's anticircumvention provisions nominally apply only to technological controls over copyrighted works. But providers of public domain works can easily evade that limitation, whether by coincidence or design, by appending a relatively trivial amount of copyrighted content. A publisher might add a new illustration or brief introduction to a public domain novel. Or the publisher might package copyrighted material together with public domain works in a single online database, and secure entry to the database with a technological control. In those instances, the copyrighted material might add little to what are essentially public domain works. Nevertheless, the DMCA would proscribe circumvention even to gain access to expression that is in the public domain.

MASS-MARKET CONTRACT

Contract law is poised to join control technology and the DMCA in marginalizing copyright's safety valves. Many Web sites contain standard terms and conditions of use that, among other provisions, require users to waive rights they would otherwise enjoy under copyright law. Digital technology also makes possible the use of "viral contracting," embedding in each digital copy contractual terms that purport to bind any user of the copy.[60] These developments may gain additional force from state law validating standard mass-market licenses that treat fair use, the idea/expression dichotomy, and other copyright limitations as mere contractual default rules. Although the law in this area remains in flux, a number of leading cases have held valid and enforceable nonnegotiable, mass-market licenses that impose access and use restrictions far exceeding those that content providers could otherwise obtain under copyright law.[61]

If such contracts continue to be held enforceable, copyright industries' ability to sidestep copyright limitations will increase dramatically as more and more expression becomes available primarily online. When you buy a book at a bookstore, you do not enter into a contract with the author, publisher, or bookseller regarding how you may use it. Your rights to read the book, make notes in it, copy expression or ideas from it, or dispose of it through sale, rent, or gift are all determined by the scope and limitations of the copyright holder's rights and your property rights in the physical copy of the book you bought. But if you want to download an ebook, read text, hear music, or watch videos on a commercial Web site, you will invariably have to click your agreement (or the Web site proprietor will simply assert that your use of the site means that you have given your agreement) to terms like these:

You may not modify, publish, transmit, display, participate in the transfer or sale, create derivative works, or in any way exploit, any of the content, in whole or in part. No copying, redistribution, retransmission, publication or commercial exploitation of downloaded material will be permitted without the express written permission of NetLibrary and the copyright owner.[62]

You may not store materials retrieved from *The New York Times* in a machine-readable form for more than 90 days.[63]

You may access and display Material and all other content displayed on this Site for non-commercial, personal, entertainment use on a single computer only. The Material and all other content on this Site may not otherwise be copied, reproduced, republished, uploaded, posted, transmitted, distributed or used in any way unless specifically authorized by Warner Bros. Online.[64]

Gone is your privilege to store, copy, modify, transmit, or display in any of a multitude of ways that might constitute fair use. Gone is your right to make whatever use you desire of any material that is in the public domain.

SUM: TECHNOLOGICAL PROTECTION MEASURES

Perhaps courts would refuse to enforce egregiously overreaching adhesion contract provisions, holding them void as against public policy or preempted by the Copyright Act. Maybe the DMCA's trumping of fair use will prove vulnerable to First Amendment challenge (more on that in chapter 8) or possibly Congress will amend the Act to eliminate its more onerous ramifications. But unless tempered by further legal developments, this nascent paracopyright regime, an amalgam of technological controls, the DMCA, and mass-market adhesion contract, will effectively give content providers perpetual, proprietary control over all access and use of expressive content they make available in digital form.

Content providers might not actually exercise that control or might exercise it in a relatively benign fashion. The motion picture, music, and publishing industries insist that they will gladly sell a full menu of options for access, ranging from pay-per-use to unrestricted downloads, at prices reflecting consumer demand for each option. However, the extent and nature of content providers' control will depend entirely on consumer acceptance of technological controls, the efficacy of encryption technology, and the providers' practical ability to enforce their paracopyright rights. Unless courts or Congress applies copyright's free speech safeguards to the DMCA and mass-market licensing, even the vestigial remnants of copyright's limited duration, the idea/expression dichotomy, and the fair use doctrine will have little bearing in the digital arena.

Personal Uses

As Justice Oliver Wendell Holmes famously remarked, copyright "restrains the spontaneity of men where but for it there would be nothing of any kind to hinder their doing as they saw fit. It is a prohibition of conduct remote from the persons or tangibles having the right."[65] With the recent extension of copyright to individuals' noncommercial, personal uses of cultural expression, that sense of burdensome restraint has pervaded our homes, offices, private spaces, and even familial relations to an extent that Holmes could never have imagined.

Until the advent of photocopiers, VCRs, cassette recorders, and other consumer copying equipment, copyright's principal concern was the infringing competitor who might invest the large sums required to print and sell unauthorized copies to the public. The individual who took the trouble to hand-copy all or part of a book for her own use posed no real threat to the publisher's ability to market the author's work. The same was true of those who sold or lent used copies or, as was common at the time of the Framers, those who read newspapers aloud, sang songs, or played music in family, church, inn, or social gatherings. The purchase or borrowing of a used copy, some time after the work came onto the market, was unlikely to substitute for the purchase of a new copy. Nor were public recitation and performance.

Until quite recently, then, copyright allowed considerable room for noncommercial personal use—for reading, sharing, performing, and copying. That immunity has sometimes been de jure and sometimes merely de facto. But the result has been the same. We have been free to read, view, or listen to the books, videos, and sound recordings we own as often as we like. We can also lend, share, or give them away. We can, indeed, make copies, whether by hand, photocopier, VCR, cassette player, CD burner, or computer, for ourselves and for our friends. We can play music at a party or show movies on TV. We can sing in the shower or at the bus stop. We can read poetry aloud in the park. We can create collages and use popular songs to write parodies and perform them at social gatherings. Not all of those activities are necessarily noninfringing. Yet we engage in them, as though our natural prerogative, with hardly a second thought.

Digital technology is radically changing that equation, leading copyright into unparalleled conflict with "the spontaneity of men." Digital technologies for personal copying and communication can readily substitute for purchases of copyrighted works, threatening copyright industries' traditional businesses as never before. And partly to defend their existing markets and partly to secure new ones, copyright industries increasingly deploy technological controls, backed by the DMCA and mass-market contract, that give them far-reaching power to track, meter, control, and cabin personal uses.

At the same time, the Internet brings a vast new arena of expression and global communication within the embrace of what millions of Internet users experience as their personal, private, self-expressive domain. We typically use our computers and access the Internet while at home or in our personal workspace. Perhaps for that reason, downloading, mixing, and exchanging music files, cutting and pasting text, and posting cartoons over the Internet have, for many people, much the same texture as videotaping a TV show, handwriting notes in the margins of one's book, listening to one's stereo, singing in the shower, or talking on the phone. And once online, making use of copyrighted material often feels no different than partaking of the wealth of expression and information that millions place on the Web for others to share freely.[66] So long as these uses are conducted without monetary compensation, they feel like the sort of innocuous private conduct or face-to-face conversation that is an integral part of our daily noncommercial activity. More than that, they are part of our creative appropriation of mass culture, the way we define ourselves in relation to the images and sounds of mass media that surround us. To make such acts infringing, to give legal power and technological tools to copyright owners to meter and control those acts, feels like a gross impingement on our privacy, personal liberty, and self-expression.

Pushing out a bit further, much the same is true with respect to the online equivalents of social and local political gatherings. Free Republic is a self-styled "online gathering place for independent, grass-roots conservatism"; the Web site, you will recall, was held to infringe newspapers' copyrights by allowing visitors to post copies of articles believed to exemplify the biases of the "mainstream liberal media." Devotees of *Star Trek* write their own stories featuring *Star Trek* characters and create their own videos by combining sundry clips from *Star Trek* episodes with a poignant or humorous sound track, and then post their creations on unofficial fan club Web sites. Users of "browser companions" share their annotations and comments regarding third-party Web sites. MySpace.com contains a multitude of personal Web pages in which (mostly) young people intersperse their personal statements, pictures and comments of friends, and icons of popular culture: pictures, popular songs, and snippets of text. When newspaper criticism, fan fiction, companion annotations, or bits of popular culture are posted on the Web, they are potentially available for dissemination to millions of Internet users. But in practice, few but the occasional amateur video hit on YouTube are viewed by anyone outside of friends or close-knit core participants. For many, those Internet fora have the feel of something akin to reading aloud and exchanging opinions in a small face-to-face, social setting or, in the case of MySpace, inviting a friend into one's dorm room. These are realms in which copyright industry cease-and-desist letters and infringement actions are perceived as overbearing intrusions.

But digital technology also brings the potential to make that intrusion a commonplace occurrence. Digital technology gives copyright industries the ability to encode works to control access and copying, digitally watermark them to track and charge for duplications and alterations, and ferret out unlicensed online uses of protected content. If widely deployed and protected against circumvention, such measures would enable copyright industries not only to protect their traditional markets but also to stem much of the leakage inherent in the predigital copyright system. Copyright industries hope to use such technological protection measures to gain effective proprietary control over even noncommercial personal uses and sharing of cultural works. They hope to require permission and payment each time a work is perceived or transferred, whether between individuals or from one device to another.

Now, in describing the growing conflict between copyright and personal use, I do not mean to suggest that individuals have a natural right of free access and copying just because digital communications and personal computer technology make that possible. As Jane Ginsburg rightly observes, to treat the free-wheeling Internet as our inherent baseline for permissible personal uses ignores the fact that prior to the advent of digital technology or, for that matter, video recorders and photocopiers, individuals' practical ability to engage in personal copying was exceedingly limited and posed no threat to copyright markets or incentives.[67] Just because digital technology and consumer electronics now make possible easy consumer copying and distribution does not mean that copyright law must step aside while widespread file sharing or posting for download erodes copyright-backed incentives for the creation of new works.

By the same token, however, neither do copyright industries have an intrinsic right to control access and personal copying merely because encryption technology might make it possible for them to do so. We must ensure that copyright's free speech safeguards, no less than the copyright incentive, remain vibrant in the digital arena. Indeed, the shared goals of copyright and the First Amendment may well require that copyright doctrine be redrawn to *loosen* copyright holders' control over nonmarket speech that builds on copyrighted expression. As I discuss further in the next section, digital technology weakens the normative and economic justification for copyright holders' proprietary control. It enables individuals to play a far more active, assertive, and effective role in our system of free expression. And, by drastically reducing the costs of producing and distributing expression, it undermines a primary rationale for proprietary copyright, the need for centralized, capital-intensive investment in making original expression available to the public.

That is not to say that copyright should be cast aside. As we will shortly see, both copyright law and media enterprises continue to serve free speech objectives in the digital arena, even if partly supplanted by nonmarket, nonproprietary, "bottom-up" speech. But adapting copyright doctrine to digital technology requires that we recalibrate copyright's balance to reflect, not stifle, digital technology's empowerment of individual speakers. Just as copyright law need not countenance massive uncompensated copying of copyrighted works simply because file swappers perceive that activity to be a personal liberty, neither should we aim to give copyright holders the broad legal and technological control to re-create the predigital market structure and mass-media-to-passive-consumer model of public discourse in the digital environment.

New Media

A Blackstonian copyright does not merely burden creative appropriators and personal users. It is also a tool for incumbent copyright industries to stifle competition from new media distributors. As I detail in chapter 6, incumbent copyright industries have a long history of lobbying and litigating for expansive copyright protection in order to entrench their market dominance and traditional business models. That history ranges from the London Stationers' efforts in the eighteenth century to obtain perpetual copyright protection to prevent competition from provincial publishers, to studio and record label lawsuits against Napster, MP3.com, and YouTube.

The major copyright industries' use of copyright as a competitive restraint burdens speech and expressive diversity. Throughout copyright history, new media have sought to reach a critical mass audience by distributing popular works, while simultaneously making available a far broader range of expression than provided by industry incumbents. That leaves lawmakers with a dilemma. Allowing the new media freely to exploit copyrighted expression might eviscerate the incumbents and the incentive to invest in new expression. Yet, blocking new media's access to existing works would deter investment in new media and content distribution technologies, thus stifling new outlets for expression and ossifying existing patterns of expressive power.

In response, until the last decade or so, the law has sought to mediate between the incumbent copyright industries and new media. Conflicts were resolved either against the copyright industries (where lawmakers perceived no great harm to the incumbents' existing markets) or by crafting a compulsory license imposing a reasonable fee on the new media in return for allowing it to use copyrighted works. Congress and the courts recognized that, by giving incumbent copyright industries a veto over new technologies for disseminating expression, proprietary copyright would both delay implementation of those technologies and solidify the incumbents' hold over the market.

As I further discuss in chapter 6, that measured approach is all the more warranted given the changes wrought by digital technology. In the age before ubiquitous personal computers and the Internet, only large media firms had the wherewithal to produce creative works and distribute them to a mass audience. Major film studios, record labels, television and radio broadcasters, and print publishers came to dominate our cultural landscape because they have the funds and infrastructure to mass-produce, package, and distribute authors' creations. But digital technology radically changes that equation by drastically reducing the cost of production and distribution. Today, the economics are such that anyone can be an author and publisher. And the infrastructure that is required for mass distribution, the Internet and its wireless counterparts, was built by telecommunications companies (with considerable government subsidy), not the major copyright industries.[68] So while the major media firms have a real stake in the content they have produced and acquired, there is no economic or policy justification for enabling them to use proprietary control over that content to parlay their dominance over distribution in the predigital world into hegemony over digital dissemination as well. It serves copyright's purpose to require new digital distributors to compensate studios, labels, and publishers for disseminating their works. It runs counter to those purposes—and to our interest in expressive diversity—to give copyright industry incumbents a legal tool to suppress today's new media, especially now that digital technology makes vibrant competition and the proliferation of outlets for speech a real possibility.

But under onslaught from the incumbent copyright industries, the courts and Congress seem to be moving in exactly the opposite direction. The time-tested measured approach, accommodating emerging technologies and incumbent copyright industries, is succumbing to a rearguard defense of Blackstonian proprietary copyright. Typical of this move is the Ninth Circuit's ruling and reasoning in *A&M Records v. Napster, Inc.*[69] In that lawsuit, the plaintiff major record labels portrayed Napster as an opportunistic thief of their hard-earned property for providing an online service that enabled users to trade music files. Napster responded that it had repeatedly sought to obtain a license from the labels, but that they had colluded to refuse to deal with the upstart new media. According to Napster and others, the major labels established and exclusively licensed their own online joint ventures, not just to corner the market in online distribution of music, but to slow online distribution altogether and thus stave off competition to their highly profitable core business of selling CDs.

The trial court found Napster's allegation of record industry restraint of trade quite plausible. As Judge Patel iterated in granting Napster's request for discovery on issues of record label antitrust violations and copyright misuse, "Even on the undeveloped record before the court, these joint ventures look bad, sound bad, and smell bad."[70] Despite this stench of anti-competitive collusion, however, the Ninth Circuit refused to fashion a compulsory license by limiting the record label plaintiffs' relief for Napster's contributory copyright liability to an award of reasonable damages. Absent an injunction, the court reasoned, "[p]laintiffs would lose the power to control their intellectual property; they could not make a business decision not to license their property to Napster."[71] Napster was thus driven out of business before it could pursue discovery on the labels' anticompetitive collusion.

Invoking a similar conception of copyright as property, the Southern District of New York held MP3.com liable for enabling subscribers to access songs on subscriber-owned CDs via the Internet.[72] MP3.com made it possible for CD owners to listen to their CDs away from home without having to carry their CDs with them. The company argued that by making CD content portable, it both served consumers and fostered CD sales. The court rejected that argument with the back of the hand, insisting that "[c]opyright . . . is not designed to afford consumer protection or convenience but, rather, to protect the copyrightholders' property interests." It also dismissed the relevance of MP3.com's possible "positive impact" on CD sales, holding that "a copyrightholder's 'exclusive' rights . . . include the right, within broad limits, to curb the development of such a derivative market by refusing to license a copyrighted work or by doing so only on terms the copyright owner finds acceptable." (The court also cited evidence that the record labels were in fact willing to license CD portability services, but after the labels drove MP3.com out of business, no licensed company has offered such a service.) As in *Napster,* the court also resolutely declined to limit its remedy to damages approximating a reasonable license fee. Indeed, partly as a warning to other new media distributors, it imposed a sizable $53.4 million statutory damage award for the company's "willful infringement."[73]

Finally, in June 2005, the Supreme Court held that Grokster and its codefendant suppliers of peer-to-peer file-trading software would be contributorily liable for actively inducing file traders to infringe copyright.[74] Courts have long ruled that one who actively and directly induces another to infringe a particular work, such as by providing an acquaintance with a purloined manuscript, knowing that the recipient intends to copy it, is liable for contributory liability for that infringement. The *Grokster* Court applied that rule, for the first time, to mass-market business models, with potentially devastating ramifications for consumer electronics and new media firms.[75]

Prior to *Grokster,* in the 1984 "Betamax" case, the Supreme Court had set out what is widely regarded as a technology-friendly safe harbor: suppliers of "staple articles of commerce" are not liable for their customers' copyright infringements, even when the supplier knows that some consumers will use the good to infringe, so long as the good is "capable of a substantial non-infringing use."[76] The *Grokster* Court ruled, however, that even if a product has a substantial noninfringing use, one who distributes it "with the object of promoting its use to infringe copyright, as shown by clear expression or other affirmative steps taken to foster infringement, is liable for the resulting acts of infringement by third parties." While the *Grokster* holding is far from clear about what conduct constitutes "active inducement" in that context, it suggests that selling a product with express intent that it be used to infringe and possibly even failing to disable a product's capacity for infringing uses would qualify.[77]

On that reading, many new media distributors and home copying manufacturers of the past, quite possibly including Sony in marketing its Betamax (and certainly Apple Computer in advertising its computers' usefulness to "rip, mix, and burn"), would have been held liable for contributory infringement. The *Grokster* ruling thus ignores the venerable tradition in which new media firms are able to provide new platforms for distributing, perceiving, and creating expression in part by tapping into consumer demand for existing, popular works. Prior to the recent proprietary turn, courts and Congress found ways to accommodate new media's unlicensed uses of copyrighted works within the larger goal of promoting rigorous competition and a dynamic, robust system of free expression. The *Grokster* Court's incorporation of the active inducement rule into the mass market context substitutes an absolutist, moral disfavor of new media's "bad motive" for the perceived need to balance competing interests. The Betamax rule aimed to foster investment in new media technologies while preserving the copyright incentive. *Grokster*, in effect, makes copyright holders' "property rights" a trump; it gives copyright holders a veto over any new media that openly enables consumers to copy and distribute existing expression.

Congress's turn toward proprietary copyright in the new media context has been somewhat more subtle but equally dramatic. It also centers on the Copyright Act's compulsory license provisions, which, as noted above, give specified media, ranging from satellite TV operators to public broadcasters, the right to distribute copyrighted expression without copyright holder permission upon paying royalties at the rate determined by the Act. The Copyright Act encourages the parties involved to reach voluntary agreement on the royalties to be paid. But absent such an agreement, it provides that the statutory royalty amounts are to be determined by administrative proceedings.

Here is where Congress's turn toward proprietary copyright comes into play. Until recently, the Copyright Act has consistently required the administrative body to follow a multifactor social utility standard designed to maximize the availability of creative works to the public.[78] In setting the compulsory license rate, the body must seek to assure both the copyright holder a "fair return for his or her creative work" and the compulsory licensee a "fair income under existing economic conditions." In so doing, the administrative decision maker must assess the relative roles of the copyright holders and licensees in making the copyrighted works available to the public in light of their respective creative contribution, technological contribution, capital investment, cost, and risk.

As part of the DMCA, however, Congress veered away from that broad fair return/fair income standard to one designed to mimic market bargains in which the copyright holder enjoys a full proprietary right. The DMCA revamped the compulsory license for digital transmission of sound recordings, basically Internet radio or "webcasting." In so doing, Congress replaced the fair return/fair income standard with one based on "market rate." The Copyright Act now provides that the compulsory license for webcasting be set at a rate that "would have been negotiated in the marketplace between a willing buyer and a willing seller."[79] The "market rate" standard does not guarantee the new media licensee a "fair income" and thus operates as a disincentive to invest in the new media. Indeed, the Copyright Royalty Board, the new administrative body entrusted with determining the "market rate" webcaster license royalty, has emphasized, without apology, that the "market rate" can be expected to put some webcasters out of business. According to the Board, "To allow inefficient market entities to continue to use as much music as they want . . . without compensating copyright owners on the same basis as more efficient market participants trivializes the property rights of copyright owners" and would deviate from the "willing buyer/ willing seller standard of the Copyright Act."[80]

The result is a disaster for noncommercial and small, independent webcasters—and for expressive diversity. Congress carved out an initial lower rate for such webcasters, who could not have continued in existence if required to pay the administratively determined market rate.[81] But that temporary respite has expired, and the Copyright Royalty Board has just ruled that small commercial webcasters and all noncommercial webcasters with more than an average of 218 simultaneous listeners for any given month must pay the same per performance rate as large commercial webcasters, including those affiliated with advertiser-supported terrestrial radio stations.[82] That "marketplace" royalty rate for streaming sound recordings, designed to stand for copyright holders' "property rights," will indeed silence many college and public Internet radio stations as well as music-oriented commercial webcasters.

Sum: Copyright's Expansion

Copyright began as a narrowly tailored, short-term prerogative designed to promote the printing of original expression. It now threatens to metamorphose to a rotund, Blackstonian property right. Copyright law must keep step with new technologies and markets for creating and distributing original expression. Indeed, as digital technology promises to upend traditional means and institutions for disseminating knowledge and culture, copyright law must adapt more radically than ever before. But copyright law's need to adapt does not correlate with the dramatic propertization of copyright holders' rights. Copyright's untoward expansion betrays copyright's core principles rather than faithfully translating those principles to new conditions.

| Is Copyright "the Engine of Free Expression"?

In our haste to disseminate news, it should not be forgotten that the Framers intended copyright itself to be the engine of free expression. By establishing a marketable right to the use of one's expression, copyright supplies the economic incentive to create and disseminate ideas.

—Harper & Row Publishers, Inc. v. Nation Enterprises,
471 U.S. 539, 558 (1985)

COPYRIGHT'S "MARKETABLE RIGHT" helps to underwrite our system of free expression in three fundamental ways. First, copyright serves what I term a "production function." It provides an economic incentive for the creation and dissemination of original expression. Second, copyright has an important "structural function." It supports a sector of authors and publishers who look to the market, not government patronage, for financial sustenance and who thus gain considerable independence from government influence. Third, copyright has an "expressive function." By encouraging authors, it reinforces the social and political importance of individuals' new, original contributions to public discourse.

Copyright's production, structural, and expressive functions are not merely means by which copyright law promotes free speech. They are also useful metrics for measuring the extent to which copyright actually furthers that end. They are tools for asking whether today's copyright law, given its current configuration and the market and technological universe in which it operates, still serves as a vital "engine of free expression."

I argue in this chapter that copyright continues to underwrite free speech through each of its production, structural, and expressive functions. In making my case, I counter the contention that the Internet renders copyright unnecessary to promoting speech and inherently deleterious to First Amendment values. Yet I also question and qualify copyright's "engine of free expression" moniker. Copyright's support for free speech is far more complex and, in some ways, more limited than the Supreme Court's often-cited paean suggests.

Copyright's "Engine" in Context

In denominating copyright as "the engine of free expression," the Supreme Court made both a historical statement regarding the Framers' intent and a descriptive observation about copyright's continuing role. How accurate is the Court's account? Did the Framers in fact view copyright as the engine of free expression? Does copyright indeed serve as the engine of free expression today?

Certainly, the Framers broadly understood that copyright is part and parcel of what we now think of as our system of freedom of expression. The Constitution gives Congress the power to enact copyright legislation for a stated purpose: "To Promote the Progress of Science." Importantly, the Framers saw that objective not merely as the advancement of learning for its own sake. Rather, they were animated by the belief that copyright's support for the diffusion of knowledge was essential to individual liberty and democratic government. As President Washington declaimed in his address to Congress in support of the first copyright act, the Act of 1790, copyright's promotion of science and literature would help to secure a

> free constitution . . . [b]y convincing those who are entrusted with public administration that every valuable end of government is best answered by the enlightened confidence of the public; and by teaching the people themselves to know and value their own rights; to discern and provide against invasions of them; to distinguish between oppression and the necessary exercise of lawful authority.[1]

Nevertheless, the Supreme Court's pronouncement in *Harper & Row* that the Framers intended copyright to be *the* engine of free expression is a gross overstatement. At the time of the founding and early Republic, copyright law was only one part of the federal government's support for the diffusion of knowledge. First and foremost, the 1790 Act did not accord copyright protection to newspapers, which then, as today, made up a vital part of public discourse.[2] The new federal government promoted newspaper printing and delivery not by granting exclusive rights in content but through substantial state subsidy, primarily in the form of government printing contracts and heavy investment in a postal system accompanied by preferential postal rates for the press. The importance of the latter should not be underestimated: by 1832, newspapers accounted for 95 percent of the weight of postal communication, but only 15 percent of postal revenue.[3] Indeed, far from recognizing intellectual property rights in news stories, the federal government subsidized newspapers' *sharing* of their content. It provided free postal delivery for newspaper publishers to exchange their papers with one another, largely to facilitate editors' common practice of using nonlocal news items from other papers to fill their columns.[4]

Even copyright's support for the publishing of books, which was the primary aim of the first copyright statute, was scant by today's standards. As noted in chapter 4, the 1790 Act made copyright protection unavailable for foreign works and, even for domestic works, contingent on meeting some stiff procedural requirements, including depositing copies with the local district court and the secretary of state. As a result, during the first decade of federal copyright law, only 556 works were copyrighted out of some 13,000 that were published. Indeed, as late as 1820, reprints of British books made up 70 percent of all published titles.[5]

In the Framers' era, in short, the primary instruments for the diffusion of knowledge were not copyrights but government subsidy and the reprinting of public domain newspaper articles and books. The Framers did intend that copyright would ultimately be *an* engine of free expression. But they certainly did not contemplate that it would be the sole or even most powerful engine. One could say, indeed, that at the Founding copyright law served the goal of disseminating knowledge as much by providing for an exceedingly limited scope, duration, and subject matter of copyright protection as by the grant of exclusive rights itself.

Having said that, I do not want to draw overly broad conclusions about copyright's past or present importance from its early limited role in the United States. After all, most British books that made up the bulk of U.S. publishing through much of the nineteenth century were created and originally published under the protection of UK copyright law, even if they were in the public domain in this country. So we cannot say that the United States reaped the benefits of British books, or that those books would have even been created, absent any copyright at all. Moreover, newspapers are more in need of copyright today, when their entire contents can be instantaneously mirrored on competitors' Web sites and their advertising revenues siphoned off by search engine news aggregators, than at the Founding, when a paper's stories were old news by the time others reprinted them and news clipping services were a labor intensive, manual operation. My point, then, is merely to put the Supreme Court's often-cited Framers'-intent claim within its proper, modest confines, not to negate copyright's historical or present role in underwriting original speech.

It is at a starting point within those modest confines, somewhere between the *Harper & Row* Court's grandiose overstatement, on the one hand, and complete negation, on the other, that I pursue the question of whether copyright serves as *an* engine of free expression. The Framers did view copyright law as one mechanism among several by which the state can underwrite original speech, procure contributions to the store of knowledge, and further the vitality of public debate. I now turn to the three fundamental ways that copyright does so: its production, structural, and expressive functions. I ask for each whether copyright continues to yield the free speech benefits envisioned by the Framers.

Copyright's Production Function

Beginning with the first modern copyright statute, England's Statute of Anne of 1709, copyright law has been premised on the intuition that authors and publishers will not make works available to the public unless they can prevent others from making copies, at least for a limited time.[6] Definitive empirical support for that intuition is difficult to come by. Accordingly, commentators dating back to Adam Smith have generally found justification for copyright in economic theory.[7] Economic analysts posit that copyright provides authors and publishers with a financial incentive to produce and disseminate creative expression. It does so by preventing "free riders" from undermining the market for books, paintings, sound recordings, films, and other works of authorship.

Contemporary copyright incentive theory is grounded in our understanding of "public goods." Like national defense, crime prevention, and other so-called public goods, creative expression is nonrivalrous and imperfectly excludable. Typical tangible consumer goods, like apples, pens, and cars, can only be used by one or a very small number of persons at a time and are depleted within a limited time span. If I see you about to eat a juicy red apple and am determined to get one for myself, I have only two options: I can go buy another one or deprive you of yours before you finish it. But one person's use of a public good does not deplete the good or otherwise prevent anyone else from enjoying it. If I hear you whistling a catchy tune, I can walk away whistling the same tune without any need to silence you, and we can both whistle the tune as often as we like.

Partly as a result of this nonrivalrous character, the supplier of a public good is generally unable to exclude those who do not pay for the good from enjoying its benefits. If you pick twenty apples from a tree, you can hold them all in your physical control and, if you choose to sell them, extract a payment for each apple. But even if you charge me for the privilege of hearing your tune, once the tune is in my head (or I have a recording of it), any further use and copying by others is out of your control. And, unlike an apple, there is virtually no physical limit on the number of other people who can use the tune without paying for the privilege. Given that inability (or great difficulty) to exclude such "free riders," the supplier of a public good cannot recover the costs of producing and supplying it by spreading those costs among the consuming public. Absent a solution to nonexcludability, such public goods will often be underproduced or not produced at all.

Of course, you might not have invested much time at all in composing your little tune, and you might not care if others copy it. But other creative works—books, articles, films, television programs, paintings, popular songs, and symphonies—may require a considerable investment of time and money to produce. And just as important, the social value of an author's work lies not only in its creation but also in its distribution to the public. For many works, the cost of bringing the work to a mass audience, including the costs of selecting which works to publish, editing and packaging the work, financing impecunious authors, and marketing, far exceeds the cost of creation. If competing publishers can free ride by making and distributing copies of such works without paying the costs of producing and distributing the first copy, few will want to invest in the initial distribution. The same is true if millions of consumers can make their own copies without paying their share of "first-copy" costs, the costs of initially creating and bringing the work to the public.

Copyright law offers a solution to the nonexcludability problem. It gives authors an exclusive right in certain uses of their works and enables authors to license or transfer that right to their publishers. Armed with this enforceable right to exclude, authors and publishers may recover their costs by selling copies, television broadcasts, and other forms of access to their works. In that manner, copyright spurs the creation and distribution of literature, art, music, television and radio programming, films, articles, and many of the texts, sounds, and images transmitted over the Internet. Those works populate our public discourse and animate our system of free expression.

Yet copyright is not always the only or best solution to the nonexcludability problem. Indeed, current conditions raise a serious question regarding whether the copyright incentive is really needed to underwrite our system of free expression. Prominent commentators have long cast doubt on the universal applicability of copyright's incentive rationale, arguing that many works would be created and disseminated without any copyright protection whatsoever—and certainly without the bloated scope of protection available under the Copyright Act of 1976.[8]

That critique has particular strength when applied to the Internet. The Internet and other digital technologies have drastically reduced the cost of disseminating and creating cultural works. As a result, they have spawned a vast sector of authors who do not rely on the copyright incentive (and, equally important, do not rely on publishers who rely on the copyright incentive) to create and disseminate original expression. Indeed, much of the rich cacophony of expression available on the Internet, both cultural and overtly political, is distributed without any claim of copyright by its author (or at least without any effort to use copyright to prevent copying).

Many speakers post their literary, artistic, audiovisual, and musical creations on the Internet without any expectation of monetary remuneration or career advancement. They simply want to communicate their ideas, knowledge, or artistic expression to anyone who might care to look or listen. The primary cost for such speakers is in creating their works, although even on that score digital technology is making widely affordable the creation of works, such as sound recordings and films, that were once prohibitively expensive for most individuals. Once a work is posted on the Internet, distribution is essentially cost-free. Granted, a work may be unlikely to reach a mass audience without considerable marketing or payment for prominent placement in Internet search engine search results. Nonetheless, many volunteer speakers reach a significantly broader audience, certainly in terms of geography if not absolute numbers, than do their street corner pamphleteer counterparts—and with far less investment of time and labor. Moreover, as we see on YouTube and other online sites, peer recommendations, lists of user favorites, and other such word-of-mouth equivalents can sometimes substitute for marketing, making amateur creations into popular hits with no advertising expenditure whatsoever. The result of those drastically reduced creation, distribution, and marketing costs is an explosion of voluntary speaker–generated content, including blogs, short videos, music recordings, photographs, fan fiction, and machinima.

In addition, as Yochai Benkler has convincingly demonstrated, digital technology creates unprecedented possibilities for volunteers to combine their efforts to create complex works.[9] For various types of projects, the Internet enables large numbers of people to make relatively small individual contributions that can be integrated into a finished product. Such modular projects include Wikipedia, the online encyclopedia that relies on volunteers to create, edit, and update entries (and that, according to a recent academic study, rivals *Encyclopedia Britannica* for its accuracy); Project Gutenberg's digitization of public domain texts, which relies on thousands of volunteer scanners and proofreaders; the NASA Clickworkers Web site, where site visitors mark and classify craters on Mars; and much open-source software. In each instance, enough people have sufficient personal motivation to volunteer a discrete amount of their time and skill, and the Internet makes it sufficiently inexpensive to coordinate and integrate those widely distributed, modular efforts, such that no copyright incentive is necessary to bring about the finished product.

In yet other instances, Internet speakers do hope to get paid but nevertheless produce and give away content for free. Academics and service professionals might do so for reputational gains and career advancement. Others may give away content as a loss leader for related goods and services. Most musicians, for example, make far more money from performing in concerts than selling records.[10] If they can contain the costs of marketing and sound recording production, it might make sense for many to provide free digital downloads of their music as a promotion for the sale of concert tickets or band-related merchandise.

Finally, digital technology might enhance possibilities for earning money directly from providing content but without relying on copyright protection. One such mechanism is advertising through sponsorship or product placement. Sponsors whose ads are firmly embedded within a sound recording, film, or novel should be eager for as many people as possible to gain copies of the work. So long as content providers have a reliable mechanism for tracking or estimating the audience size (and such mechanisms are already used to measure peer-to-peer downloads), they should not care who makes and distributes copies.

That is *not* to say that all works that are created today would continue to be created without the copyright incentive. Clearly, some types of works are suited neither to noncopyright business models nor to volunteer authorship, whether individual or modular collaborations. Nor are alternative, non-copyright business models necessarily more desirable than copyright. For example, we might not want our cultural expression to be populated with product placement advertising or devalued by treating it as a mere give-away for selling other products.[11] But be that as it may, the Internet does create unprecedented opportunities for noncopyright creation and dissemination of expression. From all appearances, even if Congress were to repeal the Copyright Act, we would continue to enjoy a surfeit of speech and wide diversity of opinion.

Where does that leave us? It seems that the continued claim that copyright's production function helps to underwrite our system of free expression must rest on an argument about copyright's *incremental* free speech benefits: if we are to believe in copyright's continuing speech-enhancing efficacy, we must posit that (1) the copyright incentive generates the creation and dissemination of original expression over and above the rich array of speech that would be available even without copyright, and (2) this additional, copyright-incented expression has independent First Amendment value. The issue boils down to whether there is First Amendment value in what Jane Ginsburg calls "sustained works of authorship," those works that require a material commitment of time and money to create.[12] Whatever the wonders of digital creation and distribution, many, many works continue to fall within this category. Among other types of expression, numerous full-length motion pictures, documentaries, television programs, books, products of investigative journalism, paintings, musical compositions, and highly orchestrated sound recordings constitute such sustained works of authorship. It is generally far too expensive and time-consuming to create such works, let alone create with the considerable skill, care, and high quality that the best of such works evince, to rely on volunteer authors.

In economic incentive terms, sustained works of authorship involve far greater first copy costs than do many works created by volunteers. Nor can many sustained works be divided into the discrete, easily assembled modules that lend themselves to peer production. Moreover, the same digital technology that enables a great deal of volunteer, dispersed creation also drastically reduces the cost and ease of unlicensed copying and distribution. It is highly likely, therefore, even more in the digital age than previously, that substantially fewer sustained works of authorship will be created without some protection against the ruinous effect of competitor and massive home copying.

Many such works make important contributions to our public discourse. With all our complaints about commercial, mass-media pulp, we can undoubtedly each name examples of copyright-supported sustained works of authorship that have greatly enriched our lives, provoked laughter or anguish, and shed light on important issues of the day. So copyright's production function continues to yield significant, if "incremental," free speech benefits. Of course, that is not to say that a copyright of today's capacious scope, or even a proprietary right as opposed to a right to remuneration, is needed to provide the incentive to create such works. But without some mechanism for compensating authors and publishers, we would likely have far fewer sustained works of authorship, and our system of free expression would be the poorer for it.

Copyright's Structural Function

Copyright does not serve merely to attain a desired quantity of creative expression. It also underwrites a particular type of speech and speaker. Copyright supports a market-based sector of authors and publishers, those who look to paying audiences (and advertisers) for financial sustenance. It fosters those sustained works of authorship that would unlikely be created if not for the opportunity to market copies and other forms of access.

Copyright's qualitative, structural function, its support for market-based authors and publishers, has traditionally lain at the heart of copyright's role as an engine of free expression. Yet today, some commentators suggest that copyright's underwriting of commercial media may well be inimical to First Amendment values. I begin with copyright's traditional role as understood by the Framers and then move to current conditions, market realities, and technology.

For the Framers, copyright served largely to avoid the corruptive, censorial influence of government and elite patronage. Copyright provided the financial wherewithal for authors and publishers to create and disseminate expression, information, and opinion without having to curry favor from ministers and nobles, or their potential counterparts in the new Republic. Together with the government's across-the-board subsidy of newspaper distribution through the post office (providing preferential rates for all newspapers regardless of viewpoint), copyright law was designed to underwrite a strong, self-reliant, expressive sector with roots outside the state. It is that expressive sector—both a guard against the abuse of state power and an independent, nongovernmental site for public discourse—that is so central to our tradition of freedom of speech and freedom of the press.

We can fully grasp the political and cultural potency of copyright's structural function only in historical context. Prior to the first modern copyright statutes in the eighteenth century, writers and artists were heavily dependent on royal, feudal, and church patronage for their livelihoods.[13] This dependency undermined expressive autonomy and thwarted the development of a vital, freethinking intelligentsia. As Voltaire described it: "[E]very philosopher at court becomes as much a slave as the first official of the crown."[14]

The patronage system also served to embed public discourse firmly within the hierarchical order of medieval and early modern Europe. During the Middle Ages, literature and art were commonly commissioned and controlled for purposes of public mystification.[15] They were designed to impress upon their audience the dominant status of the patron, whether it was a king, noble, or church. Later, within the framework of late Renaissance neo-classicism, the patronage system fostered a view of the arts as a "gentleman's calling," tailored to aristocratic tastes and far removed from common social experience and creative sensibility.[16]

It was not until the eighteenth century that there emerged a comprehensive sphere of public communication that was both independent of monarchy, aristocracy, and church and capable of challenging their political and social dominance. That sphere was largely made up of printed materials—newspapers, pamphlets, and books—that received their primary financial support not from official patronage but from readers and audiences. Freed from capricious and overbearing patrons, writers enjoyed a new, broad latitude to choose their own subject matter and find their own voice.[17] The burgeoning reading public gradually shook off the influence of those who had used their control of art and literature to reinforce their traditional authority and power.[18] As it moved from patronage to market support, this sphere of communicative exchange generated, for the first time, a sense of "public opinion," the set of beliefs and norms elaborated in debate and discussion that citizens recognize as something they hold in common.[19]

The notion of public opinion, mediated by printed materials and emerging from autonomous citizen interaction outside of official, hierarchical organs, was central to early understandings of liberal democracy.[20] It emerged with particular force in early eighteenth-century America, where this print-mediated public space defined the goals of the people and called government officials to brook for deviating from them. In so doing, it centered the ultimate power of democratic rule in the autonomous institutions of civil society, which would direct and maintain a vigilant watch on elected representatives. Within democratic theory, it effectively shifted the locus of citizen deliberation from the sovereign assembly of classical republicanism to the rough-and-tumble of the pen and the press.

Modern copyright arose with and contributed to the emergence of this print-mediated public square. Prior to the enactment of the Statute of Anne, the printing privileges that the Crown granted to members of the London Stationers' Company had served as an instrument of centralized control and censorship.[21] With the expiration of the notorious Licensing Act and the advent of modern copyright, however, authors gained a limited exclusive right to print copies of their works, with the explicit statutory purpose of encouraging learning through the widespread dissemination of original expression.[22] For the first time, authors could hope to earn their bread from the sale of their work to the public, and to do so through independent publishers who stood apart from the censorial arm of the state and the intermeddling of aristocratic and ecclesiastic patrons. As Oliver Goldsmith declared in 1760: "[Writers] have now no other patrons but the public, and the public collectively considered, is a good and a generous master."[23]

The emergence of a market in printed expression encouraged authors to challenge civic and religious authority, in part because rebelliousness and irreverence attracted paying readers.[24] It also greatly enhanced print's democratic character and democratizing influence. The noncommercial literature of letters and political pamphlets in colonial America was ordinarily addressed to a small, educated elite and was composed in a florid style punctuated with classical references that had meaning only for a few. But the establishment of markets for literary works encouraged authors to write for a broader audience.[25] Thus, the unprecedented best-seller success of Thomas Paine's pamphlet *Common Sense* in 1776 was due, in Paine's own estimation, to his calculated effort to reach the common reader by using "language as plain as the alphabet" and by replacing classical references with biblical ones.[26] This "descent" of literature "from the closets of philosophers, and the shelves of polite scholars" to the community at large, while a source of despair for some, was generally viewed as a necessary predicate for representative democracy, the future of which depended on an educated and informed citizenry.[27]

When the Framers drafted the Copyright Clause and the Copyright Act of 1790, they took as self-evident that the diffusion of knowledge and exchange of view through a market for printed matter was a pillar of public liberty.[28] They were fully immersed in a culture that identified print with republican government and resistance to tyranny. The Framers believed that a copyright-supported national market for authors' writings (together with generous subsidies for newspapers) was vital to maintaining public vigilance against undue government encroachment, while also forging a sense of national identity. As James Madison aptly put it, "A popular Government, without popular information, or the means of acquiring it, is but a Prologue to a Farce or a Tragedy; or, perhaps both."[29]

Part and parcel of this vision was an understanding that democratic governance requires not simply the diffusion of knowledge per se but also an autonomous sphere of print-mediated citizen deliberation and public education. The Framers well understood the dangers of patronage. They had strongly opposed the model of a government-controlled "hireling press," such as existed in eighteenth-century England.[30] They had also seen firsthand the transformation of the American print industry as it emerged, in the mid-eighteenth century, from its servile dependency on colonial government and church largesse to become, with the support of a broad-based readership, a powerful and highly combative force in public affairs.[31] It was only by maintaining their fiscal independence that authors and publishers could continue to guard public liberty. For the Framers, therefore, copyright's importance lay in its structural, as well as production, function. By underwriting a flourishing national market in authors' writings, copyright would help to secure authors' and printers' freedom from the corruptive influence of state, church, and aristocratic patronage.

———

Today's copyright-supported media are very different from those that the Framers viewed as the pillars of popular constitutionalism and watchdog against official tyranny. In the early Republic, book publishers and newspaper printers were widely dispersed cottage industries. Presses were hand-driven and paper handmade, each little changed from the fifteenth century. In line with that small-scale craft enterprise, book publishers relied heavily on advance subscriptions and arrangements with publishers from other regions to sell each others' books. Newspapers were generally small weeklies, often published by a single printer and apprentice, and required an investment of only a few hundred dollars. These diverse, limited-circulation presses served as vibrant wellsprings of local political association and opinion.[32]

It was only in the late nineteenth and early twentieth centuries that there began to emerge the commercial mass media that so dominate public discourse today. Major cost-cutting, time-saving advances in technologies for printing and producing paper, the emergence of the telegraph, the advent of sound recordings and motion pictures, and the invention of radio and television broadcasting, together with a myriad of government policies that favored large-scale commercial media, ultimately transformed the early Republic's barely self-supporting, locally based public sphere into a mass-market industrial enterprise.[33] In recent decades, economies of scale and other market conditions have accelerated that mass-market trend. Today's "copyright industries"—publishers, motion picture studios, and record labels—are, for the most part, large business concerns, typically under the roof of global media and entertainment conglomerates. Those copyright-supported commercial mass media enjoy an agenda-setting power rivaling that of public officials.

In the view of many commentators, the power, ubiquity, and profit orientation of today's commercial mass media undermine the democratic character of public discourse.[34] The question, then, is whether the claim that copyright serves as an engine of free expression in performing its structural function—underwriting a robust, financially independent, nongovernmental expressive sector—still has purchase. I argue that it does, although as with copyright's production function, copyright's contributions to First Amendment values in this regard are more modest and incremental than the Supreme Court's "engine of free expression" moniker suggests.

To begin with, although today's bloated copyright does fuel commercial mass-media domination of public discourse, copyright also provides support for numerous freelance writers, filmmakers, musicians, and artists, as well as small-scale publishers, studios, and record labels. For many individual creators, the possibility of earning income from the sale of their work enables them to devote substantially more time to creative pursuits, perhaps even to quit their day job. For today's cottage industry publishers and independent studio and labels, copyright can make it possible to find and thrive in niche markets and to distribute original expression through a variety of channels. Many freelance creators and cottage industry producers and distributors rely on copyright primarily for building reputation and as a supplement to revenue from other sources, rather than for mass-market exploitation and licensing. Documentary filmmakers, for example, may rely on copyright's exclusive rights to raise private financing for production, but aim to sell their finished product to public broadcasters or educational institutions. Nonetheless, copyright's structural function extends to the invaluable support it provides for this diverse sector of independent authors and publishers. The key is to tailor copyright to continue that support while minimizing the speech burdens that copyright tends to impose disproportionately on independent authors and publishers and on nonmarket speakers.

Moreover, copyright operates as an engine of free expression even in supporting large-scale commercial mass media. Commentators present trenchant criticisms of the copyright-supported media and entertainment conglomerates. But despite their many shortcomings, copyright-supported media play an important, constitutive role in our system of free expression. In particular, as I will presently demonstrate, the commercial mass media fulfill this vital free speech role in ways that neither peer communication on the Internet nor government-subsidized media can match.

First, the shortcomings: critics level a multipronged indictment against the commercial mass media.[35] In their view, the media not only fail to provide the information and reasoned debate that a democratic polity needs but do just the opposite by fostering rampant escapism, consumerism, and political inertia. Most basically, critics insist, the dominance of commercial media inevitably skews public discourse toward those with the financial means to own a printing plant, television station, motion picture studio, or record label, and, on the consumer demand side, those who can readily pay for content and buy advertised products. Commentators also charge that commercial media, particularly those supported by advertising, tend to spew out bland, uncontroversial expression, designed to put audiences in a buying mood and to attract a broad cross section of viewers, readers, and listeners without unduly offending any of them. They contend that the media, far from spurring citizen vigilance and political activism, engender a widespread sense of complacency and a diminished capacity to envision potential challenges to the status quo. The news media, critics assert, even fall short of their cherished role as guardian against state corruption and tyranny. Reporters' dependence on government officials for information, politicians' adeptness at news management, and news media obligations to corporate parents and shareholders too often blunt the media's watchdog bite. Further, given media firms' attention to the bottom line, much of what passes for news reporting today is more spectacle than information, more entertainment than measured analysis of important public issues.

PEER COMMUNICATION

I do not dispute the broad criticisms of the commercial media. And certainly the best of Internet peer reporting and communication casts the media's inadequacies in sharp relief. Digital networks encompass a growing multitude of Web sites, blogs, virtual communities, and e-mail listservs that fulfill much the same function as the Framers' ideal public sphere, while requiring neither copyright-based market support nor government patronage. Those widely dispersed arenas for bottom-up reporting and discussion have become vibrant centers for exchange of information and opinion about vital issues of the day and focal points for citizen activism, leading enthusiasts to question the First Amendment need for commercial mass media.

Furthermore, as Yochai Benkler has detailed, the mass media's limitations from a free speech perspective are far more fundamental than profit-motive distortion and selling to the lowest common denominator of audience interest. The mass media, whether the advertiser-supported ABC or the government-funded BBC, have traditionally operated on an industrial, one-way hub-and-spoke model in which speech is produced and packaged at the center, by a small set of hierarchical organizations, and then distributed out to audiences at the edge. Individuals in that model are passive recipients of finished media goods, not active participants in ongoing conversation, expressive creativity, informing public opinion, and shaping culture.[36]

Digital network communication, in contrast, provides countless outlets for speakers of all shapes and stripes to express their views. And no less important than this sheer multiplicity and diversity of speech, digital networks offer a radically different process and character of discourse. Blogs, collaborative creations like Wikipedia, online spaces like YouTube for individuals to post and critique one another's creative works, and numerous other fora are sites for ongoing conversation, debate, and sharing of information and creative expression. Their contents are ever growing and changing as participants add new entries and observations, correct misinformation, and subject previous entries to often searing criticism. This discourse is far more transparent and its production more embedded in mutual social relations than the mass-media model. Moreover, for many such sites, discussants focus on what interests them without regard to building audience share or, indeed, whether the texts, graphics, video, or music they create and exchange are marketable. As Benkler eloquently summarizes: "What emerges in the networked information environment . . . will not be a system for low-quality amateur mimicry of existing commercial products. What will emerge is space for much more expression, from diverse sources and of diverse qualities. Freedom—the freedom to speak, but also to be free from manipulation and to be cognizant of many and diverse options—inheres in this radically greater diversity of information, knowledge, and culture through which to understand the world and imagine how one could be."[37]

Yet, as I will presently enumerate, whatever their evident flaws and the Internet's apparent wonders, commercial media continue to offer indispensable speech benefits. At bottom, our system of free expression is best served by a *plurality* of types of media and models of discourse. Ideally, each medium and model will complement the others. Each type of speaker and speech community will fill in gaps where the others fall short, and each will call the others to account for their failures.

Peer digital network speakers fall short of providing an adequate substitute for the mass-media's critical Fourth-Estate role in a number of respects. Indeed, in many ways, bloggers, peer reporters, and grassroots organizers are parasitic on the mass media for making significant contributions to public discourse. First, individual yeomen speakers generally lack the resources to serve as effective watchdogs against government myopia and oppression. Nor, typically, can they adequately expose corporate unlawfulness, labor union corruption, and political party self-aggrandizement. Just as the press has evolved since the early Republic from cottage industry to global enterprise, so have many other businesses, political associations, and, indeed, government itself. Today, liberal democratic nations encompass multiple concentrations of power. Only an equally powerful press—not just daily newspapers but a full array of publishing houses, film studios, and broadcasters—can consistently check other entities' and associations' deployment of their power by exposing it to the light of public opinion. Indeed, only a *mass* media can both catalyze and, to a degree, embody public opinion in the face of government authority and corporate fiefdom.[38] To be certain, the ability of geographically dispersed individuals rapidly to gather and share information through digital technology and network communication gives them an unprecedented capacity to uncover, expose, and rally against public official and corporate wrongdoing. But peer reporting is unlikely to serve as more than a complement to the mainstream press. Individual bloggers and YouTube video creators lack the institutional mission, financial resources, and sheer force of voice often needed to engage in sustained scrutiny and call the powerful to account.

Moreover, in addition to their watchdog function, media enterprises serve an indispensable role in laying a foundation for public discourse. Liberal democratic governance requires not merely a cacophony of expressive output from diverse sources but also a robust give-and-take among contrary views. It requires some measure of *public* discourse, some means for identifying issues of widespread concern, and some forum for confronting opposing perspectives.[39] Mass media provide numerous focal points for such discursive exchange and agenda-setting. News stories, op-ed pages, pundit debates, letters to the editor, book and movie reviews, and many of the books and feature films that are the subject of those reviews are prime examples. Together they present a forum for deliberation and debate, a place where readers, viewers, and listeners often come across opposing views.

Digital network discussion, in contrast, appears to be highly fractured and balkanized. A study of political blogs during the 2004 election found, for example, that only some 15 percent of the links of conservative and liberal bloggers were to blogs across the political divide.[40] Moreover, unlike news stories, op-ed pages, and pundit debates, views from opposing camps can generally be found only by following a link; they are not interspersed side by side. To the extent that relative insularity is indicative of Internet discussion generally, it raises the concern that digital networks present an exceedingly polarized—and polarizing—discursive realm, one in which individuals do little more than reinforce existing preferences, speaking only to those who share common views and interests, rather than engaging in discourse across the political and cultural spectrum.[41]

In addition, the fact that mass-media content is generally filtered and edited has positive as well as negative ramifications. Out of the Babel of competing issues, concerns, and voices in our highly complex world, media filtering delimits a range of passable opinion and actively contributes to shaping a rough consensus regarding what are the important public issues that need to be addressed. In so doing, the mass media both narrow the public agenda to a limited set of resonant issues and frame those issues by highlighting certain angles and subtexts while ignoring others.[42] That narrowing and framing necessarily exclude many perspectives, concerns, and voices. But public debate on a national level in a highly pluralistic, advanced democratic state cannot proceed without some measure of broad public consensus on the major priorities of the day. While the multitudinous online fora in the digital network sphere present invaluable arenas for discursive exchange on a myriad of issues of intense interest to particular discussants, they supplement, and perhaps influence, rather than replace the mass media's delineation of the public agenda.

In that regard, digital network discussion about current events itself draws heavily upon mass-media agenda-setting. The 2004 election study found that political bloggers link far more heavily to articles from mainstream news media than to other blogs. Another study found that leading blogs tend to discuss the same stories that appear in the mainstream media, albeit from a different angle and presenting different information. Indeed, the blogs' primary focus is *commentary* on mainstream news; of relevance to both agenda-setting and relative capacity to serve as a watchdog, only 5 percent of the postings on the sites involved original reporting.[43]

Granted, the flow of influence regarding which issues are worthy of discussion is far from unidirectional. Like grassroots political action, peer-created content sometimes finds its way into media reporting and agenda-setting. Individuals' video footage of public figures' gaffes, violent crime, and terrorist acts moves from handheld cameras to YouTube to television. And blog commentary increasingly impacts the direction of media coverage, with respect to both the salient subtopics concerning a given issue and the choice of stories to follow. In some cases, mainstream news outlets respond directly to blog discussion, whether by reporting on bloggers' fresh perspectives or reacting to charges of news media plagiarism or error.[44] More broadly, the commercial news media have adopted the blogosphere as their own, incorporating blogs and online reader discussion as integral features of their Web sites. Both the impact of the peer reporting on media coverage and the media's embrace of blogs and online discussion suggest that the mass-media filter need not be as impervious and hierarchical as critics suggest. Peer communication serves as an incubator for issues to percolate to the mass media, which by then reporting on an issue, stamps it with the media's authority and force.

That leads to another significant function of media filtering: providing a reasonable assurance of the reliability of information. Without trusted intermediaries to serve as filters and guides, citizens who are awash in information would likely face considerable difficulties in evaluating that information's accuracy. The Internet does provide new mechanisms for peer-to-peer, search engine, and freelance filtering and accreditation. And there are instances in which Web sites post revelatory documents, video clips, or photographs that "speak for themselves." But those digital network–based alternatives to mass-media filtering and fact-checking tend to be narrowly focused and, as evidenced by the deliberate distortion and political chicanery that repeatedly find their way past Wikipedia's volunteer screeners, of limited efficacy.[45] Bloggers and other participants in Internet discussion simply do not have the financial resources needed to check the facts for many stories.

No less important, bloggers and peer reporters also lack the traditional news media's institutional commitment to professional, industry-wide standards of quality, candor, and accuracy. Papers' reputations and journalists' careers can fall to ruin on ethics violations or grossly inaccurate reporting. No such institutional constraints apply to peer reporters. Indeed, stories have already surfaced of political and corporate operatives putting bloggers on their payroll or even masquerading as nonpartisan, objective bloggers themselves.[46] Purportedly spontaneous, amateur YouTube videos have likewise been revealed to be carefully scripted promotions.[47] At this point, then, despite market distortions and biases, the mainstream news media, and certainly their elite representatives like the *New York Times* and the *Washington Post,* remain a generally more reliable source for the information upon which both individual elucidation and public discourse depend.[48]

To reemphasize, in highlighting the commercial mass media's continuing constitutive role in public discourse, I do not mean to dismiss the unique contribution of Internet-based peer communication. Digital networks greatly enhance individuals' ability to bring information to light, mobilize for political action, and exert influence on government officials, political parties, and market entities. In a number of instances the Internet has been used to great effect both to bring information to light and to raise an issue onto the public agenda. The Internet-based campaign to expose Diebold Election Systems' cover-up of security vulnerabilities in its electronic voting machines, capped by Diebold's ultimately futile attempt to use copyright law to prevent the Web posting of its damning internal e-mails, is one often touted example. But in most cases bloggers and other volunteer speakers on the Internet rely heavily on the mass media, whether as a source of information or for giving credence and force to their message, or both.

Indeed, on closer inspection, the Diebold case is no exception. The Diebold security vulnerabilities were first brought to light in a working paper authored by computer scientists at Johns Hopkins University. That study received extensive coverage in national and local news media. So did Diebold's response, Diebold executives' Republican Party connections, the revelation that the lead author of the Johns Hopkins study had ties to a Diebold competitor, state governments' follow-up investigations, and the presence of Diebold documents on the Internet. It appears that some synergistic combination of media reporting and Internet grassroots organizing exerted the pressure that helped induce government officials to reconsider their adoption of Diebold equipment.

In short, copyright's structural function—its support of professional authors and financial independent commercial media—continues to have purchase in the digital era. Digital network communication serves an important constitutive role in giving individuals voice and spurring citizen activism. And in the best of worlds, the blogosphere's influence will act as a check on media failings, thus enhancing the copyright-supported media's contribution to public discourse. But at the end of the day, copyright-supported, financially robust commercial media still supply an invaluable and unequaled layer of accreditation, fact-checking, agenda-setting, sustained investigative reporting, and representing public opinion before powerful decision makers.

GOVERNMENT-FUNDED MEDIA

Much the same can be said of the relationship between copyright-supported and government-funded expression. The Framers' profound concern about the corruptive influence of government patronage applies only in part to government-funded expression in the modern democratic state. Even aside from investing in communications infrastructure (like the establishment of the post office in the early United States), democratic countries provide significant state subsidies directly for the creation of expression, ranging from public broadcasting to visual art. Those subsidies are valuable components of our system of free expression. Indeed, the democratic character of public discourse may well depend upon state subsidies for speech that might otherwise receive scant attention in an unregulated media market.[49] Moreover, democratic countries have created mechanisms for insulating subsidy recipients from political pressure. Far from the court hirelings that the Framers feared, today's BBC, PBS, and recipients of grants from the National Endowment for the Arts enjoy considerable editorial independence and expressive autonomy.

Nevertheless, the Framers' concerns are not entirely unfounded, even in liberal democracies. In the antebellum United States, for example, lucrative government contracts, ranging from those for printing laws and government documents to concessions for the supply of twine, printed forms, and wrapping paper for the post office, came to be used as a tool by parties in power to purchase press loyalty. Such patronage transformed many newspaper editors into "political professionals, people for whom printing was a way to make a living out of politics, rather than the other way around."[50] As John Quincy Adams described the alignment of newspapers behind presidential hopeful and then Adams ally, William Crawford:

> The *National Intelligencer* is secured to him by the belief of the editors that he will be the successful candidate, and by their dependence upon the printing of Congress, ... the *Democratic Press,* of Philadelphia, because I transferred the printing of the laws from that paper to the *Franklin Gazette;* and several other presses in various parts of the Union upon principles alike selfish and sordid.[51]

Opposition politicians railed against such patronage and its accompanying shackling of the press. They rightly charged that the patronage system transformed the party press into a "government press" and that, at the very least, press liberty is compromised when "the favor of power is essential to the support of the editors."[52] But once in power, those critics used the very same tools to reward their loyal supporters and curry favor with newspapers whose future support they sought. It was not until the Civil War, the establishment of the Government Printing Office, and the emergence of a strong nonpartisan press that press patronage as an overt federal government policy came to an end.[53]

In modern times as well, incidents abound of even democratic governments seeking to use their power of the purse to extract influence over the speech of state-funded media. As evident from the repeated politically motivated threats from Congress to cut funding for PBS and the Bush administration's recent efforts to transform the public broadcaster's programming through political appointments to the Corporation for Public Broadcasting (which provides government funds to the broadcaster), mechanisms for insulating state-funded broadcasters from government and political party interference have proven to be only partly successful.[54] In some instances, public broadcasters' internal supervisory organs have become politicized along party lines. In others, governments have exerted direct pressure on public broadcasters to alter broadcasting content. Indeed, even with the purest motives, democratic governments have struggled with setting rational, neutral criteria for distributing subsidies to artists and the press.[55]

At bottom, then, the Framers' basic intuition remains cogent today. Circumscribed government subsidies for the creation and dissemination of expression are a valuable, democracy-enhancing measure of a modern democratic state. But even in a representative democracy, massive state involvement would likely present a serious impediment to expressive autonomy and freedom of information. Were authors and publishers to become largely dependent on state beneficence, we would expect to see an attendant vitiation of critical autonomy and expressive diversity. Even if some state intervention is a necessary counterweight to market-based hierarchy, a strong, self-reliant expressive sector whose roots are outside the state still constitutes an indispensable ingredient of our system of free expression. More particularly, like the digital network–commercial media dyad, state-funded and copyright-supported media ideally interact synergistically, each as a watchdog against the abuses, failings, and biases of the other.

Jeffrey Wigand

The story of former tobacco company executive Jeffrey Wigand illustrates many of the points I have made in this section, including the corruptive dangers of media conglomeration, the structural importance of commercial mass media (particularly the news media, but also cultural expression and entertainment), and the potentially synergistic speech-enhancing interplay among commercial media and other speakers.[56] Wigand served as vice president for research and development at cigarette maker Brown & Williamson from 1988 to 1993. During his tenure, he discovered that, despite repeated public denials and testimony under oath to the contrary, leading tobacco company executives had long known that the nicotine in cigarettes is an addictive substance and had, indeed, added ammonia-based compounds to cigarette tobacco to enhance nicotine's addictive effect. In 1995 Wigand relayed his discoveries to a reporter for the widely watched CBS newsmagazine 60 *Minutes* and agreed to be interviewed on the program. In so doing, he violated his Brown & Williamson nondisclosure agreement, at his considerable financial and personal risk.

Instrumental in Wigand's decision to divulge the tobacco company's misdeeds despite that risk was CBS's promise to indemnify him for any liability to his former employer. No less important, Wigand was willing to pay a personal price in order to present his findings before millions of prime-time television viewers.[57] It is highly unlikely that Wigand would have exposed Brown & Williamson at his own peril without the backing and mass audience of a major media outlet. Even if he had, perhaps by posting information and documents on his personal Web site, his story may well have been lost in the chorus of tobacco company denials (if they had even bothered to respond) and against the backdrop of blogs and crank Web sites presenting sundry allegations that few find credible even when true.

Yet, there is more to the Wigand story. CBS management initially scuttled the Wigand interview shortly before it was to appear on 60 *Minutes.* Instead, CBS aired a redacted version of the story, minus Wigand. Apparently, CBS did not want to risk having to pay a multibillion-dollar damage award to Brown & Williamson, especially since that contingency would have reduced CBS's share price at a time when the company was negotiating to be acquired by Westinghouse. Additional, and more insidious, corporate entanglements might have also contributed to the decision. Laurence Tisch, CBS's chairman at the time, was also an owner of Lorillard Tobacco Company, and his son Andrew was Lorillard's president. In fact, Andrew Tisch was one of the tobacco executives who had sworn before Congress that nicotine was not addictive, and Wigand was a witness in the perjury investigation regarding that testimony. At that time, moreover, Lorillard was negotiating with Brown & Williamson to buy six of its brands. In sum, CBS's broadcast of the Wigand interview might have caused CBS and Laurence Tisch considerable financial loss and might have helped send Tisch's son to jail, facts that could hardly have been lost on the CBS lawyers and executives involved in the decision to cancel the Wigand broadcast.

The circumstances surrounding CBS's cancellation of the Wigand interview graphically illustrate the potential vulnerabilities and limitations of the media-as-watchdog model, especially in an age of increasing media consolidation and conglomeration. But three months after the Wigand interview was to have aired, CBS reversed its decision to scuttle the interview, and the broadcast dealt a significant blow to the tobacco industry. Significantly, it was the presence and coverage of competing media that pushed a reluctant CBS to reassert its watchdog role. CBS broadcast the Wigand interview only after the *New York Times* had detailed CBS's capitulation in a front-page story and castigated CBS in an editorial, the *New York Daily News* had obtained and reported on the transcript of the omitted interview, and the *Wall Street Journal* had published Wigand deposition testimony containing his central allegations.[58] Moreover, critical media coverage did not end with the CBS broadcast. Most notably perhaps, in the motion picture *The Insider* (1999), Disney/ABC presented a widely acclaimed dramatized version of the entire Wigand episode, castigating CBS for the network's striking, if temporary, abdication of its journalistic integrity.[59] That contemporaneous and subsequent coverage by competing media enterprises, an instance of such enterprises exposing each other's wrongdoing, may deter such lapses in the future.

Digital network communication and publicly funded media also played a secondary role in this story. In May 1994, Stanton Glantz, a University of California professor of medicine and antitobacco activist received an anonymous donation of some 4,000 pages of Brown & Williamson documents. Glantz delivered copies to a *New York Times* reporter, and the *Times* promptly authored a feature story about their contents, including evidence that executives had long known of nicotine's addictive properties. In addition, in July 1995, Glantz and the University of California posted the voluminous, internal tobacco company documents on the Internet. That posting certainly made it more difficult for the tobacco industry to deny press reports. Moreover, in 1995 the Internet was still in relative infancy. It is probable that had this story broken today, bloggers would have spurred broader treatment in the mainstream press.

For their part, publicly funded broadcasters were involved principally in scrutinizing CBS's initial refusal to air the Wigand interview and laying bare its implications for commercial news media. Mike Wallace appeared on the PBS interview program *The Charlie Rose Show* on November 13, 1995, the night after *60 Minutes* had aired its redacted version of the tobacco story. Wallace admitted that CBS had been "dead wrong" for "caving in." A week later, NPR's *All Things Considered* broadcast a panel discussion featuring a news reporter, a First Amendment expert, and lawyers for Wigand and Brown & Williamson. Finally, in April 1996, PBS's *Frontline* aired a retrospective on the episode focusing on how similar pressures on commercial media might distort news coverage.

The moral I wish to draw from this story is certainly not that "all's well that ends well," that we can complacently rely on an increasingly conglomeratized mass media to expose corporate wrongdoing. Rather, the Wigand story illustrates both that mass-media entities are critical to exposing corporate wrongdoing *and* that media's propensity and capability to act as watchdog cannot be taken for granted.

Our copyright, media, and telecommunications laws must accordingly support a multiplicity of expressive sources. As Judge Learned Hand rightly insisted, our First Amendment interest in a free press demands "the dissemination of news from as many different sources, and with as many different facets and colors as is possible."[60]

In that vein, a robust system of free expression requires interplay among a wide variety of speakers, including commercial mass media, government-subsidized noncommercial media, independent studios and record labels, cottage-industry publishers, political and nonprofit associations, universities, professional and semiprofessional authors, street corner pamphleteers, and peer discussants, creators, bloggers, video-makers, and reporters online.[61] To one extent or another, each of these speakers offsets, complements, and checks the abuses of power, gross inaccuracies, and failings of the rest. Like other speakers, much of the commercial, copyright-supported media play a unique and vital role within this complex mix. Certainly, our system of expression must include considerable space for decentralized, peer expression on the Internet. But that is not to say that we should aspire, even as a liberal democratic ideal, to an egalitarian expressive universe composed entirely of yeomen speakers or any other single type of speaker.

Copyright's Expressive Function

Copyright does not further free speech interests merely by providing pecuniary incentives and support. It also symbolically reinforces certain values and understandings that underlie our commitment to free speech.

As a number of commentators have convincingly argued (though not without thoughtful opposition), law often serves an expressive or symbolic function above and beyond regulating or providing incentives for conduct.[62] Antidiscrimination law, for example, may have symbolic importance beyond whatever discriminatory conduct it actually proscribes. In enacting and applying such law, Congress and the courts effectively express our society's official condemnation of discrimination based on race and various other classifications. Similarly, the law might forbid certain market transactions, such as selling body parts or children for adoption, not merely to avoid harmful consequences that might ensue but to make a statement about human dignity. Laws that protect endangered species, forbid hate speech, and require recycling also have important symbolic dimensions over and above their regulation of conduct per se. Such laws give vent to and help crystallize collective understandings and norms. In turn, by giving legal imprimatur to certain values, they shape future perceptions and choices.

And so with copyright. Like other legal forms and processes, copyright is not simply a means for translating social policy into conduct-ordering rules. Copyright law also affirms certain social roles, values, and understandings of individual capacity and negates others. Thus, over and above its practical import, copyright plays a compositional role in our understanding of authorship and of the place of individual expression within our cultural and political matrix.

Of course, like other statements, norms, and laws, copyright's meaning is both contestable and mutable. A law can mean one thing for an advantaged group and something quite different for those on society's margins. A law's expressive statement and symbolic import can also change over time. Much like well-worn novels or works of art, legal regimes are variously understood and interpreted in the face of evolving social norms, political circumstances, and technological conditions. As I will shortly discuss, copyright increasingly stands for values and understandings quite different from those represented by copyright's historical and conceptual core. But I first consider that core.

Copyright law's symbolic potency is manifest in its constitutional pedigree. As enshrined in the constitutional authorization to secure authors' rights, copyright embodies three conceptual pillars of liberal democracy, each intertwined with collective understandings of the importance of freedom of expression. The first is the Enlightenment ideal of the self-expressive, morally responsible, and transformative individual. The Copyright Clause provides for protection for creators of original works of authorship, not publishers who reprint long-existing works, as was the case in England through the seventeenth century. In so doing, the clause underscores the value of fresh ideas and of individual contributions to our public discourse. More broadly, modern copyright suggests, in line with the Enlightenment ideal and in contrast to premodern traditionalism, that people are capable, through the constructive power of language and reason, of wresting control of their thinking away from established authority and of taking responsibility for their own words and deeds.[63] It insists that each individual has his own distinct personality and expressive style. Individuals may thus author new ideas and cultural forms rather than submissively follow time-honored precepts.

Second, of particular valence for the Framers, copyright's emphasis on authorship draws upon republican understandings of individuals' expressive contributions to public deliberation. Authors, in this view, are a nation's "virtuous citizens," educators and spokespersons who elucidate the political, cultural, and aesthetic issues that shape a polity. As John Quincy Adams's verse proclaimed:

> Behold the lettered sage devote
> The labors of his mind
> His country's welfare to promote
> And benefit mankind.[64]

Authorship, in this view, is an exercise of "self-responsibility," the ability critically to examine social norms as an independent moral agent, within the framework of political concern for the public good. Individual expression is the pillar of scientific progress and public liberty. Individual authors play a vital role not only in the dissemination of knowledge but also in personifying and inspiring public vigilance against tyrannical encroachment.

Third, copyright encapsulates the Enlightenment ideal of progress, central to American constitutionalism.[65] That ideal is expressly set forth in the Copyright Clause, with its overriding purpose of promoting the "progress of science," broadly understood to include all products of the mind. It embodies the belief that the accumulation of knowledge and deployment of reason will advance human welfare, not only in the material but also in the political realm. In this view, as Thomas Jefferson wrote, "the diffusion of knowledge among people" is the most effective guarantee of "free and good government."[66] That understanding, in turn, serves as a conceptual cornerstone for freedom of expression. It posits that "error of opinion may be tolerated where reason is left free to combat it," that the remedy to be applied to falsehood and fallacy is "more speech, not enforced silence."[67]

Copyright law, in short, has traditionally expressed the very conceptual understandings and ideals that animate the First Amendment and, indeed, liberal democracy. Yet, copyright is in danger of straying from that expressive meaning. In fact, it seems that copyright is increasingly perceived as a hindrance, if not a forbidding obstacle, to individual moral agency, contributions to public discourse, and self-expression. Rightly or wrongly, copyright is widely viewed as the tool by which the greedy and the powerful seek to exact payment for each and every use of our common cultural heritage, or to squash controversial and critical reformulations of that heritage. In the popular imagination, copyright has become ASCAP threatening to sue the Girl Scouts for singing songs around the campfire and Disney suing day care centers for showing its movie videos to preschoolers. Copyright is record labels suing thousands of teenagers and their unwitting grandparents, and targeting celebrated amateur artists who creatively remix and combine popular songs. It is television producers sending cease-and-desist letters to Web sites where fans create and exchange their own stories about their favorite characters. It is book publishers pitted against university libraries seeking to make their stores of knowledge freely searchable over the Internet. It is the Martin Luther King estate extracting payment and insisting on control over documentary footage of the civil rights leader's "I Have a Dream" speech on the Capitol Mall.

Copyright's new meaning arises from a combination of copyright's sharp expansion, copyright holder overreaching, and the growth of individuals' nonmarket sharing of information and expression over the Internet. As Jessica Litman has forcefully argued, people understand and share the basic norms that underlie copyright.[68] They believe that commercial piracy is wrong, as is plagiarism. But they do not believe that the law makes *them* outlaws. They make little distinction between sharing conversation, sharing information over the Internet, and downloading, cutting, pasting, and sharing material they find on the Web. And they cannot accept that copyright law would so severely circumscribe their right to enjoy, use, and express themselves through the words, music, and images that constitute our culture.

If copyright is to regain its traditional symbolic import, copyright law will have to be recalibrated in line with its basic norms. In that context, the copyright industries' rearguard campaigns to educate the public about copyright's worth, including such initiatives as encouraging students to put a copyright notice on their homework assignments and preparing a program for Boy Scouts for earn a "Respect Copyrights Activity Patch," are both way off the mark and destined for failure.[69] To earn public recognition and esteem, copyright law will rather have to focus once again on fostering individual self-expression. It will have to provide for remuneration and respect for authorship without imposing excessive proprietary control over self-expression.

Conclusion

Copyright indeed serves as *an* engine of free expression. Copyright underwrites speech and speakers of central importance to our system of free expression. Yet to recognize that copyright is but one of several engines is to make copyright a more true and effective engine. First Amendment values are best served by a lively interplay among copyright-supported speakers and a wide array of nonmarket and quasi-market speakers, ranging from bloggers to publicly funded broadcasters. Even within the copyright-supported arena, moreover, copyright best fuels expressive diversity and robust debate by underwriting a strong, vibrant sector of independent authors, publishers, studios, newspapers, record labels, and new media—rough modern-day equivalents of the Founders' cottage industry printers and booksellers—to pose a constant challenge to media conglomerates.

As we will see further in the next chapter, that desired multiplicity of speakers suggests the need for copyrights of modest proportions. A copyright law animated by free speech principles must enable creators and distributors of original expression to look to paying audiences for financial sustenance. But it must also leave ample room for speakers and media that stand apart from the commercial media conglomerates that have come to dominate public discourse largely through their control of vast inventories of copyrighted works. Ultimately, copyright best serves as an engine of free expression when narrowly tailored to that end.

| Copyright's Free Speech Burdens

COPYRIGHT PREVENTS SPEAKERS RANGING from the young journalist Alan Cranston to hip-hop artist Biz Markie from expressing themselves through the salient texts, stories, songs, sounds, and images that populate our culture. Copyright thus imposes a significant burden on expressive diversity and autonomy. That does not mean that copyright must always give way before countervailing speech concerns. But the paramount importance of free speech does oblige us to minimize copyright's speech burdens whenever we can do so without forsaking copyright's constitutive role as engine of free expression.

That basic principle is far easier to state than to apply. When are copyright's speech burdens intolerable? When, in contrast, might they be a price we willingly pay for copyright's support for those authors and publishers who look to the market for financial sustenance? To begin to answer those questions, we need to understand more precisely when and how copyright burdens speech.

We can divide copyright's speech burdens into three distinct yet interrelated categories. First, copyright imposes what I somewhat loosely term a "censorial" speech burden.[1] Because of copyright, speakers are often unable to convey their message effectively and audiences unable to obtain access to certain expressive works. In some such cases, like those of Alice Randall, the Philadelphia Church of God, and the Air Pirates, copyright owners avowedly seek to silence another person's chosen manner of expressing, receiving, or distributing an idea. In many others, speakers engage in self-censorship rather than incur the risk of being sued.

Second, copyright imposes a "prohibitive cost" speech burden. As Jon Else discovered, even a copyright owner who is willing to license sometimes insists on a license fee that a particular speaker can ill afford. In fact, speakers ranging from documentary filmmakers to Google often face prohibitive costs in simply locating copyright holders and negotiating copyright permissions, let alone paying the license fees. As we will see, prohibitive cost speech burdens are analytically distinct from censorial. But the result is the same: regardless of the copyright holder's willingness to license, the speaker is muted and the speech unheard.

Third, over and above its chilling effect in individual cases, copyright results in a "distributive" speech burden. The copyright regime as a whole—including copyright's proprietary character, established patterns of copyright ownership, and the structure of copyright-holding industries—imposes differential burdens on different types of speakers. Copyrights in popular expression are frequently controlled not by individual authors but by large media conglomerates.[2] These congeries of motion picture studios, television networks, cable television operators, record labels, print publishers, and music publishers dominate markets for expression and, hence, much of public discourse. The result is that highly concentrated copyright industries controlling vast inventories of copyrighted works enjoy the preponderance of copyright's benefits. And copyright's free speech burdens fall most heavily on individuals and independent speakers.

To be certain, major motion picture studios, publishers, and record labels must also regularly contend with rights conflicts and clearance barriers. But, overall, for these large, commercial repeat players, copyright's burdens have more the tenor of a cost of doing business than the irremediable stifling of self-expression. The majors can generally overcome rights conflicts by procuring licenses, cross-licensing, litigating, buying errors and omissions insurance, or, worse comes to worst, simply moving on to the next project in a long line of possible opportunities. With some notable exceptions, moreover, the typical copyright-industry firm's primary interest in any given project, like in its own "properties," is to earn a profit rather than convey a message. Media conglomerates are beholden to their shareholders. Consequently, their decisions regarding what expression to produce must be driven by expected contribution to the bottom line, not the inherent desire to make a statement about the world. For commercial media, copyright's burdens impact market strategy and profitability. For individuals and independents, particularly non-market speakers, copyright more frequently burdens speech that is a substantive end in itself.[3]

Furthermore, copyright's distributive speech burden does not lie only in the statistical likelihood that those holding copyrights will be media conglomerates and those unable to build upon copyright-protected expression, individual or independent speakers. Rather the incumbent industries have repeatedly deployed their formidable copyright arsenals as a tool to stifle competition from emerging new media and thus to maintain their dominant market position in the production and distribution of music, television programs, movies, journals, and books. The industries' top-heavy configuration, coupled with their repeated use of copyright to foreclose competition, amplifies copyright's censorial effect and raises entry barriers to prospective new speakers and distributors.

We now examine copyright's censorial, prohibitive cost, and distributive speech burdens in more detail. While some aspects of copyright's speech burdens are quite straightforward, others are surprisingly complex.

Copyright's Censorial Speech Burden

Absent an exception or limitation to their proprietary rights, copyright holders are generally free to withhold permission from using their works as they wish. Copyright holders not infrequently exercise that discretion to suppress a speaker's use of copyright-protected expression. Copyright holders have various motives for doing so. In some instances, closest to the core of what we generally think of as "censorship," the copyright holder suppresses speech to avoid criticism, prevent the disclosure of embarrassing information, or stifle the speaker's political or cultural message. In others, the copyright holder simply responds aggressively to unwanted competition. Commercial media firms commonly block speech that they suspect could impair the market value of a work in their copyright portfolio, undermine product development and merchandising opportunities, threaten their traditional business models, or challenge their dominance over the market for distributing cultural expression.

Whatever the motive, a copyright law that grants copyright holders exclusive, proprietary rights in original expression and provides for only tepid exceptions to those rights inevitably results in manifold private censorship. As we have seen, a speaker's effective dissemination of a message often requires incorporating and building upon, or liberally copying from, another's expression. Yet copyright holders too often seek to use their proprietary control of expression to silence the speaker.

The Randall, Cranston, Philadelphia Church of God, and Air Pirates cases are prime examples, but others abound. Several involve Stephen Joyce's repeated use of copyright to obstruct scholarly work about the writing and life of his grandfather James Joyce.[4] Most recently, Joyce browbeat publisher Farrar, Straus & Giroux to delete more than 30 pages of documentary material from Stanford University professor Carol Loeb Shloss's 400-page book about the mental illness of James Joyce's daughter and its impact on his work. That in turn led some leading reviewers to take Shloss to task for the "dearth of data" supporting her otherwise "poignant" and "valuable" thesis.[5] Likewise, the Church of Scientology has repeatedly threatened or brought copyright infringement lawsuits against critics who post secret church texts on the Internet to unveil church foibles. It has also taken on search engines, Internet service providers, and newspapers that facilitate or report on such postings.[6] In another infamous case of outright suppression, Lord Ashdown, former leader of Great Britain's Liberal Party, brought a successful copyright claim against a British newspaper that had published excerpts from minutes of a highly controversial, confidential meeting at which Ashdown discussed forming a new coalition cabinet with the prime minister.[7] And apparently driven by commercial motives, Mattel and Disney continue to use copyright aggressively to suppress subversive uses of their copyrighted characters.[8]

In these cases, as in many other instances of copyright holders' private censorship, speakers copy a copyright holder's work in order to expose the original author's odious ideas or character, convey more precisely the author's thoughts or thought patterns, engage in pointed cultural critique, illustrate an argument, add credibility and poignancy to news reporting, or engage in religious practice. As with Alice Randall's sequel and Alan Cranston's annotated translation, one cannot say that such copying is absolutely necessary for the speaker to make his or her point. After all, speakers can almost always describe the contents of the plaintiff's work entirely in the speaker's own words. But in many cases, no less than with Randall and Cranston, the speech in question would be far less effective, far less believable, and of far less value to the intended audience without reproducing substantial portions of the author's work.

As we have seen, judicial solicitude for speech does sometimes lead courts to allow defendants to build upon existing copyrighted work to convey their message. But given the vagaries of copyright's purported free speech safety valves, each defendant speaker who eventually prevails must engage in risky, expensive litigation to defend his entitlement to speak. Not surprisingly, in countless other instances, independent and nonmarket speakers discontinue conveying their chosen message, or simply engage in self-censorship from the get-go, rather than face the expense and risk of litigation.[9]

That speaker self-censorship is an often overlooked but vital point. Copyright holders regularly exploit a speaker's fear of litigation, heightened by general uncertainty about when speech that borrows something from existing expression infringes copyright, to claim far greater copyright protection than they would likely obtain if forced to press their claim in court. William Patry and Richard Posner have recently collected some striking examples, which, as they aptly point out, "could be multiplied indefinitely."[10] Among them, the Copyright Society of the U.S.A. brazenly—and incorrectly—advises filmmakers that there is *never* a fair use or de minimis defense to copying even just a few seconds of a movie or television program: "If film clips or photographs from motion pictures, television programs, or other sources are used, consent is required from the copyright owner to use clips or photographs in a motion picture, no matter how de minimis or short."[11] Then there is the typical book publisher warning: "No part of this book may be reproduced in any form or by any means, electronic or mechanical, including photocopying, without the written permission of the publisher"—found even in books containing considerable public domain material and purporting to apply even to copying that might actually constitute fair use. ASCAP's zealous insistence that summer camps pay public performance royalties for allowing their campers to sing copyrighted songs around the campfire is another, notorious, example. And not surprisingly, as the Chilling Effects Clearinghouse documents, media industry copyright holders regularly send cease-and-desist letters to operators of fan fiction Web sites "informing" the operator that the site's contents infringe the holder's "valuable" rights, even when the operator may well have a colorable claim of fair use.[12]

To make matters worse, Farrar, Straus & Giroux's capitulation before Stephen Joyce's threatened lawsuit is quite typical. The intermediaries on which speakers depend to reach a broad audience—record labels, studios, broadcasters, and publishers—often impose an additional layer of censorship. Speech intermediaries' management and legal counsel generally hold a far more tenuous commitment to conveying the speaker's message and artistic project than held by the speaker. They also bend over backward to avoid incurring copyright infringement lawsuits unless the commercial potential of producing the speaker's work clearly outweighs the costs and risks of litigation. Consequently, many intermediaries take a position toward their own authors that mirrors the aggressive stance they adopt toward third parties: they insist that their authors identify each and every clip, passing reference, or quotation from preexisting works, and then delete or obtain licenses for even those that are quite likely fair use, de minimis, or otherwise noninfringing.[13]

Given those "clear it or cut it" strictures, speakers who wish to reach a broad audience often have little choice but to self-censor even in advance of any express copyright holder threat. The hip-hop artists and documentary filmmakers canvassed in chapter 2 are telling examples. Far from championing speakers' creative appropriation and recasting of salient elements of our cultural heritage, intermediaries tend to impose yet another filter on speech.

Further, there is yet another quite common, yet not widely recognized, contributor to that excessive, speech-stifling caution. Postproduction and editing decisions are often conducted under the shadow—or even with the active participation—of an errors and omissions insurance carrier. One might suppose at first glance that errors and omissions coverage, by which speech intermediaries, independent producers, and speakers may insure against the risk of infringement, would provide some cushion for standing up for and perhaps testing the limits of fair use. But even more than speech intermediaries, errors and omissions insurance companies' overriding interest is in avoiding infringement litigation. Insurance carriers, in turn, takes pains to pass on that speech-chilling risk averseness to their speech intermediary clients and, ultimately, to the creative speakers themselves. Documentary filmmakers complain, for example, that if they make one "mistake," incorporating a clip or shot that brings a copyright infringement lawsuit, they will be denied errors and omissions coverage not only for the entire film in question but for all future projects.[14]

Finally, it bears emphasizing that copyright holders take advantage of the asymmetric incentives of speakers and intermediaries by pressing to hold a broad array of intermediaries liable for speakers' copyright infringements. And, predictably, intermediaries, ranging from providers of Internet access to publishers and studios, typically respond by overdeterrence, purging any material that copyright holders claim is infringing.

The notice-and-take-down provisions of the Digital Millennium Copyright Act are a case in point.[15] Those provisions, which Congress enacted in 1998, codify a compromise in which copyright industries and telecommunications companies agreed, in effect, to deputize Internet service providers (ISPs) to enforce copyrights against ISP subscribers. The provisions immunize an Internet service provider from liability for infringing material that a subscriber places on an ISP server so long as the ISP removes that material upon receiving a "take-down" notice from the copyright holder. A parallel provision immunizes Internet search engines from liability for linking to infringing material if the search engine removes the link upon receiving the copyright holder's notice.

As might be expected, the safe harbor provisions have led to the removal from the Internet of considerable material, both infringing and noninfringing. Copyright holders are not shy about sending out DMCA take-down notices, and risk-averse ISPs and search engines regularly remove subscriber content in the face of dubious copyright infringement claims.[16] In its effort to quash the college students' Internet posting of documentary evidence of voting machine security flaws, Diebold Election Systems sent out take-down notices to dozens of ISPs, not only those hosting Web sites that posted the damning Diebold e-mails but also those that merely linked to the documents or even just provided Internet service to other ISPs that hosted sites that linked to the documents. All but one ISP recipient, a nonprofit online civil liberties organization, meekly complied, this despite the court's subsequent ringing endorsement of the students' fair use and free speech right to post the Diebold emails.[17]

The problem, as copyright holders are acutely aware, is that ISPs, search engines, and other intermediaries have little incentive to expend time and money contesting sweeping demands that can be met by sacrificing a marginal user of their services. As Google feebly explained after cutting links to sites of a Church of Scientology critic in the face of a take-down notice from the church, "Had we not removed these URLs, we would be subject to a claim for copyright infringement, regardless of its merits."[18] Indeed, in defense against Viacom's billion dollar lawsuit claiming that Google-owned YouTube facilitates massive infringement and is thus ineligible for the DMCA safe harbor despite scrupulously complying with take-down notices, Google recently deployed digital filters that preemptively block many creative mashups as well as users' exact copies of TV show segments from appearing on the site. First Amendment doctrine generally imposes significant constraints on suppressing speech by targeting vulnerable or indifferent intermediaries. Yet such "censorship by proxy" is now a prime feature of copyright law.[19]

In sum, one cannot appreciate the full ambit of copyright's speech burden without taking the circle of censorship and self-censorship into account. Copyright's speech-chilling effect arises from a complex interplay of bloated copyright holder entitlements, forbidding litigation costs, copyright holder overclaiming, media's clearance culture, speech intermediaries' overdeterrence, and widespread uncertainty about just how expansive are copyright holder rights at the intersection of fair use, the idea/expression dichotomy, de minimis uses, substantial similarity, and a host of other nebulous doctrines that may or may not circumscribe copyright in any given instance. Copyright holders already enjoy an excessively expansive domain of proprietary control under the literal letter of today's copyright law. The confluence of the factors I have discussed effectively magnifies that control through a penumbra of censorship and self-censorship extending far beyond even that which copyright holders would likely obtain if they had to litigate their copyright infringement claims in court.

Copyright's Prohibitive Cost Speech Burden

Copyright's "censorial" speech burden is just one source of copyright's chilling effect on speakers and speech intermediaries. In other cases, like that of Jon Else's run-in with Twentieth Century Fox, the copyright holder appears to have no direct censorial motive but demands a license fee that makes it prohibitively expensive for the would-be speaker to obtain permission to build upon or transmit the copyright-protected expression. As a result, that speech does not take place.

While the speech-stifling consequence is the same regardless of the copyright holder's motive, it is far from intuitively obvious that we ought to treat prohibitive license fees as a speech burden on a par with deliberate copyright holder censorship. After all, "free" speech does not necessarily mean "costless" speech. And copyright is hardly unique in rendering speech more expensive, at times prohibitively so. A speaker may be unable to afford various goods, ranging from a computer to a printing press, needed for effective speech. Yet we do not normally limit property rights in those goods in order to give speakers the entitlement to own or use them. So why should copyright be viewed differently? Why should prohibitive license fees be an additional ground for carving out free speech safety valves from copyrights?

There is no simple, across-the-board answer to those questions. Prohibitive license fees in fact are often (but not always) properly understood as an intolerable speech burden. Yet, as we will presently see, that conclusion follows only from a careful exploration of how copyright markets operate. It also hinges on free speech policy, specifically various value judgments about which mix of speakers and speech our copyright regime should foster.

To begin, let us reconsider the case of Jon Else. Say that Else envisioned shooting a highly poignant scene that required air travel to a remote location or the use of a top-of-the-line movie camera that he could not afford. Else might qualify for government or foundation funding to meet those production costs. Or, as he actually did, he might hope to sell his documentary to the federally subsidized Public Broadcasting Corporation. Such public fiscal support for noncommercial expression is an important part of our system of free expression. But if Else's funding falls short, as it did with regard to Fox's license fee, Else has no claim against those who manufacture, sell, or own production equipment or other tangible inputs (like air travel tickets) he needs to express his message. The owners' property rights give way neither to Else's interest in effective speech nor to our collective interest in expressive diversity.

So why might we regard Fox's license fee as an unacceptable burden on speech, but not similarly view a prohibitively expensive movie camera? There are two basic reasons. The first and most straightforward is that copyright law regulates speech. The second, which is actually far more complicated than some observers seem to assume, is that copyright law creates an artificial scarcity in the popular expression that speakers often need for effective speech.

COPYRIGHT IS SPEECH REGULATION

Property rights in tangible goods impose only incidental burdens on speech in discrete circumstances. In contrast, copyright law directly and deliberately targets speech. This distinction parallels that which First Amendment doctrine draws between "general conduct regulation" and "speech regulation." General conduct regulation consists of laws of property, contract, business organization, traffic, taxes, and other such matters. Those laws typically govern nonspeakers as well as speakers and do not usually impose any burden on speech. It is only when they happen to affect a speaker in a particular context that a speech burden may incidentally arise.

Courts do not apply First Amendment scrutiny to true general conduct regulation.[20] That rule reflects a broad sense that our interest in free speech and expressive diversity, powerful though it may be, cannot pervade every act and social relation that is subject to the law. A journalist rushing to cover a story, even a story of clear public import, cannot enjoy a legal privilege to commandeer a stranger's car, race through red lights, and drive over others' yards. Nor does Jon Else enjoy a privilege to pilfer Fox's top-of-the-line movie cameras, even if that means that the film he envisions will not be made.

On the other hand, courts typically apply some measure of heightened First Amendment scrutiny to regulations that directly target speech.[21] First Amendment jurisprudence holds that government should not target speech and that individuals should not face punishment for speaking absent very good reason. This is especially so when government aims to suppress or favor the speaker's message or subject matter; courts subject such "content-based" regulation to "strict scrutiny" and almost always strike it down as constitutionally infirm. Yet courts also scrutinize, albeit somewhat less rigorously, regulation that targets speech in an apparently noncensorial, content-neutral manner. Such regulation, which can range from imposing decibel limits on rock concerts to permitting broadcasting only within the frequencies set forth in a Federal Communications Commission (FCC) license, poses a palpable danger that lawmakers faced with a complex array of issues and constituencies may intentionally or inadvertently give short shrift to the general public interest in free speech and expressive diversity. It also presents an opportunity for government to favor certain speakers over others, to dole out to politically powerful media exclusive entitlements to produce and disseminate expression through a variety of communications channels.

Copyright is speech regulation. It touches directly and consistently on a broad spectrum of speech, including literature, art, film, television broadcasts, photographs, political polemic, model laws and regulations, original selections and arrangements of data, and other such expression. Moreover, as I will soon enumerate, copyright is heavily involved in allocating speech entitlements among various speakers and categories of speech. Fox's right to exclude Jon Else from using *The Simpsons* is a fundamental feature, not some unintended, incidental effect, of copyright law.

For some commentators that is enough. The very fact that copyright law targets speech and prevents a speaker from articulating his message in the words, sounds, and images of his choosing is, in and of itself, grounds for concluding that copyright imposes an unacceptable, indeed unconstitutional, speech burden, regardless of any claim that copyright ultimately serves to foster speech.[22] In that view, First Amendment protection against such incursions on a particular individual's expressive autonomy trumps virtually all regulatory objectives, including delimiting and distributing speech entitlements to enhance the vitality of public discourse and provide a rich field for other individuals to learn, enjoy, and exercise their autonomy. Jon Else's liberty to communicate his imaginative vision stands above any utilitarian calculus, even one that would insist that Fox might not produce programs like *The Simpsons* if compelled to give away licenses to all comers.[23]

To similar effect, but with very different reasoning, another strain of free speech theory would support Else's right to use his shot of *The Simpsons* at a price he could readily afford on the grounds that the capacity to speak should be distributed as widely and equally as possible, without regard to the speaker's ability to pay. That view stems from a concern that radical inequality in control over resources vital to shaping public discourse runs counter to both poor persons' expressive autonomy and the democratic ideal of political equality.[24] Among other means to address that concern, some commentators insist that property rights that are inherently central to speakers' ability to reach a public audience should be subject to what has been termed a "free speech easement," the right of individuals or groups to use that essential property to speak.[25] Few can afford a press; those who cannot should enjoy some right of access to vital channels of communication.[26]

That distributive objective has received considerable acceptance in law and policy. It is partly reflected in various speech easements over a broad range of property deemed vital to speech. Newspapers have been required to devote column space for individuals wishing to reply to editorials that criticize them. Shopping centers have been required to allow leafleting and signature gathering. Broadcast, cable, and other telecommunications licensees have been required to provide unaffiliated speakers with broadcast time, entire channels, or network capacity. Such carriage and access requirements have aimed to promote expressive diversity and robust debate on important public issues even at the cost of depriving the licensee or other property owner of a portion of its communications capacity for speech of its own choosing.

Some such requirements have fallen into disfavor as being counterproductive, tainted by government favoritism, or no longer necessary given the possibility of "cheap speech" over the Internet.[27] Indeed, courts have invalidated some speech easements as unconstitutional abridgments of the burdened party's speech.[28] But other carriage and access requirements have been extended and upheld. And the Supreme Court has made a point of reminding us that the basic goal of broadly distributing speech capacity remains central to First Amendment policy, even if specific mechanisms for attaining that goal sometimes miss the mark.[29]

Copyright is heavily involved in questions of speech distribution. Copyright law is facially neutral in the sense that impecunious authors as well as Fortune 500 corporations can own copyrights. But in practice large media conglomerates own vast inventories of the culturally salient copyrighted works that inform the language of much individual expression. They also have greater resources than most individuals to buy or cross-license rights and to litigate when threatened with a copyright infringement lawsuit. On balance, therefore, if Fox and other media conglomerates enjoy a broad, proprietary entitlement—including the right to deny the use of their expression absent payment of a bargained license fee—Jon Else and other nonwealthy, independent speakers will have lesser opportunities for effective speech.

At the same time, copyright doctrine's distributional impact is not necessarily unidirectional. As the record labels and movie studios loudly remind us, large media firms are far from impervious to untrammeled, nonpaying uses of their copyrighted works.[30] Giving Jon Else and lots of other non-wealthy speakers a right to use Fox's existing work without permission might undermine Fox's licensing market and thus diminish the company's capacity to produce and disseminate its own expression.

In sum, copyright's shape and reach sharply impact the mix of speakers and speech that populates our public discourse. Moreover, unlike property rights in land and most tangible goods, speech distribution lies at the very definitional core of copyright holder rights. The term "free speech easement" suggests a carve-out from a preexisting, pre-set proprietary right. But the issue in copyright is not whether Else should have an easement to use property from which he would otherwise naturally be excluded. Rather, the question of whether Jon Else should have a right to use *The Simpsons* in his background shot is one of delimiting the baseline entitlement of the copyright holder to begin with. Copyright has no natural baseline. It is a limited entitlement designed to further a specific policy objective: promoting multifarious contributions to public discourse and the store of knowledge. Defining and delimiting copyright—determining copyright's duration and scope and delineating the bounds of fair use, compulsory licenses, and other free speech safeguards—is thus inherently a choice about how best to further that objective. As such, that choice necessarily implicates fundamental normative questions of free speech policy regarding the desired balance between commercial and noncommercial expression and between wealthy and poor speakers.

My assessment of copyright's speech burden follows far more from distributive considerations than the absolutist claim that the First Amendment renders copyright unsupportable whenever it impairs expressive autonomy. As I have argued elsewhere, so long as copyright law does not aim to suppress a given message or subject matter, which it does not, copyright is not per se unconstitutional or unacceptable.[31] Copyright law plays an important role in underwriting our system of free expression. To the extent that copyright must impose some speech burdens in order to yield significant speech benefits, the absolutist view could well impede, not further, First Amendment objectives.

For some readers, I recognize, that calculus is beside the point: an individual's expressive autonomy must trump the broader social good, certainly with respect to copyright and perhaps more generally. In that view, an individual's right to use existing expression in her speech must prevail, even if that means that over time we will have less original expression. The speaker must prevail, indeed, even if that entails diminished speech opportunities for other individuals who can speak only if adequately compensated and for others who would have gladly paid the copyright holder's price for using or gaining access to that forgone original expression. That is a defensible position, yet one that raises issues of philosophy and constitutional doctrine extending beyond the scope of this book. Hence, I will here simply posit that, in principle, copyright's overall free speech goals and benefits can justify copyright's imposition of costs that are prohibitive for some speakers.

The key, as we will presently see, is to identify those circumstances in which countenancing copyright's prohibitive costs actually serves free speech goals. That equation is necessarily less clear-cut than viewing a speaker's desired use of existing expression as an absolute trump over copyright. It requires that we evaluate copyright's prohibitive cost speech burden in light of copyright's overall impact on our system of free expression, including on the paramount aim of fostering expressive diversity. We must determine whether, given our fundamental First Amendment values and objectives, copyright's free speech benefits warrant particular speech burdens that copyright imposes. At the very least, Fox's ability to impose a license fee that is prohibitively costly for Jon Else and other similarly situated speakers must be necessary to achieve the free speech benefits to which copyright law and the First Amendment jointly aspire. If not, the burden that Else and other speakers suffer is, indeed, intolerable.

COPYRIGHT CREATES ARTIFICIAL SCARCITY

The second reason for treating prohibitive license fees differently from costly film production equipment is that unlike property rights in most tangible goods, copyright law creates an *artificial* scarcity in existing expression. That reason may appear at first to be purely an economic equation. Indeed, the question of whether copyrights create artificial scarcity and, concomitantly, lead to the "deadweight loss" characteristic of monopolies lies at the heart of the economic analysis of copyright law, a dominant school of American copyright scholarship. As we will discover, however, that question, too, ultimately revolves upon qualitative First Amendment policy judgments about what mix of speech and speakers copyright should underwrite.

In a market economy, suppliers facing rigorous competition are typically driven to sell goods at the lowest price at which it is possible to produce and distribute them and, in the aggregate, to supply sufficient quantities to meet all consumer demand at that price. If some tangible goods are scarce for some consumers, it is due to limitations in available raw materials or in manufacturing or distribution capacity that limit supply and/or drive up the market price. In addition, most tangible goods are rivalrous; like an apple that is gone once eaten, they cannot be shared among many people. So if poor consumers cannot pay the market price for a tangible, rivalrous good, we normally assist them, if at all, by subsidizing their purchasing power or, perhaps, subsidizing greater supply. We do not generally address scarcity in tangible, rivalrous goods through price regulation, limiting suppliers' property rights, or requiring mass sharing.

Likewise with the top-of-the-line camera that Jon Else would like to use in our hypothetical scenario. Such cameras are no doubt extraordinarily expensive because they contain state-of-the-art components and reflect strict levels of quality assurance in their manufacture.[32] Such cameras would be prohibitively expensive for most consumers and thus scarce even if produced and sold in a highly competitive market. And absent an unlikely charitable act, no major motion picture studio will put its top-of-the-line cameras at Else's disposal. It is because of the high cost of production and rivalrous character of each top-of-the-line camera that Else may have to shoot his film with a camera of lesser cost and quality.

In contrast, once Fox makes *The Simpsons* publicly available, the show can be readily shared by millions at virtually no additional cost, whether by posting and viewing entire episodes on the Internet or incorporating brief shots in documentary films. No single person's enjoyment of the work detracts from anyone else also accessing and enjoying it. It is Fox's exclusive right, not the inherent scarcity of *The Simpsons* as an expressive good, that potentially puts access out of reach for many consumers and speakers.

So how are we to judge Fox's $10,000 license fee? Does any positive price that puts access out of reach for any speaker cause "artificial scarcity" and thus give rise to an intolerable speech burden? In economic parlance, artificial scarcity occurs, for nonrivalrous as well as rivalrous goods, when the supplier charges not just any positive price but more than the "competitive price" for the good, or, more precisely, when the price charged for the good reflects the supplier's "market power." I will presently explore what those key terms, "competitive price" and "market power," might actually mean in the copyright context. We begin with some basic principles.

Suppliers are said to have "market power" when, due to a certain invulnerability to competitive market forces, they are able, over more than an insignificant period of time, profitably to charge higher than the "competitive price" for a given good or service.[33] When market conditions or the law enables a supplier consistently to charge more than the competitive price, the supplier effectively reduces output, depriving some consumers who would otherwise purchase the good or service under competitive conditions. That deprivation is termed "deadweight loss."

Copyright holders' ability to charge a "supracompetitive price" lies at the heart of copyright's prohibitive cost speech burden. Copyright might provide an incentive for the creation and dissemination of much original expression. But where copyright confers market power, it also brings about a scarcity that would not exist but for copyright law. Some people who would have been willing to purchase a copy (or license) of a copyrighted work at the competitive price now will not purchase it at all. In short, when copyright confers market power, it brings about the suboptimal production, consumer deprivation, and societal "deadweight loss" characteristic of monopolies.

It is thus copyright holders' exercise of market power through charging supracompetitive prices that renders the scarcity that copyright causes truly "artificial," as distinct from the scarcity inherent even in highly competitive markets for tangible, rivalrous goods. To the extent Fox can insist on a $10,000 license fee for a 4.5-second background shot of *The Simpsons* because it enjoys market power, Else's need to delete the shot is fairly characterized as a burden on speech, in a way that Else's need to forgo buying an expensive camera or shoot on location in Paris would not. (More precisely, it is copyright's dual character as speech regulation and font of market power that underlies this distinction. Even if camera producers or airlines enjoy market power, we would not generally view their supracompetitive prices as a speech burden unless their market power derived from a law that targets speech.)[34]

Now for some readers, no doubt, my suggestion that copyright confers market power raises a red flag, and rightly so. The question of whether, when, and how copyright holders enjoy market power is actually highly complex, far more so than copyright critics sometimes seem to assume. To begin with, copyright does not always—or even usually—confer market power. There is little or no consumer demand for the vast majority of expressive works. Indeed, the holders of copyright in most works can hardly give them away, let alone charge a positive price. So at most copyright makes market power possible only for those works, like *The Simpsons,* for which there is substantial and durable demand.

Yet, neither is it the case, as some have suggested, that only audience demand, not copyright, confers market power for popular works.[35] To the extent copyright holders can charge a supracompetitive price for popular works, copyright operates just like any exclusive concession or monopoly. No monopolist can charge a supracompetitive price for a good that consumers do not want. Rather, it is always the *confluence* of significant consumer demand and an absence of rigorous competition that enables supracompetitive pricing. So the pertinent question is whether publishers, studios, record labels, and other copyright holders enjoy sufficient protection from competition (whether from copiers or producers of competing books, movies, or sound recordings) to raise prices above competitive levels for those works for which there is significant consumer demand.

There are, in turn, two parts to that question. First, what is the "competitive price" for original, copyright-protected expression? Before we can establish whether copyright holders price *above* competitive levels, we need to determine what the competitive levels are. Second, as measured against our "competitive price" benchmark, do copyright holders of popular works in fact charge supracompetitive prices for more than a transitory duration? Or at least, in the absence of hard data that would make such price comparison possible, does it appear that those copyright holders enjoy sufficient protection against competition to enable them consistently to charge supracompetitive prices? As we will see, while those sound like purely economic questions, they actually cannot be answered apart from free speech policy.

What Is the "Competitive Price" for Original Expression?

Commentators often contend that copyright causes deadweight loss because it enables copyright holders of commercially successful works to charge more than the "marginal cost" of providing copies of or access to the work. That assertion draws upon textbook economics, which, indeed, typically defines competitive price as the "marginal cost" of producing a good, in other words, the cost of producing one more unit of a good, not taking into account the producer's investment in production facilities. When the good is a book, the marginal cost would equal the cost of printing and distributing one more copy. In the case of text on a Web site, the marginal cost would be virtually nothing—only the negligible cost of transmitting the text over the Internet to one more user. In neither event would marginal cost reflect the author's "first-copy" costs, the investment in creating the text that is to be distributed.

The marginal cost metric makes sense in the many contexts in which authors, like many amateur bloggers and YouTube video creators, have no need or expectation of recovering their first-copy costs (or can recover those costs by selling associated goods like advertising and lecture fees). In such cases, the supramarginal cost pricing that copyright makes possible does not serve to spur creation or further dissemination and thus imposes a deadweight loss. But for those works that would never be created and disseminated in the first place unless authors and publishers could strive to recover their first-copy costs by excluding copyists, we need a more nuanced measure of competitive price and market power. For those works, marginal cost pricing cannot be the proper measure of competitive price because marginal cost pricing would not sustain any market at all. Given the relatively high first-copy costs of producing sustained works of authorship, like investigative journalism and full-length feature films, and the low marginal costs of distributing such works—indeed the negligible marginal costs of disseminating them over the Internet—authors could never recover their first-copy costs if they adopted marginal cost pricing. Copyright holders, then, price above marginal cost because they have to if they are to stay in business, not because they have market power. Hence, the mere fact that Fox charges something above marginal cost to use *The Simpsons* does not necessarily mean that its price is supracompetitive and thus that Fox's copyright *artificially* deprives Else of his opportunity to speak.

In that respect, markets for original expression are much like any markets characterized by scale economies, that is, where producers incur high upfront fixed costs and where the more of the product is supplied, the lower its per unit incremental cost. When scale economies are present, firms cannot recover their fixed costs if they price at their declining per unit incremental, or marginal, cost. Such firms would be condemned to destruction if they adopted marginal cost pricing. As a result, competitive pricing for scale economy firms more closely approximates the *average* per unit price required to recover fixed costs (plus incremental costs) than it approximates marginal cost pricing.[36]

So at least where copyright is in fact necessary to spur a work's creation or dissemination, a better measure of competitive price would be the average price required for the copyright holder to recover its first-copy costs, plus any marginal costs. Copyrighted works must be priced at an amount calculated to enable the copyright holder to recover the costs both of producing the first copy and of producing and distributing subsequent copies.[37]

Yet, although average cost thus provides an analytically more accurate benchmark for measuring competitive price than marginal cost, the average cost metric is far more difficult to apply in practice. Unlike marginal cost, average cost can only be estimated, not calculated with any precision. Even if we can accurately quantify first-copy and incremental costs, we can rarely know in advance how many copies of a work will be produced over its commercial lifetime and thus what fraction of first-copy costs to allocate to each copy.

That is not all: even the average cost metric fails to capture the full complexity of copyright markets unless we include some multiplier for risk of failure, for copyright holders' investment in many works that turn out to be commercial flops. Why should this be? After all, every producer faces a risk of commercial loss. And competitive pricing is not generally understood to include a risk multiplier; under ideal conditions of perfect competition, producers cannot raise prices above marginal (or average) cost to cushion against possible losses.

The reason, media firms have long argued, is that markets for expressive works are fundamentally different. Producers of expression—studios, labels, and publishers—face extreme uncertainty and risk. Accordingly, media firms must be able to price to earn revenues far in excess of average cost for successful works in order to make up for losses on flops.[38] As Landes and Posner rephrase the industry argument (without necessarily accepting it in full), "Because demand is uncertain, the difference between price and marginal cost of the successful work must not only cover the cost of expression but also compensate for the unavoidable risk of failure."[39]

In this view, even though Fox's $10,000 license fee for a 4.5-second background shot seems excessive when compared with license fees for most works, it might actually be the "competitive" price. Fox needs to earn pure profit—a lot of pure profit—on its hits to make up for the considerable losses it unavoidably incurs investing in the many television programs and movies that do not enjoy sustained and widespread audience demand. Fox might procure insurance for risk of failure if such insurance were available. But in the absence of such insurance, Fox must, in effect, self-insure by banking on its occasional megahits.

We will shortly assess just how much of a risk multiplier is truly warranted. For now, the important point to keep in mind is that once we accept the basic premise, as I think we must, that copyright holders as a whole need profits from commercially successful works to balance out inevitable losses from other works that turn out to be flops, our analysis of competitive pricing becomes exponentially more complex. It means, first, that we can no longer assess pricing and production costs on a discrete, work-by-work basis. Rather, we need to view the aggregate of a copyright holder's works as a single economic unit. The sum total of the prices charged for all uses of any work in the copyright holder's portfolio must be sufficient to yield revenues equal to the sum total of the copyright holder's marginal and actual production costs for all its works. So we can only evaluate Fox's $10,000 license fee in the context of Fox's, or perhaps a hypothetical average copyright holder's, entire portfolio, risk management, and pricing strategy. Apart from that context, we have no baseline for determining whether Fox's fee is supracompetitive.

Second, once we think about "competitive pricing" in terms of an entire portfolio rather than an individual work, we realize that our true metric must be aggregate copyright holder *profits,* not pricing per se. In the real world, moving away from the ideal of perfect competition found in economics textbooks, copyright holder pricing must be sufficiently high (and, by implication, copyrights must be sufficiently robust) to generate "normal profits." "Normal profits" are that return on investment required to keep copyright holders in business. That means, essentially, that, on average, copyright holders must earn profits from marketing their works that at least equal what they could garner from some "typical" alternative venture.[40] Otherwise, it will not be worth their while to produce and disseminate original expression. In the real world, investors and firms spurn ventures that do not consistently earn some margin of profit over costs. No firm wants to be in the business of selling a pure commodity, a staple product that faces rigorous price competition that drives prices and profits to pure competitive levels. Of course, some cottage industry publishers, independent studios, and individual investors might invest in original expression partly for glamour, social recognition, and the love of discovering and disseminating works of art and literature, just as many authors have myriad nonpecuniary motivations. But overall, as the recent sales of numerous cottage industry publishers and independent studios to media conglomerates attest, we can expect no more of commercial, for-profit copyright industries than we do of other industries. As a matter of copyright economics, our determination of copyright holders' competitive pricing must take into account not only copyright holders' actual profits but also their opportunity costs, profits that they might reasonably earn by diverting their resources to alternative ventures.

Third, we need to look at the *sources* of the copyright holder's profit. Undoubtedly, Fox earns the lion's share of its revenue from television advertising, audience receipts, and product merchandising, not licensing short background shots to documentary filmmakers like Jon Else. If Fox can earn normal profits without charging Jon Else $10,000, does that mean that Fox's license fee is supracompetitive? Or should our analysis contemplate that Fox may earn normal profits with whatever pricing strategy it sees fit, including slightly lower prices for consumers and advertisers but higher license fees for speakers like Jon Else? Our premise that "competitive pricing" necessarily entails that some revenue sources make up losses from others makes such questions inevitable.

That leads us back to an important theme of this chapter. Although our average cost metric for competitive pricing begins as an objective (even if not precisely calculable) measure of actual costs incurred in producing and distributing a given expressive work, adding the risk multiplier invariably implicates far more open-ended, fundamental questions of speech policy. How much revenue above cost (however defined) should copyright aim to accord creators and distributors of creative expression? To what extent should copyrights be set to enable commercial media firms to earn supranormal profits and thus to induce them to invest in creating more original expression rather than turning to alternative, nonspeech ventures? How much investment in commercially risky expression should our copyright regime tolerate or, indeed, seek to encourage? Should copyrights give way before some authors,' publishers,' and investors' nonpecuniary motivations? Which users of copyrighted expression should have to pay a premium to subsidize other users and copyright holder investment in expression that results in losses? Should we favor lower licensing fees for nonmarket speakers like Jon Else at the expense of higher prices for audiences and advertisers? These questions cannot be answered—and thus the competitive price benchmark for copyright-protected expression cannot be defined—without making value judgments about the types and mix of expression and speakers we want our copyright system to foster. In short, our very determination of copyright holders' "competitive" price ultimately turns as much on speech policies as on any objective, purely economic assessment of risk, average cost, or what are "normal" profits.

We will return to these distributive speech issues at the end of this chapter. We now turn to the second element of artificial scarcity: the question of copyright holders' market power. Are copyright holders able to sustain supracompetitive prices (however defined) to an extent and for a duration that we deem significant? As we will presently see, that side of the seemingly purely economic equation, no less than defining "competitive price," must likewise take account of the policy goals that copyright shares with the First Amendment.

Market Power: Are Copyright Holders Able to Charge Supracompetitive License Fees?

Given the considerable difficulty in identifying the competitive price for many products and services, analysts typically assess the competitiveness of the relevant market and the extent of producer profitability, rather than pricing per se, to determine whether producers enjoy market power. If producers face rigorous competition (or even the constant threat of potentially rigorous competition from new entrants) in the relevant market, they cannot charge supracompetitive prices for an extended period. The same applies to markets for books, movies, music, and art. Whatever we might hypothesize is the "competitive price" for original expression, copyright law cannot confer market power in popular and iconic works unless copyright holders enjoy considerable immunity from competition in markets for those works.

In that vein, the starting point for understanding the competitiveness of copyright markets is the concept of "monopolistic competition." On one hand, copyright law gives copyright holders a quasi monopoly in the market for any given work; copyright precludes others from selling copies of the work without copyright holder permission. But, on the other hand, each copyright holder competes in the broader market for expressive works of the same or similar genre. Copyright confers no monopoly in that broader market.

Hence, the extent of copyright holders' market power—and thus of copyright holders' prohibitive cost speech burden—depends largely on whether that broader market is fully competitive. A fully competitive copyright market consists of multiple producers capable of distributing expressive works that although distinct from one another in many respects are regarded by consumers as approximate equivalents. Competition from expressive works that consumers regard as approximate, even if not perfect, substitutes for a given work will erode a copyright owner's power to charge a supracompetitive price for that work. In turn, such competition would sharply curtail copyright's potentially chilling effect on speech, at least where the copyright holder has no censorial intent.

Building on those precepts, some commentators contend that copyright alone can almost never confer a significant degree of market power for any given work.[41] They argue that even though copyright prevents competition from copiers (so that no one but Fox can distribute *The Simpsons* or license its characters), competition from other works that are close enough substitutes (perhaps roughly similar satirical animated television programs like *South Park* and *Family Guy*) imposes ample market constraint to keep pricing within reasonably competitive levels.

I think that argument is wrong, certainly as applied to licensing popular expression to speakers, as opposed to selling copies to consumers. As I will presently amplify, those licensing markets are far less competitive than the commentators assume. But, first, it is important to put that factual dispute in some conceptual context: our conclusions about whether copyright holders enjoy market power (or "too much" market power) derive largely from why we are asking.

There is no such thing as "market power" in the abstract. In real-world markets, where the ideal economics textbook conditions of perfect competition give way to a host of market frictions and imperfections, suppliers are almost always able to charge somewhat above the competitive price.[42] So the question becomes, How much above competitive price are we willing to tolerate? The answer depends largely on context. What policies are we seeking to further? Which legal regime are we operating under, and what are the costs of using that regime to combat market power? What are the goods in question? How important is it that consumer deprivation in a particular market segment be minimized? Or, conversely, how necessary is the prospect of supracompetitive pricing to induce investments in producing the good in the first place?

That context-specific understanding is important because the term "market power" is typically used within the framework of antitrust law and policy, and most antitrust scholars posit that a single copyright holder's ability to charge a supracompetitive price for use of a given expressive work seldom constitutes "market power" in a conventional antitrust sense.[43] Yet this conclusion, which appears to inform commentators' skepticism about copyright's propensity to confer market power, largely reflects the particularities and limitations of antitrust law. Antitrust lawyers generally define the relevant market as a group of potentially competing products, not a single product. And they believe that even very popular expressive works have colorable, even if imperfect, substitutes that constrain prices sufficiently so that antitrust enforcement, an expensive and highly imprecise instrument, is not worth the candle.[44]

But we are not assessing copyright holders' potential power over price in the context of antitrust law, with its specific regulatory goals and limitations. Rather, our concern is speech. To the extent a copyright holder may profitably charge a supracompetitive price even for a single work, some speakers who otherwise would have access will be denied the ability to build upon that work in conveying their message and creating new speech. Given the paramount importance of free speech (as well as copyright law's greater capacity for fine-tuning than antitrust's), we should thus less tolerate copyright holder power over price than we might in the antitrust context. We must assess copyright holders' power over price against the benchmark of the particular, shared policy goals of copyright and the First Amendment. Competition among copyright holders and expressive works might sufficiently constrain prices to make antitrust enforcement unwarranted, but not enough to obviate the need for robust free speech safety valves that limit the holders' exclusive rights.

There is ample evidence that holders of copyrights in popular and iconic expression for which there is substantial, enduring demand, like *Gone with the Wind* and *The Simpsons,* enjoy sufficient power over price to raise serious free speech concerns. Key copyright markets are highly concentrated, and potential new competitors face considerable barriers to entry. At the same time, because of the peculiar shape of consumer demand for original expression, the works that audiences and speakers most value lack colorable substitutes. Finally, as an additional indication of market power, major copyright industries appear to earn substantial economic rents, profits well in excess of those that one would expect in a competitive market.

Together, these factors present quite compelling evidence that copyright holders enjoy at least some power to set prices for popular and iconic works, cushioned from the full impact of competitive forces that would otherwise force competitive pricing. To the extent that is so, copyright's prohibitive costs are fairly understood as burdens on speech. The very works that typically have the greatest resonance for audiences, and thus that speakers most wish to build upon in communicating their own message or artistic sensitivity, are those that copyright law renders artificially scarce. (I put aside for the moment the question of whether the power to set supracompetitive prices for iconic works is needed to make up for losses on flops.)

WEAK FIRM COMPETITION. Without rigorous challenge from existing competitors, or at least easy entry for potential new ones, even producers of relatively substitutable expression are unlikely to offer it at prices that would undercut each other's market power. When one or a small number of firms dominate the market and new entrants face considerable difficulty in challenging incumbents, we would expect incumbent industries to charge consumer prices and license fees well in excess of competitive levels.[45]

Copyright markets range from fine art to full-length motion pictures and exhibit varying structures and levels of competitiveness. Accordingly, a complete analysis of copyright market competitiveness and copyright holder market power would require in-depth industry-by-industry study that is beyond the scope of this book. By all accounts, however, a number of major copyright markets—markets for the very mass-media-produced popular culture that serves as the lingua franca for much self-expression and artistic comment—are characterized by weak interfirm competition and considerable barriers to entry.

Copyrights in popular expression are generally controlled not by individual authors (or at least not solely by individual authors) but by firms, including motion picture studios, record labels, print publishers, music publishers, and their affiliates. And typical of economy-of-scale markets, these copyright industries tend to be highly concentrated, increasingly under the roof of large media conglomerates. As I detail later in this chapter, a number of copyright industry sectors, particularly sound recording, television, motion picture, for-profit academic journal, and book publishing industries, face the oligopolist dominance of a handful of firms. In those sectors, the "major" labels, studios, and book publishers both hold rights to vast inventories of works that serve as inputs to new expression and have traditionally controlled the channels for distributing expression to the public, although digital technology threatens to undermine that control. They also hold critical advantages over small independents in financing production, distribution, marketing, and promotion. To add to these natural advantages, moreover, industry incumbents have long used copyright strategically as a vehicle for erecting barriers before new firms that wish to challenge their dominance. Indeed, copyright industry efforts to suppress competition have repeatedly been the subject of antitrust actions and have several times been held to run afoul of antitrust law.

Copyright industry concentration, anticompetitive collusion, and entry barriers have greatly restricted competition among producers of possible substitutes. For that reason alone, the media conglomerates that dominate major copyright markets are likely to enjoy considerable market power or, more precisely, will enjoy market power if they are able to parlay their copyright-buttressed advantages in predigital markets into the digital arena as well.

DEARTH OF SUBSTITUTES. Even if copyright industries were more competitive, holders of copyrights in iconic works like *Gone with the Wind* would enjoy market power as a result of the dearth of substitutes for such works. Popular, iconic works—including novels, newspapers, songs, movies, and televisions programs, as well as many scholarly publications—are considerably less substitutable than toasters, toothbrushes, and other such consumer goods. As a result, competition from other expressive works will constrain prices to a far less extent than in fully competitive markets.

Markets for expression offer a considerably greater quantity of goods, yet are nevertheless less competitive, than markets for many other products. The reason is that consumer demand for creative expression tends to follow a winner-take-all, "power law" distribution; the lion's share of consumer demand at any given time is for a relatively small number of works.[46] The U.S. motion picture industry is fairly typical of markets for books, recorded music, and other expressive works: consistently, fewer than 20 percent of first-run movies earn 80 percent of box office gross and fewer than 5 percent earn about 85 percent of all profit.[47] Studies suggest, moreover, that this highly skewed consumer demand endures over time. Best sellers tend to show extraordinary staying power relative to other works, and cumulative ongoing demand for particular works, authors, and recording artists follows the same power-law distribution as demand for recent hits.[48] Further, the power-law distribution holds not only across broad media categories, such as movies, books, music recordings, and video games, but also within specific expressive genres, such as high-budget action movies and shoestring documentaries.[49]

Significantly, that highly skewed demand also characterizes digital distribution, including usage patterns of purely Internet-based expression like blogs and Web sites.[50] Digital technology does foster a "long tail" of numerous niche works, each of which generates a small but nontrivial demand. But while digital technology thus makes it possible to profit even from niche works that would have previously been taken off the shelf, it does not reverse the economic and cultural dominance of the relatively few works still positioned at the top of the sharp peak of greatest audience demand.[51]

The skewed distribution of demand for expressive works flows partly from expression's character as an "experience good." Consumers cannot judge the value of an expressive good until they have actually experienced it themselves or been apprised of the opinions of others who have seen, read, or heard it. As a result, consumers tend to rely heavily on branding and marketing campaigns when a new work is first released and on the response of early audiences increasingly thereafter. For that reason, consumer demand for expressive works is especially prone to herd behavior and information cascades. Those who have not yet seen a new movie or read a new book tend to base their purchase decisions on what they perceive to be early audiences' response, as derived from some combination of marketing buzz, word of mouth, written criticism, and news reports of the best-selling hits.[52]

Expression's power-law distribution has a strong cultural element as well. Informational and cultural works share characteristics of "solidarity" and "associative goods."[53] "Solidarity goods," like the president's State of the Union address or a popular movie, have value for the individual viewer largely because they are consumed by many people. "Associative goods," like country clubs and institutions of higher education, have value for the individual consumer largely because they are also consumed by a certain select category of other people. Part of what consumers pay for when they buy solidarity or associative goods is the benefit they glean from the fact that other people—or certain other people—are also enjoying the same good.

Such goods thus have value far greater than each individual's personal benefit from consuming the good. To the extent that a given product has solidarity or associative value, a second product that few others—or few others of a particular group—are consuming would be an inadequate substitute for the first even if the two products are quite similar to one another.

Newspapers, movies, books, songs, and television shows that are read, watched, and listened to by many people in a particular social group are classic solidarity and associative goods. We do not read a newspaper or book, watch a movie or television show, or even listen to a song merely because of the solitary, personal benefit and enjoyment it gives us. Rather, we generally want to read, see, and hear at least in part what we think others of our social group are reading, seeing, and hearing. We want to experience cultural events and phenomena jointly with others and to share a common basis for conversation with our friends and colleagues. We also want to know what others think is important, current, and of interest, and to show others in our social group that we also are "in the know." As a result, our demand for popular, opinion-leading, or prestigious expression is likely to be considerably less elastic than is the case with consumer goods that merely provide more atomistic, solitary benefits.[54]

Of particular importance for free speech concerns, the solidarity and associative force of culturally seminal works may be stronger for speakers—those who wish to convey, refer to, critique, learn from, or reformulate existing expression in creating their own—than it is for those whose use is more passively consumptive. Effective speech commonly entails building upon specific works that have particular salience for the intended audience. Existing works of authorship, ranging from scholarly texts to cartoon characters, may embody a significant part of the discourse, understandings, standards, norms, and even definition of social and professional groups. And some expressive works have, of course, come to populate and inform the very language of mass culture.

Without the ability to borrow from such key works, authors can neither participate in the joint conversation that defines their social or professional group nor, in some cases, successfully engage a mass audience. Alice Randall could not have effectively conveyed her message by writing a sequel to a little-known Civil War saga. The Free Republic could hardly post articles from small-town newspapers to target the liberal bias of the mainstream, establishment press. Jon Else's stagehands-playing-checkers scene loses some of its poignancy without the background shot of the instantly recognizable icon of lowbrow popular culture, Homer Simpson. In none of these cases do the speakers have an adequate substitute upon which to build their own expression. Certain expressive works are central for conveying a speaker's message or for individual or group definition.

Moreover, the speaker's self-expression often requires the use of a particular work quite apart from whether some other expression would be reasonably salient to the speaker's intended audience. Alice Randall was outraged not just with racism in our culture but specifically with *Gone with the Wind*'s perpetuation of racist stereotypes. *The Simpsons* is what was actually on the screen when Jon Else filmed the stagehands playing checkers. Dedicated Trekkies who post their own creative spin-offs of *Star Trek* episodes on fan fiction Web sites are passionate about that particular television program. Such speakers cannot bargain with copyright holders by insisting that they could convey their message equally well building on substitute expression if the copyright holder fails to offer an affordable license fee.

RISK AND RENT. I now return to the question of whether copyright industry risk must be factored in when determining competitive price and, therefore, market power. The major movie studios, record labels, and trade book publishers claim that they must earn excess profits from commercially successful works to make up for inevitable losses on flops. Does that claim hold water? Do those industries need to charge prices that would otherwise be far in excess of competitive levels on some works in order to earn "normal profits" overall and thus to continue in the business of producing expression?

The answer, in short, is that, while some degree of risk should be taken into account, the industry claim to a significant risk multiplier for popular, iconic works like *The Simpsons* appears greatly to overstate the true competitive price benchmark. To understand why, we need more closely to examine copyright markets and how copyright industries actually respond to risk. The major, mass media copyright industries appear to manage risk without need of significant excess profits on successful works. The industries also appear to earn significant economic rents, overall profits far in excess of that required to keep them in business.

Copyright Industry Risk. The broad factual premise behind the industry's claim is correct: markets for expressive works are indeed characterized by considerable uncertainty and risk. Copyright holders are generally unable to predict in advance which new works will be among the relatively rare hits that generate the lion's share of total revenues and which will be the exceedingly more common failures.[55] Expressive works, as we have seen, are "experience goods": no work is exactly like another, and no one knows for certain how much consumers will value new works they have yet to read, hear, or see. Moreover, consumer valuation is relative, not absolute. A work's popularity depends in part on what other works of its genre are released at the same time, as well as other sundry contingencies. Consequently, as one Hollywood insider famously described the motion picture business, "Nobody Knows Anything" about which scripts and film productions will yield a box office hit.[56]

To be certain, copyright industries are not alone in facing the risk of new product failure. Studies show that from 37 to more than 80 percent of all new consumer goods and between 20 and 40 percent of new industrial goods fail in the market.[57] But copyright industries face failure rates at the top end of that spectrum. They also rely far more heavily on revenues from new products than most manufacturers.[58] In addition, each studio, publisher, and record label competes against a constant stream of new releases, while in most industries, avoiding markets that are laden with other new products is a key determinant of new product success.[59]

Yet although copyright industries face greater risks than most, they also have means to lessen and manage risk, and thus remain profitable, short of earning vastly excessive, supracompetitive profits on successful products. Most important, while it is in fact extraordinarily difficult to foretell which movie, book, or record album will be the next blockbuster hit, it is not the case that "Nobody Knows Anything" about how to better the odds for at least some modicum of success. Studies show, for example, that sequels of hit movies, books by previously best-selling authors, and albums by star recording artists correlate positively with enhanced prospects for success, even though they far from guarantee sustained consumer demand or profitability.[60] Likewise with celebrity authors' first books and movies that enjoy a combination of high production budgets and high-profile stars, especially when those works are accompanied by major marketing campaigns and carefully calibrated simultaneous release in thousands of bookstores or movie theaters across the country.[61] Given their brand recognition, publicity "buzz," and ubiquitous placement, such works can often earn significant gross revenues upon their initial release even if they are soon after spurned by the public. Genre can also make some difference. Family-oriented movies tend, on average, to do better than their R-rated counterparts.[62] And movies likely to sell well overseas (particularly action movies with relatively little dialogue) or presenting stories and characters that lend themselves to product placement advertising and merchandising have the potential for ancillary revenue that can far exceed U.S. domestic box office receipts.[63] Finally, even among the works that are more likely to achieve some success, industries armed with computer-tracked sales data can cut their losses, and thus improve overall profitability, by quickly pulling those works that show signs of weakness in any given market.[64]

With the notable exception of failing to produce more family films, large media firms regularly pursue these recipes for (somewhat enhanced chances for some degree of) success. Indeed, critics often take today's media conglomerates to task for chasing after blockbuster hits and formulas for past success, exalting branding and marketing over producing quality product, and abruptly dropping support for works that fail to generate significant consumer demand immediately upon release.[65] So while we might lament the strategies that large media firms follow to reduce risk, such strategies are in fact available.

That brings up a crucial point, to which I will return later: despite long-standing speculation and industry claims that the greater the copyright-generated revenue, the more copyright industries will invest in diverse, commercially risky works, there is no reason to think that awarding media firms broad copyrights will induce them to depart from their current, overwhelmingly conservative risk-management strategies. Media firms might use additional revenue to produce a greater *quantity* of works (or they might invest in ventures unrelated to cultural production).[66] But any additional works they produce and in which they invest most of their marketing dollars would likely be heavily weighted toward more of the standard fare that carries instant author, star, and title brand recognition for a mass audience.[67]

The industries' standard-fare business model is sometimes derided as irrational herd behavior, in which entertainment firms impulsively mimic others' recent successes in selecting new creative projects. But it is primarily an economically rational vehicle for managing risk and earning a share of mass audience profits. Indeed, while the mass media copyright industries' heavy reliance on standard, brand recognition product might be lamentable from the perspective of creativity and expressive diversity, it is quite typical of the way other industries manage their own risks of new product failure.[68] In sum, the standard-fare model is likely to remain firmly entrenched in entertainment industries' corporate culture. The notion that more copyright will induce the industries to produce more diverse expression has little empirical or theoretical basis.

Copyright Industry Rents. The availability of risk-management strategies is not the only reason to question industry claims that copyright must be sufficiently broad to yield immense "excess" profits on blockbusters to defray losses on other works. It also appears that key copyright markets produce significant economic rents. Comparing major copyright industry profit margins with that of other ventures is one indication. According to several reports, today's media conglomerates generally earn profits of up to 20 percent, and in certain niches even up to 35 percent.[69] In contrast, a FCC study from 2000 found that average profits for the 500 largest industrial corporations were just 6.8 percent.[70] Likewise, supermarket retailers typically face profit margins of around 4 percent and consumer electronics manufacturers of only 1 to 3 percent.[71] Even ExxonMobil enjoyed profit margins of "just" 16 percent in 2005, a record year for oil industry profits.[72]

Those figures are suggestive but admittedly tentative. Data on industry profit margins vary considerably and, especially in the entertainment sector, are highly dependent on obtuse, industry-specific accounting practices.[73] Moreover, given heavy media industry debt, cash flow might be a more relevant criterion than net profit, although a cash flow metric suggests even greater media profitability. Perhaps more revealing, investors' valuation of copyright industries reflects a belief that copyright in fact supports firms' supranormal profits. A recent study of publicly traded copyright industry stock prices found that expansions in copyright protection due to Copyright Act amendments and decisions in high-profile copyright cases generate significant excess returns on copyright firm equity.[74]

Rent-seeking and rent dissipation are additional indicators that the major copyright industry firms earn economic rents. Economists teach us that the prospect of earning economic rents induces firms to expend considerable resources in capturing them. Indeed, in competing to capture rents, firms, in the aggregate, will eventually spend amounts that equal, or even exceed, the rents to be captured. As a result, at least in fully competitive markets, the rents will be dissipated and firms on average will garner just normal profits, the competitive rate of return.[75] So regardless of whether a firm ultimately ends up with supranormal profits, evidence that firms in that industry spend excessive amounts in the effort to attain supracompetitive returns suggests that they are in fact earning (but then dissipating) economic rents.

Copyright industries not only dissipate rents but do so in ways that can only be regarded as socially wasteful, certainly from the perspective of the shared goals of copyright and the First Amendment. First, as is typical of oligopolies, media firms invest extraordinary sums in promotion and marketing.[76] In recent years, the motion picture, book publishing, and sound recording industries have been plagued by a marketing arms race that has fueled drastic increases in promotion budgets for many works.[77] Major motion picture marketing costs have mushroomed more than fivefold in the last two decades, far greater than the rate of inflation. Today, advertising and publicity typically add 50 percent or more to the cost of releasing a new feature film.[78] The amounts major labels and publishers now spend on promoting new record albums and books are similarly excessive. They not uncommonly exceed production costs by several orders of magnitude.[79]

We would expect copyright industries to have somewhat higher marketing expenses than those selling typical consumer goods. After all, copyright holders must continually market new expressive works, each with unique characteristics. But as commentators have rightly emphasized, much of the industries' marketing expenditures can only be understood as socially wasteful rent-seeking and rent dissipation.[80] The escalating marketing costs are largely defensive; each studio, label, and publisher perceives it necessary to meet competitors' increasingly lavish promotional campaigns, with direct marketing expenditures ranging from traditional advertising, to sponsoring publicity tours, to "payola," making direct or indirect payments to radio stations, retail stores, and other consumer gatekeepers to buy prominent play or placement for media products.[81] Nor can copyright industry promotion accurately be regarded as helpfully informing consumers of new works. The marketing strategy capitalizes on the character of expression as an experience good. It aims to lure large audiences immediately upon the work's release, so that significant sales can be achieved even if the work bombs and subsequent consumer demand sharply decreases. As one observer colorfully describes the typical movie extravaganza, "By the time we've all seen that it sucked, it's a hit."[82] Whether by industry design or coincidence, the marketing arms race also imposes a significant entry barrier before independent publishers, studios, and labels that lack the resources to compete with media conglomerate promotion. The costs of marketing new releases have become prohibitive for smaller companies, further entrenching the market dominance of the majors.[83]

Second, and closely related to marketing, publishers and movie studios pay exorbitant amounts to celebrity authors and actors. Economists generally agree that differences in talent cannot explain the extraordinary premiums that star actors and, certainly, celebrities who are first-time authors (and who, indeed, sometimes delegate actual authorship to ghostwriters) command.[84] Of course, celebrity participation often enhances consumer demand. Yet even so, the amounts media firms typically pay celebrities far exceed most recipients' opportunity cost, the amount required to induce the celebrity to participate—at least what would be required but for the recent bidding wars that have grossly raised celebrity expectations and demands.[85] Hence, much of the premiums paid for celebrity and star branding, like the exorbitant sums paid for advertising, constitute socially wasteful rent dissipation and evidence that copyright markets generate those rents to begin with.

Third, the vociferousness with which entertainment conglomerates litigate and lobby government to expand their copyrights is typical of firms that dissipate economic rents by seeking laws and regulations that enable them to earn still more. Record labels' early attempts to stifle competition from digital dissemination of music and entertainment industry lobbying for the Copyright Term Extension Act are but two recent examples. Economists tell us that monopolists' dissipation of rents by lobbying government to entrench protection against competition constitutes a primary social cost of monopoly.[86] Obviously, not every firm that lobbies government is a monopoly. But observers' rightly view copyright industries' concerted campaigns to lengthen and expand copyright protection as paradigmatic rent-seeking.[87]

Fourth, as I will shortly discuss, major copyright industry incumbents have a history of colluding and using their copyrights to impose barriers to entry of possible competitors. Even more than lobbying, such efforts are indicative of firms that dissipate rents to protect and entrench their protection from competition. Copyright industry concentration, of which the industries' massive copyright holdings are a contributing factor, is both a source for entertainment conglomerate rents and a vehicle for further rent-seeking.

Sum: Copyright and Artificial Scarcity

To conclude, our measure of competitive pricing for seminal works should include *some* multiplier for the inherent risk and uncertainty in markets for original expression. In all likelihood, however, the risk multiplier need not be nearly as high as the industry claims and others have sometimes assumed to be warranted. Indeed, the indications that copyright law enables media firms to earn substantial economic rents suggest that the prices and license fees that copyright holders charge for popular works are supracompetitive, even when revenues from those works are viewed as but a part of the copyright holder's overall profits. As such, copyright does indeed appear to enable market power and cause artificial scarcity in the very iconic works that serve as fundamental building blocks for self-expression. Beyond that, moreover, the mainstream copyright industries tend to dissipate their rents not by investing in more risky expression but in ways that are socially wasteful and even inimical to expressive diversity.

That market analysis does not yield an exact yardstick to measure whether Fox's $10,000 license fee, opposed to, say, a $5,000 fee, reflects Fox's market power and thus imposes an intolerable speech burden on Jon Else. It does suggest, however, that we should delimit copyright so that, on the margins, relatively more oppositional and nonmarket creative appropriation is permitted.

My conclusion partly stems from the showing that copyright holders generally enjoy market power in pricing iconic works. But as I will discuss later, it also follows from a straight free speech policy trade-off. We would want to tailor copyright law to allow greater oppositional and nonmarket creative appropriation of iconic expression even if that causes a reduction in entertainment conglomerate rents that in turn results in somewhat less conglomerate investment in new expression. Depending on how we tailor copyright law, either Fox will have the prerogative to charge license fees that are prohibitively expensive for noncommercial speakers like Else or noncommercial speakers will be able to use some of Fox's expression without paying a bargained-for rate (or anything at all). We must choose one or other. And it better serves expressive diversity to provide speakers like Else an opportunity to convey their message and artistic imagination than accord Fox slightly greater economic rents to invest in more mainstream commercial expression.

TRANSACTION COSTS

Copyright holders' market power is not the only source of copyright's prohibitive-cost speech burden. The proliferation of copyright holders' proprietary rights can make it prohibitively expensive for prospective licensees to obtain all the permissions needed to use, modify, or distribute creative expression, even absent copyright holders' insistence on a supracompetitive price. In numerous cases, the sheer time and expense of determining which rights must be cleared, determining who controls those rights, locating the appropriate rights holder, valuing the needed license, and negotiating a license put rights clearance beyond the would-be speaker's reach. Such transaction costs can effectively stifle speech even where the copyright holder and speaker might have otherwise come to terms for a license. As we have seen, the expense of clearing numerous copyrights can thwart even well-endowed new media like Google.

Speakers who seek a copyright license to incorporate, build upon, or distribute existing expression typically face significant costs in locating the appropriate rights holders and negotiating the terms of use. There is no mandatory system for registering copyright ownership or recording ownership transfers. In fact, unlike the United States, which maintains and provides incentives for participation in a voluntary registration and recording system, most countries have no such system at all. As a result, especially with old works, it can be extremely difficult to determine who owns the copyright in the work, let alone locate that person once identified.

The United States Copyright Office has recently issued a report that identifies this "orphan works" problem as a serious impediment to productive and beneficial uses of existing expression.[88] Under the current proprietary copyright regime, the burden is generally on the person who wishes to incorporate or distribute copyrighted expression to obtain the copyright holder's permission. Failure to do so is no defense even in the face of great difficulty locating the appropriate rights holder. And, as the report notes, for "[m]any users of copyrighted works who have limited resources or are particularly risk-averse . . . the risk of liability for copyright infringement, however remote, is enough to prompt them simply to not make use of the work." (The Copyright Office has proposed legislation to address the orphan works problem, but, as I discuss in chapter 9, that proposal, even if adopted, falls short.)

Locating and obtaining permission from a single copyright owner can be costly enough. Yet, securing the right to use a given work for a given purpose often requires obtaining licenses from multiple parties. Many items of cultural expression are composed of more than one "work of authorship" for copyright purposes. For example, each song on a CD consists of both the underlying musical composition and the sound recording of the performance of the song. A motion picture consists of the screenplay, direction, cinematography, score, background artwork, and set design. Moreover, the screenplay might be based on a short story, novel, or nonfiction book. Each of those contributions and components is subject to a separate copyright, which may or may not be owned by the same person or firm that owns the rights in the others.

In addition, the bundle of rights that make up the copyright in each work are fully divisible by right, national territory, duration, and media of exploitation, and each component may be separately transferred. A novelist might grant the exclusive North American book publication rights to one publisher, the North American first serial rights to another, the North American paperback rights to yet another, the electronic rights to another, the rights in other countries to other publishers, the dramatization rights to different parties in different territories, the motion picture rights to a film studio, the translation rights in various languages to various parties in various territories, and so on. And if the speaker wishes to use a work in new technological distribution media that did not exist when the author transferred a given right, it is often difficult to tell whether the transferee obtained the right to exploit the work in that new media. As we have seen, that is one of the obstacles that Google would face if required to clear the rights to include books in Google Book Search; it has only been within the last decade or two that publishers have explicitly acquired rights in electronic distribution and in some jurisdictions even a license to use a work in "any manner, medium, form, or language" might not be enough to cover distribution media that did not exist at the time the license was executed.[89]

That is not all: the would-be speaker may wish to incorporate more than one work in her own expression. If she is making a documentary film, she may need to clear rights to use multiple graphics, art, bits of film, musical compositions, sound recordings, works of architecture, and screenplay. If she creates a song composed of digital samples from previous recordings, she will need to obtain licenses from the copyright holders in each sound recording and underlying musical composition.

The multiplicity of copyright holders and divisible copyright components can greatly increase the cost of obtaining all the copyright licenses required for transformative expression, in some circumstances prohibitively so. The transaction cost barrier that arises from the proliferation of needed licenses exemplifies the "tragedy of the anti-commons" identified by Michael Heller and others.[90] When a resource is subject to too many property rights held by too many parties, the resource will tend to be underexploited, if at all. That phenomenon arises on occasion with respect to tangible property; it is a common and serious impediment to the exploitation of copyright-protected works.

The tragedy of the anti-commons is especially prevalent in the digital arena. Prospective digital uses typically involve combinations of multiple works and rights. Moreover, rights holders often voice overlapping claims about which rights are actually implicated by various digital uses. For example, streaming songs over the Internet implicates a public performance right, in both the underlying musical composition and the sound recording. As if that is not complex enough, music publishers and record labels argue that Internet streaming implicates the right to copy as well because streaming entails the making of temporary copies on various computers. Conversely, digital downloads—where users download songs from a central server onto their computers or MP3 players—clearly involve the right to copy. But performing rights societies ASCAP and BMI contend that a download also implicates the right of public performance because the song is transmitted for eventual user listening.[91] As numerous commentators and policy makers have lamented, such multiple, overlapping claims, coupled with the sheer cost of clearing rights from numerous parties, significantly retard the development of licensed uses of a broad array of expression.[92]

Copyright's Distributive Speech Burden

A Blackstonian copyright does not merely stifle the speech of numerous, sundry individuals. Rather, given the skewed distribution of copyright holdings, copyright's speech burdens fall far more heavily on certain categories of speakers than on others. Copyright industries controlling vast inventories of copyrighted works enjoy a disproportionate share of copyright's benefits. And most of copyright's free speech burdens, most of the time, fall on individuals and independent speakers, particularly those who want to recast a popular work in order to criticize it, alter or contest its meaning, or simply use it as a building block for personal expression and creativity.

Copyright's "distributive speech burden" has both a static and a dynamic dimension. The static dimension is what I have described so far. At any given time, large firms, increasingly under the roof of media conglomerates, typically control the copyrights that individuals and independent speakers need to license for effective speech. As we will shortly see, that skewed distribution pervades our system of free expression and constricts expressive diversity. The dynamic dimension centers on copyright's role in fueling and perpetuating copyright industry concentration. Proprietary copyright is not the only centripetal force operating in markets for expression, but it is a significant factor in entrenching media conglomerate domination of public discourse.

COPYRIGHT'S DISTRIBUTIVE SPEECH BURDEN: STATIC DIMENSION

Effective speech very often requires the use of existing expression. Hence, those who control copyrights in vast content catalogs tend to have far greater power to shape public discourse than those who do not. The oligopoly structure of the principal copyright-holding industries, coupled with copyright's expansive scope, greatly magnifies that unequal distribution of expressive power.

The copyright industries that dominate public discourse have reached levels of concentration that are deleterious to both competition and expressive diversity. As of this writing, four major labels control some 85 percent of the U.S. record industry market (held at four rather than three only because regulators refused to approve the merger of EMI with Time Warner), six major studios consistently garner well over 80 percent of domestic box office market share, and ten publishing houses enjoy oligopoly domination of the trade and paperback book markets.[93] Further, almost all the dominant firms in each area are part of a media conglomerate with affiliates in the other areas. These affiliates, which include content producers, aggregators, and distributors, extend and solidify the dominant firms' control of the market. To complete that picture, "Big Six" media giants—CBS Viacom, Time Warner, NBC Universal (a unit of General Electric), Sony, News Corporation, and Disney—own all the major movie studios, the two largest record labels, and three of the top ten trade book publishing houses.[94] A seventh global media conglomerate, Bertelsmann, is the largest trade book publisher, the largest record label (as part of its joint venture with Sony), and 50 percent owner of Europe's largest operator of independent television stations. The Big Six conglomerates also own all five U.S. television networks and sixty-four cable television networks, which together account for 98 percent of U.S. prime-time television advertising revenues.[95] Not surprisingly, that oligopoly extends to television programming as well as distribution. Together with Liberty Media, which owns approximately 18 percent of News Corporation and 4 percent of Time Warner, the Big Six own more than four-fifths of prime-time programming.[96] Likewise with motion pictures. Together with their dominance in film production, the Big Six own motion picture distribution arms that earn some 96 percent of U.S. movie theater rentals, reflecting the fact that independent studios must rely on the majors to get their films to theaters. Finally, the Big Six's radio station holdings garner 65 percent of all U.S. radio advertising revenues.[97]

That industry concentration tends to narrow public discourse on a number of fronts. First, as one would expect from publicly traded companies that must answer to shareholders, there is considerable anecdotal evidence that media conglomerates, far more than independent publishers, labels, and studios, focus on the bottom line.[98] As a result, critics charge, the conglomerates are inclined to produce "safe" content designed to appeal to the lowest common denominator of the consumer public and to tailor content toward marketing products of their corporate affiliates.

Second, content providers are likely to share a fundamental conservatism in licensing transformative or competing uses of items in their respective inventories. Media conglomerates are in the business of managing their content portfolios. Their goal is to build upon existing inventory, exploit synergies with corporate partners, and selectively license content in ways that will maximize the value of the inventory as a whole. Media conglomerates accordingly have a strong incentive to avoid controversial reformulations of their content that might (1) subvert that content's carefully cultivated conventional meaning, (2) diminish its commercial value or the value of other inventory items, or (3) potentially compete with planned uses of that or other content by conglomerate divisions and corporate partners.[99] Far from licensing controversial or competing uses of their inventory, media enterprises thus aggressively seek to stifle such uses.

Firms' efforts to silence expression that might conflict with affiliates' business interests or impair the value of another work in the firm's catalog add a significant dimension to copyright's censorial speech burden. Among the more egregious examples, HarperCollins breached its agreement to publish the memoirs of Chris Patten, the last British governor of Hong Kong, under order from Rupert Murdoch, the controlling shareholder of Harper-Collins's corporate parent, who was concerned about the memoirs' impact on his media interests in China.[100] Likewise, Comedy Central pulled a scheduled rerun of a *South Park* episode that had mercilessly lampooned Tom Cruise and his avid belief in Scientology. Comedy Central's corporate affiliate, Paramount (both owned by Viacom), was set to release *Mission: Impossible III,* the latest in a movie franchise starring Cruise, and Cruise had reportedly threatened to halt his promotional activities for the movie.[101] One can only imagine the numerous other such instances that go unreported.

Moreover, given media conglomerates' common conservatism, prospective speakers seeking to reformulate popular expression in controversial ways are unlikely to find substitutes when denied a license by a given content owner. Consider the Air Pirates' short-lived counterculture treatment of Mickey Mouse and friends. The chances are nil that the comic book creators could have avoided Disney's wrath by obtaining a license from Disney competitor Warner Bros. to portray Bugs Bunny or from Mattel to portray Barbie engaged in sex and illicit drug taking. Indeed, studio licenses commonly contain a nondisparagement clause forbidding the licensee to use the licensed material in any way that casts the studio or motion picture industry in an unfavorable light.

Finally, copyright industries' vertical integration, the merger of firms that produce expression with those that distribute it to the public, provides media conglomerates with the opportunity and incentive to favor their own content over that of competitors and independents. Vertical integration, indeed, has been fueled largely by copyright industries' desire for congenial and preferential distribution channels coupled with distributors' desire to gain inexpensive and favored access to affiliate content. That is not surprising. In an industry with a small number of competitors (and, like content production, the content distribution sector is highly concentrated), no firm can afford the high risk of being denied access to distribution or product.[102] The other side of that coin is that vertical integration makes it more difficult for unaffiliated speakers—those who do not control distribution channels—to reach an audience. As we shall shortly see, the industry's control over distribution, in which copyright law plays a major role, also raises a significant entry barrier before new firms that might otherwise challenge industry incumbents' dominant position and provide outlets for a broader range of speakers and expression.

COPYRIGHT'S DISTRIBUTIVE SPEECH BURDEN: DYNAMIC DIMENSION

Copyright industry concentration both exacerbates copyright's speech burdens and is further fueled by an expansive copyright. Copyright contributes to industry concentration in two basic ways. First, as Yochai Benkler has underscored, basic economics tells us that copyright and copyright industry dominance likely have a snowball effect.[103] Second, copyright serves as a barrier to entry before prospective new distributors of original expression.

Snowball Effect

Since virtually all speech incorporates inputs, learning, or inspiration from prior speech, those who already own exclusive rights in vast inventories of expression enjoy decided commercial advantages over those who do not. In creating new expression, media conglomerates can often exploit their extensive copyright holdings to recycle, build upon, and incorporate portions of existing works at below-market or even marginal cost. A major movie studio, for example, can issue sequels and remakes of its hit films, produce television series based on its films, incorporate music owned by its record label and music publisher affiliates, and make motion pictures based on titles owned by its affiliate book publishers at far lower costs than if it had to obtain all required licenses from independent copyright holders. Similarly, different business units under a common corporate umbrella can exploit a new work across several media, license free, as when Disney packages a children's story as a movie, comic book, TV cartoon, computer game, and sound track. Finally, as they have in their online distribution joint ventures, large media firms can also use their copyrights to cross-license content from one another and from other copyright holders.

In contrast, nonconglomerates, including individuals, educational institutions, noncommercial media, documentary filmmakers, cottage-industry publishers, and independent studios and labels, must generally negotiate a license and pay the copyright-buttressed price to incorporate existing video clips, songs, graphics, or text in their new expression. Hence, the typical nonentertainment-conglomerate speaker not only has fewer financial resources than any of the majors but also has to pay more for inputs from existing works that resonate with a broad audience. And the more expansive copyright's scope and duration, the greater the chance that any given use of existing expression will require a copyright license and thus the more pronounced copyright's disproportionate impact.

The conglomerates' vast copyright holdings give them significant competitive advantages in reaching consumers as well. Conglomerates are far more able than independents to bundle together vast numbers of works of a given genre in a single package, a facility that has proven a significant advantage for commercial success in both traditional and online distribution.[104] Conglomerates' control over large content repertoires also assists them in placing their works with unaffiliated distributors and retailers. As Douglas Gomery notes, for example, "Seagram's Universal Pictures might not sell movies to Time Warner's HBO unless Time Warner's cable franchises book Universal's (partially owned) U.S. television network."[105] Jon Else or even a small independent producer of more commercial films would lack that powerful bargaining chip.

On average, the copyright-driven competitive advantages make expressive activity far less profitable for independents than for media conglomerates. With an expanded copyright, therefore, conglomerate expression will increasingly dominate over nonconglomerate—and we would expect that to occur even absent other factors that contribute to media consolidation. Over time, one would thus expect that speakers and expressive activity will follow the money, moving from the nonconglomerate sector to the conglomerate, thus further spurring media concentration. The flurry of conglomerate acquisitions of independent book publishers, record labels, and movie studios in recent decades may be an indication of that centripetal force. Also tellingly, perhaps, several years after Disney shut down the Air Pirates, one of the underground comic group's lead cartoonists joined Disney's product merchandising art department.[106]

Entry Barriers

To view motion picture studios, record labels, and book publishers merely as copyright-holding content producers misses an important dimension of how copyright serves to consolidate large media firms' dominance. The major firms act not merely as producers but also as distributors. They maintain nationwide and, in some cases, global networks for the sale and rental of hard copies and the broadcast of television and radio programming. Indeed, it is the industry's control of distribution, through corporate affiliates and vertically integrated subsidiaries, that constitutes the core of their power and a key source of their revenue.[107] Even well-financed, commercially successful independents, like DreamWorks, find it difficult to remain in business without integrating with a major that has a distribution arm.

Significantly in that regard, copyright industries do not use vertical integration with distributors merely to favor their own content; they use copyrights as vertical restraints to foreclose potential competitors in content distribution as well. That practice has a long history, as old as modern copyright law itself. It stems back to the London Stationers' ultimately fruitless battle, lasting through most of the eighteenth century, to maintain their dominance over the British book trade. Parliament let the Stationers Company's statutory monopoly over book publishing expire in 1695 and replaced it with a short-term copyright pursuant to the Statute of Anne of 1709. The Stationers responded by colluding to control the market. They agreed to establish and mutually respect one another's extralegal exclusive rights to publish new and existing books. Then, when emerging provincial booksellers refused to abide by this collusive restraint on trade, the Stationers went to court, claiming a perpetual common-law copyright in books whose statutory copyright had expired. The Stationers' efforts ended in defeat only when the House of Lords held, in 1774, that the Statute of Anne had preempted any common-law copyright.[108]

Similar incumbent industry efforts to expand the bounds of copyright protection to foreclose rivals have been repeated several times over in the United States, especially as new distribution technologies have emerged.[109] In each instance, the copyright industry incumbent has argued, with varying degrees of success, that the new technology may not be deployed without a copyright license. In so doing, incumbents have typically sought either to bar entry outright or to charge license fees that would have the effect of impeding distribution technology deployment and innovation. While couched as a claim against the "piracy" of copyrighted content, the industry effort has been as much or more about maintaining control over the means by which audiences gain access to content.

Consider these examples.[110] In the late nineteenth and early twentieth centuries, sheet music publishers sought to use copyright to counter, and then control, what they viewed as a major competitive threat, distributors of music in mechanically recorded form. When the Supreme Court held that mechanical renditions of music (in particular, player piano rolls) do not infringe the copyright in underlying musical compositions, the publishers lobbied Congress to amend the Copyright Act. In the 1920s, ASCAP, a society representing sheet music publishers, composers, and songwriters, targeted commercial radio broadcasters, alleging that broadcasts of live music performances constituted an independent public performance of the musical composition and thus required a separate copyright license. ASCAP prevailed in its copyright infringement litigation but was eventually required by an antitrust decree to license all radio broadcasters on "reasonable" terms subject to judicial oversight.[111] In the 1960s and 1970s, incumbent broadcasters brought infringement actions against cable television operators for transmitting off-air television for programming. When the Supreme Court ruled against the broadcasters,[112] they, too, lobbied Congress to amend the Copyright Act in their favor. In 1976, the major motion picture studios sued Sony Corporation, contending that the consumer electronics manufacturer was contributorily liable for enabling users of its Betamax to copy television programs at home. The Supreme Court held that Betamax users engaged in fair use.[113] But in recent years the studios have brought similar lawsuits against manufacturers of digital video recorders and have lobbied Congress and the FCC to mandate "broadcast flag" technology that would prevent home copying of programs from digital TV broadcasts.[114] Likewise, the record labels have sought to enforce their copyrights, or to lobby Congress to make it possible to enforce their copyrights, against radio broadcasters, manufacturers of digital audio recorders and MP3 players, MP3.com, webcasters, and suppliers of peer-to-peer file-trading software and services. Most recently, movie studios, news media, and book publishers have sought to limit the use of their works by search engines, such as Google, and have sued social networking and video-sharing service sites like MySpace and YouTube.

As is evident in the studios' dealings with Google and YouTube, their interest is not merely in preventing unlicensed uses of their content but also in "trying to protect their decades-old way of doing business—controlling not only their programming but the advertising revenue and distribution outlets."[115] Viacom's lawsuit against Google and YouTube comes in the wake of the parties' failure to agree on terms for licensing Viacom content on YouTube, a failure that can be explained largely by Viacom's unwillingness to relinquish the premium for controlling distribution. The recently announced News Corp.–NBC Universal partnership to establish an alternative to YouTube and to license their content only to Google's rivals stems from a similar motive. As one media analyst put it, "The media companies don't want to be forced to only work with one distribution entity."[116]

Incumbent media firms' desire to avoid subservience to a potential new media behemoth is understandable. But their repeated use of proprietary copyrights to drive out rivals to their own distribution business and to impede content delivery platforms that threaten their established distribution channels has rightly raised regulatory concerns. Indeed, motion picture studios, record labels, music publishers, and broadcasters have a long history of running afoul of antitrust authorities when they have colluded to suppress competition.[117] In several instances over the past century, moreover, Congress has stepped in to broker a compromise allowing proprietors of new content delivery platforms to engage in limited distribution of copyrighted works in return for paying a statutory fee rather than having to obtain copyright holders' consent.[118] In the case of ASCAP and the radio broadcasters, much the same was accomplished in court through the ASCAP (and, later, BMI) antitrust consent decrees.

As crafted by Congress or the courts, the compulsory licenses aim to maintain copyright law's economic incentives to create and disseminate new expression. But they deprive incumbents of the use of copyright to foreclose potential rivals, whether directly, by refusing to license, or indirectly, by expropriating the surplus that provides an incentive for the development of new content delivery platforms. And, almost across the board, from cable television's multiple channels to webcasters' niche programming, by freeing new technological distributors from copyright incumbents' vertical restraints, the compulsory licenses have created alternative outlets for independent speakers and helped to foster expressive diversity.

Not surprisingly, however, copyright incumbents continue to seek to enforce proprietary copyright against new technology media. And, as we saw in chapter 4, both the courts and Congress have recently tilted toward the incumbents' position of copyright as inviolable property. As a result, a number of new media, including MP3.com, peer-to-peer file-trading systems, and user-generated video sites, have been enjoined from further infringing copyright (or facilitating others' infringement) and then driven out of business when the copyright industry plaintiffs refused to license.[119] It remains to be seen how the industry lawsuits against their powerful, well-heeled rival, Google, will play out—whether courts will similarly apply a Blackstonian vision of copyright or whether some combination of courts and Congress will spur a compromise.

In sum, proprietary copyright has emerged as a principal bottleneck to competition from new media distributors in the digital arena. And copyright's continued use as a vertical restraint threatens to extend media incumbents' control over distribution just when the economics of digital markets undermine the traditional basis and justification for that control. In the analog, hard-copy world, copyright industry distributors rightly earn a premium because their vast networks are critical to getting original expression to audiences. In addition, the substantial cost of establishing a large-scale distribution network, as much or more than copyright law, often prevents the entry of serious competitors. But digital technology changes all that. Distribution now costs next to nothing. Any studio, label, publisher, or, most important, individual author can make a work available to a global audience simply by posting it on a Web site or releasing it onto a peer-to-peer network.

Copyright industries may still play an important function in that universe by selecting, financing, editing, aggregating, and marketing original expression. But industry incumbents would face considerable competition in providing those services. In an untrammeled digital playing field, major media conglomerates would no longer enjoy a stranglehold over the market by virtue of the significant investment required and scale economies inherent in analog distribution. Moreover, digital technology also drastically reduces production and, possibly, even marketing costs associated with creating and disseminating original expression. The economics of digital distribution, in short, would seem to dictate a highly competitive, decentralized sector for producing and disseminating creative works.

However, neither traditional nor new media distributors can effectively compete with copyright industry incumbents without access to the vast catalogs of existing works over which a proprietary copyright gives the incumbents control. Cable television began by retransmitting off-air television broadcasts. It was only when cable obtained a solid footing that it emerged as a vast source of new content, far exceeding that which was previously available.

Much the same is true of new media. The creators of search engines, peer-to-peer platforms, content aggregation and repackaging software, user-generated content sites, and devices that make content portable must enable users to read, see, and hear the works that are of interest to them. Like Google Book Search, indeed, much of their value lies in providing access, in usable form, to a wide swath, if not the entirety, of our cultural heritage (as well as new, popular expression). At some point, we would expect new media distributors to provide alternative outlets for creators, speakers, and independent studios, labels, and publishers and thus to foster greater expressive diversity. Indeed, Web sites like YouTube already feature thousands of amateur video shorts, and peer-to-peer networks provide outlets for numerous garage bands. But to attract the critical mass of audience needed to attain commercial viability, they must typically also provide existing copyrighted expression for which there is already consumer familiarity and demand. Like their analog predecessors, ranging from cable television to radio broadcasters, developers of digital distribution technologies are far better positioned to offer outlets for a broad spectrum of new, independent speech if they can initially make available familiar, mainstream works unhindered by copyright holders' exclusive rights.

Let me be clear: I do not mean to suggest that new technological media should necessarily have the right to aggregate and distribute copyright-protected works without compensation. Absent some form of remunerating copyright holders, the untrammeled deployment of new technologies for distributing and accessing copyrighted-protected expression might undercut copyright's incentive to create original expression. But Blackstonian copyright is not the solution either. That amounts to giving copyright holders a veto over new technological media. The expansive proprietary rights that copyright industries repeatedly seek and use as vertical restraints impose an unjustifiable burden on independent speech.

| The Propertarian
Counter-Argument

S OME SCHOLARS AND POLICY makers claim that an expansive, proprietary copyright not only imposes merely trivial speech burdens but,
indeed, represents the best means for resolving the tension between copyright and free speech. As Paul Goldstein forcefully puts it: to extend copyright "into every corner where consumers derive value from literary and
artistic works" is the "best prescription for connecting authors to their audiences."[1] A broad, proprietary copyright, Goldstein argues, would thus
"promote political as well as cultural diversity, ensuring a plenitude of
voices, all with the chance to be heard."

As I will presently delineate, supporters of this Blackstonian property
position advance a number of arguments in its favor. Some posit that a
combination of expansive copyright protection and digital technology will
enable copyright holders to engage in individualized price discrimination, in
other words, to charge each consumer what that person is able and willing to
pay for access to copyright-protected expression. In that way, they contend,
copyright's deadweight loss (and speech burden) would be sharply reduced if
not essentially eliminated. Others insist that a broad copyright will induce
more investment in creating expressive works and will thus bring more
competition and reduced market power. Still others posit that a proprietary
copyright will force authors to differentiate their expression from existing
works, thus promoting expressive diversity.

Much of the propertarian argument—the notion that an expansive copyright would actually enhance expressive diversity—has an air of unreality,

divorced from the actual workings of copyright markets. We have already seen a number of respects in which the argument is far off the mark. First, far from giving play to a plentitude of voices, the copyright industries' predominant business model is to produce and heavily promote celebrity-studded mainstream expression. There is no reason to think that an expansive copyright would induce the industry to depart from its economically rational risk-management strategy. Second, a proprietary copyright backed by judicial remedies that enforce exclusivity by broad injunction and onerous damage awards gives copyright holders greater power to intimidate speakers and speech intermediaries into forgoing speech that is actually noninfringing. Third, the proliferation of broad copyrights leads to the "tragedy of the anti-commons"; it fuels multiple, often overlapping claims and thus greatly increases the costs of obtaining copyright permissions. Finally, a Blackstonian copyright contributes to copyright industry conglomeration and serves as a tool for conglomerate incumbents to entrench their domination of public discourse by imposing entry barriers before emerging speakers and distributors.

I now consider the propertarian arguments and highlight some additional ways in which those arguments ring hollow.

Price Discrimination

Consumers have different preferences and willingness to pay for copyrighted expression, as do those who wish to build on existing expression in their own speech. Copyright industries typically go some ways toward meeting this variable demand by product versioning and price discrimination. Book publishers, for example, issue books serially, first in hardcover, then trade paperback, then mass-market paperback, and charge considerably higher prices for the first two than the additional costs of production would warrant. That way, those consumers who especially value reading a book when it first comes out will pay a premium for that privilege, while readers who are happy to wait or who cannot afford the hardcover price can pay a lower price for a trade paperback or, by waiting still longer and bearing with slightly less attractive design, a bargain-basement price for an eventual mass-market paperback edition. Under that scheme, more readers may eventually purchase the book, and the publisher can extract a greater share of consumer surplus than if the publisher sold just a hardcover edition.

Propertarians embrace such price discrimination as a way to drastically reduce copyright's deadweight loss and thus lessen copyright's free speech burdens.[2] In so doing they paint a far rosier portrait of price discrimination's potential than warranted by the several-tiered product versioning that media firms offer today. Mindful of the limited reach of today's bluntly targeted pricing, the propertarians suggest that digital technology makes possible near-perfect price discrimination, a regime in which copyright owners would tailor access and license fees to each individual's ability and willingness to pay. In theory, digital technology enables suppliers to amass a wealth of information about individuals' consumer preferences and, through digital rights management, to divide up products into multiple versions and uses. Once media firms apply that technology to pricing, if I value the right to download The Beatles' *Sgt. Pepper's* album at $5, Fred values the right to listen to a stream of the album at $2, and Jon Else values the right to include a background shot of Homer Simpson in his film at $1,500, that is what we will each pay, no more, no less. If you and Steven Spielberg value those rights, respectively, at $50, $20, and $15,000, you will each pay that tenfold amount.

Under a regime of individualized price discrimination, copyright holders would capture all possible profit from their works, and some users would pay more. But each consumer who wishes to acquire access to a given work would be able to do so. So would every speaker who wishes to acquire a license to build upon existing expression in creating her own. As a result, propertarians argue, so long as copyright owners are able to pursue their incentive to price discriminate, we have little to fear from copyright expansion.

In fact, propertarians do not merely posit that we have little to fear from copyright expansion. They hold that the pervasive deployment of copyright-law-backed "digital rights management" technology is a necessary condition to enabling copyright owners to engage in effective price discrimination.[3] It is only by asserting hermetic control over every use of copyright-protected expression that copyright holders can both exact payment at the amount each user values and have confidence that low-valuing users who buy copies or access at a low price will not engage in "arbitrage," reselling the product to high-valuing users at a price that undercuts that of the copyright holder. In this seemingly paradoxical view, the broader copyright holders' legal and technological control, the greater will be public access to existing expression. Only if they are armed with hermetic control will copyright holders be able to eliminate copyright's deadweight loss by tailoring prices to consumers' ability and willingness to pay.

If the propertarian argument seems counterfactual, that is because it is. After all, what was stopping Fox from reducing its license fee to a price that Else would have been willing to pay? Surely Fox did not fear that Else would turn around and sell the footage to Steven Spielberg. Moreover, Else's story is not at all atypical. As numerous nonprofit choral groups, filmmakers, theater companies, and textbook authors can attest, major copyright holders often refuse to offer reduced-price licenses—or simply fail to respond to license requests—even when the result of their refusal is that the would-be licensee will be unable to use the work and the copyright holder will lose a potential avenue for profit.

Why is this so? Why do copyright holders fail to price discriminate (or, in the case of Fox, fail to price discriminate sufficiently) when the result is that they will not receive any license fee at all? The primary reason is that price discrimination is costly to implement. Determining user valuations, setting differential pricing, designing product and distribution systems to enable differential pricing, and creating and enforcing prohibitions against arbitrage require considerable information, labor, and financial and organizational resources. That substantial expense does not prevent copyright holders from engaging in fairly gross, across-the-board differential pricing schemes, principally based on releasing works in different formats for different markets over time. But the costs of implementing and administering differential pricing pose a severe impediment to more refined price discrimination, particularly that required to license noncommercial speakers.

Significantly, moreover, those costs tend to skew what copyright holder price discrimination does take place. Copyright holders who price discriminate are generally less likely to reduce prices for low-income users than simply raise the prices they charge to high-end users who are able and willing to pay the considerable sums that copyright holders need to recover their price discrimination costs.[4] Partly for that reason, economic analysts point out that the welfare effects of imperfect price discrimination are highly variable and uncertain.

Propertarians imagine that digital technology will drastically reduce the cost of differential pricing and thus make near-perfect price discrimination possible. But even if digital technology can lower price discrimination costs with respect to readers, listeners, and other end users of expressive works, a proposition that has yet to be proven, it would be of little effect where the "consumer" is a speaker who wishes to build upon, reformulate, or otherwise incorporate existing expression in new speech. Copyright holders typically need to engage in a costly, individualized, nonautomated assessment of what price to charge such speakers for a copyright license. Transformative uses involve widely varying combinations of the copyright holder's expression and the speaker's independent expression. Transformative uses also have a broad range of possible impacts on the commercial prospects for other works in the copyright holder's content portfolio, ranging from parodies that make a laughingstock of the copyright holder's work to secondary uses that might enhance the work's value. Copyright holder pricing for licensing such uses thus generally reflects a costly case-by-case assessment of numerous factors, including the speaker's anticipated audience, the extent and nature of the speaker's independent expression, the degree of creative control that the copyright holder retains, and the perceived need to police the licensed use to make certain it remains within the agreed bounds.

Digital technology would do little to lessen the cost of such individualized negotiations. Further, even in a regime of highly refined price discrimination, the copyright holder's license price for a transformative use must reflect not only the speaker's willingness to pay but also the copyright holder's assessment of the risk that the speaker's use will impair the work's value. Indeed, the offered license price will also reflect the reluctance of mid-level decision makers in copyright industry firms to risk a supervisor's wrath for having granted a discount from standard pricing. For those reasons, it is hardly surprising that copyright-holding firms often price higher than what many low-income and nonmarket speakers can pay.

In sum, even to the limited extent that digital technology might pave the way for greater price discrimination in the end-use consumer market, the prospect of refined differential pricing for transformative speech is highly unlikely. The notion that copyright holders will price discriminate in ways that will significantly ameliorate copyright's speech burden if only they are given the legal and technological tools to do so is little more than a pipe dream.

Misconstruing Expressive Diversity

Propertarians argue that requiring speakers to create entirely new expression rather than borrowing from others will enhance expressive diversity. David McGowan raises that possibility with respect to Alice Randall.[5] He suggests that our discourse might actually be more robust and diverse if Randall had to vent her anger by writing her "own novel" rather than parodying *Gone with the Wind.* Conversely, he asks, "If she is capable of writing her own novel would a rule that allows her to copy Margaret Mitchell induce her to forgo her own voice to piggyback on the popularity of *Gone with the Wind*?" More broadly, Christopher Yoo argues that a broad, proprietary copyright will spur the creation of a greater variety of expressive works as creators seek to differentiate their products from existing works in order to compete for market share. Professor Yoo also contends that we need not be concerned with the media concentration that copyright fosters because large media firms produce expressive works of diverse genres.[6]

Such arguments are grounded in an exceedingly narrow and wooden understanding of expressive diversity. The notion that speech woven from the fabric of existing works is necessarily less creative and less diverse than that which incorporates not a line or scene from its predecessors flies in the face of some of the greatest, most inspired art, literature, and music in the Western canon. After all, as Landes and Posner rightly underscore, Chaucer, Shakespeare, and Milton lifted from earlier works with zest. Yet what those luminaries "*did* with inherited or borrowed themes and sources—which if the originals were under copyright today would constitute copyright infringement—exemplified a higher order of creativity than is commonly attained by works of literature that are fully original in the copyright sense."[7] For these authors' contemporaries, no doubt, their creativity and distinctiveness lay precisely in their blatant quotation and brilliant reworking of recognized stories, lines, and themes. Much the same is true of modernist and present-day creative appropriators.

Nor, as I discussed in chapter 3, is expressive diversity at all coterminous with product differentiation. It may be just the opposite in fact. To successfully challenge prevailing understandings and stereotypes perpetuated by mainstream, popular expression often requires a partial *melding* of expressive product rather than complete product differentiation. Consider Alice Randall. What if she had written a novel that was fully differentiated from *Gone with the Wind* in the sense that her novel borrowed no expression whatsoever from the civil war saga? Or what if she wrote in an entirely different genre, say a scholarly article or op-ed piece that lambasted racism and the racist stereotypes perpetuated in Margaret Mitchell's work? To do so would have been far less effective, far less self-expressive, and far less enriching of robust debate than to do what she did: upend Mitchell's idealized portrait by deploying its very story line, scenes, and characters to reimagine them from the viewpoint of a slave.

If we define differentiation as the absence of copying expression, Randall's oppositional speech was quite deliberately less than fully differentiated from the target of her ire. Yet, like the creative appropriations of many artists and dissenters who recast mainstream speech, her at once highly derivative and powerfully subversive expression is a crucial element of expressive diversity. Indeed, that derivative-yet-subversive recipe plays a significant and growing role in public and private discourse as millions of individuals use affordable digital technology to remix, modify, and manipulate popular mass media sounds, images, and texts, and then share their derivative creations with others. From feminist fan fiction to mashups that meld white-bread music with hip-hop, creative appropriation gives individuals a voice, a means to challenge the ubiquity of mass media culture and the prevailing mores, ideology, and artistic judgments it represents—or simply to use widely recognizable, mainstream cultural icons as linguistic building blocks for new art, literature, and political commentary.

That welter of bottom-up creative appropriation, like Alice Randall's work and Shakespeare's, makes clear that product differentiation, in the sense of the absence of borrowing copyrightable elements from existing expression, cannot serve as a metric or proxy for "expressive diversity." (For that matter, as I soon discuss, a speaker can copy existing copyrightable elements and still create a differentiated product even in the pure economic sense; much unlicensed creative appropriation serves an entirely different audience than that of the underlying work or any derivative works the copyright holder would likely license.) Certainly, much decidedly derivative creative expression has no less value for autonomous self-expression and a robust exchange of ideas than does commercial media's production of fully differentiated product or genre. Expressive diversity demands speech "from diverse and antagonistic sources," not speech created as if walled off from the speaker's cultural milieu.

Consumer Demand Does Not Yield Expressive Diversity

The propertarians assert that extending copyright into "every corner where consumers derive value from literary and artistic works" will enhance expressive diversity. That claim is based on the idea that the prices people pay for goods serve as a signal to producers of what goods people want. As applied to the claim that Blackstonian copyright supports expressive diversity, that pricing system rationale unfolds as follows:

1. Consumers have diverse tastes.
2. The prices consumers are willing to pay for expressive works and uses of those works reflect consumer tastes.
3. The license fees prospective creative appropriators and distributors of copyrighted expression are willing to pay reflect, on average, their accurate assessment of consumer demand for their planned use.
4. Consumer preferences can be accurately signaled through pricing only when consumers and prospective licensees must pay for each use

of the work and the copyright holder is free to set prices in accordance with consumer demand.

5. Therefore, an expansive copyright (and paracopyright) that requires payment for each use will signal the full spectrum of consumer demand and will induce creators and copyright holders to meet that diverse demand.

Whatever the pricing system's capacity to signal consumer preferences and induce producers to respond to those preferences in other markets, the propertarians fail to account for a number of factors that distort pricing signals in markets for expression. These include, as we have already seen: (1) the concentrated structure of copyright industries and markets; (2) the inherent "Nobody Knows Anything" uncertainty in determining which new works consumers will most highly value; (3) copyright holders' inability to use highly refined price discrimination to measure the intensity of consumer preferences; (4) tragedy of the anti-commons, orphan works, and other transaction cost barriers to obtaining licenses to use existing expression in new speech that consumers would want; and (5) digital technology's drastic reduction on the costs of distribution, production, remixing, storage, and measuring audience preferences, making it possible to serve a wide spectrum of preferences without need of pricing signals.

It is also highly questionable, even apart from market distortions, whether the prices consumers pay for various works and uses could ever serve as a valid and accurate proxy for expressive diversity.[8] First, consumer purchasing decisions reflect ability as well as willingness to pay. An expressive mix based entirely on consumer pricing signals would thus be skewed toward the tastes of the wealthy. Second, mass-media products, which embody a combination of information, social mores, and artistic convention, may well color consumer taste as much as reflect it. As Ed Baker aptly notes, "[T]he media are among the powerful determinants of people's values and preferences," and the media have every incentive to foster preferences that increase consumer demand for the products of mass-media firms and their advertisers.[9] Third, as a number of scholars have emphasized, individuals' purchasing decisions do not necessarily align with decisions they make in other contexts.[10] Individuals may value having a far broader range of expression available than they are personally interested in purchasing.

That last point is worth emphasizing because it has particular importance for speakers who wish to build on existing works in creating their own. It means that potential licensees may place a value on a license that is considerably lower than optimal because they cannot capture all of the social value of their prospective use. Oppositional and other transformative expression that is not controlled by the owner of the source material carries a social value far in excess of the aggregate price that consumers would pay to read, view, or listen to it. Robust public debate, the spread of knowledge, and the questioning of cultural hierarchy are of paramount importance to a democratic society. Accordingly, I benefit from the ability of secondary authors to reformulate and challenge the social meaning of cultural icons, to expose corrupt or racist practices of powerful institutions, and to publish biographical material about public figures even if I never personally purchase or even see the transformative work. If transformative speakers could expect to capture that social value in the sale of their transformative expression, they might be able and willing to pay a higher price for a license to make it. But to the extent speakers cannot capture that value (and I cannot imagine we would want a regime that monetized individuals' interest in democratic discourse), speakers' private value—the amount they are likely to offer for a license—will not reflect the societal benefit that would accrue from their transformative expression. As a result, some socially valuable transformative speech will not be created.

In sum, the notion that a Blackstonian copyright will lead to greater expressive diversity is highly dubious. To require Jon Elses and Alice Randalls to obtain a bargained-for copyright clearance for each and every use of existing expression will diminish, not engender, diverse, socially valuable expression.

An Expansive Copyright Leads to Clustering

Copyright impacts the mix of speech that constitutes our public discourse. Copyright law primarily fosters a select category of expression: sustained works of authorship that are best funded through the market. In so doing, an expansive copyright tends to diminish the creation and dissemination of certain other categories of expression, particularly noncommercial expression that builds upon copyright-protected works and that would itself be created without the copyright incentive.

But that is not all. A copyright of broad scope tends to skew even the mix of expression that *is* created in response to copyright law. The economic literature on product differentiation tells us that an expansive copyright does not merely foster greater overall investment in original expression. It also leads to diversion of demand from existing works.[11] Like the numerous radio stations that compete for a slice of the Top 40 market, publishers and others attracted by the economic rents that a broad copyright makes possible tend to invest in expressive works that are close substitutes for proven, commercially successful hits. It typically makes more sense for an entrant to seek to siphon off even a small percentage of the mainstream market than to attempt to forge a new niche market. As a result, we would expect to see excessive entry and clustering in already popular genres. As economists put it, "When there are many firms competing for monopoly rents, and market conditions are such that rents can be obtained even with some degree of competition, the rent-seeking behavior of competing monopolists dissipates the social surplus by overproduction of too many similar items."[12] That mainstream demand diversion, moreover, appears to be especially strong when marginal costs are low relative to fixed costs, as they are in many copyright markets, increasingly so in an era of digital distribution.

The economic analysis of demand diversion matches and provides a richer explanation for what many perceive to be the herd behavior of movie studios, television networks, record labels, and book publishers in chasing after blockbuster hits by producing copycats of the same genre. In conjunction with speech policy, it also tells us something about copyright's optimal scope. At some level of copyright protection, copyright's welfare benefits sharply diminish. Beyond the minimal scope and duration that might provide an economic incentive for the creation of numerous works of most genres, making copyright even broader will likely result only in more close substitutes. Like the reality TV shows that have proliferated in recent years, these substitutes will typically be sufficiently differentiated to avoid copying copyrightable expression even if they sometimes copy the basic underlying, noncopyrightable idea. But any new work of an already crowded genre will likely add little, if at all, to consumer welfare—or to public discourse.[13] Indeed, given the power-law distribution of consumer demand for expression (a point to which we will return shortly), the vast majority of new works in a given genre are highly unlikely to reach a significant audience.

Some commentators have maintained that a regime of expansive copyright scope that gives the copyright holder the exclusive right to make derivative works and vaguely similar "reproductions" of a popular work forces competitors to differentiate their works and thus mitigates demand diversion.[14] But just as propertarians mistake product differentiation (in the sense of an absence of borrowing from copyrightable expression) with expressive diversity, so do they wrongly conflate building on existing expression with consumer substitutability and demand diversion. There is actually no reason to assume that new works that are differentiated in the sense that they incorporate no copyrightable expression from existing works are less likely to divert demand than are new works that creatively appropriate from existing works. A new, wholly noninfringing reality TV show is far more likely to divert demand from others of that genre than is a mashup that mixes copied segments of reality TV shows with those of *I Love Lucy* and *Seinfeld* to say something about trends in popular culture.

Granted, some derivative works might constitute mutually redundant expression, at least in the economic sense. Major motion picture studios' competing sequels of a popular film all aimed at the same mainstream audience are one obvious possibility. Yet other creative appropriations, especially those created by oppositional or noncommercial speakers, are far less likely to substitute for the original work, or even for derivative works that the copyright holder would be expected to license, than would "copyright-differentiated" works of the same media and genre. *The Wind Done Gone* hardly substitutes for *Gone with the Wind* or any of its authorized sequels.[15] Like the new reality TV show, animated sitcoms *Family Guy, King of the Hill, Drawn Together, American Dad!, Futurama,* and *South Park* are much more likely to divert demand from *The Simpsons* (and each other), even assuming that they do not incorporate any copyrightable expression from that show, than is the background shot of Homer Simpson appearing fleetingly in Jon Else's PBS documentary about a Wagner opera.

I am not suggesting that multiple works in the same commercial genre have no value for speech. The issue, rather, is one of marginal benefit versus cost. At some point, more copyright yields minimal additional speech and consumer welfare benefits. While doing so, it also impedes the creation of some truly differentiated creative appropriations.

Clustering Does Not Reduce Market Power

Drawing on the economics of monopolistic competition, some commentators contend, counterintuitively, that a *broad,* proprietary copyright actually *reduces* copyright holders' market power.[16] It does so, they contend, by enabling holders of copyrights in commercially successful works to earn excess returns on their investment. Such supracompetitive profits soon attract other creators and publishers to produce additional new works that are relatively close substitutes for the commercially successful expression. That new entrant competition, in turn, forces a price reduction for all works, ultimately bringing prices down to fully competitive levels.

That argument is both unappealing and unconvincing. It is unappealing because, whatever its import for copyright's prohibitive-cost speech burden, a broad, proprietary copyright, encompassing exclusive rights over more transformative speech and lasting for a longer time, gives copyright holders greater occasion and ability to deliberately suppress expression. And, as we have seen, the expression that copyright holders deliberately target is likely to be the oppositional and iconoclastic uses that are so vital to our system of free expression.

The argument is unconvincing, among other reasons,[17] because the market structure for expressive works makes it unlikely that a given new entrant will significantly compete with the culturally salient, popular works that often serve as building blocks for new speech. Given the power-law distribution of consumer demand for expression, only a small number of works will maintain popular, culturally salient status no matter how many quasi imitations are produced. None of the antebellum period harlequin novels inspired by *Gone with the Wind* even begin to discipline the market for that classic. Likewise with efforts to imitate other iconic works. The imitations that proponents of a broad copyright claim will vitiate copyright holders' market power are far more likely to fall somewhere far down the long tail of consumer demand than to present a serious competitive threat to culturally salient classics.

Moreover, even where the winner-take-all market does, over time, yield a small number of colorable substitutes, that hardly constitutes a fully competitive market for would-be creative appropriators. Given the highly skewed power-law distribution, only a very few expressive works of any given genre attain and retain cultural salience. That top-heavy structure likely renders speaker demand for iconic works relatively inelastic and copyright holder market power significant no matter how many new entrants are attracted by the prospect of garnering supracompetitive profits for themselves.[18]

Sum: Copyright's Speech Burdens, Economics, and Speech Policy

Today's bloated copyright is far from optimal from either a free speech or economic welfare perspective. The very copyright expansion that, on the margins, supports production of additional works of little or no value significantly impedes noncommercial, oppositional, and bottom-up creative appropriation. As we saw in chapter 6, an expansive proprietary copyright also fuels copyright holders' market power, media concentration, and copyright industry's socially wasteful rent-seeking and rent dissipation.

Yet from a pure economic efficiency standpoint, the fact that copyright is far from optimal does not necessarily give cause for alarm. In sharp contrast to the ideal of perfect competition, some degree of market power and oligopoly is very much the norm in our economy, as is the overwhelming dominance of large firms' products over those of small producers and nonprofit organizations.[19] It is not certain that a broad copyright pushes copyright markets much farther below the competitive optimum than are many other markets. It might be that copyright markets are typical of many others in which some degree of deadweight loss, consumer deprivation, rent-seeking, and static inefficiency is a necessary condition for capital investment and innovation.

What distinguishes copyright, however, is that copyright governs speech. When copyright engenders oligopoly, it gives media conglomerates inordinate power over public discourse. When copyright imposes barriers to entry, it stifles new media distributors and aggregators, leaving creators dependent on entrenched incumbents to reach their audiences and leaving audiences without new outlets for more varied expression and immeasurably useful tools for learning, like Google Book Search. When copyright results in deadweight loss, it deprives users of access to information and speakers of the ability to build on existing expression in creating their own.

Copyright law and the First Amendment jointly aim to promote expressive diversity, not product differentiation or consumer welfare per se. Speech that creatively appropriates, refashions, builds upon, and recodes popular, mainstream expression may indeed enhance consumer welfare. But the value of diverse political and artistic viewpoints lies largely in our fundamental extraeconomic commitments to individual self-expression and democratic discourse. Hence, resolving the questions of how much copyright holders' market power and copyright industry concentration we should tolerate, how much copyright holder private censorship we should abide, and what shape and breadth we should allow copyright to assume must ultimately depend on free speech policies and concerns.

So what shape should copyright take? As I have argued, a robust system of free expression requires a multiplicity of types of speakers, ranging from commercial mass media, to publicly subsidized news and cultural expression, to documentary filmmakers, bloggers, and writers of fan fiction. Importantly, that list very much includes the types of speech and speakers that copyright underwrites: authors who can earn a living from creating original expression and publishers who can earn enough from audiences to invest in sustained works of authorship, including investigative reporting, feature films, lengthy biography, historical studies, and fiction, free from dependence on the subsidy of government or wealthy, partisan patrons. Granted, the First Amendment import of commercial mass media (and to some extent even professional authors) is diminished in a digital world in which the costs of production, dissemination, and collaboration are a fraction of that required to produce and distribute analog, hard copies. The age in which our system of free expression required entities with sufficient capital to own a printing press, physical distribution network, massive studio, or broadcast station in order to produce and distribute expression and information to a mass audience is no longer. Nonetheless, as we saw in chapter 5, professional authors and commercial mass media play and, I suspect, will continue to play, an important role in our system of free expression.

That suggests, in turn, that, contrary to the view of copyright's severest critics, free speech policy countenances, and even celebrates, some degree of copyright holders' expressive and market power. If we are to have works of authorship that are expensive to produce and if we want some of those works to be produced without reliance on patronage, individuals and firms must be able to recover their average costs (including some risk factor). Indeed, if we expect commercial media firms to remain in business in the face of market realities and alternative investment opportunities, they must probably even earn supranormal profits.

But that is true only to a point, and we are far past that point. Today's commercial mass media conglomerates occupy a considerably wider swath of public discourse than warranted by their incremental contribution to speech. At this juncture, our fundamental interest in expressive diversity is far better served by tailoring copyright to give freer play to nonmarket and oppositional creative appropriation than to march onward toward the Blackstonian property right that copyright industries and propertarian commentators favor. As we have seen, expanding proprietary copyright is more likely to produce marginal works in already crowded mainstream commercial genres than to give voice to a full range of ideas and artistic sensibilities. Blackstonian copyright might induce product differentiation; it does not underwrite expressive diversity.

Through their ownership of broad, proprietary copyrights in vast inventories of cultural building blocks, indeed, copyright industry incumbents drive out other speakers and new media distributors. As such, copyright threatens to stand as the principle bottleneck before the unprecedented blossoming of bottom-up creative appropriation, oppositional speech, and aggregation of knowledge in accessible form that digital technology makes possible. If industry incumbents succeed in using copyright to bring creative appropriators and new media platforms to heel, the last century's dominance of our system of free expression by the commercial mass media may well continue into the next, even when the economics of production and distribution can no longer justify that skewed shape.

In sum, copyright must be tailored to serve our fundamental interest in uninhibited, robust, and wide-open debate from diverse and antagonistic sources. That shared goal of copyright and the First Amendment is best furthered by charting a middle ground between Blackstonian copyright and no copyright. At the very least, copyright's multifaceted speech burdens counsel strongly against expanding copyright holders' rights. Copyright law should enable creators and media enterprises to earn ample remuneration from the market without affording them broad, proprietary veto over oppositional speakers, nonmarket creative appropriators, and new media distributors.

That is the principle. I sketch in some of the contours in chapters 8 and 9.

| Copyright and the First
Amendment

T HE FIRST AMENDMENT PROVIDES that "Congress shall make no
law ... abridging the freedom of speech." Copyright abridges speech.
Because of copyright, speakers are often unable effectively to convey their
message, and audiences are deprived of valuable expression.

Yet that does not necessarily mean that the First Amendment places
limits on copyright's application and scope. First Amendment doctrine is
highly complex and First Amendment protections far more qualified than
the amendment's sweeping, absolute language suggests. In fact, government
regulation imposes many speech burdens that do not give rise to any justiciable claim under the First Amendment.

Nevertheless, as I argue in this chapter, copyright law does implicate
traditional First Amendment concerns and courts should accordingly apply
the First Amendment to cabin copyright holder prerogatives where necessary to protect speech. At the very least, even if the First Amendment is not
applied as an external constraint, Congress and the courts should interpret
and develop copyright doctrine in line with First Amendment values.

Courts have recognized that copyright can abridge speech and thus that it
raises First Amendment concerns, but they have almost never actually imposed First Amendment limitations on copyright. In fact, most courts have
summarily rejected First Amendment defenses to copyright infringement
claims. In almost every instance, they have assumed that First Amendment
values are fully and adequately protected by limitations on copyright holder

rights within copyright doctrine itself.[1] As a result, they hold, no independent First Amendment scrutiny is called for.

The courts are correct that, in principle, copyright's free speech burden could be ameliorated by various safeguards within copyright law itself. But as we have seen, copyright's much-touted internal free speech safety valves in fact fall far short of their promise. As a result, copyright doctrine has proven inadequate to protect free speech. The notion that copyright's uncertain fair use privilege, ever-vague idea/expression dichotomy, and not-so-limited term serve as effective proxies for the First Amendment is judicial formalism at its worst. On paper, those doctrines stand for First Amendment values. In practice, they provide far less than the resolute guarantees that the First Amendment demands, guarantees that in other areas of law provide a robust penumbra of protection so that speakers need not engage in self-censorship to avoid the risk of liability.

Nor can we rely on lower courts, many of which fall prey to a Blackstonian view of copyright, or on Congress, with its predisposition to dispense rents to copyright industries, to rehabilitate copyright from within. Consequently, First Amendment scrutiny is both warranted and, I suspect, necessary to restore an appropriate balance between copyright holder prerogatives and free speech. At the very least, the First Amendment should be applied to ensure that copyright's traditional free speech safety valves actually accomplish their task.

Copyright's exoneration from external First Amendment scrutiny not only ignores the actual workings of copyright law and practice but is also sharply out of step with the rest of First Amendment doctrine. During the very period that courts have trumpeted copyright's categorical immunity, they have subjected a wide array of other intellectual property and private causes of action to First Amendment scrutiny. Courts have brought the First Amendment to bear on the laws of trademark, trade secret, the right of publicity, defamation, the right of privacy, tortious interference with business relations, intentional infliction of emotional distress, a private right of action for damages caused by illegal wiretapping, and, in some instances, personal and real property. First Amendment scrutiny does not always mean that the speaker prevails. But to avoid a potentially "chilling effect" on valued speech, courts often place formidable barriers before individuals seeking to vindicate proprietary or personal rights.

Moreover, in marked contrast to the judicial exoneration of copyright, courts do not ordinarily consider a body of law's internal free speech safeguards to obviate the need for First Amendment scrutiny. Courts have regularly applied First Amendment restrictions to other private rights, including intellectual property rights that, like copyright, have built-in mechanisms designed to protect free speech interests. Even prior to First Amendment intervention, for instance, trademark law generally denied trademark owners the right to prevent the unauthorized use of their marks for news reporting, commentary, parody, and artistic expression. Similarly, the right of publicity has long been subject to a privilege to use a person's name or likeness for the dissemination of news or as part of artistic expression. Yet despite these internal free speech protections, courts subjected trademark and the right of publicity to further, independent First Amendment constraints.[2] Likewise, common law defamation and right of privacy were remolded to conform with First Amendment strictures despite internal doctrine that already limited aggrieved persons' redress in order to protect free speech. For example, common law libel recognized a privilege of fair comment on matters of public concern and a qualified privilege for news dealers and bookstores to transmit defamatory matter published by a third person.[3] Nonetheless, the Supreme Court constitutionalized the law of defamation, holding that the First Amendment requires (1) shifting the burden of proof from the defendant to the plaintiff on the issues of falsity and fault for making a false statement, (2) precluding any liability for defaming a public figure absent malice, and (3) precluding strict liability and, absent a showing of malice, punitive damages even for defaming a private person, at least when the defamation involves more than a purely private matter.[4] Surely, the First Amendment ought to have something to say about copyright doctrine as well.

To be certain, not everything we might think of as "speech" is protected as such under the First Amendment. Corporate proxy statements, fraudulent misrepresentation, and criminal conspiracy are prime examples. But copyright law touches directly and consistently on literature, art, film, television broadcasts, photographs, political polemic, criticism, scholarship, and other expression lying at the core of First Amendment protection. Copyright is also heavily involved in the structuring and operation of traditional First Amendment media. In contrast to the regulation of general conduct and of forms of expression effectively deemed "nonspeech" for First Amendment purposes, indeed, copyright law's entire focus is on providing some speakers with the legal entitlement to restrict others' speech. Accordingly, copyright law falls squarely within the realm of those types of speech-burdening regulations that generally do implicate the First Amendment.

Courts' persistent immunization of copyright from First Amendment scrutiny is thus a striking anomaly. Their failure even to ask whether copyright's traditional safety valves are sufficient to pass First Amendment muster stands in sharp contrast to other closely analogous areas of First Amendment doctrine. At the very least, courts should, as they have in other areas, apply the First Amendment prophylactically to ensure that the enforcement of copyright holders' rights does not chill valued speech. Courts understandably do not wish to interpret and apply First Amendment tests to the particular facts at hand in every copyright infringement action. But as with defamation, privacy, and other torts, they could refashion key facets of copyright doctrine to comport more consistently and rigorously with First Amendment requirements without having repeatedly to entertain First Amendment defenses to copyright infringement claims.

The Supreme Court Speaks: Eldred v. Ashcroft

The most recent and conclusive statement on the relationship between copyright and the First Amendment is the Supreme Court's January 2003 decision in *Eldred v. Ashcroft.*[5] In *Eldred,* a 7-to-2 majority of the Court rejected a First Amendment challenge to the Sonny Bono Copyright Term Extension Act (CTEA) of 1998. The *Eldred* majority conceded that lower courts have spoken too broadly when declaring copyrights categorically immune from First Amendment challenges. But in rejecting Eldred's challenge, the Court held that when "Congress has not altered the traditional contours of copyright protection, further First Amendment scrutiny is unnecessary."[6]

By that ruling, the Supreme Court perpetuated copyright's aberrant treatment. *Eldred* did put to rest the sweeping (and ludicrous) suggestion that no Copyright Act provision could possibly run afoul of the First Amendment. (After all, what if Congress amended the Copyright Act to provide that only registered Republicans enjoy copyright protection?) But in holding that First Amendment scrutiny is unwarranted when "Congress has not altered the traditional contours of copyright protection," the Court almost entirely closed the door on further First Amendment challenges to traditional copyright law.

The Court's explanation for its holding is no less disappointing than the result. *Eldred* shows remarkably little understanding of, or appreciation for, the First Amendment values at stake in copyright's burdening of speech. The majority's opinion also gives further credence to lower court justifications for exonerating copyright from First Amendment review, some of them no less doctrinally and logically unsound than the broad statement that copyrights are categorically immune from First Amendment scrutiny.

At the same time, almost in spite of itself, *Eldred* actually goes some way toward bringing copyright law within the First Amendment fold. Despite the Court's abjuration of First Amendment scrutiny for traditional copyright, the decision leaves room for the First Amendment both to inform copyright jurisprudence and to oversee Copyright Act amendments that do alter copyright's traditional contours. Most broadly, in rejecting (or at least qualifying) copyright's categorical immunity, the Court explicitly recognized that, in principle, copyright does implicate the First Amendment. Further, the Court's opinion also suggests some specific ways in which the First Amendment might yet circumscribe copyright holder prerogatives.

For better or for worse, the Supreme Court's decision in *Eldred v. Ashcroft* likely sets the framework for First Amendment challenges to copyright for years to come. That is not to say that *Eldred* determines the question of whether, as a matter of policy, copyright law should be tailored to minimize free speech burdens. Free speech policy, we must keep in mind, is not coterminous with the complex array of rules, presumptions, tests, and standards that constitute First Amendment doctrine. First Amendment doctrine reflects the constraints of judicial administrability and judicial sensitivity to the prerogatives of coordinate branches of government as much as it concerns the protection of First Amendment values. At least formally, even if *Eldred* sharply narrows the field for justiciable First Amendment claims, it says nothing about the broader policy question of how copyright law should be designed to best serve our "system of freedom of expression." Nevertheless, given the Court's prominence, its dismissive characterization of copyright's free speech burdens may well have influence over policy makers as well as judges.

We now turn to a closer, critical examination of the *Eldred* decision and what it portends for copyright, the First Amendment, and free speech.

BACKGROUND

Eldred v. Ashcroft differs from most previous cases involving copyright and the First Amendment. *Eldred* arose not as a defense to a particular copyright infringement claim but as a facial First Amendment challenge to new copyright legislation. The Sonny Bono Copyright Term Extension Act amended the Copyright Act to extend the copyright term for an additional twenty years. The term extension applied not only prospectively, to works created after the CTEA's effective date, but also retrospectively, to subsisting copyrights in existing works.

In January 1999, a group of archivists and publishers of public domain material filed a complaint seeking to enjoin then Attorney General Janet Reno from enforcing the CTEA. The complaint posed two constitutional challenges to the Act. The first was that the term extension exceeded Congress's enumerated power under the Copyright Clause. The second, the sole ground we will consider here, was that the Act contravened the First Amendment.

Both the trial court and the District of Columbia Circuit Court of Appeals summarily dismissed plaintiffs' First Amendment claims, with the D.C. Circuit holding explicitly that "copyrights are categorically immune from challenges under the First Amendment."[7] In so ruling, the *Eldred* lower courts went further than any others in immunizing copyright from First Amendment challenge. Other courts had exonerated copyright from First Amendment defenses to copyright infringement claims. The D.C. District and Circuit were the first to hold that the Copyright Act legislation and amendments are immune even from facial attack. In addition, the D.C. Circuit baldly stated that "the plaintiffs lack any cognizable first amendment right to exploit the copyrighted works of others."[8] Most other courts have characterized the copyright/free speech conflict in a more nuanced manner. They have accepted that, in principle, copyright does raise First Amendment concerns but have held that copyright's internal free speech safeguards adequately address them.

THE *ELDRED* PETITIONERS' FIRST AMENDMENT ARGUMENT

First Amendment doctrine establishes a panoply of standards and tests for determining whether speech-burdening legislation and regulation meet First Amendment muster. In particular, "content-based" speech restrictions, generally those in which the government seeks to suppress a particular viewpoint or subject matter, are subject to "strict scrutiny" and almost never upheld. Examples of content-based speech restrictions include government prohibitions of communist tracts, hate speech, and flag burning. In contrast, "content-neutral" speech restrictions are those that limit expression without regard to the speech's message or communicative impact. Classic examples include capping decibel levels at music clubs, forbidding sound trucks in residential neighborhoods, and imposing "time, place, or manner restrictions" on billboards and demonstrations. Content-neutral speech restrictions are subject to a level of judicial scrutiny that, although more rigorous than that applied to regulations that raise no First Amendment (or other special constitutional) concerns, is less exacting than the strict scrutiny applied to content-based regulation. Courts and commentators often refer to such scrutiny as "intermediate scrutiny."[9]

The *Eldred* petitioners maintained that copyright law is a "content-neutral" speech regulation and that the Copyright Term Extension Act should, therefore, be subject to "intermediate scrutiny" under the standard set forth in a number of prior cases, including, most definitively, the Supreme Court's two decisions in *Turner Broadcasting Sys., Inc. v. FCC.*[10] *Turner* concerned a First Amendment challenge to a federal law requiring cable television systems to devote a portion of their channels to the transmission of local broadcast television stations. In *Turner I,* the Court characterized those "must-carry" rules as content-neutral because they "impose burdens and confer benefits without reference to the content of speech."[11] In *Turner II,* the Court restated and applied the standard for intermediate scrutiny: "A content-neutral regulation will be sustained under the First Amendment if it advances important government interests unrelated to the suppression of free speech and does not burden substantially more speech than necessary to further those interests."[12]

The *Eldred* petitioners trained their First Amendment challenge on the Act's retrospective extension of copyright duration to subsisting copyrights in existing works. Under those provisions, even holders of copyrights in old works about to enter the public domain, like the Mickey Mouse cartoon character, were handed an additional twenty years of exclusive rights. The *Eldred* petitioners argued that the only important governmental interest previously recognized by the Supreme Court as sustaining copyright's speech restrictions—namely, providing incentives to authors to create original works—is irrelevant once a work has been created, certainly after the author has died. As the petitioners put it: "No matter what we offer Hawthorne or Hemingway or Gershwin, they will not produce anything more."[13] The petitioners then argued that the other interests that the government advanced in support of the term extension, which included providing greater income to authors' heirs, harmonizing U.S. copyright law with that of other countries, and preserving old works, were illegitimate, hypothesized after the fact, or insufficient to justify the speech burden imposed.

The Supreme Court's Ruling

The Supreme Court did not reach the merits of the petitioners' First Amendment challenge because, like the lower courts, it treated copyright as essentially outside the First Amendment scheme. Indeed, the Court gave short shrift to the conflict between copyright and free speech. Most revealing of the Court's failure to grasp the First Amendment values at stake was its explanation for why, in its view, *Turner* was inapposite to Eldred's challenge.

DISTINGUISHING *TURNER*

Turner was the primary case cited by the petitioners in support of their argument that the CTEA should be subject to intermediate scrutiny and held to fail to pass First Amendment muster. In rejecting the petitioners' First Amendment claim, the *Eldred* Court summarily dispensed with *Turner*, asserting that it "bears little on copyright." The Court reasoned that in contrast to the "must-carry" provisions at issue in *Turner*, copyright law "does not oblige anyone to reproduce another's speech against the carrier's will." Justice Ginsburg's majority opinion in *Eldred* stated, "The First Amendment securely protects the freedom to make—or decline to make—one's own speech; it bears less heavily when speakers assert the right to make other people's speeches."[14] While that statement stops short of the D.C. Circuit's blanket rejection of any cognizable First Amendment interest in copying or building upon others' copyrighted works, it runs squarely against established First Amendment precedent and wholly mischaracterizes the First Amendment values at issue in copyright's continuing expansion.

To begin with, contrary to the Court's crabbed reading, neither *Turner* nor other precedent applying intermediate scrutiny is merely about "forced speech." *Turner*, rather, is viewed to stand for the broad proposition that the government may not generally target speech for restriction, even to serve legitimate, speech-enhancing, content-neutral goals, unless the speech restriction meets the test for intermediate scrutiny.

Likewise with respect to the Court's blithe assertion that making "other people's speeches" is of secondary First Amendment import. Speakers often express themselves more fully and effectively imparting words others have written than those of their own creation. As detailed in chapter 3, there are numerous instances in which conveying another person's speech stands at the very heart of the First Amendment. Reciting the Koran or Communist Manifesto on a street corner is but one apt example. Outside the copyright context, such choices regarding which of other people's speeches best expresses one's own message enjoy full First Amendment protection, and rightly so. As the Supreme Court has previously held:

> Nor, under our precedent, does First Amendment protection require a speaker to generate, as an original matter, each item featured in the communication. . . . For that matter, the presentation of an edited

compilation of speech generated by other persons is a staple of most newspapers' opinion pages, which, of course, fall squarely within the core of First Amendment security, as does even the simple selection of a paid noncommercial advertisement for inclusion in a daily paper.[15]

Similarly and perhaps most disturbingly, the *Eldred* Court's "right to make other people's speeches" characterization grossly belittles the First Amendment costs that copyright too often imposes. Is the "right to make other people's speeches" all that was at stake in Alan Cranston's unauthorized, unexpurgated translation of *Mein Kampf*? Was Alice Randall merely repeating Margaret Mitchell's speech when Randall took aim at the racist stereotypes and idealized portrait of slavery in *Gone with the Wind*? Is the "right to make other people's speeches" all that Jon Else and his audiences lost when Else reluctantly removed *The Simpsons* from the background shot in his *Ring Cycle* documentary? What about the *City Pages* newspaper that reprinted a racist fable from a police department newsletter to expose police racism? The Church of Scientology critics who posted church texts on the Internet to unveil church foibles? The Worldwide Church of God dissidents who circulated the church founder's suppressed teachings to engage in their religious practice? The creator of the mashup, posted on the Internet on the eve of the Iraq war, featuring a recording of the song "Endless Love," played over television news images carefully selected and edited to create the appearance of President Bush and Prime Minister Blair singing the song to one another? Swiss artist Christian Marclay, whose critically acclaimed *Video Quartet,* a four-channel audiovisual collage commissioned by the San Francisco Museum of Modern Art and the Grand Museum of Luxembourg, combines some 600 sound and film clips from more than a hundred classic movies?

From political to cultural to religious to artistic to whimsical, the speech that copyright burdens is as varied, and at times as profound (and creative), as any other speech. Even if the Court were correct that "the right to make other people's speeches" receives lesser First Amendment protection, copyright often burdens far more than that right alone. Contrary to the Court's suggestion that copyright merely prevents infringers from acting as free-riding conduits for other's expression—a suggestion that has, unfortunately, already been repeated in lower courts[16]—today's expanded copyright regularly chills creative and poignant criticism, commentary, artistic insight, and self-expression. Copyright's far-ranging speech burdens implicate the First Amendment no less than does government regulation of speech that stands outside the distended ambit of copyright holders' proprietary control.

As an additional reason for absolving traditional copyright from First Amendment review, the *Eldred* Court invoked copyright law's constitutional pedigree: "The Copyright Clause and First Amendment were adopted close in time. This proximity indicates that, in the Framers' view, copyright's limited monopolies are compatible with free speech principles."[17] Like the making "other people's speeches" calculus, that rationale has already been cited by a post-*Eldred* lower court in denying a First Amendment challenge to a provision of the Copyright Act.[18] And it, too, falls apart on even the most cursory examination.

The Court's constitutional pedigree argument is right about one thing: the fact of temporal proximity. The Constitution, including the clause empowering Congress to enact a copyright statute, was ratified only two years prior to the First Amendment and the rest of the Bill of Rights. For that matter, Congress enacted the first copyright statute the very same year it adopted the Bill of Rights.[19]

But what does that tell us? While it certainly suggests that the Framers could not have intended that copyright is per se unconstitutional, the mere fact of temporal proximity does not mean that whatever copyright statute Congress chooses to enact is immune from First Amendment scrutiny. The essential point of the First Amendment is to impose limits on powers that Congress would otherwise have under the Constitution. Not surprisingly, therefore, the First Amendment has been repeatedly held to override legislation enacted by Congress pursuant to other enumerated congressional powers under the Constitution, adopted with the very same temporal proximity to the First Amendment as the Copyright Clause. For example, the Constitution expressly empowers Congress to "provide for the Punishment of counterfeiting." However, the Supreme Court has held that portions of statutes restricting the use of photographic reproductions of currency ran afoul of the First Amendment.[20] Likewise, on First Amendment grounds, the Court has stricken legislation, enacted pursuant to Congress's power under the Federal District Clause, prohibiting the public display of any flag, banner, or device on the grounds of the Supreme Court, and legislation, enacted pursuant to the Post Office Clause, restricting mailings of communist advocacy.[21] The Court has also subjected to First Amendment scrutiny legislation enacted pursuant to Congress's enumerated power under the Commerce Clause, including, among others, the granting of a special trademark right in the Olympic symbol and the must-carry rules at issue in *Turner.*[22] Copyright law enjoys no greater constitutional pedigree than any of those statutes, and all have been subjected to First Amendment review.

Nor does the Framers' understanding that "copyright's limited monopolies are compatible with free speech principles" tell us anything about whether the current Copyright Act comports with the First Amendment. As we have seen, today's turgid copyright bears only scant resemblance to the narrowly tailored short-term entitlement for which the first Congress provided. The "limited monopolies" enacted by the first Congress entailed only the exclusive right to copy books, maps, and charts. They did not extend to other works, and they prevented no one from preparing derivative works or publicly performing or displaying another person's original expression. And even those "limited monopolies" lasted for at most twenty-eight years, not for well over a century, as is typical of today's not-so-limited copyright. The Framers would not recognize today's broad proprietary entitlement as "copyright." Whether they would find it compatible with their "free speech principles" is an entirely open question.

Equally fatal for the Court's temporal proximity argument is how radically First Amendment doctrine has changed since the Founding. Our modern First Amendment jurisprudence, largely a product of recent decades, is far more solicitous of free speech interests than were the Framers. It is inconceivable, for example, that the Alien and Sedition Acts or eighteenth-century libel law would survive First Amendment muster today. The Framers' "free speech principles" bear no more resemblance to current First Amendment doctrine than does than the 1790 copyright statute to its current counterpart.

If brought to the test, the truly "limited monopolies" that the Framers envisioned—the short-term, narrow copyright of their day—would most probably meet current First Amendment strictures. But the First Amendment compatibility of the CTEA and other recent Copyright Act amendments is an entirely different question. And the fact that the Copyright Clause and First Amendment were ratified more or less contemporaneously, at a time in which both copyright and free speech rights were a pale shadow of what they are today, bears not at all on how that question should be answered.

COPYRIGHT'S FREE SPEECH BENEFITS

Following its invocation of the Framers' view of copyright's compatibility with free speech principles, the Court rehearsed another old saw of copyright's First Amendment immunity: the notion that copyright's purported role as "the engine of free expression" excuses any speech burdens copyright imposes. Like the other rationales for copyright's First Amendment immunity, the copyright-as-engine argument runs aground on the shoals of empirical examination and prevailing First Amendment doctrine. As I discussed in chapter 5, copyright's free speech benefits are considerably more attenuated than is often assumed. Copyright's speech benefits appear to outweigh its costs. But those benefits are certainly not so overwhelming as to obviate any need for First Amendment scrutiny.

Moreover, even if copyright does yield important free speech benefits, it simply does not follow that copyright should escape First Amendment scrutiny. As Mark Lemley and Eugene Volokh have pointed out, much speech-burdening regulation, ranging from defamation law to campaign finance restrictions to time, place, or manner regulation, may be characterized as speech-enhancing.[23] But the fact that speech-burdening regulation might also enhance some speech does not generally absolve the regulation of First Amendment scrutiny. Indeed, the Supreme Court recognized that the must-carry rules at issue in *Turner* aimed to achieve important free speech objectives: to "preserve access to free television programming" for those without cable and to promote "the widespread dissemination of information from a multiplicity of sources."[24] Yet the *Turner* Court exercised First Amendment review without even considering that the must-carry rules' free speech goals might somehow reduce the need for First Amendment scrutiny. As is routinely the case when courts consider a regulation that burdens some speech to enhance other speech or promote widespread speech benefits, the *Turner* Court asked whether the must-carry rules "burden substantially more speech than necessary to further those interests."[25]

So, at the very least, the *Eldred* Court's "engine of free expression" argument is sharply out of step with other First Amendment doctrine. The Court's notion that First Amendment scrutiny is less warranted because copyright law broadly aims to promote speech provides yet another example of copyright's peculiarly privileged status.

COPYRIGHT'S INTERNAL FREE SPEECH
SAFETY VALVES

Finally, the *Eldred* Court emphasized that "copyright law contains built-in First Amendment accommodations," particularly the idea/expression dichotomy and the fair use doctrine.[26] As I have already discussed, the widespread judicial notion that copyright's internal free speech safety valves substitute for First Amendment scrutiny falls apart on two counts.

First, copyright's internal safety valves are woefully inadequate to that task. At the very least, the vague, unpredictable nature of the idea/expression dichotomy and fair use privilege induces considerable speaker self-censorship.

The *Eldred* Court's Panglossian rejoinder that "every idea, theory, and fact in a copyrighted work becomes instantly available for public exploitation at the moment of publication" misses the point so apparent in the Else, Cranston, Randall, and other examples I have discussed: a speaker's ability to copy, convey, quote, or build upon a copyrighted work's particular words and images can be no less critical to the communication of her message than is access to the work's ideas. In other First Amendment jurisprudence, it is axiomatic that speakers must sometimes use particular locution to make their point. As the Supreme Court has long recognized, "[W]e cannot indulge the facile assumption that one can forbid particular words without running a substantial risk of suppressing ideas in the process."[27] Neither the idea/expression dichotomy nor the fair use privilege was of assistance to John Else, Alan Cranston, or the Worldwide Church of God dissidents. That Alice Randall's sequel was ultimately accorded fair use protection is, as I will discuss shortly, a case that proves the need for greater First Amendment intervention. In short, even if the built-in safeguards of some statutory regimes might sometimes substitute for First Amendment scrutiny, copyright's cannot.

Second, the presence of internal free speech safeguards does not ordinarily obviate the need for First Amendment scrutiny. In other areas, as I have discussed, courts regularly apply the First Amendment to ensure the adequacy of such safeguards. First Amendment doctrine generally recognizes that "the legal system is imperfect and mandates the formulation of legal rules that reflect our preference for errors made in favor of free speech."[28] The talisman of copyright's purported "built-in First Amendment accommodations" cannot justify the failure to evaluate whether today's bloated copyright comports with First Amendment constraints. In other areas, courts regularly apply the First Amendment proactively to prevent government regulation and private rights from chilling valued speech. Even with respect to trademark, defamation, the rights of publicity and privacy, and other private right regimes that already have built-in free speech safety valves, courts impose the procedural and substantive constraints to avoid "intolerable self-censorship" and the undue suppression of "speech that matters."[29] There is no reason to expect less regarding copyright.

COPYRIGHT LEGISLATION AS SUCCESSFUL
RENT-SEEKING

I now turn to a point that the *Eldred* Court was invited to consider but did not. The *Eldred* petitioners argued that the CTEA was a quintessential rent-distribution statute, a giveaway to the corporations and heirs who own existing copyrights at the expense of the public at large. That argument was reiterated in amicus briefs and found prominent expression (albeit not in so many words) in Justice Breyer's dissent. It was also expressed in comments made during oral argument even by justices who ultimately joined the majority. But the Court's First Amendment analysis fails to address it.

Clearly, the Act's most direct beneficiaries—and those most active in lobbying for its passage—were the entertainment industries that held old copyrights soon to expire if the term extension were not enacted. Nevertheless, in its rejection of the petitioners' Copyright Clause challenge, the Court implicitly found the rent-distribution argument to be unavailing. Applying a highly deferential "rational basis" standard of scrutiny to that challenge, the majority recited a number of purported rationales for the term extension and concluded, with a notable lack of enthusiasm for the government's argument, that the Court was "not at liberty to second-guess congressional determinations and policy judgments of this order, however debatable or arguably unwise they may be."

I think that the rationales the government advanced in support of the Act are largely spurious, or at least that the term extension was an overly broad, slipshod tool for advancing them. For example, while the government touted the CTEA as a vehicle for harmonizing U.S. law with the European Union Copyright Term Directive, the Act's provisions in fact heighten the disparity for the copyright terms for some works, including those created by corporate authors, that were already *longer* than the European standard prior to the Act's enactment. But that is not the point I wish to address here. My concern, rather, is that while the Court implicitly addressed the rent-distribution argument in connection with the Copyright Clause claim, it failed even to consider the issue in its First Amendment analysis.

When courts apply rational basis scrutiny, they are generally right to ignore rent distribution. Organized-interest influence and legislative bargains are, after all, endemic to our legislative process and should not generally serve as a basis for judicial intervention. But when speech interests are at stake, that is another matter. Rent distribution in the form of doling out speech entitlements to well-heeled organized interests at the expense of the speech of the citizenry at large should be cause for heightened First Amendment scrutiny.

Accordingly, the *Eldred* Court should have taken cognizance of the CTEA's rent-distribution character as yet another reason to apply intermediate First Amendment review. Unlike the other aspects of its First Amendment analysis, the Court's failure to do so does not run squarely against well-established and well-defined First Amendment doctrine. Courts have not explicitly invoked speech-entitlement rent distribution as a trigger for heightened First Amendment scrutiny. But in reviewing First Amendment challenges to speech entitlement allocations, courts have repeatedly expressed concern about the "exercise of the most naked interest-group preferences" in the area of First Amendment rights.[30] The fact that Copyright Act amendments, like other speech entitlement allocations, raise the suspicion of successful rent-seeking should thus lend considerable weight to applying heightened judicial scrutiny with respect to the speech burdens they impose.

As the Supreme Court recognized in *Turner,* "Regulations that discriminate among media, or among different speakers within a single medium, often present serious First Amendment concerns."[31] Underlying those concerns is the suspicion that the government has doled out speech entitlements to favored interest groups without adequately accounting for the speech burdens imposed on other speakers and the public at large. The *Turner* Court ultimately upheld the must-carry rules but emphasized that the local broadcasters who had lobbied for the rule effectively served as a proxy for the public at large; requiring cable operators to carry local broadcast programming both maintained expressive diversity and ensured access to television for the millions who did not have cable. In any event, the concern running through *Turner,* as well as a number of lower court decisions, that government allocations of speech entitlements to favored interest groups might unduly burden speech, echoes important tenets of First Amendment jurisprudence.

Given the central value of speech to individual autonomy and a democratic polity, First Amendment scrutiny serves the salutary function of requiring legislatures to account for the interests of speech beneficiaries who would otherwise be underrepresented in the political process.[32] Often, the underrepresented are fringe speakers and other minorities. That is a particular concern when the government targets a particular viewpoint or subject matter for suppression. But when government defines and distributes speech-related entitlements at the behest of politically powerful groups, the underrepresented may well be the numerous but widely dispersed majority, the public at large. Faced with industry associations competing for government-supplied rents, including rents taking the form of speech entitlements, the public suffers a distinct disadvantage. This disadvantage differs in character from that of fringe speakers but results from a comparable lack of political power. In contrast to well-heeled interest groups, the public consists of a large number of discrete individuals, each with a small, highly diffuse stake in the regulation at issue. As a result, the general public faces serious organizational obstacles to countering industry lobbying, and when industries lobby for speech entitlements, the underrepresented public interest in free speech is likely to be shortchanged. When Congress doles out speech entitlements, therefore, it must fall to courts applying First Amendment scrutiny to ensure that systemic political infirmities do not unduly burden speech.

First Amendment concerns regarding political process pathologies are especially pertinent to copyright legislation, which has long been notorious for its embodiment of successful industry rent-seeking.[33] Congress has repeatedly amended the Copyright Act to provide for more expansive protection for copyright industries. Legislative expansions of copyright holder rights do not merely reflect industry lobbying and influence. They often consist of outright congressional rubber-stamping of industry-drafted legislation and committee reports. As a former House Intellectual Property subcommittee staff member graphically describes it:

> Copyright interest groups hold fund raisers for members of Congress, write campaign songs, invite members of Congress (and their staff) to private movie screenings or soldout concerts, and draft legislation they expect Congress to pass without any changes. In the 104th Congress, they are drafting the committee reports and haggling among themselves about what needs to be in the report. In my experience, some copyright lawyers and lobbyists actually resent members of Congress and staff interfering with what they view as their legislation and their committee report. With the 104th Congress we have, I believe, reached a point where legislative history must be ignored because not even the hands of congressional staff have touched the committee reports.[34]

Not all interest groups lobby for greater copyright protection. Some, like those representing restaurants, bars, and retail stores that play music for their customers, have successfully lobbied for exceptions to copyright holders' rights. But Congress typically responds to politically powerful user industries by enacting narrowly tailored carve-outs for those industries. Absent from the bargaining table—and thus too often exerting little influence in copyright legislation—are the public at large and potential speakers, like the young Alan Cranston, who might someday wish to reproduce or build upon copyrighted expression in order to convey their message, often with no motive of commercial gain.

If copyright law was ordinary economic legislation, that might not be grounds for judicial intervention. But copyright law is not ordinary economic legislation. Copyright regulates speech. It thus behooves courts to ensure that when Congress doles out copyright prerogatives, it gives adequate weight to the First Amendment burdens that copyright imposes. In that vein, at the very least, the *Eldred* Court should have required the government to demonstrate that the CTEA's term extension for existing copyright holders actually served a substantial, legitimate governmental purpose and was narrowly tailored to minimize the burden the extension imposes on speech.

First Amendment Intervention after Eldred

Despite its tepid rejection of copyright's categorical immunity, *Eldred* leaves room for First Amendment intervention in copyright law in two contexts. The first involves copyright legislation that does alter the "traditional contours of copyright protection." The second concerns copyright's internal free speech safeguards.

ALTERING THE TRADITIONAL CONTOURS OF COPYRIGHT PROTECTION

As we have seen, *Eldred* holds that no First Amendment scrutiny is necessary when "Congress has not altered the traditional contours of copyright protection." That strongly suggests that First Amendment scrutiny would be warranted were Congress to alter copyright's traditional contours. In so doing, the *Eldred* Court recognized the First Amendment import of copyright's traditional free speech safeguards. In contrast to some lower court suggestions, Congress could not repeal fair use or the idea/expression dichotomy without running up against the First Amendment.

Eldred gives little indication of what other sorts of legislation the Court might view as altering the "traditional contours of copyright protection." However, one recent Copyright Act amendment would appear to readily meet that description: the anticircumvention provisions of the Digital Millennium Copyright Act (DMCA).[35]

The DMCA imposes both an access prohibition (forbidding individuals from circumventing technological measures that prevent unlicensed access to a copyrighted work) and a device prohibition (forbidding the manufacture and trafficking of devices, technology, and services that are primarily designed to assist users in circumventing technological protection measures). Although the DMCA's ultimate purpose is to assist copyright holders in exerting greater control over their works, the Act focuses on access and copy control technology, not on proscribing or penalizing acts of infringement per se. Accordingly, as the House Commerce Committee report on the amendment recognized, the DMCA's anticircumvention provisions "have little, if anything, to do with copyright law," and "represent an unprecedented departure into the zone of what might be called paracopyright."[36]

Indeed, as we saw in chapter 4, the "paracopyright" provided for under the DMCA expands content providers' control over content significantly beyond that which has traditionally obtained under the Copyright Act. First, the DMCA does not merely secure technological measures designed to prevent copyright infringement. It also enables content providers to control *access* to content, a prerogative not included among copyright holders' exclusive rights. Second, in many cases the DMCA's access and device prohibitions effectively apply even to technological measures controlling material that is not protected by copyright.[37] For example, if a content provider deploys a technological measure to control access to an electronic database containing a copyrighted work, the DMCA makes it unlawful to circumvent that technological measure even if the database also contains many public domain works. The same is true where the content provider has appended minimal copyrightable expression to an essentially public domain work (such as adding a new two-paragraph introduction to a Shakespeare play). Finally, the DMCA's access and device prohibitions apply even when circumvention is needed to use a copyrighted work in a manner that is permitted under copyright law, such as fair use. The DMCA expressly preserves the fair use privilege to engage in conduct that would infringe traditional copyright.[38] But, as courts have held, fair use is unavailable as a defense to unlicensed circumvention in violation of the DMCA even when individuals need to circumvent to engage in fair use.[39]

Congress was well aware that the DMCA's sweeping prohibitions might raise First Amendment concerns by impairing the availability of information and public domain expression and by blocking noninfringing uses of copyrighted works. The House Commerce Committee report on the DMCA warns of the development of a "legal framework that would inexorably create a pay-per-use society" and refers to testimony that "[t]hese newly created rights will dramatically diminish public access to information."[40] Yet the DMCA only pays lip service to these concerns. Purporting to preserve the fair use privilege, but making it unavailable for DMCA violations is one example of that lip service. Another is the Act's declaration that "[n]othing in this section shall enlarge or diminish any rights of free speech or the press for activities using consumer electronics, telecommunications, or computing products."[41] Since Congress lacks the authority to diminish free speech rights protected by the First Amendment, that declaration effectively means only that the DMCA does not enlarge free speech rights.

Beyond these impuissant general savings clauses, the DMCA also purports to protect First Amendment interests by delegating to the Librarian of Congress the power to suspend application of the access prohibition to the extent required to prevent undue speech burdens. The Act instructs the Librarian to determine whether the prohibition adversely impacts persons' "ability to make noninfringing uses under this title of a particular class of copyrighted works."[42] If the Librarian finds such adverse impact, he or she may suspend the prohibition for "such users with respect to such class of works for the ensuing 3-year period." In making this determination, the Librarian must devote particular attention to the availability of works for nonprofit archival, preservation, and educational purposes and for criticism, comment, news reporting, teaching, scholarship, and research.

The House Commerce Committee described the Librarian's review as a " 'fail-safe' mechanism" for ensuring ongoing access to "copyrighted materials that are important to education, scholarship, and other socially vital endeavors."[43] But the review mechanism falls so far short of that salutary goal that one can only conclude that the DMCA provisions setting up that mechanism are a product of gross negligence or a cynical abridgment of First Amendment concerns.[44]

For one, the prohibition on actual circumvention is only one aspect of the DMCA and the only provision subject to the Librarian's power to review and suspend. The device prohibition remains in full force despite any determination by the Librarian of Congress that noninfringing uses of certain classes of works will likely be adversely affected by the access prohibition.[45] The device prohibition makes unlawful the manufacture and trafficking of the very circumvention devices that all but sophisticated computer programmers need to circumvent technological access controls. As a result, even persons legally entitled to circumvent access controls will be unable to do so.

Similarly, the DMCA's device prohibitions also apply to devices designed to circumvent technology controls over uses, not merely technology that controls access. Consequently, even users with authorized access wishing to circumvent use controls in order to make noninfringing copies of copyrighted works—an act that is permitted without the authorization of the copyright owner—will generally be unable to obtain the device or service needed to make such a copy. The same is true of those wishing to circumvent use controls in order to copy public domain material that is intermingled with copyright-protected material.

Finally, although the statute directs the Librarian to consider possible adverse impacts on particular uses that lie at the core of free speech and fair use concerns, it permits the Librarian to exempt from the access prohibition only "particular classes of works" (such as physics textbooks and musical works), not particular uses or users (such as news reporting and library patrons). As a result, the Librarian faces severe constraints in his ability to blunt adverse impacts on noninfringing uses. Those constraints are strikingly evident in the Librarian's anticircumvention rule-making. Emphasizing the circumscribed scope of its authority, the Librarian has exempted only a handful of narrow classes of works. These include, for example, "computer programs protected by dongles that prevent access due to malfunction or damage and which are obsolete," "literary works distributed in ebook format when all existing ebook editions of the work . . . contain access controls that prevent the enabling of . . . the book's read-aloud function," and "sound re-cordings . . . protected by technological protection measures that . . . create or exploit . . . flaws or vulnerabilities that compromise the security of personal computers, when circumvention is accomplished solely for the purpose of good faith testing, investigating or correcting such security flaws or vul-nerabilities."[46]

In a much welcome development, the Librarian's 2006 anticircumvention rule-making also exempts "[a]udiovisual works included in the educational library of a college or university's film or media studies department, when circumvention is accomplished for the purpose of making compilations of portions of those works for educational use in the classroom by media studies or film professors."[47] As noted earlier, however, the Librarian has no author-ity to permit the manufacture or supply of software needed to circumvent technological controls on DVDs. As a result, professors must scrounge for illegal software to actually make use of their exemption from the circum-vention prohibition.

Given these defects, the DMCA's anticircumvention provisions should not pass First Amendment muster. As *Turner* states, "A content neutral regulation will be sustained under the First Amendment if it advances im-portant government interests unrelated to the suppression of free speech and does not burden substantially more speech than necessary to further those interests."[48] Even assuming that the DMCA actually serves an important government interest, it fails the requirement that speech-burdening regulation be narrowly tailored to avoid burdening more speech than necessary. Content-neutral regulation need not be the least restrictive alternative to achieving the governmental interest but must, nevertheless, burden no more speech than is "essential to the furtherance of that interest."[49]

Courts commonly find that the presence of less restrictive alternatives within the same statutory scheme indicates that a content-neutral regulation is insufficiently tailored to survive First Amendment review.[50] In that regard, the DMCA's failure to meet the narrowly tailored requirement is apparent on the face of both the Copyright Act as a whole and the DMCA in particular. Perhaps most obviously, Congress could have forbidden circumvention only when undertaken to infringe copyright. By the same token, it could have required that content providers deploy control technology only as needed to secure protection for their copyrights. The DMCA includes two such provisions, one involving broadcasters' ephemeral and archival recordings and the other, analog VCRs. Each requires that technological protection measures be configured to enable copying that is permitted under the Copyright Act.[51] Those provisions are concessions given to industry associations present at the DMCA bargaining table. If Congress had truly sought to protect the general public's First Amendment interests, it could have extended that model to all technological protection measures. It could have required, for example, that content providers enable users to circumvent for purposes of fair use or to gain access to public domain material. A recent European Union directive that also protects the integrity of digital rights management technology takes just that broad approach. It effectively obligates content providers who deploy technology controls to provide means for users to freely exercise their rights of access and use under national copyright laws.[52]

Just as obviously, Congress could have shorn up the DMCA provisions that are purportedly designed to ameliorate the Act's speech burdens. As I have discussed, by their very terms, these provisions are utterly inadequate to their task. Despite its lip service to free speech and fair use, the Act provides for no fair use defense to the access or device prohibitions. Likewise, the Librarian of Congress review mechanism is fatally circumscribed. Since the review pertains only to classes of works, not uses or users, speech interests in access and use that are not narrowly confined to a given class of works will continue to be burdened. And since the Librarian has no authority to suspend the device provisions, even users whom the Librarian exempts from the access prohibition will, in practice, be unable to gain access.

In sum, the anticircumvention provisions should not survive *Turner* scrutiny (or, for that matter, any other formulation of intermediate scrutiny that might be applied following *Eldred's* apparent narrowing of *Turner's* applicability to "forced speech"). The DMCA provisions quite clearly protrude beyond the traditional contours of copyright law; subjecting them to heightened scrutiny exposes both their internal contradictions and their capacious, unduly speech-burdening scope.

COPYRIGHT'S TRADITIONAL FREE SPEECH SAFEGUARDS

Eldred leaves room for the First Amendment to play a role *within* copyright's traditional contours as well. The *Eldred* Court appended what might be a significant footnote to its statement that First Amendment scrutiny is unnecessary when Congress has not altered copyright's traditional contours. The footnote proclaims that in both facial challenges to copyright legislation and First Amendment defenses to copyright infringement claims, "it is appropriate to construe copyright's internal safeguards to accommodate First Amendment concerns."[53] In the context of the facial challenge in *Eldred,* the footnote reiterates a cardinal rule of judicial restraint: courts should not reach constitutional issues if they can interpret a statute to eliminate doubts regarding its constitutionality. But the footnote also says something about how copyright's internal safeguards should generally be construed. It suggests that courts should interpret and define their scope in a manner that comports with First Amendment concerns. In other words, contrary to the prior suggestion of some commentators and lower courts,[54] copyright's internal safeguards do have constitutional import: even if the First Amendment imposes no external constraints on copyright, First Amendment principles must animate our understanding and application of copyright law. Indeed, only by employing that First Amendment metric can we take seriously the *Eldred* Court's proposition that copyright's traditional safeguards actually serve to protect First Amendment values.

The Eleventh Circuit's decision in the *Wind Done Gone* case, issued just over a year before the Supreme Court decided *Eldred,* presents a laudable example of that approach. The Eleventh Circuit reversed the district court's preliminary injunction forbidding distribution of Alice Randall's acerbic *Gone with the Wind* sequel. In so doing, the Eleventh Circuit repeatedly invoked the First Amendment as a lodestar for interpreting copyright law.[55] Copyright law, the court emphasized, must be construed to incorporate First Amendment values and comport with First Amendment strictures. The court underscored that the fair use privilege in particular has "constitutional significance as a guarantor to access and use for First Amendment purposes."

Accordingly, in conducting fair use analysis, "we must remain cognizant of the First Amendment protections interwoven into copyright law." Applying that First Amendment construction, the Eleventh Circuit concluded that Randall was likely to prevail on her fair use claim and that "the issuance of the injunction was at odds with the shared principles of the First Amendment and the copyright law, acting as a prior restraint on speech because the public had not had access to Randall's ideas or viewpoint in the form of expression that she chose."

The *Eldred* footnote and the Eleventh Circuit's ruling regarding *The Wind Done Gone* suggest a number of ways that the First Amendment could and should be brought to bear to revive the fair use doctrine. I will give three brief examples: the first substantive, the second involving burden of proof, and the third involving remedy. Each would lend support to the free speech approach to fair use in the face of the market-centered Blackstonian property line of fair use cases spurred by the Supreme Court's reasoning in *Harper & Row v. The Nation,* as discussed in chapter 4.

First, courts should give renewed weight in fair use analysis to the defendant's transformative expression and purpose. As the Second Circuit has recently emphasized, fair use should typically extend to uses that serve a fundamentally different expressive purpose from the original by employing the original "in the creation of new information, new aesthetics, new insights and understandings."[56] So long as the defendant copies no more than reasonably necessary for such purposes, fair use should not be defeated merely because the defendant's work competes in an actual or potential market for derivative works based on the original.

Reformulations that serve as commentary on the original or on some aspect of society at large that the original in some way embodies or reflects would fall within the ambit of such favored uses. So would borrowing to illustrate or authenticate history, biography, or news reporting, as would creative appropriation as reference or homage in artistic movements such as hip-hop or appropriation art. Copying works in ways that vastly increase the accessibility of our store of knowledge, including Google's digital scanning of books and copying short excerpts from newspaper articles in order to make those sources available for Internet search, should also qualify as a favored transformative purpose.

A First Amendment–animated fair use doctrine, in short, would typically find fair use whenever the defendant adds new expression or, like Google, value, that imbues the original with a different purpose or character in furtherance of distinct creative, critical, communicative, or informational objectives. The First Amendment would place the defendant speaker's transformative purpose, rather than harm to the copyright holder's potential market, at the center of fair use analysis. The First Amendment, not just copyright and free speech policy, should mandate that fair use doctrine be construed to accord Alan Cranston the right to create and distribute his unauthorized, highly critical translation of *Mein Kampf* even if that diminishes the market for Hitler's authorized translation.

Second, once the defendant shows a colorable claim of fair use, the burden should pass to the copyright holder to prove that the defendant has copied more than necessary for effective speech and that the defendant's use is likely to harm the actual or potential market for the copyright holder's work. Market-centered fair use doctrine places the defendant in the onerous position of proving a negative: that the allegedly infringing use—and other possible uses like it—will not even harm a market, including a market for derivative works, that the copyright holder has no concrete plans to exploit. That formidable burden unduly chills speech and is inconsistent with First Amendment goals. It also runs squarely against the standard First Amendment rule that the burden of proof as to constitutionally relevant facts—such as the veracity of an allegedly libelous statement—must be placed on those who would stifle or punish the speaker, not the speaker herself. Otherwise, as is sadly the case with the Blackstonian approach to fair use, "the possibility of mistaken fact-finding—inherent in all litigation—will create the danger that the legitimate utterance will be penalized," and that speakers will engage in broad self-censorship in order to avoid that risk.[57]

Third, where the defendant presents a colorable but unsuccessful claim of fair use, courts should generally award damages in the amount of a reasonable license fee instead of enjoining the use. In that manner, defendants will be better able to convey their message so long as they pay what is in effect a compulsory license fee set by the court. The Supreme Court has repeatedly suggested that given copyright's paramount goal of stimulating "the creation and publication of edifying matter," in cases of colorable but failed claims of fair use, courts should award damages rather than grant injunctive relief in order to further the "strong public interest in the publication of the secondary work."[58] But current copyright law constrains judges' ability to tailor damages to give the defendant a meaningful opportunity and incentive to publish the secondary work. The Copyright Act gives copyright holder plaintiffs the right to recover what amount to punitive or expropriative damages from the defendant: the plaintiff may elect to receive either statutory damages or actual damages suffered as a result of the infringement plus any profits the defendant earns from the infringement that exceed those damages.[59] If the strong public interest in publication is to be served, judges must have discretion to fashion a reasonable ongoing royalty rather than awarding sizable damages that effectively deter potential speakers from risking infringement. A constitutionalized copyright law would provide for such a possibility as a matter of First Amendment mandate.

Courts have been understandably reluctant to adopt rules that would require them to entertain First Amendment defenses in individual copyright infringement actions. As Judge Posner recently interposed, "Copyright law and the principles of equitable relief are quite complicated enough without the superimposition of First Amendment case law on them."[60] But copyright can "accommodate First Amendment concerns" without adding a layer of fact-specific, case-by-case First Amendment analysis. As courts have done in other areas, the First Amendment should be applied to mandate global changes in copyright doctrine, such as reinforcing the fair use privilege and giving judges the discretion to fashion damages in the form of reasonable royalties. Indeed, First Amendment principles, to paraphrase the Eleventh Circuit, are already interwoven into the history and framework of copyright law. To remain cognizant of those principles requires only that courts peel back copyright's recent expansion, not fundamentally modify traditional copyright doctrine. It insists that copyright be understood and construed as a limited statutory entitlement, not a Blackstonian property right.

Conclusion

The judicial immunization of traditional copyright from First Amendment scrutiny is a peculiar and pernicious anomaly. In *Eldred,* the Supreme Court largely perpetuated that anomaly, at least with respect to imposing external First Amendment constraints on traditional copyright. Nevertheless, *Eldred* leaves open considerable room for First Amendment intervention in copyright law. Copyright Act amendments, such as the DMCA anticircumvention provisions, that extend copyright holder prerogatives beyond copyright's traditional contours are precisely the type of speech regulation that, even following *Eldred,* should be subject to First Amendment scrutiny. As *Eldred* suggests, courts should also "construe copyright's internal safeguards to accommodate First Amendment concerns." Today's palsied safety valves too often intolerably exacerbate the dangers of self-censorship. Following the Supreme Court's suggestion, courts should reinvigorate copyright's safeguards in light of First Amendment strictures. Among other possible applications, they should mandate greater leeway for transformative uses of copyrighted works. They should also require that copyright holders bear the burden of proving market harm in fair use analysis and award damages in the form of a reasonable royalty where the user raises a colorable but unsuccessful claim of fair use.

Courts, as I have explained, are not the only realm in which First Amendment values should come into play in defining and delimiting copyright. Concern over copyright's speech-burdening potential should also animate congressional legislation and Copyright Office regulation and arbitration. In the next chapter, I accordingly consider how First Amendment values might color copyright law beyond what First Amendment doctrine requires. I outline a number of ways in which the Copyright Act could be modified to be more solicitous of speech while still preserving the copyright incentive's positive contribution to our "system of freedom of expression."

| Remaking Copyright in the First Amendment's Image

A COPYRIGHT LAW ANIMATED by free speech values must navigate between the shoals of proprietary lockup and digital anarchy. It must be tailored to minimize copyright's speech burdens—even beyond what might be required by First Amendment doctrine. Yet it must simultaneously serve copyright's continuing "engine of free expression" role.

In this chapter I sketch a few of the many possible alternatives for paring back speech-chilling copyright holder control while continuing to provide ample remuneration for market-based authors and media firms dedicated to producing original expression. My proposals tend toward narrowing copyright holders' proprietary entitlements. In some cases, indeed, I would convert proprietary copyrights to liability rules, rules that deny copyright holders a veto but entitle them to compensation for use of their works in an amount set by a court, statute, or administrative body. But my proposals do not all result in a net loss for copyright holders. In some areas, I propose mechanisms for payment where today copyright holders receive nothing, either because the law is uncertain regarding fair use or because copyright enforcement faces significant obstacles.

I group my discussion roughly in line with the speech burdens that the proposals address: copyright's extension to creative appropriation, copyright's inordinately lengthy term, the conflict between copyright and personal uses, the conflict between copyright incumbents and new technological media, and paracopyright. I also propose limited "moral rights" protection for creators in line with my discussion of the free speech benefits of that protection in chapter 3. All these proposals are legislative; they would further free speech policy through amendment to the Copyright Act. They are meant to supplement the First Amendment invalidation of portions of the DMCA and the constitutionalization of fair use discussed in the last chapter.

Creative Appropriation

Creative appropriation ranges from modifications and adaptations of a single work to samplings, remixes, and mashups that incorporate an array of discrete components from numerous existing works. Copyright's speech burdens are not limited to such creative appropriations: effective speech may sometimes entail copying or distributing existing expression without modification. But copyright's restrictions on speakers' ability to recast existing expression or incorporate it in a new context present the most striking and poignant examples of the copyright/free speech conflict. And that conflict has reached new breadth and intensity with the advent of digital technology, which makes it so easy for so many people to appropriate the images, sounds, and texts of popular culture and then add their own creative, self-expressive gloss, criticism, or radical retransformation. Digitization, indeed, makes technologically possible the infinite manipulability of existing works, opening up a myriad of possibilities for transformative uses.

As we have seen, through most of the nineteenth century authors were free to build on existing works so long as they made a substantial independent contribution. But today, speech that builds upon an existing work commonly runs afoul of the copyright holder's broad proprietary rights. Copyright now includes an exclusive right to make derivative works. Moreover, the reproduction right has expanded dramatically. In addition to substantial literal or near-literal copying, it now encompasses nonliteral "total concept and feel" similarity and literal copying of small fragments of the original work. To the extent copyright holders are able and willing to enforce these expansive rights, manifold instances of creative appropriation and even entire creative genres, like early hip-hop music, will be gravely hindered or suppressed.

In response to copyright's extension to derivative works, sampling, and other creative appropriations, a number of commentators have proposed that copyright holders' exclusive rights be limited to exact or near-exact copies of their works. Jed Rubenfeld argues, for example, that granting copyright holders proprietary rights to prevent modifications, reformulations, and derivative works suppresses secondary authors' "freedom of imagination" in contravention of the First Amendment.[1] Rubenfeld insists that imaginative works must be free from claims for damages as well as injunction. Rather, secondary authors should only be required to disgorge to the copyright holder the proportionate share of their profits attributable to using the underlying work. In that way, copyright holders could neither prevent nor penalize speakers from using existing works in exercising their imagination. But they would be entitled to just apportionment of any profits speakers earn from incorporating copyrighted expression into new, creative speech.

Professor Rubenfeld's proposal would go considerably farther than the First Amendment–mandated rules regarding fair use for transformative expression and judicially crafted compulsory licenses for colorable fair use that I proffered in the last chapter. Much creative appropriation would qualify neither as transformative expression nor as colorable fair use. Say, for example, that a commercial press publishes a new, unlicensed sequel of J. K. Rowling's *Harry Potter* series for a mass-market audience, or that a major motion picture studio produces an unlicensed motion picture version of a Rowling *Harry Potter* novel, and that neither unlicensed work in any way criticizes or comments on Rowling's *Harry Potter*. Each of these works would constitute creatively appropriative works of imagination. But neither would serve a fundamentally different expressive purpose from that for which Rowling created her *Harry Potter* characters, settings, and dialogue, certainly not in the same sense as would weaving *Harry Potter* characters into lesbian-themed fan fiction appearing on a nonmarket Web site or a user-generated mashup of *Harry Potter* movie clips posted on YouTube. Moreover, each commercial work would likely cause concrete, significant harm to a potential market that authors like Rowling would be reasonably expected to enter, mass-market sequels and movie versions of popular novels.

I am not at all certain that the First Amendment law mandates secondary authors' wholesale freedom to appropriate copyrighted expression beyond that which would constitute even colorable fair use. But, with the modifications I will presently discuss, Rubenfeld's proposal may well provide a solid basis for free speech policy. Even competing derivative works aimed largely at the same market can present diverse views and artistic sensibilities, as well as giving rein to secondary authors' "freedom of imagination." And while an absence of an exclusive right to prepare derivative works is likely to diminish authors' incentives to create in some instances, in others the competition might even spur creation. It has been speculated, for instance, that Miguel de Cervantes hurried to complete Part II to his classic story of Don Quixote after reading a specious sequel that ridiculed Part I and, as a result, successfully produced his finished work shortly before he died.[2]

Now for the modifications to Rubenfeld's proposal. First, eliminating the exclusive derivative right would sometimes severely undermine the incentive that copyright provides for the creation of the original work. This problem would be particularly acute whenever a creative appropriation maintains the essential content of the original work in the same or another form. For example, secondary works that are quite similar to the original, including edited books, films, and television programs, could act as market substitutes for the unedited versions. Likewise, some works, like film or television screenplays, are created only to serve as the basis for a derivative work. In such cases, giving the author the right to prevent unauthorized derivative versions may be necessary for the creation of the original.

Second, a derivative right might sometimes be necessary to avoid "multiple taker" problems.[3] Just like original expression, certain creative appropriations take a number of months or years to produce and require a significant capital investment. In some such instances, the absence of an exclusive derivative right would undermine the incentive to produce the creative appropriation. Consider, for example, the production of a motion picture based on a popular contemporary novel. Few studios would invest the tens of millions of dollars required to produce a commercial full-length feature film without the right to prevent another studio from simultaneously releasing a competing film based on the same novel.[4] In order to maintain the copyright incentive for such capital- and time-intensive creative appropriations, we may wish to accord an exclusive right to create and commercially distribute a derivative work in a given medium for a short time, perhaps five to ten years. In that way, the creator of the derivative work would enjoy a legally protected first-mover advantage. Following the short period of exclusivity, others would be free to compete with their own creative interpretations of the same underlying work.

Third, in permitting others to modify existing works, the law should take account of individual authors' personal interest in creative control and authorship credit. I discuss those "moral rights" issues later in this chapter.

Finally, if secondary authors' only liability for permitted derivative works is a judicially determined compulsory license in the amount of their profits attributable to the underlying work, they would have an incentive to pay nothing and take their chances at facing an unfavorable apportionment of profits in court in the event they get sued, rather than coming to an agreement up front.[5] To blunt that incentive, the law should impose a hefty monetary penalty on a secondary author who fails to notify the copyright owner of his intent to produce the derivative work and to pay the copyright holder's offering price for a license if the court ultimately determines that apportioned profits due to the copyright holder equal or exceed that offered price. To induce the copyright holder to make a reasonable offer, the law should also penalize the copyright holder if the judicially determined apportioned profits fall some percentage short of the offered license fee.

Such mechanisms for inducing voluntary licensing raise an important point, one that is equally applicable to the judicially crafted compulsory license that I proposed for colorable fair uses in the last chapter. Rules that empower judges to determine the license fees to be paid to copyright holders do not necessarily mean that judges, rather than the parties, will actually set the price. Rather, the parties would often bargain, and could be induced to bargain reasonably, under the shadow of a judicially imposed liability rule should negotiations fail. As in other areas of the law, moving from a property to a liability rule does not spell the end of private bargaining. After all, parties commonly settle lawsuits for damages. Liability rules merely alter bargaining positions and terms. In our context, they remove the copyright holder's veto and ability to extract a supracompetitive price by holding up the secondary author or transformative user. But rules that provide for judicially determined compulsory licenses can still provide for significant remuneration for copyright holders and, in many cases, bargained-for license terms rather than judicial fiat.[6]

Copyright Duration

It is exceedingly difficult to approximate a copyright term that would optimally promote the creation and dissemination of original expression while minimizing speech burdens. Among other factors, we must account for copyright's breadth of protection: the narrower the scope of copyright holder rights, the longer the optimal copyright term might be. But it is clear by virtually any measure that today's copyright term is inordinately long, that it imposes speech burdens without concomitant speech benefits.

Congress's recent extension of the copyright term for yet another twenty years, making the standard term seventy years after the year of the author's death, provides essentially no additional incentive for authors to create original expression. As leading economists explained in their amicus brief in support of *Eldred*'s constitutional challenge of the term extension, the present value of supplemental revenue from an additional twenty years so far in the future is negligible, even aside from discounting for any new work's highly uncertain prospects for enduring commercial success.[7] Indeed, all evidence suggests that, from the prospective author's view, the bifurcated twenty-eight-year initial term and twenty-eight-year renewal term of the 1909 Copyright Act provided more than enough incentive for the creation and dissemination of new expression. The copyrights in the vast majority of works that were published under that incentive structure were allowed to lapse after the first term (although it is unclear how many authors of those works anticipated from the outset that they would enjoy only a twenty-eight-year term).

At the same time, copyright's extended term imposes a tangible speech burden. Every year that a work is kept from the public domain is a year in which the work cannot be disseminated, recast, or incorporated into new expression without the copyright holder's permission. It is another year in which the expressive reinterpretation of works central to our cultural heritage is subject to a copyright holder's veto. Because of the 1998 copyright term extension, authors must continue to obtain a copyright license to adopt dialogue or plot from novels like *The Great Gatsby, The Magic Mountain, Peter Pan,* and *Elmer Gantry,* refashion characters like Mickey Mouse and Peter Pan, or use Tin Pan Alley songs like "Let's Do It (Let's Fall in Love)" as period-piece music for documentaries about life during the Great Depression.

Moreover, particularly for the millions of older works of less enduring popularity, it is immensely difficult, if not impossible, to trace copyright ownership and determine who holds the particular rights that must be cleared for the desired use. That problem of such "orphan works" stems directly from Congress's extension of the copyright term and repeal of any requirement that copyright holders renew or register their copyrights. The ubiquity of orphan works imposes a serious chill on the speech of numerous filmmakers, archivists, writers, musicians, and broadcasters, who regularly desist from incorporating works or bits of works, including period film footage, photographs, and sound recordings that are an invaluable part of our historical record and cultural heritage, for which the copyright owner cannot be readily identified.

COPYRIGHT AS PRESERVATION

Copyright owners sometimes argue that an extended copyright term actually enhances access by providing incentives for publishers to make old works available. As Jack Valenti, former president of the Motion Picture Association of America, envisioned it, the true orphan works problem arises from copyright's absence, not the great difficulty in locating the copyright holder: "A public domain work is an orphan. No one is responsible for its life . . . it becomes soiled and haggard."[8] Similarly, William Landes and Richard

Posner argue that just like any unowned resource, public domain works may be underused. Since no publisher can "establish a property right" in such works, "the incentives of publishers to publish and promote them may well be inadequate from a social standpoint."[9]

These advocates of a potentially perpetual copyright far overstate their case. Publishers regularly put out new editions and releases of public domain works. In fact, a comparison of public domain works from the 1910s and early 1920s with their still copyrighted counterparts from the 1920s shows that far more public domain than copyrighted works are actually distributed to the public.[10] As Mark Lemley points out, publishers' evident willingness to print and distribute public domain books, without any continuing monopoly incentive, should not surprise us. After all, we do not worry that producers of other commodities and consumer goods would fail to produce them in a competitive market. Copyright for old works, Lemley argues, is thus superfluous at best: "If people are willing to pay enough to justify printing copies of *Ulysses,* copies of *Ulysses* will be printed. And if people are not willing to pay even the marginal cost of printing, granting exclusive rights over *Ulysses* would not solve the problem."[11]

Lemley's argument holds only to a point. The maintenance, storage, and new release of some old master recordings, films, and even some manuscripts has historically required considerable capital investment. Traditional public goods economics tells us that publishers would underinvest in maintaining and releasing these old works absent an ability to recover capital investment through a continuing exclusive right to market them. But digital technology sharply reduces the need for capital investment in maintenance, storage, restoration, and new releases. Once digital copies of a work are disseminated, they can be maintained and disseminated further, or reside in virtual libraries, in mint condition, at very little cost per work. That is already true for texts. As the costs of digital storage and dissemination continue to plummet, it is also increasingly the case for music, graphics, video clips, television programs, and even full-length motion pictures. Works stored in digital form in multiple sites are forever available at a click of the mouse, with no need to invest in preparing, manufacturing, and distributing copies of new editions and releases. As more and more works become available in digital form, there is thus an ever-decreasing need for copyright to provide an incentive for publishers to continue disseminating old works.

New works are increasingly being created and released in digital form from the get-go. But what of the vast inventory of expression created before the advent of digital technology? Might copyright provide an incentive for undertaking the time and expense of converting old works to publicly available digital form? It is possible. Unlike with print editions of *Ulysses,* where every publisher bears more or less the same production costs, the publisher that is the first to convert *Ulysses* from print to digital format would bear costs that others then able to download and make free digital copies would not. For that matter, the same may be true regarding periodic demands to convert digital content to new formats for use on new devices. Despite the capacity of digital technology to make works forever available, might some form of exclusive right be needed to induce market actors to make certain that vintage works remain widely accessible as the digital formats in which they are stored become functionally obsolete?

If recent experience is our guide, the answer, it seems, is "quite possibly not." There is a wealth of evidence that subsisting copyrights in old works is more of a hindrance than a help in the digitization of our cultural heritage. Preserving and making available old manuscripts, books, sound records, works of art, and film has traditionally been the province of public libraries, educational institutions, museums, and nonprofit foundations. And such organizations, including the Library of Congress, have now turned much of their attention to digitization. The rapidly falling cost of digitizing pre-digital works, coupled with the Internet's capacity for marshaling the volunteer efforts of numerous, geographically dispersed individuals, has also spawned new digital archivists. These include the Project Gutenberg Literary Archive, which, as of this writing, holds a collection of some 20,000 electronic books, produced by hundreds of volunteers and available for free download over the Internet. They also include the Internet Archive, which houses tens of thousands of digitized and born-digital texts, music, graphics, photographs, and video, and the Carnegie Mellon One Million Book Digital Library Project, which has already scanned more than 600,000 books for free Internet access.

The vast majority of works available through such nonprofit archives are in the public domain. As the archives have emphasized, until works enter the public domain, the process of finding the copyright owner or owners and clearing rights is prohibitively time-consuming and expensive. At the same time, only a small fraction of our cultural heritage that remains protected by copyright is available to the public. A copyright owner has no incentive to maintain a work in circulation, revive an out-of-print work, or even scan or preserve copies of old works unless the expected profit from doing so exceeds that which could be garnered from marketing new works or engaging in some other business altogether. It is not surprising that a vast array of old but still copyrighted expression that would unlikely draw commercially significant audience share remains orphaned. Our best hope for preserving and making those works available, it appears, is to remove them from copyright constraint and allow nonprofit, volunteer, and publicly funded libraries and archivists freely to exploit the efficiencies of digital technology.

Or, perhaps even better, find a company that can profit from a massive investment in digitizing old books without having to obtain proprietary rights. That, of course, brings us to Google. As we have seen, Google's Book Search Project contemplates scanning and digitizing some 15 million books and documents in the collections of leading research libraries, followed by Google's display of the full text of public domain works and three-sentence snippets of in-copyright books in response to search engine queries. Google hopes to recover its up to $375 million investment through search-inquiry-targeted advertising, including ads from sellers of the books that show up in the search. Despite this potential boon for bookselling, Google's Book Search has been met with copyright infringement suits brought by major publishers and the Authors Guild.

As the Google Book Search Project suggests, commercial entities that earn revenue from providing search capabilities and other added-value services to digital content can also be expected to underwrite digitization costs. Indeed, the Google agreement is nonexclusive; it leaves the libraries free to provide access to their digital collections directly to library patrons and to allow scanning by competing search engines. In sum, all the massive digitization by Google, research libraries, government agencies, and nonprofit archives is being undertaken without exclusive rights in the digitized collections. Lingering proprietary copyright protection in old works is an impediment, not an incentive, to digitizing those works.

COPYRIGHT AND "CONGESTION EXTERNALITIES"

Of course, the problem of copyright as an impediment to the availability of old works does not apply in the same way to works of enduring popularity that retain their commercial value. We do not need research libraries or Google to keep Mickey Mouse or the songs of Cole Porter in circulation. Copyright holders have every incentive to continue to distribute and license those valuable works.

For that reason, commentators have outlined various possible mechanisms for separating out works of enduring commercial value from the vast majority of old works. The proposals generally favor giving copyright owners rights to extend their copyrights though periodic renewal, but would impose renewal fees as a means of dissuading those whose works having little market value from renewing.[12] Landes and Posner even propose a copyright of indefinite duration, a regime in which copyright owners could retain copyright protection for a profitable work for as long as they are willing to pay a periodic renewal fee.[13]

Yet just because copyright owners could be expected to continue to distribute works of enduring commercial value does not mean that a lengthy copyright term for those works is needed or warranted, especially in light of the free speech burdens that copyright imposes. In support of a potentially infinite copyright term for valuable works, Landes and Posner raise the banner of "congestion externalities." They argue that absent the copyright holder's proprietary control, multiple and diverse recastings and creative interpretations of popular works would rob those works of their unique meaning, thus eviscerating their economic and social value. To prevent that dilution of meaning, in other words, Disney must have exclusive, proprietary control over Mickey Mouse, just as the Margaret Mitchell estate must control *Gone with the Wind*—and Beethoven's and Shakespeare's heirs be given a veto over all interpretations and recastings of those authors' works—for so long as the works continue to have substantial economic value.

Landes and Posner are wrong on two counts. First, many public domain works are subject to a vast array of reformulations, sequels, and interpretative presentations without any seeming diminution in their expressive power and social value. Consider the numerous and highly varied interpretations and adaptations of Shakespeare. Shakespeare's works are hardly tarnished by such modern permutations as *West Side Story, Rosencrantz and Guildenstern Are Dead,* and *Shakespeare Classic Comics,* not to mention innovative productions recasting the plays in different times and locales. Likewise with respect to the varied interpretative performances of Beethoven and Bach, or even the replication of paintings by van Gogh and Matisse on coffee mugs.

Second, and, I think, more important, a vibrant culture is not a static culture. Even if competing uses and versions cause the Mickey Mouse character to lose some of its clarity or come to represent something very different from its original image—and even if *West Side Story* does forever color our view of Romeo and Juliet—so be it. Art and culture must inevitably change and grow. New versions and interpretations replace the old. Some classics fall by the wayside, and some remain central to our cultural heritage. Indeed, even classics that remain "unadulterated" are necessarily understood quite differently by modern audiences than by the original readers, listeners, and viewers. Landes and Posner's "congestion externality," the potential loss of economic value for any given cultural work resulting from diverse creative reformulations, is a central feature, not a bug, of a robust system of free expression. Even if a period of broad, proprietary control is needed to provide an incentive for authors like Margaret Mitchell to write novels and enterprises like MGM to invest large sums in creating motion picture versions of popular novels, once that incentive purpose is satisfied, we are far better off with an open contest of multiple uses, editions, and interpretative recastings than an heir's or corporation's perpetual veto.

PROPOSALS FOR REFORM

What, then, is to be done about today's absurdly lengthy copyright term? Ideally, copyright should be returned to the bifurcated twenty-eight-year initial term and twenty-eight-year renewal term for published works in force prior to the 1976 Copyright Act, with a term of the life of the author plus five years for unpublished works, to give authors the prerogative to withhold works from publication while they are alive and authors' heirs an incentive to publish those works soon after the author's death. But since 1989, the United States has been required by the Berne Convention to maintain a term of at least the life of the author plus fifty years for works from other countries. Moreover, Congress is unlikely to rescind the extra twenty years that the Copyright Term Extension Act added for both foreign and U.S. works on top of that minimum requirement. Accordingly, there have been a number of proposals to blunt the speech-burdening effects of the long term without actually repealing it. Thoughtful proposals include introducing the passage of time as a factor favoring fair use and requirements that copyright holders must periodically renew their copyright in order to enjoy the full twenty years added by the CTEA.

Most recently, the U.S. Copyright Office has sought to address the problem of orphan works. It has proposed legislation that would limit the copyright holder's monetary remedy to "reasonable compensation" (what the Copyright Office defines as an arm's length, willing buyer–willing seller license fee) when (1) prior to the infringement, the infringer tried but failed to locate the owner despite having "performed a good faith, reasonably diligent search," and (2) during the course of the infringement, the infringer "provided attribution to the author and the copyright owner."[14] Those who infringe copyrights in orphan works "without any purpose of direct or indirect commercial advantage" would be exempt from monetary liability. A copyright owner could obtain an injunction to prohibit further use of the work that was previously orphan, but not where the infringer has "prepared or commenced preparation of a derivative work that recasts, transforms or adapts the infringed work with a significant amount of the infringer's expression" and pays "reasonable compensation" for ongoing use.

All these proposals take steps in the right direction, but none comes close to the significant reduction in the copyright term that free speech policy truly warrants (even if the *Eldred* Court is correct that the First Amendment does not so require). In particular, the Copyright Office proposal has far more limited ambitions. Most obviously, the proposal does not aim to ameliorate the burden on speech imposed by lengthy copyright protection for works, including culturally salient icons like *Gone with the Wind,* for which the copyright owner may be easily found but unwilling to license the speaker's desired use, whether at all or at a price that is not prohibitive. Nor does the Copyright Office proposal address the problem of vintage licensing agreements that leave unclear to the original parties and their successors, as well as to prospective users, who holds the authority to give permission to adapt or disseminate the work in a new technology such as the Internet.

Indeed, the Copyright Office proposal does not even adequately solve the problem of orphan works. The reason is that the proposal aims as much as possible to mimic the rubric of a proprietary copyright regime, in which the burden is on the user to affirmatively seek out and obtain permission and copyright holders are entitled to hold out for the price they are willing to receive. Hence, rather than reinstituting a modified form of renewal or even requiring copyright holders to post updated ownership and contact information on a publicly available registry, the Copyright Office would put the onus on the speaker who wishes to use an orphan work to meet the nebulous requirement of a "good faith, reasonably diligent search." The proposal would also put the speaker at risk of having to pay a judicially determined arm's length license fee if the copyright owner should ever come out of the woodwork. Granted, the proposal would exempt uses made without "any purpose of direct or indirect commercial advantage" from that potential liability. But given Congress's and courts' niggardly interpretation of "noncommercial" uses, under which failing to pay the "customary price" constitutes a commercial use, risk-averse speakers will be hard-pressed to rely on that exemption. A documentary filmmaker who sells a broadcasting license to PBS might be found to have made a commercial use of multiple orphan clips included in the film and face liability for the license fees for past and future use measured by the willing-seller rather than fair-return standard.

Documentary filmmakers and other cottage industry speakers can ill afford those uncertainties and risk of exposure. At a minimum, Congress should place some onus on copyright holders to facilitate rights clearance by requiring that they list their works and contact information on a public registry. With respect to most foreign works, international treaty obligations would preclude requiring such a formality as a condition of copyright protection. But Congress could provide a remedial inducement for compliance by setting a discrete, nominal cap on the reasonable compensation that a speaker must pay after having unsuccessfully attempted to identify and locate a copyright owner who failed to list on a public registry. That way, speakers—and their financers, distributors, and errors-and-omissions insurers—can account for the maximum risk of incorporating orphan works.

Consumptive Uses

The explosion of individuals' sharing and remixing popular songs and movies over the Internet brings the tension between copyright and speech to millions of homes. Many embrace the collection, exchange, and transformation of existing works as part and parcel of the individual liberty, self-expression, and creative collaboration for which we celebrate the Internet. Others fear that file swapping poses a mortal threat to authors, artists, and copyright industries, threatening to still many of the creative voices that fill our system of free expression.

The peer-to-peer controversy has degenerated into a steadily intensifying war of words and legal action. The copyright industries have successfully shut down a number of peer-to-peer networks and user-posted-content Web sites and continue to bring lawsuits against others. They have also sought to compel search engine, telecommunications, and consumer electronics companies to disable unlicensed peer sharing and posting of copyright-protected works. The industries have targeting tens of thousands of individual files traders as well.

Yet, despite this multipronged attack, unlicensed file swapping continues apace. Copyright industries still hope to push unlicensed file sharing out of the mainstream through a combination of litigation, third-party policing, digital rights management, and enticing alternatives. But they have generally despaired of stamping out the phenomenon altogether.

As I discussed in chapter 3, much file sharing is little more than the passive consumption of entertainment consumer goods (without paying for them), and thus does not constitute "speech." Yet file sharing implicates free speech interests nonetheless. File sharing is not just downloading music and movies for free. For many, it is a vehicle for discovering works that are otherwise not available, exploring entire new genres, making personalized compilations, participating in online discussion about cultural expression, and posting creative remixes, sequels, and modifications of popular works. Moreover, the unlicensed availability of popular copyrighted works on file sharing and user-posted-content sites like YouTube helps to draw a sufficiently large audience to render those sites viable platforms for a plethora of user-created content as well. In that manner, user file sharing helps to underwrite alternative outlets for speakers in an otherwise highly concentrated media sector.

At bottom, then, seen as part of the broader picture of peer expression over the Internet, the problem with file sharing is not that it takes place—and takes place on a massive scale—without copyright holders' permission, but that it takes place without compensating authors or copyright holders. In this context, as in others I have discussed, it would serve free speech policy to convert copyright from a right of proprietary control to a right to receive compensation. Copyright law should not serve as a tool for media incumbents, or for media-licensed distributors of digital content (whether media joint ventures or, depending on how the YouTube and Book Search litigation pans out, emerging powerhouses like Google), to parlay mass media dominance into digital markets. Nor should copyright be available to suppress the wellspring of peer-created remixes and mashups that digital technology makes possible. At the same time, neither should untrammeled file sharing be allowed to eviscerate revenues for creators and media firms that look to the market for sustenance and a degree of editorial independence.

In that vein, following on existing statutory licenses, both in the United States and in other countries, I have elsewhere set out a detailed blueprint that would allow largely unrestricted noncommercial file sharing while remunerating copyright owners.[15] Under that plan, noncommercial file sharing and remixing would be privileged uses (with "noncommercial" defined as not receiving monetary compensation). And since noncommercial file sharing and remixing would not be infringing, those who provide products and service used for such activities would not face third-party liability for enabling, inducing, or profiting from infringement. In return, providers of services and devices the value of which is substantially enhanced by peer-to-peer sharing of copyrighted works would be charged a statutory fee—what I term a noncommercial use levy—set as a percentage of gross revenue. Likely candidates for the levy would include Internet access; peer-to-peer software and services; computer hardware; platforms and Web sites for user-posted content like YouTube; software like TiVoToGo that enables users to transfer copied television programs to a personal computer and from there to the Internet; consumer electronic devices (such as CD burners, MP3 players, and digital video recorders) used to copy, store, transmit, or perform downloaded files; and storage media (like blank CDs) used with those devices. According to a variety of estimates, including my own, a levy averaging some 4 percent of gross retail revenue would well compensate copyright holders for net income they actually stand to lose as a result of unhindered noncommercial file sharing.[16] Once collected, levy proceeds would be allocated among copyright holders in proportion to the popularity of their respective works and of user-modified version of their works, as measured by digital tracking and sampling technologies.

The noncommercial use levy would give noncommercial users and creators freedom to explore, share, compile, and modify many of the expressive works that populate our culture. Yet in compensating copyright owners for displaced revenues, the levy would continue to underwrite the creation and dissemination of new original expression.

Significantly, moreover, the levy would fund a far broader spectrum of creators than under our current copyright industry–dominated system. Peer distribution provides a ready, inexpensive vehicle for creators to reach audiences and track audience preferences, free from major copyright industries' control of distribution channels and moneyed influence on mass media and retail outlets. Although mass-media products dominate file-trading networks, audience consumption patterns in those networks also exhibit a phenomenal, "long tail," demand for many, many works and genres that have traditionally been ignored in copyright industry–controlled distribution focusing on blockbuster hits. And media dominance appears to be far weaker on user-generated video Web sites; a recent study indicates that mass media content makes up only a small fraction of YouTube's most popular videos.[17] In short, in a robust, legally sanctioned peer-to-peer file-sharing universe, dissident and independent writers, musicians, and filmmakers would have unprecedented opportunities to develop such dedicated, if often relatively niche, followings—and to garner a share of levy proceeds.

Moreover, those who wish to develop and invest in new distribution media for noncommercial sharing of copyrighted works would no longer face the prospect of a copyright holders' veto. Like the several distribution media that operate subject to statutory licenses under the Copyright Act, they would have to remunerate copyright holders but would not need copyright holder permission to facilitate the distribution of copyrighted works. In that way, new digital media will be brought within the framework of Congress's traditional compromise for new distribution technologies: removing the bottleneck of a proprietary copyright (and, with it, incumbent copyright industries' ability to torpedo new technologies that threaten their market dominance and existing business models) while still requiring payment to copyright holders.

A noncommercial use levy, to be certain, would entail administrative costs and some cross-subsidization of peer file sharing by those with computers and

Internet access who do not engage in that activity. But the costs of a levy must be compared with the enforcement costs, criminal penalties, and speech burdens that copyright industries hoping to stem the peer-to-peer tide would impose on file sharers and a host of third parties, ranging from venture capitalists to Internet service providers to suppliers of peer-to-peer software, that provide direct or indirect support for file sharing. Furthermore, cross-subsidization would be far less of a problem in a legally sanctioned peer-to-peer world than it might appear today. If noncommercial peer-to-peer file sharing were legal, more people would use peer networks to access a wide variety of creative expression. And levies could be targeted toward those services and devices most likely to be used to share copyrighted content.

Google: Digital Archives and Search Engine Aggregators

As the Google Book Search and Google News litigation make clear, copyright conflicts with the work of digital archivists and search engine firms on multiple fronts. Digital archives and search engines hold the promise of making all recorded information and expression, from today's news to ancient cultural artifact, readily available and accessible the world over. But proprietary copyright, the need to obtain clearances to include in-copyright material, would leave gaping holes in that universal digital library.

At the same time, with some exceptions, digital archives look less like the modern-day Alexandrian library and more like commercial competitors when they move beyond legacy works, those created before the widespread availability of digital technology. As hard-copy production and distribution give way to digital, the unlicensed posting of books, newspaper articles, sound recordings, and videos on digital archive and search engine sites comes increasingly to supplant copyright markets. Future creators may well disseminate their works entirely online. In that world, to give Google the untrammeled privilege to re-post online works and earn revenue from selling access or advertising would undercut the creator's copyright incentive.

The resolution of this conundrum varies with circumstance. Yet the underlying principle should be constant. Copyright should be delimited to account for the relative roles of copyright holders and information aggregators in making creative works available to the public in light of their respective creative contribution, technological contribution, capital investment, cost, and risk.[18] As in other areas, copyright should be calibrated to provide market-based authors and media with ample remuneration, but not the right to impose a bottleneck on new means for making expression widely available and accessible.

Let us begin with legacy works. Copyright should be tailored to remove the barriers that it currently imposes on digitizing, archiving, and making available en masse the millions of legacy books, articles, documents, sound recordings, photographs, paintings, and motion pictures that constitute our cultural heritage. As we have seen, it is primarily libraries, universities, nonprofit archivists, volunteers, and for-profit search engines, not copyright holders, that have invested the time, money, and technology in undertaking that task.

Copyright's barriers would only partly be lessened by ameliorating the problem of orphan works. As noted earlier, for many legacy works, the problem is not that they are orphan per se but that it is unclear who holds the rights to license the work's digital reproduction, distribution, and display (or, in the case of music or film, performance). For most publishing license agreements drafted more than a decade or so ago, the contract is unclear and copyright case law conflicted regarding whether the author retains electronic distribution rights or transfers them to the publisher. The same is true with music publishing agreements, recording contracts, and some agreements regarding contributions to films. Even if a copyright claimant lists a work on a public registry and thus removes that work from the category of orphan works, without clarity regarding whether that claimant can actually grant permission to include a work in a digital archive, the work will languish in its predigital form.

To remedy that problem, Congress should facilitate the establishment of umbrella, one-stop collective licensing organizations to grant digital rights permissions and remit proceeds to rights holders.[19] As it has in other areas, Congress should also determine what portion of the proceeds should be allocated to which rights-holder groups. In principle, in line with copyright law's support for authors, Congress should provide that, absent express license terms to the contrary, digital rights in legacy works remain with the author. Beyond that, particular solutions might vary from industry to industry.

In that vein, Congress should provide that the millions of legacy books that are currently out of print can be digitized and made freely available on a noncommercial basis by a nonprofit library or archive without any need to obtain a copyright license; in effect such legislation would determine (as courts might anyway) that such noncommercial uses of out-of-print works are per se fair use. A commercial firm's scanning of out-of-print books on behalf of a nonprofit institution would fall within that privilege, but the firm's online display of the books would not. A commercial firm that wishes to display the entire text of a non-orphan, in-copyright, out-of-print legacy book would have to obtain a license from the applicable collective licensing organization. That organization, in turn, would be required to grant licenses on reasonable terms that reflect the relative contributions and investment of the firm and author. In absence of agreement, the reasonable terms would be determined by a panel of copyright royalty judges, as currently set forth in the Copyright Act with respect to other statutory licenses.

Google, then, would be both in need of and eligible for such a statutory license were it to display the entire text of in-copyright, out-of-print legacy books as part of its Google Book Search Project. What about displaying new books and in-copyright, non-orphan legacy books that remain in print? These would be subject to proprietary copyright and the copyright holder's right to refuse to license.

At the same time, Google's scanning and public display of mere snippets of in-copyright books, whether still in print or not, should be fair use. Markets for books are certainly not harmed by Google's use. If anything, Google's book scanning and display of short snippets in response to users' search inquiries will kindle demand for many featured books. Nor does anyone write or publish a book in reliance on anticipated license revenues from this type of virtual card catalog,[20] and nothing in Google's project prevents publishers from licensing the online display of longer portions of their books, as many do under Google's Book Partners Program. Moreover, the Book Search Project's value lies almost entirely in Google's considerable investment in aggregating and applying its search engine technology to millions of books. Any benefit to the author or publisher of any given book is a windfall, especially for books that are currently out of print.

Google News's copying and display of short snippets—the headlines and the first couple sentences—of articles from newspaper Web sites should also be a permitted fair use. But Google News does raise some difficult free speech policy concerns. As I discussed in chapter 2, Google News is a tremendously valuable news aggregation service. However, it could well siphon off advertising revenue from the very newspapers and newspaper Web sites that underlie the service. That threat does not arise from Google's copying of short snippets from newspaper articles per se. Few who would otherwise turn to the article itself would find the headline and first couple lines a satisfactory substitute. But those who read their news online may well go to Google's news aggregation Web site rather than the Web site of a single newspaper or news agency to find the articles of interest to them. Essentially, Google News might harm newspapers by commoditizing them, by appropriating reader loyalty from particular papers to itself. Google's automated search and display of article snippets is what enables it to provide its news aggregation service several orders of magnitude more efficiently than manual news clipping and summaries. But, again, it is the Google News service as a whole, not Google's minimal copying of expression, that might harm the newspapers.

How, then, should a copyright law animated by First Amendment values respond? Part of copyright's purpose and its engine of free expression function is to encourage investment in producing expression. That purpose is ill served by allowing a search engine aggregator to appropriate the value of newspapers' investment in the articles they post on their Web sites. But to hold a search engine firm liable for displaying short snippets of online material could well cripple the very tool that makes the Web so valuable, the ability to quickly find information of interest and import from among the billions of pages that are available.

All in all, First Amendment values are best furthered by holding Google News's replication of headlines and opening sentences to be fair use. Newspapers will have to respond, as some have already begun to do, by attempting to strengthen customer loyalty and providing more attractive content and features on their Web sites. Newspapers might even compete with Google by providing their own niche news aggregation services, perhaps powered by their editorial judgment, as an adjunct to their own stories and columns. And rather than cannibalize its service by usurping advertising revenues from the newspaper Web sites that Google News aggregates, Google might come to partner with newspapers in advertising and producing content. These scenarios certainly have their minefields as well as opportunities, but at bottom, as in other areas, copyright should serve to promote the creation and dissemination of expression, not prop up traditional business models.

Finally and importantly, according search engine aggregators with limited privileges to copy and display in-copyright content, whether as fair use or under a statutory license, would serve a dual purpose. It would not only prevent copyright holders' from using proprietary copyright to hold up highly valuable services like Google Book Search and Google News. It would also preserve competition in the market for search engine aggregators by preventing Google or another search engine giant from procuring exclusive rights to display seminal content.

Paracopyright

Armed with digital encryption and enforceable mass-market licenses, copyright holders could readily elide the speech-enhancing limitations I have discussed, as well as other copyright limitations, both existing and proposed. As we have seen, digital rights management technology can be deployed to control expression for which copyright has expired and to prevent uses that, while privileged under copyright law, are unauthorized by the content provider. Mass-market licenses, such as Web site terms and conditions that purport to bind all site visitors, can similarly contain provisions that negate user privileges sanctioned by copyright law. Or digital control technology and mass-market licenses can be combined. A motion picture studio, for example, might make movies available for viewing via a studio-controlled Web site, where encryption blocks access to the site absent the viewer's agreement to a standard license and blocks copying any portion of the movie that is viewed even where such copying might constitute fair use or where the movie is in the public domain. Existing law would not merely permit the studio to use encryption and contract to expand its proprietary control; it would provide legal backing for that expansion. With the notable exception of the Copyright Office's recent rule-making exemption for film teachers, the DMCA would prohibit users' circumvention of the studio's technological access controls, even where undertaken for uses that would otherwise be privileged under copyright law.

Digital control technology and mass-market license can be useful tools for enforcing copyright and clarifying users' obligations under copyright law. But speech-enhancing limitations to copyright holders' rights should not be mere default rules susceptible to override at the hands of technological control and adhesion contract. Speakers should enjoy the actual right and ability to engage in privileged uses of creative expression, not merely a formal right that digital content providers can readily elide. To that end, the use of technological controls to block privileged uses should be prohibited— or, at the very least, it should be legal to circumvent and to market circumvention tools as required to effectively engage in privileged uses. Similarly, provisions of mass-market licenses that purport to override copyright limitations should be per se unenforceable.

It is unclear whether the First Amendment mandates the ability of users to circumvent encryption in order to engage in digital copying that constitutes fair use. As the Second Circuit has noted, the First Amendment does not necessarily guarantee the right to speak or gain access to information using the best available technology.[21] From the perspective of First Amendment doctrine, it may be that those who wish to use movie clips in their speech must splice from a videocassette or film the clip on their television screen rather than making a direct digital copy. But even if First Amendment doctrine falls short, free speech policy dictates that speakers have the opportunity to use digital technology to engage in fair use and other uses of copyrighted expression that are privileged under copyright law. A copyright law animated by First Amendment values must promote expressive diversity even where First Amendment doctrine might not require it.

Limited Moral Rights

A central part of copyright's role as an engine of free expression is to provide a possible livelihood for individual authors and to promote the value of individual expression and contributions to public discourse. Of particular importance to the latter, many authors feel deeply affronted—indeed, devalued—when others modify their work without permission or disseminate their work without giving authorship credit. The continental European doctrine of moral rights protects this personal interest by according authors certain inalienable rights to control the timing and manner in which their creative works are disseminated to the public. United States law contains only very limited recognition of authors' nonpecuniary interest in creative control.[22] While an author who retains the copyright in her work can prevent unlicensed modifications and dissemination, she generally loses that right upon transferring the copyright and must look instead to a hodgepodge of contract, unfair competition, and defamation law to find even a pale semblance of the European moral right.

To the extent the European regime gives authors a broad right to prevent creative appropriations of their existing works, it, no less than proprietary copyright, unduly impedes such expression. But the law can—and should—give some accommodation to authors' interest in creative control, without excessively burdening creative speakers. As under Professor Rubenfeld's proposal regarding derivative works, the holder of the copyright in the underlying work (and, presumably, through the copyright holder, the author) should receive a share of the derivative author's profits attributable to the underlying work, providing at least some monetary compensation for the loss of creative control.

In addition, those who disseminate a creative appropriation should be required to label it as an unlicensed modification of the original work. To the extent feasible, indeed, as Jessica Litman has proposed, the modified version should be accompanied by "a citation (or hypertext link) to an unaltered and readily accessible copy of the original."[23] Those requirements would serve to accord authorship attribution for the underlying work, avoid confusion regarding which is the "authentic," copyright holder–authorized version, and refer interested persons to the underlying work so they can see what has been changed. Digital technology may well ease the burden of compliance. In fact, it might entail nothing more than leaving intact the copyright management information that is digitally embedded in the underlying work when portions of that work are incorporated in the creative appropriation. (The DMCA already prohibits the intentional removal or alteration of copyright management information.)[24] Moreover, the precise requirements should depend on context, following a reasonableness standard rather than a hard-and-fast rule. They might be eased for uses that are noncommercial or that occur in settings that make the source obvious to all readers and viewers, such as in fan fiction Web sites devoted to posting derivative works based on a particular television series.

Importantly, according such limited moral rights protection would do more than merely assuage authors' feelings. It would also promote First Amendment values. For one, a requirement that creative appropriators take reasonable steps to accord authorship credit for underlying works and ensure that audiences understand the source of the modified version can help to protect authors' interest in avoiding "forced speech." As I argued in chapter 3, while authors do not have a cognizable speech interest in preventing another from modifying their creative expression or using it in a context that is not to their liking, they do have such an interest in preventing the impression that they endorse a message they find repugnant.

Of interest, French moral rights doctrine, generally one of the most protective of authors' creative control, draws just this balance with respect to parodies. In striking contrast to the Ninth Circuit's *Air Pirates* decision, for example, a French court held that cartoons portraying *Peanuts* characters in obscene situations infringed neither the copyright holder's adaptation right nor the author's moral right of integrity.[25] So long as the parody is a distinct, independent work, clearly not that of the parodied author, the parodist's right of free expression trumps the author's moral right.[26]

In addition to labeling to avoid false endorsement, according authorship credit has the salutary benefit of encouraging the creation and dissemination of original expression and underscoring the value of individual contributions to culture and public discourse. Our culture gives significant weight to authorship attribution. Even authors who are happy to distribute their work freely, without compensation or other control, almost universally insist on receiving authorship credit. Creative Commons provides a good example. That organization makes it possible for authors to release their work to the public under a variety of standard licenses with various combinations of terms that generally permit far greater liberty of use than is typical of commercially distributed copyrighted works. Creative Commons has estimated that, as of February 2005, authors chose licenses requiring attribution some 94 percent of the time and, in contrast, chose licenses prohibiting the making of a derivative work less than one-third of the time.[27] As Rebecca Tushnet has observed, authorship attribution is a powerful norm among fan fiction communities as well (as are express disclaimers of any endorsement by the owner of the copyright in the underlying work).[28] Documentary filmmakers also underscore the importance of authorship attribution in their best practice guidelines.[29]

In sum, the limited moral rights protection I have described would further First Amendment values by promoting individual authorship. It would do so, moreover, without unduly burdening speakers' ability to build upon existing expression in conveying their own.

Conclusion

As Justice Brennan eloquently expressed in his dissent in *Harper & Row v. Nation,* "The copyright laws serve as the 'engine of free expression,' only when the statutory monopoly does not choke off multifarious indirect uses and consequent broad dissemination of information and ideas. To ensure the progress of arts and sciences and the integrity of First Amendment values, ideas and information must not be freighted with claims of proprietary right."[30] Viewing copyright through that free speech lens is critical to recovering copyright's delicate balance and faithfully translating copyright's core principles to the digital arena. It also requires that we place copyright in its proper context, as part of a multifaceted regime of laws, regulations, government subsidies, and communication technologies and practices that make up our system of free expression.

Copyright can indeed be an engine of free expression. But for copyright to fulfill that potential, we must realize that copyright is far from *the* engine of free expression. Copyright law has a continuing, constitutive role, in both traditional media and the digital arena, for fostering a wide array of original works of authorship, ranging from full-length feature films to investigative journalism, and underwriting a robust, fiscally independent sector of authors and publishers. Yet while those market-supported works and speakers make vital contributions to public discourse and culture, they best serve First Amendment values in lively interplay with publicly funded art and broadcasting and the welter of nonmarket blogs, Web sites, and peer communication that populates digital networks.

Our system of free expression requires not just a diversity of content but a plurality of types of speech and speakers. It must embrace commercial mass media, cottage industry publishers, professional authors, publicly funded artists and media, nonprofit organizations and political activists, and a host of sundry creators and discussants who exchange their opinions, expression, and personal reworkings of bits and pieces of popular culture without any expectation of monetary remuneration.

A copyright animated by the First Amendment would further that diversity and plurality by affording authors a tailored mix of exclusive rights and rights of compensation only. In contrast, today's increasingly bloated set of Blackstonian proprietary rights too often serves as a tool for private censorship, a burden on nonmarket and semimarket speech, and a bottleneck for incumbent copyright industries to ward off new media and other potential challengers. As experience teaches us, copyright law truly serves as an engine of free expression when it limits the reach of copyright holder control no less than by spurring the creation of original works of authorship.

Preface

1. JOHN MILTON, AREOPAGITICA (John W. Hales ed., Oxford University Press 1961) (1644). *See also* JOSEPH LOWENSTEIN, THE AUTHOR'S DUE: PRINTING AND THE PREHISTORY OF COPYRIGHT 185–209 (University of Chicago Press 2002) (contending that Milton actually supported a Stationers' copyright, but that others nevertheless used *Areopagitica* to favor authors over Stationers).
2. *On the Means of Preserving Public Liberty*, NEW-YORK MAG., Jan. 1790.
3. *See, e.g.*, COPYRIGHT AND FREE SPEECH: COMPARATIVE AND INTERNATIONAL ANALYSES (Jonathan Griffiths & Uma Sutherland eds., Oxford University Press 2005); Bernt Hugenholtz, *Copyright and Freedom of Expression in Europe, in* THE COMMODIFICATION OF INFORMATION 239 (Neil Netanel & Niva Elkin-Koren eds., Kluwer Law Int'l 2002).

Chapter One

1. Harper & Row, Publishers, Inc. v. Nation Enters., 471 U.S. 539, 558 (1985).
2. *See* David D. Kirkpatrick, *A Writer's Tough Lesson in Birthin' a Parody*, N.Y. TIMES, Apr. 26, 2001, at E1.
3. *See* Suntrust Bank v. Houghton Mifflin Co., 136 F. Supp. 2d 1357, 1369 (N.D. Ga. 2001), *rev'd,* 252 F.3d 1165 (11th Cir. 2001).
4. Melville B. Nimmer, *Does Copyright Abridge the First Amendment Guarantees of Free Speech and Press?,* 17 UCLA L. REV. 1180, 1181 (1970).
5. Amy Harmon, *The Supreme Court: The Context; A Corporate Victory, But One That Raises Public Consciousness,* N.Y. TIMES, Jan. 16, 2003, at A24 (describing the Supreme Court's ruling in Eldred v. Ashcroft, 537 U.S. 186 (2003)).
6. Robert S. Boynton, *The Tyranny of Copyright?,* N.Y. TIMES MAG., Jan. 25, 2004, at 40.

7. Turner Broad. Sys., Inc. v. FCC, 520 U.S. 180, 226–227 (1997); FCC v. Nat'l Citizens Comm. for Broad., 436 U.S. 775, 799 (1978) (both quoting Associated Press v. United States, 326 U.S. 1, 20 (1945)).

8. Under the Copyright Act of 1909, still in force in 1936, the copyright term lasted twenty-eight years from publication, plus another twenty-eight years if the copyright owner renewed the copyright for the second term. Thus, even if the copyright in *Gone with the Wind* was renewed (which it was), the novel would have entered the public domain in 1992.

9. Copyright law used to require as a condition to copyright protection that authors affirmatively assert their copyright in published works by placing a copyright notice on publicly distributed copies of the work. In the King estate's lawsuit against CBS, the Eleventh Circuit held that the broadcast of King's speech on nationwide television did not constitute a "general publication" of the work and, therefore, did not effect a forfeiture of his copyright despite King's failure to affix a copyright notice on advance copies he had distributed to the press. The court noted, however, that CBS would prevail on that issue at trial if it proved, as seemed plausible, that King had made the advance printed copies available to the public at large (and not just the press) or had authorized the speech's distribution in the Southern Christian Leadership Conference newsletter without the requisite copyright notice. Estate of Martin Luther King, Jr., Inc. v. CBS, Inc., 194 F.3d 1211 (11th Cir. 1999). The case settled before trial. For illuminating discussion of how Congress's subsequent elimination of formal requirements for copyright protection, encompassing both the notice requirement and the requirement that copyright be renewed after the first twenty-eight-year term, has effectively expanded copyright holder rights, see Christopher Sprigman, *Reform(aliz)ing Copyright,* 57 STAN. L. REV. 485 (2004).

10. I assess the causes of copyright expansion elsewhere. *See* Neil W. Netanel, *Why Has Copyright Expanded?, in* 5 NEW DIRECTIONS IN COPYRIGHT LAW (Fiona Macmillan ed., Edward Elgar, forthcoming 2008).

11. 2 WILLIAM BLACKSTONE, COMMENTARIES *2. Scholars note that Blackstone himself must have recognized that description as hyperbole, even as applied to real property. Robert C. Ellickson, *Property in Land,* 102 YALE L.J. 1315, 1362 n.237 (1993).

12. Brief for Motion Picture Studio and Recording Company Petitioners, Metro-Goldwyn-Mayer Studios Inc. v. Grokster, Ltd. at 8, 13, 545 U.S. 913 (2005) (No. 04-480).

13. The anticircumvention provisions that Congress enacted are complex. I describe the basics in chapter 4.

14. LAWRENCE LESSIG, THE FUTURE OF IDEAS 9 (Random House 2001).

15. Richard Siklos, *Push Comes to Shove for Control of Web Video,* N.Y. TIMES, Apr. 1, 2007, at sec. 3, p. 8; John Jurgensen, *Rewriting the Rules of Fiction,* WALL ST. J., Sept. 16, 2006, at 1.

16. As Larry Lessig has cogently argued, "fidelity" to a legal regime's original purpose, principles, and, indeed, meaning requires "translation" in light of new circumstances, not rote application of literal doctrine and text. *See* Lawrence Lessig, *Fidelity in Translation,* 71 TEX. L. REV. 1165 (1993). *See also* Daniel A. Farber, *Conflicting Visions and Contested Baselines: Intellectual Property and Free Speech in the "Digital Millennium,"* 89 MINN. L. REV. 1318, 1345 (2005) (concluding that in light of the radical changes wrought by the Internet, "[w]e cannot meaningfully translate copyright rules to the digital world without considering the goals of the copyright regime").

Chapter Two

1. Eldred v. Ashcroft, 537 U.S. 186, 191 (2003). I discuss and show the fallacy of the Court's characterization in chapter 8.
2. Houghton Mifflin Co. v. Noram Pub. Co., Inc., 28 F. Supp. 676 (S.D.N.Y. 1939). For Cranston's version of the case's underlying facts, see Anthony O. Miller, *Court Halted Dime Edition of "Mein Kampf": Cranston Tells How Hitler Sued Him and Won,* L.A. TIMES, Feb. 14, 1988, at 4.
3. That is not to say that the demise of Cranston's translation deprived Americans of all access to Hitler's manifesto. Bowing to a firestorm of criticism over its expurgated translation, Houghton Mifflin had licensed the publisher Reynal & Hitchcok and the New School of Social Research to produce a complete, annotated translation. That scholarly, thousand-page tome was published shortly before Cranston's, but its potential readership was far more limited than that of Cranston's popularly priced, thirty-two-page exposé. *See* Jay Worthington, *Mein Royalties,* 10 Cabinet 112 (Spring 2003), *available at* http://www.cabinetmagazine.org/issues/10/mein_royalties.php; ADOLF HITLER, MEIN KAMPF (Reynal & Hitchcock 1939).
4. Worldwide Church of God v. Phila. Church of God, Inc., 227 F.3d 1110, 1113, 1119 (9th Cir. 2000), *cert. denied,* 532 U.S. 958 (2001) (internal quotation marks omitted) (describing the church's position).
5. *Id.* at 1119.
6. *Id.* at 1115 (quoting Harper & Row, Publishers, Inc. v. Nation Enters., 471 U.S. 539, 558 (1985)).
7. My depiction of Else's story is based on a telephone interview conducted with John Else, Professor, UC Berkeley (Feb. 2003). I first heard the story from Larry Lessig.
8. One Fox representative did offer to reduce the fee to $9,000, still far higher than what Else paid to clear other rights.
9. PATRICIA AUFDERHEIDE & PETER JASZI, CTR. FOR SOCIAL MEDIA, UNTOLD STORIES: CREATIVE CONSEQUENCES OF THE RIGHTS CLEARANCE CULTURE FOR DOCUMENTARY FILMMAKERS (2004), *available at* http://www.centerfor socialmedia.org/files/pdf/UNTOLDSTORIES_Report.pdf.

10. *See* Declan McCullagh, *Will This Land Me in Jail?*, C/NET NEWS.COM, Dec. 23, 2002, http://news.com.com/2010–1028–978636.html.

11. Egilman v. Keller & Keckman, LLP, 401 F. Supp. 2d 105 (D.D.C. 2005); I.M.S. Inquiry Mgmt. Sys., Ltd. v. Berkshire Info. Sys., Inc., 307 F. Supp. 2d 521 (S.D.N.Y. 2004).

12. Free Republic, http://www.freerepublic.com /home.htm (last visited Jan. 7, 2007).

13. L.A. Times v. Free Republic, 54 U.S.P.Q.2d 1453, 1472 (C.D. Cal. 2000).

14. Walt Disney Prods. v. Air Pirates, 581 F.2d 751, 753 (9th Cir. 1978) (internal quotation marks omitted).

15. THE VIBE HISTORY OF HIP HOP (Alan Light ed., Three Rivers Press 1999); SIVA VAIDHYANATHAN, COPYRIGHTS AND COPYWRONGS 132–40 (New York University Press 2001).

16. JOSEPH G. SCHLOSS, MAKING BEATS: THE ART OF SAMPLE-BASED HIP-HOP (Wesleyan University Press 2004).

17. As Public Enemy's Hank Shocklee expressed in an interview: "A guitar sampled off a record is going to hit differently than a guitar sampled in the studio. The guitar that's sampled off a record is going . . . to hit the tape harder. It's going to slap at you. Something that's organic [i.e., the guitar played in the studio] is almost going to have a powder effect. It hits more like a pillow than a piece of wood. So those things change your mood, the feeling you can get off a record." Kembrew McLeod, *How Copyright Law Changed Hip Hop: An Interview with Public Enemy's Chuck D and Hank Shocklee,* STAY FREE!, Issue 20, Fall 2002, at 24, *available at* http://www.stayfreemagazine.org/archives/20/public_enemy.html.

18. David Sanjek, *"Don't Have to DJ No More": Sampling and the "Autonomous Creator,"* 10 CARDOZO ARTS & ENT. L.J. 607, 616 (1992) (quoting Greg Tate, *Diary of a Bug,* VILLAGE VOICE, Nov. 22, 1988, at 73).

19. Olufunmilayo B. Arewa, *From J. C. Bach to Hip Hop: Musical Borrowing, Copyright and Cultural Context,* 84 N.C. L. REV. 547, 630 (2006).

20. Bridgeport Music, Inc. v. Dimension Films, 410 F.3d 792 (6th Cir. 2005). *Bridgeport Music* involved a three-note sample, and the Court purported (1) not to "provide a definitive answer" regarding whether a single-note sample would infringe and (2) to leave open the possibility of a fair use defense. But the Court's rejection of any de minimis defense for copying sound recordings and its touting of a new "bright line rule" of "[g]et a license or do not sample" leave little doubt that, in that Court's view, a commercial sampler's single-note sample of a sound recording requires permission from the copyright owner.

21. *Id.* at 801.

22. *Id.*

23. DONALD S. PASSMAN, ALL YOU NEED TO KNOW ABOUT THE MUSIC BUSINESS 297 (Free Press, 5th ed. 2003); Josh Norek, Comment, *"You Can't Sing*

without the Bling": The Toll of Excessive Sample License Fees on Creativity in Hip-Hop Music and the Need for a Compulsory Sound Recording Sample License System, 11 UCLA Ent. L. Rev. 83, 89–91 (2004). *See also Fight for Your Right to Sample?; Why the Beasties' Best Album Could Never Happen Today,* ENTERTAINMENT WEEKLY, Nov. 19, 2004, at 40.

24. McLeod, *supra* note 17, at 24 (quoting Public Enemy artist, Chuck D).

25. *See* SCHLOSS, *supra* note 16, at 176–77 (describing the copyright-driven practice of altering samples so they are unrecognizable).

26. Arewa, *supra* note 19, at 601–07.

27. Malcolm Gladwell, *Something Borrowed: Should a Charge of Plagiarism Ruin Your Life?,* NEW YORKER, Nov. 22, 2004, at 45.

28. Kevin Kelly, *Scan This Book!,* N.Y. TIMES MAGAZINE, May 14, 2006, at 42, 45.

29. *See* S. M. Shafi and Rafiq A. Rather, *Precision and Recall of Five Search Engines for Retrieval of Scholarly Information in the Field of Biotechnology,* WEBOLOGY, Aug. 2005, http://www.webology.ir/2005/v2n2/a12.html.

30. *See* Google Book Search "vision," http://books.google.com/googlebooks/vision .html (last visited Jan. 4, 2007).

31. A 2005 study found that Google's five initial library partners had approximately 10.5 million unique books, or about one-third of the 32 million unique books in the collections of the some 9,000 libraries worldwide whose collections are cataloged in the OCLC Online Computer Library Center's WorldCAT bibliographic database. *See* Brian Lavoie et al., *Anatomy of Aggregate Collections: The Example of Google Print for Libraries,* D-LIB MAGAZINE, Sept. 2005, http://www.dlib.org/dlib/september05/lavoie/09 1avoie.html. I have roughly, and I think conservatively, extrapolated from that study to estimate some 15 million unique books to account for the collections of the libraries of the University of California, University of Wisconsin, and the Universidad Complutense Madrid, which have signed with Google since that study was completed.

32. *Compare* John Markoff and Edward Wyatt, *Google Is Adding Major Libraries to Its Database,* N.Y. TIMES, Dec. 14, 2004, at A1 (estimating ten dollars per book) *with* Jonathan Band, *The Google Library Project: Both Sides of the Story,* in PLAGIARY: CROSS-DISCIPLINARY STUDIES IN PLAGIARISM, FABRICATION, AND FALSIFICATION, Feb. 8, 2006, *available at* http://www.plagiary.org/Google-Library-Project.pdf (estimating twenty-five dollars per book based on Microsoft's announced scanning costs for its proposed digitization project).

33. Given that foreign copyright laws might be even more restrictive than U.S. copyright, Google will scan only public domain books in library collections outside the United States.

34. Press Release, Association of American Publishers, Google Library Project Raises Serious Questions for Publishers and Authors (Aug. 12, 2005), *available at* http://www.publishers.org/press/releases.cfm?PressReleaseArticleID=274.

35. Industry analysts have reportedly questioned the wisdom even of Google's substantial investment in scanning millions of books, let alone bearing the expense of obtaining copyright clearances. *See* Band, *supra* note 32, at 8.

36. For this point, as well as for the information in the rest of this paragraph, see Brief Amici Curiae of the American Association of Law Libraries, et al., at 21–26, Eldred v. Ashcroft, 537 U.S. 186 (2003) (No. 01–618). Books published prior to 1923 are in the public domain. The brief cites a study showing that only 1.7 percent of all books registered for copyright between 1927 and 1951 remain in print. I see no reason why the in-print percentages for the years 1923–1926 would differ substantially from the period studied.

37. Greg Sandoval, *Newspapers Want Search Engines to Pay,* C/NET NEWS.COM, Feb. 1, 2005, http://news.com.com/Newspapers+want+search+engines+to+pay/2100–1025_3–6033574.html. Google has reached an accord, similar to its AFP settlement agreement, with three other news agencies, including Press Association of Britain, Canadian Press, and The Associated Press. *See* Reuters, *Google Shift on Handling of News,* N.Y. TIMES, Sept. 1, 2007, at B2.

38. Mazer v. Stein, 347 U.S. 201, 219 (1954) ("Sacrificial days devoted to such creative activities deserve rewards commensurate with the services rendered.").

Chapter Three

1. For a listing of many of the various understandings and citations to their principal proponents, *see* Frederick Schauer, *The Boundaries of the First Amendment: A Preliminary Exploration of Constitutional Salience,* 117 HARV. L. REV. 1765, 1786 (2004). For a brief critical summary of free speech theories, see ERIC BARENDT, FREEDOM OF SPEECH 1–36 (Oxford University Press, 2d ed. 2005); Kent Greenawalt, *Free Speech Justifications,* 89 COLUM. L. REV. 119, 121–24 (1989).

2. ALEXANDER MEIKLEJOHN, FREE SPEECH AND ITS RELATION TO SELF-GOVERNMENT 75 (Harper 1948).

3. *See, e.g,* CASS R. SUNSTEIN, DEMOCRACY AND THE PROBLEM OF FREE SPEECH 121–65 (Free Press 1993) (favoring a two-tier First Amendment that recognizes the primacy of political speech and includes within the ambit of political speech only "art and literature that have the characteristics of social commentary").

4. Hurley v. Irish-Am. Gay, Lesbian & Bisexual Group of Boston, 515 U.S. 557, 569 (1995). *See also* Schad v. Borough of Mount Ephraim, 452 U.S. 61, 65 (1981).

5. ALEXANDER MEIKLEJOHN, POLITICAL FREEDOM: THE CONSTITUTIONAL POWERS OF THE PEOPLE 255–57 (Harper 1960).

6. *See* ALAN BULLOCK, HITLER AND STALIN: PARALLEL LIVES 426–27 (HarperCollins 1991) (describing totalitarian repression of artistic expression); FRANCES STONOR SAUNDERS, THE CULTURAL COLD WAR: THE CIA AND THE WORLD OF ARTS AND LETTERS (New Press 2000) (documenting the

CIA's covert funding of select academic conferences, magazines, and cultural activities in postwar Europe); Marci A. Hamilton, *Art Speech,* 49 VAND. L. REV. 73, 96–101 (1996).

7. The classic treatment of this issue is Lawrence G. Sager, *Fair Measure: The Legal Status of Underenforced Constitutional Norms,* 91 HARV. L. REV. 1212 (1978).

8. THOMAS I. EMERSON, THE SYSTEM OF FREEDOM OF EXPRESSION 3–5 (Random House 1970). *See also* BARENDT, *supra* note 1, at 104–08 (arguing from a comparative law perspective that, even as a constitutional matter, the right to free speech may entail positive rights to government support as well as a negative liberty right against government censorship).

9. PAUL STARR, THE CREATION OF THE MEDIA: POLITICAL ORIGINS OF MASS COMMUNICATIONS 83–94 (Basic Books 2004).

10. STUART BENJAMIN ET AL., TELECOMMUNICATIONS LAW AND POLICY (Carolina Academic Press 2001).

11. *See* Turner Broad. Sys., Inc. v. FCC, 520 U.S. 180, 190 (1997); FCC v. Nat'l Citizens Comm. for Broad., 436 U.S. 775, 799 (1978).

12. *See* 17 U.S.C. §§ 108–22.

13. *See* Tim Wu, *Copyright's Communications Policy,* 103 MICH. L. REV. 278 (2004); Jessica Litman, *Revising Copyright Law for the Information Age,* 75 OR. L. REV. 19, 29 (1996); Yochai Benkler, *Intellectual Property and the Organization of Information Production,* 22 INT'L REV. L. & ECON. 81 (2002); Diane Leenheer Zimmerman, *Information as Speech, Information as Goods: Some Thoughts on Marketplaces and the Bill of Rights,* 33 WM. & MARY L. REV. 665 (1992).

14. The recognition of the virtue of robust debate among diverse viewpoints has roots in the free speech writings of John Milton and John Stuart Mill. *See* JOHN MILTON, AREOPAGITICA 126 (J. C. Suffolk ed., University Tutorial Press 1968) (1644) ("Let [Truth] and Falsehood grapple; who ever knew Truth put to the worse, in a free and open encounter."); JOHN STUART MILL, ON LIBERTY AND OTHER ESSAYS 59 (John Gray ed., Oxford University Press 1998) (1869) ("[I]it is only by the collision of adverse opinions that the ... truth has any chance of being supplied.").

15. The Supreme Court has repeatedly recognized our "profound national commitment to the principle that debate on public issues should be uninhibited, robust, and wide-open." New York Times Co. v. Sullivan, 376 U.S. 254, 270 (1964).

16. *See generally* JAMES SUROWIECK, THE WISDOM OF CROWDS (Anchor 2005); Cass R. Sunstein, *Deliberative Trouble? Why Groups Go to Extremes,* 110 YALE L.J. 71 (2000).

17. On industry in general, *see, e.g.,* JOSEPH A. SCHUMPETER, CAPITALISM, SOCIALISM, AND DEMOCRACY 81–106 (Harper, 3d ed. 1950) (maintaining that monopolists are more likely to innovate because they can exploit scale economies in research and development and appropriate the full value of their inventions); Kenneth Joseph Arrow, *Economic Welfare and the Allocation of*

Resources for Innovation, in ESSAYS IN THE THEORY OF RISK-BEARING 144 (American Elsevier Pub. Co., 3d ed. 1976) (contending that monopolists may tend to be relatively risk-averse rather than innovative because they have more to lose than competitors); F. M. Scherer, *Antitrust, Efficiency, and Progress,* 62 N.Y.U. L. REV. 998, 1011 (1987) ("Although there are fairly simple and well-accepted generalizations as to which market structures stimulate the most rapid pace of innovation, the question of what progress rate is socially optimal, and . . . which market structure driving it is best, is extremely complex and poorly settled.").

18. *See* BRUCE M. OWEN & STEVEN S. WILDMAN, VIDEO ECONOMICS 101–50 (Harvard University Press 1992) (finding that traditional commercial media's congenital bias against minority tastes and in favor of large audiences' tastes is exacerbated in media characterized by firm concentration and in media supported by advertising); Joel Waldfogel, *Preference Externalities: An Empirical Study of Who Benefits Whom in Differentiated Product Markets* 30 (National Bureau of Econ. Research Working Paper No. 7391, 1999), *available at* http://www.nber.org/papers/W7391 (finding that majority preferences tend to crowd out minority ones in markets, like media markets, characterized by large fixed costs and preferences differing sharply across consumers).

19. The classic studies, based on economic modeling and narrow assumptions, are Peter O. Steiner, *Program Patterns and Preferences, and the Workability of Competition in Radio Broadcasting,* 66 Q.J. ECON. 194 (1952); Jack H. Beebe, *Institutional Structure and Program Choices in Television Markets,* 91 Q.J. ECON. 15, 15–17 (1977). Later commentators have reflexively invoked those studies without reference to the studies' narrow assumptions. *See, e.g.,* Schurz Communications, Inc. v. FCC, 982 F.2d 1043, 1054–55 (7th Cir. 1992) (Posner, J.) ("It has long been understood that monopoly in broadcasting could actually promote rather than retard programming diversity."); Jim Chen, *The Last Picture Show (On the Twilight of Federal Mass Communications Regulation),* 80 MINN. L. REV. 1415, 1448–49 (1996) (asserting that the "positive correlation between concentration and diverse programming testifies to the unpredictability of regulatory strategies that aim to offset uneven levels of market power" in media markets).

20. *See, e.g.,* Christopher S. Yoo, *Architectural Censorship and the FCC,* 78 S. CAL. L. REV. 669, 693–99 (2005); Matthew L. Spitzer, *Justifying Minority Preferences in Broadcasting,* 64 S. CAL. L. REV. 293 (1991).

21. C. Edwin Baker, *Media Structure, Ownership Policy, and the First Amendment,* 78 S. CAL. L. REV. 733, 735 (2005). *See also* C. EDWIN BAKER, MEDIA CONCENTRATION AND DEMOCRACY: WHY OWNERSHIP MATTERS (Cambridge University Press 2006).

22. *See* Turner Broad. Sys., Inc. v. FCC, 520 U.S. 180, 190 (1997); FCC v. Nat'l Citizens Comm. for Broad., 436 U.S. 775, 799 (1978).

23. STEVEN H. SHIFFRIN, DISSENT, INJUSTICE, AND THE MEANINGS OF AMERICA xi (Princeton University Press 1999); STEVEN H. SHIFFRIN, THE FIRST AMENDMENT, DEMOCRACY, AND ROMANCE 96 (Harvard University Press 1990).

24. For a cogent explication of this point, see YOCHAI BENKLER, THE WEALTH OF NETWORKS: HOW SOCIAL PRODUCTION TRANSFORMS MARKETS AND FREEDOM 137–38, 166–70 (Yale University Press 2006).

25. *See* Ellen Goodman, *A Right to Mock Tara,* WASH. POST, May 5, 2001, at A19 (reporting that the Mitchell estate asked Pat Conroy to write an official sequel subject to those conditions).

26. *See, e.g.*, Jane C. Ginsburg, *Recorded Remarks in Panel Discussion: The Constitutionality of Copyright Term Extension: How Long Is Too Long?,* 18 CARDOZO ARTS & ENT. L.J. 651, 701 (2000) ("The First Amendment is certainly about the freedom to make your own speech. Whether it is about the freedom to make other people's speeches again for them, I have some doubt.").

27. Eldred v. Ashcroft, 537 U.S. 186, 191 (2003).

28. Jack M. Balkin, *Digital Speech and Democratic Culture: A Theory of Freedom of Expression for the Information Society,* 79 N.Y.U. L. REV. 1, 4 (2004).

29. *Id.* Terry Fisher and others aptly call this practice of appropriating and recasting mass-media expression "semiotic democracy." WILLIAM W. FISHER III, PROMISES TO KEEP: TECHNOLOGY, LAW, AND THE FUTURE OF ENTERTAINMENT 28–31 (Stanford University Press 2004).

30. This and other examples are enumerated in Rebecca Tushnet, *Copy This Essay: How Fair Use Doctrine Harms Free Speech and How Copying Serves It,* 114 YALE L.J. 535, 572 (2004).

31. Ed Baker similarly maintains that under the Speech Clause of the First Amendment, "speech freedom is a liberty—not a market—right." Professor Baker thus concludes that "a prohibition on a person's commercial use of another's copyrighted material, unless the rule is adopted for constitutionally impermissible reasons, should not be seen as an abridgment of her speech freedom." C. Edwin Baker, *First Amendment Limits on Copyright,* 55 VAND. L. REV. 891, 903 (2002).

32. FREDERICK SCHAUER, FREE SPEECH: A PHILOSOPHICAL ENQUIRY 94 (Cambridge University Press, 1982).

33. Greenawalt, *supra* note 1, at 121–24. *See also* SCHAUER, *supra* note 32, at 5–12.

34. *See, e.g.,* EMERSON, *supra* note 8, at 18; SCHAUER, *supra* note 32, at 92–101. Thoughtful First Amendment scholars posit that the constitutionality of legislation that restricts expressive conduct should turn on government motive rather than attempting to define whether conduct is speech or pure conduct. They argue that the First Amendment forbids government from regulating activity with the motive of restricting speech and that, so long as that motive is absent, regulation passes First Amendment muster even if some people

cannot express their views effectively as a result. *See, e.g.,* Jed Rubenfeld, *The First Amendment's Purpose,* 53 STAN. L. REV. 767 (2001); Elena Kagan, *Private Speech, Public Purpose: The Role of Governmental Motive in First Amendment Doctrine,* 63 U. CHI. L. REV. 413 (1996). Of note here, those arguments pertain to First Amendment doctrine, not free speech policy, which entails questions of whether government should promote certain activities, not just whether a given government regulation abridges speech. In addition, the government motive arguments also require that we distinguish between speech and conduct; they ask whether the government regulates with the aim of restricting speech or something that is not speech.

35. *See, e.g.,* Tushnet, *supra* note 30, at 570 (emphasizing that "[p]ersonality may also be expressed inseparably from copying").

36. Sony Music Entm't v. Does 1–40, 326 F. Supp. 2d 556, 564 (S.D.N.Y 2004).

37. As the Supreme Court emphasized in upholding the FCC's "fairness doctrine" requirement that radio and television broadcasters air responses to personal attacks involving controversial issues, "It is the right of the viewers and listeners, not the right of the broadcasters, which is paramount." Red Lion Broad. Co. v. FCC, 395 U.S. 367, 390 (1969).

38. *See* Turner Broad. Sys. v. FCC, 520 U.S. 180, 189 (1997) (upholding Congress's "must carry" rules requiring cable television systems to dedicate some of their channels to local broadcast television stations as serving the important governmental interest of "preserving the benefits of free, over-the-air local broadcast television"). Among scholars, Rebecca Tushnet has placed particular emphasis on the central role of copying, access, and library distribution in our system of free expression. *See* Tushnet, *supra* note 30; Rebecca Tushnet, *My Library: Copyright and the Role of Institutions in a Peer-to-Peer World,* 53 UCLA L. REV. 977 (2006).

39. This paragraph draws from Geoff Boucher, *Ex-Door Lighting Their Ire,* L.A. TIMES, Oct. 5, 2005, at A1.

40. *See* David McGowan, *Some Realism about the Free-Speech Critique of Copyright,* 74 FORDHAM L. REV. 435 (2005). The quotation in the following sentence is from an entry in Townshend's weblog that has since been removed. *See An Image Inconsistent with His Lifestyle,* CANBERRA TIMES, July 17, 2004, at B09.

41. A New York court dismissed the composers' complaint. Shostakovich v. Twentieth Century-Fox Film Corp., 80 N.Y.S.2d 575 (Sup. Ct. 1948), *aff'd,* 87 N.Y.S.2d 430 (1st Dept. 1949). But a French court, applying the continental European doctrine of moral rights, found in favor of the composers and ordered the film seized. Soc. Le Chant de Monde v. Soc. Fox Europe et Soc. Fox Americaine Twentieth Century, Judgment of Jan. 13, 1953 [1953] 1 Gaz. Pal. 191 [1954] D.A. 16, 80 (Cour d'Appel Paris).

42. *See* McGowan, *supra* note 40, at 438.

43. Justin Hughes, *The Philosophy of Intellectual Property,* 77 GEO. L.J. 287, 359 (1988).

44. Randall P. Bezanson, *Speaking through Others' Voices: Authorship, Originality, and Free Speech*, 38 WAKE FOREST L. REV. 983 (2003); Jed Rubenfeld, *The Freedom of Imagination: Copyright's Constitutionality*, 112 YALE L.J. 1, 29 (2002).

45. Whitney v. California, 274 U.S. 357, 377 (1927) (Brandeis, J., concurring).

46. Hurley v. Irish-Am. Gay, Lesbian and Bisexual Group of Boston, Inc., 515 U.S. 557, 573 (1995).

47. Riley v. Nat'l Fed'n of the Blind, 487 U.S. 781 (1988); Pacific Gas & Electric Co. v. Public Utilities Comm'n of Cal., 475 U.S. 1 (1986) (holding that a state agency cannot require a utility company to include a third-party newsletter in its billing envelope); Wooley v. Maynard, 430 U.S. 705 (1977) (holding unconstitutional a state law that required New Hampshire motorists to display the state motto "Live Free or Die" on their license plates); West Virginia Bd. of Ed. v. Barnette, 319 U.S. 624 (1943) (holding unconstitutional a state law requiring schoolchildren to recite the Pledge of Allegiance and to salute the flag).

48. A number of courts have posited that a copyright owner's exclusive right of first publication, the right to determine whether, when, by whom, in what literal form, and under what conditions a work will be released to the public, furthers the author's First Amendment right to refrain from speaking. *See* Harper & Row, Publishers, Inc. v. Nation Enters., 471 U.S. 539, 559 (1985); Schnapper v. Foley, 667 F.2d 102 (D.C. Cir. 1981), *cert. denied*, 455 U.S. 948 (1982); Estate of Hemingway v. Random House, Inc., 244 N.E.2d 250, 255 (N.Y. 1968). Yet no court has suggested that the author's interest in avoiding compelled speech is implicated in copyright's exclusive rights to exploit a work subsequent to publication.

49. Rumsfeld v. Forum for Academic and Institutional Rights, Inc., 126 S. Ct. 1297 (2006).

50. Ed Baker has cogently distinguished individuals' autonomous speech from the largely market-driven speech of advertisers and commercial media and has detailed the implications of this distinction for First Amendment law and policy. *See* C. EDWIN BAKER, HUMAN LIBERTY AND FREEDOM OF SPEECH 199–234 (Oxford University Press 1989).

51. IMMANUEL KANT, Von der Unrechtmassigkeit des Buchernachdruckes, in IMMANUEL KANTS WERKE 213, 213–16 (Ernst Cassirer ed., 1913). For discussion, *see* Neil Netanel, *Copyright Alienability Restrictions and Enhancement of Author Autonomy: A Normative Evaluation*, 24 RUTGERS L.J. 347, 374–77 (1993).

Chapter Four

1. THE FEDERALIST NO. 43, at 272 (James Madison) (Clinton Rossiter ed., 1961).

2. The complete title of the first federal copyright statute was: "An Act for the encouragement of learning, by securing the copies of maps, charts, and books,

to the authors and proprietors of such copies, during the times therein mentioned." Act of May 31, 1790, ch. 15, § 1, 1 Stat. 124, 124.

3. Books, plays, and other texts that were not "published," meaning printed and distributed to the public, remained protected by common-law copyright under state law. Owners of common-law copyright in unpublished works generally enjoyed the exclusive right to copy, publicly perform, or possibly even modify such works, although in some circumstances those rights might be deemed partly waived even by acts falling short of publication.

4. Act of May 31, 1790, §§ 3–4, 1 Stat. 124, 124. *See also* Wheaton v. Peters, 33 U.S. (8 Pet.) 591, 665–68 (1834) (stating that the 1790 Copyright Act required the author or copyright owner to comply with all four of the provisions as set out in sections 3 and 4 of the Copyright Act of 1790 in order to have a valid copyright).

5. PAUL STARR, THE CREATION OF THE MEDIA: POLITICAL ORIGINS OF MASS COMMUNICATIONS 90 (Basic Books 2004).

6. 2 Stat. 171 (April 29, 1802).

7. 4 Stat. 36 (Feb. 3, 1831).

8. David Nimmer, *The End of Copyright,* 48 VAND. L. REV. 1385, 1416 (1995).

9. Act of May 31, 1790, ch. 15, § 1, 1 Stat. 124, 124.

10. Act of Feb. 3, 1831, ch. 16, 4 Stat. 436.

11. Act of Mar. 4, 1909, ch. 320, § 23, 35 Stat. 1075, 1080.

12. A Copyright Office study of copyright renewal, completed in 1960, found that only about 15 percent of subsisting copyrights were being renewed. Barbara A. Ringer, *Renewal of Copyright, in* 1 STUDIES ON COPYRIGHT 503, 617 (Arthur Fisher mem. ed., 1963).

13. Actually, between 1962 and 1974, Congress passed a series of laws that incrementally extended subsisting copyrights. It did so in anticipation of modifying the copyright term as part of the general copyright revision ultimately enacted in 1976.

14. 17 U.S.C. § 302 (1994). Works created, but not published or copyrighted prior to January 1, 1978, and works in which copyright already subsisted on January 1, 1978, are protected for different terms pursuant to sections 303 and 304, respectively.

15. Sonny Bono Copyright Term Extension Act, Pub. L. No. 105-298, § 102, 112 Stat. 2827, 2827–28 (1998).

16. *See* Brief of Amici Curiae George A. Akerlof et al., Eldred v. Ashcroft, 537 U.S. 186 (2003) (No. 01-618); Christopher Sprigman, *Reform(aliz)ing Copyright,* 57 STAN. L. REV. 485, 522 (2004).

17. Stowe v. Thomas, 23 F. Cas. 201 (C.C.E.D. Pa. 1853) (No. 13,514).

18. For an insightful and detailed discussion of courts' gradual move from a focus on defendants' contributions to a view that copyright owners are generally entitled to control any use of expression from which they might profit, see

Glynn S. Lunney, Jr., *Reexamining Copyright's Incentives-Access Paradigm,* 49 VAND. L. REV. 483, 534–40 (1996).

19. Sheldon v. Metro-Goldwyn Pictures Corp., 81 F.2d 49, 56 (2d Cir. 1936), *cert. denied,* 298 U.S. 669 (1936).

20. *See* MELVILLE B. NIMMER & DAVID NIMMER, 3 NIMMER ON COPYRIGHT, § 13.03[A][1][b], at 13–36 (2005).

21. On substantial similarity, see Swirsky v. Carey, 376 F.3d 841 (9th Cir. 2004). On subconscious copying, see Three Boys Music Corp. v. Bolton, 212 F.2d 971 (2d Cir. 1991); Bright Tunes Music Corp. v. Harrisongs Music, Ltd., 420 F. Supp. 177 (S.D.N.Y. 1976).

22. *See* Metcalf v. Bochco, 294 F.3d 1069, 1074–75 (9th Cir. 2002) (holding that the presence of generic similarities and common patterns was sufficient to defeat defendant's motion for summary judgment under the Ninth Circuit's extrinsic test); Three Boys Music Corp. v Bolton, 212 F.3d 477, 485–86 (9th Cir. 2000) (substantial similarity in combination of five unprotectible elements in popular songs).

23. Peter Pan Fabrics, Inc. v. Martin Weiner Corp., 274 F.2d 487, 489 (2d Cir. 1960).

24. 17 U.S.C. § 106(2) (1994).

25. Roth Greeting Cards v. United Card Co., 429 F.2d 1106, 1110 (9th Cir. 1970) (holding that defendant's imitative greeting card may be infringing even though it copied neither copyrighted text nor copyrighted artwork). *See also* Sturdza v. United Arab Emirates, 281 F.3d 1287, 1297–99 (D.C. Cir. 2002) (dealing with architectural work); Hamil Am. Inc. v. GFI, 193 F.3d 92, 101–02 (2d Cir. 1999), *cert. denied,* 528 U.S. 1160 (2000) (rejecting "the broad proposition that 'in comparing designs for copyright infringement, we are required to dissect them into their separate components, and compare only those elements which are in themselves copyrightable.'"); BMS Entm't/Heat Music LLC v. Bridges, 2005 WL 2675088 (S.D.N.Y. 2005) (holding that similarity in total concept and feel in combination of unoriginal elements in song can infringe).

26. *See* Shine v. Childs, 382 F. Supp. 2d 602, 615 (S.D.N.Y. 2005) (describing the Second Circuit's "'more discerning' ordinary observer test").

27. Arnstein v. Porter, 154 F.2d 464, 473 (2d Cir. 1946). *See also* Shaw v. Lindheim, 919 F.2d 1353, 1360–61 (9th Cir. 1990) (holding that the Ninth Circuit's intrinsic test for substantial similarity is inherently subjective and thus the exclusive province of the jury). On the "turbid waters of the 'extrinsic test' for substantial similarity," see Metcalf v. Bochco, 294 F.3d 1069, 1071 (9th Cir. 2002); Swirsky v. Carey, 376 F.3d 841, 848 (9th Cir. 2004).

28. Newton v. Diamond, 388 F.3d 1189, 1195 (9th Cir. 2004).

29. Feist Publ'ns v. Rural Tel. Serv. Co., 499 U.S. 340, 349–50 (1991) (citing the fundamental objectives of copyright law laid out in Art. I § 8, cl. 8 of the Constitution).

30. *See, e.g.,* Metcalf v. Bochco, 294 F.3d 1069, 1074–75 (9th Cir. 2002).

31. 4 MELVILLE B. NIMMER & DAVID NIMMER, NIMMER ON COPYRIGHT § 13.03[E][1][b] & [3] (2006).

32. Nichols v. Universal Pictures Corp., 45 F.2d 119, 122 (2d Cir. 1930).

33. Ringgold v. Black Entm't Television, Inc., 126 F.3d 70 (2d Cir. 1997).

34. LAWRENCE LESSIG, THE FUTURE OF IDEAS 4 (Random House 2001) (discussing actions against the films *Twelve Monkeys, Batman Forever,* and *The Devil's Advocate*).

35. Folsom v. Marsh, 9 F. Cas. 342 (C.C.D. Mass. 1841). For a fascinating account of this seminal copyright case, see R. Anthony Reese, *The Story of Folsom v. Marsh: Distinguishing between Infringing and Legitimate Uses,* in INTELLECTUAL PROPERTY STORIES 253 (Jane C. Ginsburg & Rochelle Dreyfuss eds., Foundation Press, 2006).

36. 17 U.S.C. § 107 (2001).

37. Campbell v. Acuff-Rose Music, Inc., 510 U.S. 569, 578 n.10 (1994) (quoting Pierre N. Leval, *Toward a Fair Use Standard,* 103 HARV. L. REV. 1105, 1134 (1990)).

38. Campbell v. Acuff-Rose Music, Inc., 510 U.S. at 575 (quoting Emerson v. Davies, 8 F.Cas. 615, 619 (No. 4,436) (CCD Mass.1845)).

39. Campbell v. Acuff-Rose Music, Inc., 510 U.S. at 575.

40. 471 U.S. 539 (1985) (holding that a story in the *Nation* that included quotations, paraphrases, and facts drawn from a manuscript by former president Gerald Ford was not fair use under the Copyright Act).

41. Harper & Row, Publishers, Inc. v. Nation Enters., 723 F.2d 195, 208 (2d Cir. 1983).

42. *Id.* at 561. At the time *Harper & Row* was decided, the question of how the burden of proof was to be allocated in fair use litigation was a matter of substantial disagreement among courts and commentators. *See* Wendy J. Gordon, *Fair Use as Market Failure: A Structural and Economic Analysis of the Betamax Case and Its Predecessors,* 82 COLUM. L. REV. 1600, 1624 n.135 (1982). It was not until Campbell v. Acuff-Rose Music, Inc., that the Supreme Court stated explicitly that because fair use is an "affirmative defense," the party asserting fair use bears the burden of proving the absence of market harm. 510 U.S. at 590.

43. *See* Campbell v. Acuff-Rose Music, Inc., 510 U.S. 569 (1994) (remanding case involving alleged parody fair use for further findings on whether the defendant had met the burden of proving absence of harm to potential markets for derivative works of plaintiff's song). These ramifications of *Harper & Row*'s characterization of fair use as an affirmative defense were not spelled out explicitly by the Court in that case. In fact, somewhat contradicting its depiction of fair use as an "affirmative defense," the Court in *Harper & Row* stated that to "negate" fair use, the copyright holder "need only show that if the challenged use 'should become widespread, it would adversely affect the

potential market for the copyrighted work. ' " 471 U.S. at 568 (quoting Sony Corp. of America v. Universal City Studios, Inc., 464 U.S. 417, 451 (1984)).

44. *See* Castle Rock Entm't, Inc. v. Carol Publ'g Group, Inc., 150 F.3d 132 (2d Cir. 1998) (finding no fair use for trivia book on *Seinfeld* TV series even though producers had no plans to enter that market); A&M Records, Inc. v. Napster, Inc., 239 F.3d 1004, 1015 (9th Cir. 2001) (describing Napster users as engaged in a disfavored "commercial" use of copyrighted music because they "get for free something they would ordinarily have to buy").

45. *See, e.g.,* Worldwide Church of God v. Phila. Church of God, Inc. 227 F.3d 1110 (9th Cir. 2000) (holding that the absence of market harm in no way guarantees fair use where a church offshoot distributed writings of a deceased church leader whose writings had since been repudiated by the mainstream church); Salinger v. Random House, Inc., 811 F.2d 90 (2d Cir. 1987) (finding biographer's quotations from unpublished letters of publicity-shunning author not fair use); Religious Tech. Ctr. v. Netcom On-Line Comm'cn Servs., Inc., 923 F. Supp. 1231 (N.D. Cal. 1995) (holding that Internet posting of Church of Scientology documents by a vocal church critic was not likely to be fair use).

46. *See Campbell,* 510 U.S. at 590 (citing *Harper & Row,* 471 U.S. at 561, in support of holding, in case involving commercial parody, that fair use is an affirmative defense and that the applicability of fair use must thus be proven by defendant); Fair Use of Copyrighted Works, H.R. Rep. No. 102–836, 102d Cong., 2d Sess. 3 n.3 (1992) (insisting that the burden "is always on the party asserting the defense, regardless of the type of relief sought by the copyright owner," and criticizing cases that have suggested otherwise). At the preliminary injunction stage, it is not certain whether the rule that defendant bears the burden of proving fair use overcomes the rule that a plaintiff moving for a preliminary injunction has the burden of proving likelihood of success on the merits. *See* A&M Records, Inc. v. Napster, Inc., 239 F.3d 1004, 1015 n.3 (9th Cir. 2001) (citing authorities on both sides and declining to rule either way).

47. *See, e.g.,* Dep't of Commerce Info. Infrastructure Task Force, Intellectual Property and the National Information Infrastructure: The Report of the Working Group on Intellectual Property Rights 82 (1995) (suggesting that technological means of tracking transactions and licensing should lead to reduced application and scope of the fair use doctrine); Paul Goldstein, Copyright's Highway: From Gutenberg to the Celestial Jukebox 203 (Stanford University Press 2003) (asserting that fair use should be invoked only in cases of bilateral market failure, which in the coming age of nearly costless collective and digital licensing will rarely, if ever, occur).

48. Universal City Studios, Inc. v. Corley, 273 F.3d 429, 458 (2d Cir. 2001). As I discuss in chapter 8, in *Eldred v. Ashcroft,* the Supreme Court noted in rejecting a First Amendment challenge to the Copyright Term Extension Act that "it is

appropriate to construe copyright's internal safeguards to accommodate First Amendment concerns." This implies, contrary to the Second Circuit's suggestion, that fair use and other free speech safeguards on copyright do in fact have constitutional import and should be interpreted and applied in line with First Amendment values.

49. Suntrust Bank v. Houghton Mifflin Co., 268 F.3d 1257, 1260 (11th Cir. 2001).

50. Mattel Inc. v. Walking Mountain Productions, 353 F.3d 792, 803 (9th Cir. 2003). *See also* Online Policy Group v. Diebold, Inc., 337 F. Supp. 2d 1195, 1200 (N.D. Cal. 2004).

51. Bill Graham Archives v. Dorling Kindersley Ltd., 448 F.3d 605, 615–15 (2d Cir. 2006). *See also* Blanch v. Koons, 467 F.3d 244, 253 (2d Cir. 2006) (favoring fair use for speech employing the original as raw material "in the creation of new information, new aesthetics, new insights and understandings").

52. As David Nimmer's comprehensive study of fair use concludes: "So which is it, fair use or unfair use? . . . [T]he problem with the four factors is they are malleable enough to be crafted to fit either point of view. Where does that leave us? . . . In the end, reliance on the four statutory factors to reach fair use decisions often seems naught but a fairy tale." David Nimmer, *"Fairest of Them All" and Other Fairy Tales of Fair Use,* 66 Law & Contemp. Prob. 263, 287 (2003).

53. Lawrence Lessig, Free Culture: How Big Media Uses Technology and the Law to Lock Down Culture and Control Creativity 187 (Penguin Press 2004).

54. As James Gibson points out, that clearance culture may also contribute to further narrowing of fair use, since courts often look to prevailing licensing practices to determine whether there is a market that would be harmed by the defendant's use of the plaintiff's copyrighted work without obtaining a license. James Gibson, *Risk Aversion and Rights Accretion in Intellectual Property Law,* 116 Yale L.J. 882 (2007).

55. After a storm of protest, Adobe modified its restrictions and explained that they were never intended to have the onerous effect that their literal reading would suggest. *See* Lessig, *supra* note 53, 147–53.

56. Pub. L. No. 105–304, sec. 103, § 1201, 112 Stat. 2860, 2863–65 (1998).

57. For discussion, see Julie E. Cohen, *The Place of the User in Copyright Law,* 74 Fordham L. Rev. 347, 359–60 (2005); R. Anthony Reese, *Will Merging Access Controls and Rights Controls Undermine the Structure of Anticircumvention Law?,* 18 Berkeley Tech. L.J. 619, 650–51 (2003).

58. In practice, the public's liberty of access, free from copyright holder constraint, has begun to erode in the digital arena even aside from the DMCA. When I view an article or listen to a song on my computer, an electronic version of the work temporarily resides in my computer's random-access memory. Several courts have thus extrapolated that the mere act of accessing

a work on a computer reproduces a "copy" of the work. *See, e.g.,* MAI Systems Corp. v. Peak Computer, Inc., 991 F.2d 511, 518 (9th Cir. 1993); Intellectual Reserve, Inc. v. Utah Lighthouse Ministry, 75 F. Supp. 2d 1290, 1294 (D. Utah 1999). If that line of cases applies, merely reading a text, watching a TV program, or listening to a recorded song on a Web site constitutes the making of a "copy" and thus infringes copyright unless de minimis, fair use, or, as is often deemed to be the case today, pursuant to the copyright holder's express or implied permission.

59. The DMCA provides that nothing in its anticircumvention provisions "shall affect rights, remedies, limitations or defenses to copyright infringement, including fair use, under this title." 17 U.S.C. § 1201(c)(1). However, that clause has been interpreted by courts to apply only to traditional copyright actions, not to actions for violation of the DMCA anticircumvention provisions. *See, e.g.*, Universal City Studios, Inc. v. Corley, 273 F.3d 429, 443–44 (2d Cir. 2001); Sony Computer Entm't of Am., Inc. v. GameMasters, Inc., 87 F. Supp. 2d 976 (N.D. Cal. 1999).

60. Margaret Jane Radin, *Online Standardization and the Integration of Text and Machine,* 70 Fordham L. Rev. 1125, 1141 (2002).

61. *See, e.g.,* Altera Corp. v. Clear Logic, Inc., 424 F.3d 1079, 1089–90 (9th Cir. 2005); Bowers v. Baystate Technologies, Inc., 320 F.3d 1317 (Fed. Cir. 2003), *cert. denied,* 539 U.S. 928 (2003); ProCD. Inc. v. Zeidenberg, 86 F.3d 1447 (7th Cir. 1996); Meridian Project Sys. v. Hardin Constr. Co., LLC, 426 F. Supp. 2d 1101 (E.D. Cal. 2006).

62. NetLibrary's TitleSelect Website, Terms of Use Agreement, ¶3.B., http://extranet.netlibrary.com/TitleSelect/process.asp (last visited Dec. 12, 2005).

63. Terms and Conditions for the Use of LexisNexis Services, Supplemental Terms for Specific Materials, Nov. 15, 2005, at ¶42 (N.Y. Times).

64. Warner Bros. Terms of Use, http://www2.warnerbros.com/main/privacy/terms.html?frompage=movies (last visited Apr. 19, 2006).

65. *See* White-Smith Music Publg. Co. v. Apollo Co., 209 U.S. 1, 19 (1908) (Holmes, J., concurring).

66. *See* Jessica Litman, *Sharing and Stealing,* 27 Hastings Comm. & Ent. L.J. 1 (2004).

67. *See* Jane C. Ginsburg, *From Having Copies to Experiencing Works: The Development of an Access Right in U.S. Copyright Law,* 50 J. Copyright Soc'y U.S.A.113 (2003).

68. The Internet began as a U.S. Department of Defense initiative. *See* Steve Bickerstaff, *Shackles on the Giant: How the Federal Government Created Microsoft, Personal Computers, and the Internet,* 78 Tex. L. Rev. 1, 38 (1999). Its use remains heavily subsidized by the public fisc and by telecommunications regulations maintaining cross-subsidies from telephone and other non-Internet services. *See id.* at 45–55, 82–83; Jonathan Weinberg, *The Internet and "Telecommunications Services": Access Charges, Universal Service Mechanisms and Other*

Flotsam of the Regulatory System, 16 YALE J. ON REG. 211 (1999); Philip J. Weiser, *The Ghost of Telecommunications Past*, 103 MICH. L. REV. 1671, 1673 (2005).

69. A&M Records v. Napster, Inc., 239 F.3d 1004 (9th Cir. 2001).

70. *In re* Napster, Inc. Copyright Litig., 191 F. Supp. 2d 1087, 1109 (N.D. Cal. 2002).

71. A&M Records v. Napster, 239 F.3d at 1029.

72. UMG Recordings, Inc. v. MP3.com, Inc., 92 F. Supp. 2d 349 (S.D.N.Y. 2000).

73. UMG Recordings, Inc. v. MP3.com, Inc., 2000 U.S. Dist. LEXIS 17907 (S.D.N.Y. 2000).

74. MGM Studios Inc. v. Grokster, Ltd., 545 U.S. 913 (2005).

75. It is perhaps for that reason that the *Grokster* Court stated that it was importing its active inducement rule from the Patent Act rather than relying on traditional copyright doctrine. 545 U.S. at 936–937.

76. Sony Corp. of Am. v. Universal City Studios, Inc., 464 U.S. 417, 442 (1984).

77. The Court cited the defendants' failure to "develop filtering tools or other mechanisms to diminish the infringing activity using their software" as one factor establishing active inducement, but it stated in a footnote that such a failure would not be sufficient in and of itself to support liability absent "other evidence of intent." MGM Studios Inc. v. Grokster, Ltd., 545 U.S. at 939, 939 n.12.

78. *See* 17 U.S.C. § 801(b)(1) (2001).

79. 17 U.S.C. § 114(f)(2)(B) (2000). For application of that standard, see Rates and Terms for Eligible Nonsubscription Transmissions and the Making of Ephemeral Reproductions, 37 C.F.R. § 261 (2003). *See also* Recording Indus. Ass'n of Am. v. Librarian of Congress, 176 F.3d 528, 533–34 (D.C. Cir. 1999) (rejecting the recording industry's claim that the pre-1998 law required a market rate standard and noting that Congress did adopt that rate prospectively in the DMCA).

80. In the Matter of Digital Performance Right in Sound Recordings and Ephemeral Recordings, Docket No. 2005–1 DRB DTRA 19 n.7 (U.S. Copyright Royalty Board, Mar. 2, 2007).

81. Small Webcaster Settlement Act of 2002, 107 Pub. L. No. 321, Sec. 3(a)(2), 116 Stat. 2780 (Dec. 4, 2002), codified at 17 U.S.C. § 114(f)(5)(E).

82. In the Matter of Digital Performance Right in Sound Recordings and Ephemeral Recordings, Docket No. 2005–1 DRB DTRA 19–20 (rejecting any distinction between small commercial webcasters and other commercial webcasters), 46 (royalty rate for commercial webcasters), 60–61 (royalty rate for noncommercial webcasters) (U.S. Copyright Royalty Board, Mar. 2, 2007). The noncommercial webcasters must pay the commercial rate for all transmissions that exceed the equivalent of 218 simultaneous listeners per month and a flat rate of $500 per month for transmission below that threshold.

Chapter Five

1. United States Copyright Office, Copyright in Congress 1789–1904, Copyright Office Bulletin No. 8, 115–16 (T. Solverg ed., 1905) (quoting *U.S. Senate Journal,* 1st Cong. 102–04).

2. *See* Clayton v. Stone, 5 F. Cas. 999, 1003 (C.C.S.D.N.Y. 1829) (No. 2872) (denying copyright protection to newspaper financial reports in part on grounds that daily newspapers' incompatibility with copyright deposit and registration requirements indicated that Congress did not intend to include them within scope of copyrightable "books").

3. *See* RICHARD R. JOHN, SPREADING THE NEWS: THE AMERICAN POSTAL SYSTEM FROM FRANKLIN TO MORSE 38 (Harvard University Press 1996); RICHARD B. KIELBOWICZ, NEWS IN THE MAIL: THE PRESS, POST OFFICE, AND PUBLIC INFORMATION, 1700–1860S 71 (Greenwood Press 1989).

4. PAUL STARR, THE CREATION OF THE MEDIA: POLITICAL ORIGINS OF MASS COMMUNICATIONS 90 (Basic Books 2004).

5. *Id.* at 122.

6. For a historical account of economic approaches to copyright, see Gillian K. Hadfield, *The Economics of Copyright: An Historical Perspective,* 38 COPYRIGHT L. SYMP. (ASCAP) 1 (1992).

7. Adam Smith lauded the temporary monopoly granted to authors and their assigns under the Statute of Anne as an efficient means of stimulating book production: "[I]f the book be a valuable one the demand for it in that time [i.e., the copyright period] will probably be a considerable addition to his [i.e., the author's] fortune. But if it is of no value the advantage he can reap from it will be very small." Adam Smith, *Lectures on Jurisprudence; Report of 1762–63, in* ADAM SMITH, AN INQUIRY INTO THE NATURE AND CAUSES OF THE WEALTH OF NATIONS 754 n.69 (Oxford University Press, R.H. Campbell & A.S. Skinner eds., 1976) (1776).

8. *See, e.g.,* Stephen Breyer, *The Uneasy Case for Copyright: A Study of Copyright in Books, Photocopies, and Computer Programs,* 84 HARV. L. REV. 281, 322–23 (1970) (concluding that "the basic case for copyright protection of books is weak" and arguing that this "suggests that a heavy burden of persuasion should be placed upon those who would extend such protection," including extending protection against photocopying and to computer programs); Lloyd L. Weinreb, *Copyright for Functional Expression,* 111 HARV. L. REV. 1149, 1211 (1998) (contending that copyright derives more from convention than actual incentive benefit).

9. Yochai Benkler, *Coase's Penguin, or, Linux and the Nature of the Firm,* 112 YALE L.J. 369 (2002).

10. WILLIAM W. FISHER III, PROMISES TO KEEP: TECHNOLOGY, LAW, AND THE FUTURE OF ENTERTAINMENT 19–20, 54–59 (Stanford University Press 2004); Raymond S. Ku, *The Creative Destruction of Copyright: Napster and*

the New Economics of Digital Technology, 69 U. CHI. L. REV. 263, 306–09 (2002).

11. A seminal work on the untoward influence of advertising on our system of free expression is C. EDWIN BAKER, ADVERTISING AND A DEMOCRATIC PRESS (Princeton University Press 1994).

12. Jane C. Ginsburg, *Putting Cars on the "Information Superhighway": Authors, Exploiters, and Copyright in Cyberspace,* 95 COLUM. L. REV. 1466, 1499 (1995).

13. PETER GAY, THE ENLIGHTENMENT: AN INTERPRETATION — THE SCIENCE OF FREEDOM 57–65 (Alfred A. Knopf 1969); JOSEPH LOEWENSTEIN, THE AUTHOR'S DUE: PRINTING AND THE PREHISTORY OF COPYRIGHT 27–88 (Univ. of Chicago Press 2002).

14. GAY, *supra* note 13, at 63 (quoting Voltaire) (internal quotation marks omitted).

15. James Curran, *Communications, Power and Social Order, in* CULTURE, SOCIETY AND THE MEDIA 201, 203–10 (Michael Gurevitch et al. eds., Methuen 1982) (describing medieval Catholic Church's use of architecture, sculpture, paintings, stained glass windows, and books to uphold its power).

16. *See* HAROLD J. LASKI, THE AMERICAN DEMOCRACY 394 (Viking Press 1948); MICHAEL WARNER, THE LETTERS OF THE REPUBLIC: PUBLICATION AND THE PUBLIC SPHERE IN EIGHTEENTH-CENTURY AMERICA 132–38 (Harvard University Press 1990). Prior to the neoclassical period, popular culture and elite culture were intermingled to a greater extent. *See* PETER BURKE, POPULAR CULTURE IN EARLY MODERN EUROPE 277 (New York University Press 1978) (noting that Shakespeare had played to noblemen and apprentices alike). It was not until the spread of print and the "rediscovery" of popular culture among late eighteenth-century and early nineteenth-century Romantics that the neoclassical disjunction between elite and popular culture was, to some degree, attenuated. *See id.* at 3–22.

17. *See* VICTOR BONHAM-CARTER, AUTHORS BY PROFESSION 1911, 5–32 (William Kaufmann 1978); GAY, *supra* note 13, at 58–65.

18. *See* CATHY DAVIDSON, REVOLUTION AND THE WORD: FROM THE INTRODUCTION OF PRINTING UNTIL THE COPYRIGHT ACT 42–45 (Oxford University Press 1986) (describing how growth, in late eighteenth-century and early nineteenth-century America, of proto–mass audience for books, especially those, such as novels, that did not require official exegesis, eroded the pulpit model of authority and led to "democratization of mind"); *see also* JOHN B. THOMPSON, THE MEDIA AND MODERNITY 56–62 (1995) (discussing the role of early print capitalism and the nascent reading public in eroding the power of the Catholic Church and contributing to the emergence of the modern state in sixteenth- and seventeenth-century Europe).

19. My discussion of this sphere of print-mediated public opinion draws heavily upon Charles Taylor, *Modes of Civil Society,* 3 PUB. CULTURE 95, 108–09 (1990); *see also* JOYCE APPLEBY, CAPITALISM AND A NEW SOCIAL ORDER: THE REPUBLICAN VISION OF THE 1790S 76–78 (New York University Press 1984)

(noting the centrality of print in grassroots politics in early United States); JÜRGEN HABERMAS, THE STRUCTURAL TRANSFORMATION OF THE PUBLIC SPHERE 29–43 (Thomas Burger trans., MIT Press 1989) (1962) (chronicling the emergence of a literary public sphere in England, France, and Germany); LARZER ZIFF, WRITING IN THE NEW NATION 91 (Yale University Press 1991) (discussing generally how "the democratization of print both promoted and was promoted by the democratization of society").

20. *See* WARNER, *supra* note 16 (discussing preeminent role of understandings of print in republican ideology of eighteenth-century America); Taylor, *supra* note 19, at 108–09.

21. ADRIAN JOHNS, THE NATURE OF THE BOOK: PRINT AND KNOWLEDGE IN THE MAKING 213–65 (University of Chicago Press 1998).

22. The Statute of Anne, enacted by Parliament in 1710, was entitled "An Act for the Encouragement of Learning, by vesting the Copies of printed Books in the Authors or Purchasers of such Copies, during the Times herein mentioned." 8 Anne 19 (1710) (Eng.).

23. Letter LXXXIV, *The Citizen of the World, in* 2 COLLECTED WORKS OF OLIVER GOLDSMITH 341, 344 (Clarendon Press 1966).

24. *See* LANCE BERTELSEN, THE NONSENSE CLUB: LITERATURE AND POPULAR CULTURE 1749–1764 260–61 (Oxford University Press 1986); Curran, *supra* note 15, at 222.

25. Michael Schudson, *Was There Ever a Public Sphere? If So, When? Reflections on the American Case, in* HABERMAS AND THE PUBLIC SPHERE 143, 151 (Craig Calhoun ed., MIT Press 1992). By the end of the eighteenth century, the audience for print appears to have comprised the majority of U.S. citizens, though most could not afford to purchase many books, and many who could not read listened as printed materials were read aloud. *See* DAVIDSON, *supra* note 18, at 27–28; THOMPSON, *supra* note 18, at 60; WARNER, *supra* note 16, at 14.

26. ERIC FONER, TOM PAINE AND REVOLUTIONARY AMERICA 83 (Oxford University Press 1976) (internal quotation marks omitted). Not surprisingly, Paine was an outspoken advocate for according statutory copyright protection to authors. *See* JOHN TEBBEL, 1 A HISTORY OF BOOK PUBLISHING IN THE UNITED STATES 1630–1865 138 (R. R. Bowker Co. 1972).

27. ZIFF, *supra* note 19, at 52 (quoting SAMUEL MILLER, A BRIEF RETROSPECT OF THE EIGHTEENTH CENTURY (T. & J. Swords 1803) (internal quotation marks omitted); *see also* JAMES RALPH, THE CASE OF AUTHORS BY PROFESSION OR TRADE (Scholars' Facsimiles & Reprints 1966) (1758) (defending professional authors against charges of venality, but conceding that much commercial literature is of low quality).

28. *See* WARNER, *supra* note 16, at 122–32.

29. Letter from James Madison to W. T. Barry (Aug. 4, 1822), reprinted in 9 THE WRITINGS OF JAMES MADISON 103, 103 (Gaillard Hunt ed., G. P. Putnam's Sons 1910).

30. Jeffrey L. Pasley, "The Tyranny of Printers": Newspaper Politics in the Early American Republic 58 (University Press of Virginia 2001).

31. *See* Davidson, *supra* note 18, at 16–30 (describing emerging but uneven market economy of book publishing in early national period); Lucas A. Powe, Jr., The Fourth Estate and the Constitution 28–29 (University of California Press 1991) (depicting transformation of eighteenth-century press); Warner, *supra* note 16, at 67–70 (discussing manner in which printers, whose economic viability was threatened by the Stamp Tax, successfully galvanized public opinion against the tax by emphasizing that it was an affront to liberty of press).

32. *See* Starr, *supra* note 4, at 85, 122–27.

33. Id. at 145, 185–89, 295–384.

34. *See, e.g.*, News Incorporated: Corporate Media Ownership and Its Threat to Democracy (Elliot D. Cohen ed., Prometheus Books 2005); Robert W. McChesney, The Problem of the Media: U.S. Communication Politics in the 21st Century (Monthly Review Press 2004); Ben H. Bagdikian, The New Media Monopoly (Beacon Press 2004).

35. In this paragraph I summarize media criticism presented in one or more of the following: C. Edwin Baker, Media, Markets, and Democracy (Cambridge University Press 2002); McChesney, *supra* note 34; Cass R. Sunstein, Democracy and the Problem of Freedom of Speech (Free Press 1993); and Owen Fiss, *Why the State?*, 100 Harv. L. Rev. 781, 787–88 (1987).

36. Yochai Benkler, The Wealth of Networks: How Social Production Transforms Markets and Freedom 178–80 (Yale University Press 2006).

37. *Id.* at 168–69.

38. In a sense the media themselves often act as the public to which the democratic process responds. *See* David L. Protess et al., The Journalism of Outrage: Investigative Reporting and Agenda Building in America 244–49 (Guilford Press 1991) (noting, on the basis of detailed case studies of investigative reporting, that government officials tend to respond to investigative reporters and media exposés before interest groups or the public at large takes up the issue, treating the press as if it were the public).

39. *See* Stephen Holmes, Passions and Constraint: On the Theory of Liberal Democracy 179–81 (University of Chicago Press 1995) (discussing John Stuart Mill's thesis that a liberal state requires a robust exchange of view); Cass R. Sunstein, Free Markets and Social Justice 186–87 (Oxford University Press 1997) (contending that liberal democracy requires a realm of discursive exchange in which citizens can test their preferences and produce better collective decisions).

40. Lada Adamic and Natalie Glance, *The Political Blogosphere and the 2004 U.S. Election: Divided They Blog,* Mar. 4, 2005, http://www.blogpulse.com/papers/2005/AdamicGlanceBlogWWW.pdf.

41. For discussion of the problem of excessive insularity in the context of the Internet, see ANDREW SHAPIRO, THE CONTROL REVOLUTION 105–09 (Public Affairs 1999); CASS R. SUNSTEIN, REPUBLIC.COM (Princeton University Press 2002). Indeed, as studies of group psychology suggest, discursive insularity may well promote great polarization and extremism, not merely stasis. *See* Cass R. Sunstein, *Deliberative Trouble? Why Groups Go to Extremes,* 110 YALE L.J. 71 (2000).

42. *See* Maxwell McCombs, et al., *Issues in the News and the Public Agenda: The Agenda-Setting Tradition, in* PUBLIC OPINION AND THE COMMUNICATIONS OF CONSENT 281, 292 (Theodore L. Glasser & Charles T. Salmon eds., Guilford Press, 1995) (noting that given competition among issues for saliency among the public, the public agenda typically consists of no more than five to seven issues).

43. Project for Excellence in Journalism, 2006 Annual Report on the State of the News Media, Chapter: A Day in the Life of the Media; Blogs (2006), http://www.stateofthenewsmedia.com/2006/printable_daymedia_blogs.asp. The Project for Excellence in Journalism is an academic institute affiliated with the Columbia University Graduate School of Journalism.

44. Daniel W. Drezner and Henry Farrell, *The Power and Politics of Blogs,* July 2004, http://www.danieldrezner.com/research/blogpaperfinal.pdf.

45. *See Political Dirty-tricksters Are Using Wikipedia,* SILICONVALLEY.COM, Apr. 28, 2006, http://www.siliconvalley.com/mld/siliconvalley/news/editorial/14454525.htm (reporting that political operatives have been covertly rewriting the online encyclopedia's entries to make their bosses look good or opponents look ridiculous).

46. Lindsey Powell, Note, *Getting Around Circumvention: A Proposal for Taking FECA Online,* 58 STAN. L. REV. 1499, 1525–29 (2006); Sam McManis, *These Days You Can't Trust Some Blogs,* SACRAMENTO BEE, Dec. 21, 2006 (describing "flogs," fake weblogs that purport to chronicle an ordinary consumer's passion for a product but that are actually sponsored by corporate public relations firms).

47. The Lonelygirl15 ruse, when an actress posed as a homeschooled teenager in a YouTube video blog, is a recent much-discussed example.

48. Moreover, significantly for the relative import of traditional media versus network discussion for public discourse, the public *views* the traditional news media as far more trustworthy than bloggers and other Internet sources. *See* Princeton Survey Research Associates International, *Leap of Faith: Using the Internet Despite the Dangers; Results of a National Survey of Internet Users for Consumer Reports WebWatch* 23, 26 (Oct. 26, 2005), http://www.consumer webwatch.org/pdfs/princeton.pdf.

49. Democratic governments regularly provide direct and indirect subsidies for various forms of cultural expression, ranging from individual grants to the funding of public broadcasting. *See* David Throsby, *The Production and*

Consumption of the Arts: A View of Cultural Economics, 32 J. ECON. LIT. 1, 20–22 (1994).

50. PASLEY, *supra* note 30, at 131.

51. 6 MEMOIRS OF JOHN QUINCY ADAMS 61 (Charles Francis Adams ed. 1874–77; reprinted, Books for Libraries Press, 1969), quoted in DONNA LEE DICKERSON, THE COURSE OF TOLERANCE: FREEDOM OF PRESS IN NINETEENTH-CENTURY AMERICA 66 (Greenwood Press 1990).

52. Duff Green, U.S. TELEGRAPH, Feb. 9, 1826, quoted in DICKERSON, *supra* note 51, at 69.

53. *See* DICKERSON, *supra* note 51, at 65–71 (describing criticism and subsequent use of press patronage by John Quincy Adams and Daniel Webster); CULVER H. SMITH, THE PRESS, POLITICS, AND PATRONAGE: THE AMERICAN GOVERNMENT'S USE OF NEWSPAPERS 1789–1875, 229–48 (Univ. of Georgia Press 1977) (describing the end of press patronage).

54. *See* Paul Farhi, *PBS Scrutiny Raises Political Antennas,* WASH. POST, Apr. 22, 2005 at C01. *See also* ELI NOAM, TELEVISION IN EUROPE 96–97 (Oxford Univ. Press 1991) (chronicling decades of postwar French government attempts to influence coverage on state-run French television and radio); *Furor over IRA Film Could Put Peace Talks in Jeopardy,* THE INDEPENDENT (LONDON), July 27, 1997, at 1 (noting that under a UK government ban, Sinn Fein representatives were not allowed to speak on British television until 1993).

55. *See generally* Robert Post, *Subsidized Speech,* 106 YALE L.J. 151 (1996). *See also* ANTHONY SMITH, THE POLITICS OF INFORMATION 174 (Macmillan 1978) (noting that proposals for press subsidies in Germany have foundered on the difficulty of determining such criteria).

56. My account of the Wigand story draws heavily upon Paul Starr, *What You Need to Beat Goliath,* AM. PROSPECT, Dec. 20, 1999, at 7, and the PBS *Frontline* chronology of events, at http://www.pbs.org/wgbh/pages/frontline/smoke/cron.html.

57. Some 10 million households watch *60 Minutes* each week. Owen M. Fiss, *The Censorship of Television,* 93 NW. U.L. REV. 1215, 1217 (1999) (citing Nielsen Media Research, 1998 Report on Television (1999)).

58. *See* Bill Carter, *CBS Broadcasts Interview with Tobacco Executive,* N.Y. TIMES, Feb. 5, 1996, at B8 (reporting that CBS broadcast the interview a week after the *Wall Street Journal* had published the transcript of the Wigand deposition).

59. And of course that film has been criticized for taking liberties with the facts in order to present a more dramatic story. *See* Lawrence K. Grossman, *The Insider: It's Only a Movie,* COLUM. JOURNALISM REV., Nov./Dec. 1999, http://archives.cjr.org/year/99/6/insider-review.asp.

60. United States v. Associated Press, 52 F. Supp. 362, 372 (S.D.N.Y. 1943), *aff'd,* 326 U.S. 1 (1945).

61. *See* C. Edwin Baker, *Media Concentration: Giving Up on Democracy,* 54 FLA. L. REV. 839, 918 (2002); James Curran, *Rethinking Media and Democracy, in* MASS

MEDIA AND SOCIETY 120, 140–48 (James Curran & Michael Gurevitch eds., 3d ed., Oxford University Press 2000).

62. Commentary highlighting the law's expressive function includes Hanoch Dagan, *Takings and Distributive Justice*, 85 VA. L. REV. 741, 771–72 (1999); Dan M. Kahan, *What Do Alternative Sanctions Mean?*, 63 U. CHI. L. REV. 591 (1996); Cass R. Sunstein, *On the Expressive Function of Law*, 144 U. PA. L. REV. 2021 (1996); Richard H. Pildes, *Why Rights Are Not Trumps: Social Meanings, Expressive Harms, and Constitutionalism*, 27 J. LEGAL STUD. 725 (1998). Thoughtful critics include Matthew D. Adler, *Expressive Theories of Law: A Skeptical Overview*, 148 U. PA. L. REV. 1363 (2000); Lewis A. Kornhauser, *No Best Answer?*, 146 U. PA. L. REV. 1599, 1623–34 (1998).

63. *See* CHARLES TAYLOR, SOURCES OF THE SELF: THE MAKING OF MODERN IDENTITY 167–75 (Cambridge University Press 1989).

64. ROBERT A. FERGUSON, LAW AND LETTERS IN AMERICAN CULTURE 6 (Harvard University Press 1984).

65. I borrow heavily in this paragraph from Michael D. Birnhack's excellent article, *The Idea of Progress in Copyright Law*, 1 BUFFALO INT. PROP. L.J. 3 (2001).

66. Letter of Thomas Jefferson, 1786, quoted in Birnhack, *supra* note 65, at 21.

67. *Id.;* Whitney v. California, 274 U.S. 357, 377 (1927) (Brandeis, J., concurring).

68. JESSICA LITMAN, DIGITAL COPYRIGHT 111–21 (Prometheus Books 2001). *See also* Jessica Litman, *Sharing and Stealing*, 27 HASTINGS COMM. & ENT. L.J. 1 (2004).

69. *See* David Pierson, *Merit Badge That Can't Be Duplicated: MPAA, Scouts Team Up to Offer an Anti-Piracy Award*, L.A. TIMES, Oct. 21, 2006, at B1 (reporting on Boy Scouts program). The Recording Industry Association of America features several K–8 copyright education programs on its Web site. Recording Industry Association of America, Copyright Educational Efforts, http://www .riaa.com/issues/education/default.asp (last visited Jan. 7, 2007).

Chapter Six

1. Schauer would reserve the word "censorship" for direct government suppression of speech. *See* Frederick Schauer, *The Ontology of Censorship, in* CENSORSHIP AND SILENCING: PRACTICES OF CULTURAL REGULATION 147 (Robert C. Post ed., Getty Research Institute for the Art and Humanities 1998). He also notes that media entities' own speech often involves editorial discretion regarding which of others' speech to include. So to label as "censorship" a newspaper's or broadcaster's refusal to print or air a reply or other submission would deny the media's speech interest in editorial discretion and fly in the face of ubiquitous practice. *See* FREDERICK SCHAUER, FREE SPEECH: A PHILOSOPHICAL ENQUIRY 119–25 (Cambridge University Press 1982). But the copyright holder silencing I describe is quite different from a newspaper's refusal to print a reply to an

editorial. A newspaper has limited space, so if required to print every reply and submission, it would be unable to convey its own chosen speech. In contrast, copyrighted expression is nonrivalrous. Alice Randall's creative recasting of *Gone with the Wind* in no way impedes the Mitchell estate's continued distribution of that Civil War classic. A speaker's creative appropriation might diminish the marketability of the original work, whether by savage criticism or competing for consumer attention and dollars. But that does not stop the copyright owner from speaking.

2. *See* Maureen O'Rourke, *A Brief History of Author-Publisher Relations and the Outlook for the 21st Century*, 50 J. COPYRIGHT SOC'Y U.S.A. 425 (2003).

3. Ed Baker has eloquently distinguished the inherently market-driven speech interests of commercial enterprises from the value decisions of nonmarket speakers. *See generally* C. Edwin Baker, *Realizing Self-Realization: Corporate Political Expenditures and Redish's Value of Free Speech*, 130 U. PA. L. REV. 646 (1982); C. Edwin Baker, *Commercial Speech: A Problem in the Theory of Freedom*, 62 IOWA L. REV. 1 (1976).

4. *See* D. T. Max, *The Injustice Collector: Is James Joyce's Grandson Suppressing Scholarship?*, NEW YORKER, June 19, 2006, at 34.

5. Complaint for Declaratory Judgment and Injunctive Relief at 12, Shloss v. Estate of James Joyce, No. CV 06–3718 (N.D. Cal., Oct. 25, 2006), *available at* http://cyberlaw.stanford.edu/attachments/Complaint%20Endorsed%20Filed%206–12–06.pdf (quoting reviews). With the pro bono representation of the Stanford Center for Internet and Society's Fair Use Project, Professor Shloss sued the estate to establish her fair use right to use the deleted materials in connection with her scholarly biography of Lucia Joyce. The case settled in March 2007, after the court had denied the estate's motion to dismiss, with the estate agreeing to allow Shloss to publish the deleted materials on a Web site that would supplement her book.

6. *See* New Era Publ'ns Int'l. v. Henry Holt & Co., 873 F.2d 576 (2d Cir. 1989) (denying the application of fair use to the use of unpublished writings of a founder of the Church of Scientology in a critical biography); Religious Tech. Ctr. v. Lerma, 40 U.S.P.Q.2D (BNA) 1569 (E.D. Va. 1996) (holding not a fair use for Scientology critic to distribute Church documents on the Internet); Religious Tech. Ctr. v. Lerma, 908 F. Supp. 1362, 1366–67 (E.D. Va. 1995) (finding *Washington Post* quotation from church materials was a fair use); Religious Tech. Ctr. v. Netcom On-Line Comm. Servs., Inc., 923 F. Supp. 1231 (N.D. Cal. 1995) (holding Internet service provider potentially liable for user's infringing posting of church documents).

7. Ashdown v. Telegraph Group Ltd [2001] 4 All ER 666. Although the case was brought and decided in the United Kingdom under UK law, there is no reason to think that the result would be any different in the United States.

8. *See, e.g.,* Mattel Inc. v. Walking Mountain Prod., 353 F.3d 792 (9th Cir. 2003) (suit against Tom Forsythe's Food Chain Barbie series); Mattel, Inc. v. MCA

Records, 296 F.3d 894 (9th Cir. 2002) (trademark infringement action over song that lampooned Barbie); Mattel, Inc. v. Pitt, 229 F. Supp. 2d 315 (S.D.N.Y. 2002) (suit against customized Barbie with sadomasochistic theme); Walt Disney Prod. v. Mature Pictures Corp. 389 F. Supp. 1397 (D.N.Y. 1975) (suit against use of Mickey Mouse March in an adult movie). For discussion of threatened litigation by Mattel, see Lisa Bannon, *Barrister Barbie? Mattel Plays Rough,* WALL ST. J., Jan. 6, 1988, at B1. For reporting on Disney's loose trigger, see Nigel Andrews, *That Soared,* FINANCIAL TIMES (LONDON), Apr. 11, 1992, at IX.

9. *See* MARJORIE HEINS & TRICIA BECKLES, WILL FAIR USE SURVIVE? FREE EXPRESSION IN THE AGE OF COPYRIGHT CONTROL ii (NYU Brennan Center for Justice 2005) ("Threatening 'cease and desist' letters cause many people to give up their fair use rights"); Jean O. Lanjuow & Josh Lerner, *The Enforcement of Intellectual Property Rights: A Survey of the Empirical Literature* (Nat'l Bureau of Econ. Research Working Paper No. 6296, 1997) (stating that litigation costs fall most heavily on small firms, which may settle because they cannot afford long-term litigation).

10. William F. Patry & Richard A. Posner, *Fair Use and Statutory Reform in the Wake of Eldred,* 92 CAL. L. REV. 1639, 1654–57 (2004).

11. *Id.* at 1654.

12. *See* Chilling Effects Clearinghouse at http://www.chillingeffects.org.

13. Studios and broadcasters, for example, typically have their attorneys scrutinize motion picture cue sheets to identify any cut, background shot, or music that might pose any risk of infringement. Record labels require recording artists to identify any samples of prerecorded music. Book publishers regularly insist that authors clear even short quotations. For an illuminating depiction of this clearance culture and of how it feeds back into intellectual property doctrine, see James Gibson, *Risk Aversion and Rights Accretion in Intellectual Property Law,* 116 YALE L.J. 882 (2007).

14. In a much welcome but as yet untested development, a couple of errors and omissions carriers have recently announced that they will provide coverage for documentary filmmakers' use of clips that comply with the Documentary Filmmakers' Statement of Best Practices in Fair Use, when supported by a legal opinion or guarantee of pro bono representation. *See* Dave McNary, *Insurance for Documentary "Fair Use,"* VARIETY, Feb. 22, 2007, *available at* http://www.variety.com/article/VR1117960027.html; Patricia Aufderheide, *Insurer Accepts Fair Use Claims!,* Copyright & Fair Use Blog, American University Center for Social Media, Feb. 13, 2007, http://www.centerforsocial media.org/blogs/fair_use/insurer_accepts_fair_use_claims1/. *See also* Ass'n of Independent Video and Filmmakers et al., *Documentary Filmmakers' Statement of Best Practices in Fair Use,* Nov. 18, 2005, http://www.centerforsocialmedia.org/resources/fair_use.

15. 17 U.S.C. § 512.

16. A recent study, based on an admittedly small and nonstatistical sample, concluded that a high percentage of take-down notices have at best questionable legal basis and that "the [take-down] process is commonly used . . . to create leverage in a competitive marketplace, to protect rights not given by copyright (or perhaps any other law), and to stifle criticism, commentary and fair use." Jennifer M. Urban & Laura Quilter, *Efficient Process or "Chilling Effects"? Takedown Notices under Section 512 of the Digital Millennium Copyright Act,* 22 SANTA CLARA COMPUTER & HIGH TECH. L.J. 621 (2006).

17. *See* Farhad Manjoo, *Voting Machine Showdown,* SALON.COM, Feb. 10, 2004, http://dir.salon.com/story/tech/feature/2004/02/10/diebold_copyright/index.html.

18. Declan McCullagh, *Google Yanks Anti-Church Sites,* WIRED NEWS, http://www.wired.com/news/politics/0,1283,51233,00.html (Mar. 21, 2002) (quoting the letter from Google to the church critic).

19. For a perceptive study of First Amendment law in this area, see Seth F. Kreimer, *Censorship by Proxy: The First Amendment, Internet Intermediaries, and the Problem of the Weakest Link,* 155 U. PA. L. REV. 11 (2006).

20. When regulation that purports to regulate conduct in fact imposes a differential burden on speech, that is cause for heightened First Amendment scrutiny. *See* Minneapolis Star & Tribune Co. v. Minn. Comm'r of Revenue, 460 U.S. 575, 579–83 (1983) (holding that a state tax on ink and paper violates the First Amendment because it both singles out the press and targets a small group of newspapers).

21. For a more detailed discussion of the subject of this paragraph, see Neil Weinstock Netanel, *Locating Copyright within the First Amendment Skein,* 54 STAN. L. REV. 1, 30–35, 60–67 (2001).

22. *See, e.g.,* C. Edwin Baker, *First Amendment Limits on Copyright,* 55 VAND. L. REV. 891, 907–08 (2002) (contending that "in the case of intellectual property, the lack of necessity and the direct targeting of speech should combine to be constitutionally fatal to the legal restriction when it abridges speech freedom"); Jed Rubenfeld, *The Freedom of Imagination: Copyright Constitutionality,* 112 YALE L.J. 1 (2002) (maintaining that copyright runs afoul of the First Amendment whenever it prevents an individual from exercising imagination); Mark A. Lemley & Eugene Volokh, *Freedom of Speech and Injunctions in Intellectual Property Cases,* 48 DUKE L.J. 147, 186 (1998) (arguing that copyright is content-based speech regulation and thus should be subject to almost always fatal strict scrutiny).

23. *See* Baker, *supra* note 22, at 935 ("[F]rom the perspective of individual liberty, speech-suppressive means are impermissible even if maximizing valuable speech (as the government sees it) is the result"); Rubenfeld, *supra* note 22, at 23–24 ("The First Amendment's objective is not maximization of total speech production. . . . The Constitution cannot be economized.").

24. *See* Molly Shaffer Van Houweling, *Distributive Values in Copyright,* 83 TEXAS L. REV. 1535 (2005); Daniel A. Farber, *Property and Free Speech,* 93 NW. U. L. REV. 1239, 1239–40 (1999).

25. Noted First Amendment scholar Harry Kalven Jr. seems to have coined the term "free speech easement" in an essay expressing concern about the implications of private property law for the civil rights movement. *See* HARRY KALVEN JR., THE NEGRO AND THE 1ST AMENDMENT 141 (University of Chicago Press 1965).

26. The classic work supporting this position is Jerome A. Barron, *Access to the Press: A New First Amendment Right,* 80 HARV. L. REV. 1641 (1967). More generally, Owen Fiss's scholarship has been central to the argument that the market inadequately serves free speech values and that "to serve the ultimate purpose of the first amendment we may sometimes find it necessary to 'restrict the speech of some elements of our society in order to enhance the relative voice of others.' " *See* Owen M. Fiss, *Free Speech and Social Structure,* 71 IOWA L. REV. 1405, 1425 (1986).

27. *See* Eugene Volokh, *Cheap Speech and What It Will Do,* 104 YALE L.J. 1806 (1995); Martin H. Redish & Kirk J. Kaludis, *The Right of Expressive Access in First Amendment Theory: Redistributive Values and the Democratic Dilemma,* 93 NW. U. L. REV. 1083 (1999).

28. *See, e.g.,* Miami Herald v. Tornillo, 418 U.S. 241 (1974) (invalidating a state "right of reply" statute that required newspapers to devote column space to responses from individuals who were the subject of the newspaper's editorials).

29. In upholding the "must-carry rules" requiring cable operators to carry local broadcasters' channels, the Supreme Court emphasized that the rules aimed to achieve important free speech objectives: to "preserve access to free television programming" for those without cable and to promote "the widespread dissemination of information from a multiplicity of sources." Turner Broadcasting Sys., Inc. v. FCC, 512 U.S. 622, 646, 662-64 (1994) ("Turner I"), *rhrg den.* 512 U.S. 1278 (1994).

30. Industry claims about the extent of harm from unlicensed Internet file trading might be overstated. For example, studies have come to conflicting conclusions regarding the extent to which the recent sharp slump in record sales can be attributed to unlicensed file sharing versus other factors. *Compare* Stan J. Liebowitz, *File Sharing: Creative Destruction or Just Plain Destruction?,* 49 J.L. & ECON. 1 (2006) (contending that file sharing has significantly harmed record sales), *with* Felix Oberholzer-Gee and Koleman Strumpf, *The Effect of File Sharing on Record Sales: An Empirical Analysis,* Working paper (University of North Carolina, Department of Economics, March 2004), http://www.unc.edu/~cigar/papers/FileSharing_March2004.pdf (finding no statistically significant effect on purchases of the average record album).

31. Netanel, *supra* note 21, at 47–59 (arguing that copyright law constitutes content-neutral, not content-based, speech regulation and thus should be subject to a form of "intermediate scrutiny," not the "strict scrutiny" typically applied to out-and-out government censorship).

32. In reality, copyright's sister intellectual property regimes, patent and trademark, might well contribute to the high price as well, but I put this issue aside to simplify the analysis.

33. A supplier has market power when the supplier has "the ability profitably to maintain prices above, or output below, the competitive level for a significant period of time." United States Dept. of Justice & FTC, Antitrust Guidelines for the Licensing of Intellectual Property § 2.1 (1995).

34. Fox's character as a media firm might also be relevant to our assessment. In the early years of the motion picture industry, the major studios controlled film production through anticompetitive collusion based on their ownership and cross-licensing of patents in film production equipment. *See* Barak Y. Orbach, *Antitrust and Pricing in the Motion Picture Industry,* 21 YALE J. ON REG. 317 (2004). The breakup of that oligopolist restraint on trade would, I think, properly be considered an element of free speech policy, as well as general law preserving competitive markets. For discussion of whether antitrust law does and should take cognizance of free speech policy, see C. Edwin Baker, *Media Concentration: Giving Up on Democracy,* 54 FLA. L. REV. 839 (2002); Howard A. Shelanksi, *Antitrust Law as Mass Media Regulation: Can Merger Standards Protect the Public Interest?,* 94 CAL. R. REV. 371 (2006); Maurice E. Stucke & Allen P. Grunes, *Antitrust and the Marketplace of Ideas,* 69 ANTITRUST L.J. 249 (2001).

35. *See, e.g.,* HERBERT HOVENKAMP, FEDERAL ANTITRUST POLICY: THE LAW OF COMPETITION AND ITS PRACTICE §3.9d, at 141 (West Group, 2d ed. 1999) (stating that if most intellectual property rights have no commercial value, such rights necessarily lack market power).

36. *See* William J. Baumol and Daniel G. Swanson, *The New Economy and Ubiquitous Competitive Price Discrimination: Identifying Defensible Criteria of Market Power,* 70 ANTITRUST L.J., 661, 662 (2003); Michael E. Levine, *Price Discrimination without Market Power,* 19 YALE J. ON REG., 1, 13–20 (2002).

37. *See* Glynn S. Lunney, Jr., *Reexamining Copyright's Incentives-Access Paradigm,* 49 VAND. L. REV. 483, 584–85 (1996) (using average cost as the baseline for determining whether copyright holder earn rents (i.e., real profit); Edmund W. Kitch, *Elementary and Persistent Errors in the Economic Analysis of Intellectual Property,* 53 VAND. L. REV. 1727, 1737 (2000) (pricing must include all the costs necessary to bring the good to market).

38. That industry thesis extends back even to the 1643 London Stationers' petition to Parliament for monopoly printing privileges: "Scarce one book in three sells well, or proves gainfull to the publisher." The Humble Remonstrance of the Company of Stationers, London, to the High Court of Parliament, April 1643, *quoted in* Arnold Plant, *The Economic Aspects of Copyright in Books,* 1 ECONOMICA

167, 183 n.2 (1934). Similarly, publishers advanced the argument in support of high prices for books before the Royal Commission on Copyright in 1878: "Four books out of five do not pay their expenses.... The most experienced person can do no more than guess whether a book by an unknown author will succeed or fail." *Id.* at 183. The Recording Industry Association of America has also used the risk argument to lobby against legislated increases in the statutory rate for mechanical licenses, which affects the amounts that the record labels pay composers and music publishers. In opposing a proposed increase in 1972, the RIAA cited figures showing that, as it was, only one in five singles sold the 46,000 units needed to break even and argued that an increase in statutory rates would raise the break-even point even higher. RUSSELL SANJEK & DAVID SANJEK, AMERICAN POPULAR MUSIC BUSINESS IN THE 20TH CENTURY 223 (Oxford University Press 1991).

39. WILLIAM M. LANDES & RICHARD A. POSNER, THE ECONOMIC STRUCTURE OF INTELLECTUAL PROPERTY LAW 40 (Harvard University Press 2003). Landes and Posner seem to state the proposition as their own. But earlier, they suggest that a publisher's costs of failed books might "at least to a considerable extent" merely be "waste induced by competition for economic rents." *Id.* at 23.

40. More precisely, normal profits are those in which the firm's return on investments of capital and labor equals total opportunity cost. *See* Michael Abramowicz, *An Industrial Organization Approach to Copyright Law,* 46 WM. & MARY L. REV. 33, 51 (2004).

41. *See, e.g.,* Christopher Yoo, *Copyright and Product Differentiation,* 79 N.Y.U. L. REV. 212, 218–19 (2004); Edmund W. Kitch, *Elementary and Persistent Errors in the Economic Analysis of Intellectual Property,* 53 VAND. L. REV. 1727, 1729–38 (2000); Tom W. Bell, *Fair Use vs. Fared Use: The Impact of Automated Rights Management on Copyright's Fair Use Doctrine,* 76 N.C. L. REV. 557, 588–89, 601–08 (1998); Paul Goldstein, *Copyright,* 55 L. & CONTEMP. PROBS. 79, 84 (1992).

42. Among the various factors that enable producers to sell at somewhat above marginal costs are brand differentiation, consumer-producer information asymmetries, and consumer transportation costs. *See* HOVENKAMP, *supra* note 35, at 84; ROBERT KUTTNER, EVERYTHING FOR SALE: THE VIRTUES AND LIMITS OF MARKETS 13–14 (University of Chicago Press 1999): Jon D. Hanson & Douglas A. Kysar, *Taking Behavioralism Seriously: Some Evidence of Market Manipulation,* 112 HARV. L. REV., 1420, 1429–39 (1999).

43. *See, e.g.,* 1 HERBERT HOVENKAMP ET AL., IP AND ANTITRUST § 4.2 (Aspen 2003) (concluding that the vast majority of intellectual property rights do not confer monopoly power in a relevant economic market).

44. The Supreme Court has recently emphasized the costs, inefficiencies, and administrative burdens of antitrust enforcement in denying an antitrust challenge to a telecommunications firm's refusal to license competitors. *See*

Verizon Commc'ns, Inc. v. Law Offices of Curtis V. Trinko, LLP, 540 U.S. 398, 414–15 (2004).

45. *See* DOMINICK SALVATORE, MICROECONOMICS 376–77, 381–82, 426 (Oxford University Press, 4th ed. 2003) (discussing oligopoly market power where markets are less than freely contestable); Roger G. Noll, Napster's Copyright Abuse Defense and the Future of Digital Entertainment Downloads (unpublished manuscript, March 2006) (on file with author) (detailing history of anticompetitive collusion in recording industry oligopoly).

46. *See* F. M. Scherer, *The Innovation Lottery, in* EXPANDING THE BOUNDARIES OF INTELLECTUAL PROPERTY: INNOVATION FOR THE KNOWLEDGE SOCIETY 12 (Rochelle Cooper Dreyfuss et al., eds., Oxford University Press 2001) (best-selling popular music albums and singles); Arthur De Vany & W. David Walls, *Bose-Einstein Dynamics and Adaptive Contracting in the Motion Picture Industry,* 106 ECON. J. 1493, 1504–5 (1996) (films). *See also* A. Collins et al., *What Makes a Blockbuster? Economic Analysis of Film Success in the United Kingdom,* 23 MANAGERIAL & DECISION ECON. 343 (2002) (finding power law in film distribution revenues in the United Kingdom). *See also* Noll, *supra* note 45, at 11 (discussing absence of reasonable substitutes for many consumers for hit records and records by star artists).

47. ARTHUR DE VANY, HOLLYWOOD ECONOMICS: HOW EXTREME UNCERTAINTY SHAPES THE FILM INDUSTRY 261–64 (Routledge 2004). *See also* RICHARD CAVES, CREATIVE INDUSTRIES: CONTRACTS BETWEEN ART AND COMMERCE 256–57 (Harvard University Press 2000) (80 percent flop rate for musicals); WILLIAM W. FISHER III, PROMISES TO KEEP: TECHNOLOGY, LAW, AND THE FUTURE OF ENTERTAINMENT 77–78 (Stanford University Press 2004) (skew log normal distribution for popular and classical music CDs); Kee Chung and Raymond Cox, *A Stochastic Model of Superstardom: An Application of the Yule Distribution,* 76 REV. ECON. & STAT. 771 (1994) (popular recorded music).

48. *See* Scherer, *supra* note 46, at 13–14 (detailing the highly skewed distribution of the record sales of recording artists over a fifty-year period and in the number of available recordings of works of classical composers). In the case of successful films, staying power may reflect marketing strategy. Consumer demand for a film is built by word of mouth (and reviews) from early viewers. Rather than charging a higher admission price for films that garner excess consumer demand, and thus risking a decline in the number of people who would see the film in the opening weeks, the motion picture industry maximizes revenue by extending the film's run. *See* De Vany & Walls, *supra* note 46, at 1511. *Cf.* Gary S. Becker, *A Note on Restaurant Pricing and Other Examples of Social Influences on Price,* 99 J. POL. ECON., 1109 (1991) (noting similar strategy for restaurants, theater owners, and booksellers).

49. *See* DE VANY, *supra* note 47, at 263–64.

50. *See* Clay Shirkey, Power Laws, Weblogs, and Inequality, Clay Shirkey's Writings about the Internet, Feb. 8, 2003, http://www.shirky.com/writings/

powerlaw_weblog.html. *See also* Bernardo A. Huberman & Lada A. Adamic, *Growth Dynamics of the World-Wide Web,* 401 NATURE, 131 (1999). *But see* David M. Pennock et al., *Winners Don't Take All: Characterizing the Competition for Links on the Web,* 99 PNAS, 5207 (2002) (concluding that although the connectivity distribution over the World Wide Web as a whole is close to a pure power law, the distribution within some specific categories, while still heavily tilted toward the most popular sites, is not quite "winner-take-all"). *Cf.* YOCHAI BENKLER, THE WEALTH OF NETWORKS: HOW SOCIAL PRO-DUCTION TRANSFORMS MARKETS AND FREEDOM 241–61 (Yale University Press 2006) (contending that Web usage falls into numerous interlocking subspheres rather than a single power-law pattern).

51. In fact, given that digital distributors offer many more works than their brick-and-mortar counterparts, an even smaller *percentage* of their inventory garners the lion's share of consumer demand. *See* CHRIS ANDERSON, THE LONG TAIL: WHY THE FUTURE OF BUSINESS IS SELLING LESS OF MORE (Hyperion 2006).

52. *See* Sushil Bikhchandani et al., *Learning from the Behavior of Others: Conformity, Fads, and Informational Cascades,* 12 J. ECON. PERSPECTIVES 151 (1998).

53. Cass Sunstein & Edna Ullman-Margalit, *Solidarity in Consumption,* 9 J. POL. PHIL. 129 (2001); Henry Hansmann, *Higher Education as an Associative Good,* Yale Law and Economics Working Paper No. 231 (Nov. 21, 1999).

54. A similar cultural effect, the desire to share common icons, may underlie part of superstar actors' and musicians' market power. *See* Moshe Adler, *The Economics of Superstars: A Review with Extensions, in* 2 HANDBOOK ON THE ECO-NOMICS OF ARTS AND CULTURE (Victor Ginsburgh & David Throsby, eds., Elsevier forthcoming).

55. *See* CAVES, *supra* note 47, at 2–7, 137–41, 256–57, 315–16; DE VANY, *supra* note 47, at 220–21, 225–26, 267–71.

56. WILLIAM GOLDMAN, ADVENTURES IN THE SCREEN TRADE: A PERSONAL VIEW OF HOLLYWOOD AND SCREENWRITING 39 (Warner Books 1984).

57. *See* C. Merle Crawford, *Marketing Research and the New Product Failure Rate,* 41 J. MARKETING 51 (1977) (surveying study results). *See also* Eric Berggren & Thomas Nacher, *Introducing New Products Can Be Hazardous to Your Company: Use the Right New-Solutions Delivery Tools,* 15 ACAD. MGMT. EXECUTIVE 92 (2001) (noting that new product failure rates have not improved despite considerable academic research and management resources devoted to the issue).

58. One 1981 study of more than 700 U.S. Fortune 1000 companies estimated that new products would provide just over 30 percent of these firm's profits during the succeeding five-year period. BOOZ ALLEN & HAMILTON, NEW PRODUCTS MANAGEMENT FOR THE 1980S 4 (Booz Allen & Hamilton 1982). In contrast, some two-thirds of recording industry revenues comes from current releases. *See* Noll, *supra* note 45, at 11 n.11 (citing National Association of Recording Merchandisers 2000 Annual Survey Results).

59. *See* Billie Jo Zirger & Modesto A. Maidique, *A Model of New Product Development: An Empirical Test,* 36 MGMT. SCI. 867, 870, 880–81 (1990).

60. *See* DE VANY, *supra* note 47, at 134; Eric W. Rothenbuhler & John M. Streck, *The Economics of the Music Industry, in* MEDIA ECONOMICS 199, 217 (Alison Alexander et al., eds., 2d ed., Lawrence Erlbaum Associates 1998); Scott Stossel, *Bibliosophy,* AM. PROSPECT, Jan. 29, 2001, at 40 (the fortunes of American publishing are heavily dependent on the sales of just a few authors). As Epstein discusses, it is also often easier for studios to obtain financing for producing sequels to hit movies. EDWARD JAY EPSTEIN, THE BIG PICTURE: THE NEW LOGIC OF MONEY AND POWER IN HOLLYWOOD 234 (Random House 2005).

61. On the book business, see GAYLE FELDMAN, BEST AND WORST OF TIME:; THE CHANGING BUSINESS OF TRADE BOOKS, 1975–2002, 27–31, 68 (Columbia University National Arts Journalism Program 2003). On the movie business, see DE VANY, *supra* note 47, at 134–38; S. Abraham Ravid, *Information, Blockbusters, and Stars: A Study of the Film Industry,* 72 J. BUS. 463 (1999); Orbach, *supra* note 34; Joseph Lampel & Jamal Shamsie, *Critical Push: Strategies for Creating Momentum in the Motion Picture Industry,* 26 J. MGMT. 233 (2000).

62. *See* DE VANY, *supra* note 47, at 99–138. For the years 2001–2004, films rated G or PG have constituted between 20 and 35 percent of the top 20 grossing feature films. Films rated PG-13 have made up between 55 and 65 percent, and films rated R between 0 and 20 percent. MOTION PICTURE ASSOCIATION, U.S. ENTERTAINMENT INDUSTRY: 2004 MPA MARKET STATISTICS 16 (2005).

63. Louis Menand, *Gross Points: Is the Blockbuster the End of the Cinema?,* NEW YORKER, Feb. 7, 2005, at 82, 86. According to Motion Picture Association of America president Dan Glickman, in 2004 ticket sales for the overseas box office rose to $15.7 billion, a 44 percent increase since 2003, while domestic box office sales totaled only $9.54 billion. Sharon Waxman, *Movie Costs Drop,* N.Y. TIMES, Mar. 16, 2005, at B2.

64. That strategy has long been followed in the motion picture industry and appears to be increasingly prevalent. *See* John Horn & Rachel Abramowitz, *"Batman" Can't Begin to Rescue Film Industry,* L.A. TIMES, June 21, 2005, at A1, A18 ("If a movie doesn't do well in its first weekend, a studio will often pull the plug on its marketing resources, saving the money for its video release."); *see also* Lampel & Shamsie, *supra* note 61, at 253 (noting that movie studios' business strategy "is based on rapidly shifting investments from products that fail to catch and towards products that begin to show momentum"). It has also spread to other industries. *See* FELDMAN, *supra* note 61, at 19 (describing the impact of computerized tracking on the book publishing and bookselling business).

65. *See, e.g.,* Menand, *supra* note 63, at 82; Verlyn Klinkenborg, *Nothing but Troubling News from the World of Publishing,* N.Y. TIMES, Jan. 27, 2003, at

A24 ("Like the film and music industries, publishing is now driven wholly by the search for blockbuster books.").

66. They might also simply retain the additional revenues in the form of excess returns on investment. *See* Matthew J. Baker & Brendan Michael Cunningham, *Court Decisions and Equity Markets: Estimating the Value of Copyright Protection*, 49 J.L. & ECON. 567, 593 (2006) (noting that studies are inconclusive regarding whether additional copyright industry returns actually result in the creation of new expressive works). *Cf.* Kai-Lung Hui & I. P. L. Png, *On the Supply of Creative Works: Evidence from the Movies*, 92 AM. ECON. REV. 217, 220 (2002) (concluding that while economic incentives do generally lead to the creation of more movies, Congress's 1998 extension of the copyright term for an additional twenty years had little impact on creative activity and was thus essentially a giveaway to owners of existing copyrights).

67. Some copyright industries, notably record labels and book publishers, produce many more works than they invest significant sums in marketing. They tend to market those works that they predict will sell the best. *See* HAROLD L. VOGEL, ENTERTAINMENT INDUSTRY ECONOMICS 208 (Cambridge University Press, 6th ed. 2004) (discussing record labels).

68. Between 80 and 95 percent of new products are extensions of existing product lines or brands. *See* Srinivas K. Reddy et al., *To Extend or Not to Extend: Success Determinants of Line Extensions*, 31 J. MARKETING RES. 243 (1994). *See also* Booz Allen & Hamilton, *supra* note 55, at 8 (concluding on the basis of a survey of more than 700 Fortune 1000 companies that only 10 percent of all new products are truly innovative).

69. FELDMAN, *supra* note 61, at 23–24. A recent study of commercial publishers of academic journals found operating margins even as high as nearly 35 percent. Aaron S. Edlin & Daniel L. Rubinfeld *Exclusion or Efficient Pricing? The "Big Deal" Bundling of Academic Journals*, 72 ANTITRUST L.J. 119, 142 (2004) (reporting Reed Elsevier operating margins on journals, but cautioning that this figure is merely suggestive because accounting profits do not always indicate economic profits). *See also* C. Edwin Baker, *Media Structure, Ownership Policy, and the First Amendment*, 78 S. CAL. L. REV. 733, 737 n.16 (2005) (citing FCC studies showing similar levels of high profitability of TV network affiliates and radio broadcasters).

70. Jonathan Levy, Marcelino Ford-Livene, & Anne Levine, *Broadcast Television: Survivor in a Sea of Competition* 34 tbl.16 (Office of Plans & Policy, FCC, 37 Working Paper Series, 2002), *available at* http://hraunfoss.fcc.gov/edocs public/attachmatch/DOC-226838A22.doc.

71. The supermarket retailer data are reported in James Surowiecki, *Printing Money*, NEW YORKER, Apr. 3, 2006, at 33. The consumer electronics data: *see* Irene M. Kunii et al., *Can Sony Regain the Magic?*, BUS. WK., Mar. 11, 2002, at 72 (reporting that Sony's operating profit margins on electronics products fell to 1 percent in 2001, down from 10 percent in 1991); *see also* EACEM's

Comments on the Commission's Green Paper on Liability for Defective Products COM (1999) 396 (Nov. 1999), at 6, *available at* http://europa.eu.int/comm/internal_market/en/goods/liability/027.pdf (last visited Oct. 10, 2003) (stating that profit margins of European consumer electronics manufacturers are at most 3 percent).

72. *See* Surowiecki, *supra* note 71, at 33.

73. *See* EPSTEIN, *supra* note 60, at 106–12 (detailing the motion picture industry's obfuscatory accounting practices). In addition, copyright industry profit margins, perhaps more than those of other industries, tend to fluctuate substantially from year to year. See DAVID WATERMAN, HOLLYWOOD'S ROAD TO RICHES 30 (Harvard University Press 2005) (motion picture industry).

74. *See* Baker & Cunningham, *supra* note 66 Excess returns means that investors earn more from their investment than they would need to justify that investment. The typical measure of what investors would need is the standard return on risk-free investments.

75. *See* LANDES & POSNER, *supra* note 39, at 17–18; Mark S. Nadel, *How Current Copyright Law Discourages Creative Output: The Overlooked Impact of Marketing,* 19 BERKELEY TECH. L.J. 785, 801 (2004). This might be seen as a specific instance of Parkinson's law: "The demand upon a resource always expands to fill the resource." VOGEL, *supra* note 67, at 107–08.

76. *See* SALVATORE, *supra* note 45, at 377 (discussing oligopoly firms' tendency to compete through product differentiation and massive advertising rather than price).

77. *See* CAVES, *supra* note 47, at 321 (noting shift in book publishing toward managing promotion and competing for star authors); Fisher, *supra* note 47, at 81 (increases in motion picture production and marketing costs); VOGEL, *supra* note 67, at 107, 316–17 (sharp increase in motion picture industry and trade book marketing expenditures); Motion Picture Association, supra note 62, at 17, 20 (motion pictures).

78. According to Motion Picture Association of America president Dan Glickman, 2004 production costs for major studios' full-length motion pictures averaged about $63.6 million. And while, according to Glickman, marketing costs fell in 2004, they still averaged $34.4 million, just over 50 percent of production costs. Sharon Waxman, *Movie Costs Drop,* NEW YORK TIMES, Mar. 16, 2005, at B2. Moreover, the motion picture industry generally includes within production costs the huge advances paid to star actors and directors, even though a good portion of those sums is more accurately attributed to marketing and promotion, not production per se. Marketing costs for major studio subsidiaries, principally divisions, like Sony Pictures Classics and Miramax, that make more niche "art" and "independent" films, are much lower in absolute terms and slightly lower as a percentage of production costs. Marketing costs for those new films averaged $11.4 million in 2004, which

amounted to some 40 percent of production costs. MOTION PICTURE ASSO-CIATION, *supra* note 62, at 18, 20.

79. *See* VOGEL, *supra* note 67, at 208 (estimating marketing costs at up to $100,000 for a standard sound recording release and in excess of $500,000 for a major artist, and these figures do not include indirect promotion payments to radio stations). On skyrocketing costs to market books, including paying retail chains significant amounts for prominent placement, see Feldman, *supra* note 61, at 16–20; Randy Kennedy, *Cash Up Front,* N.Y. TIMES BOOK REV., June 5, 2005, at 14.

80. *See* Nadel, *supra* note 75, at 800–01 and the sources cited by him. *See also* Menand, *supra* note 63, at 85–87 (lamenting movie studios massive expenditures on promotion and "production value" instead of quality "content").

81. *See* Nadel, *supra* note 75, at 797–803. On payola, see CAVES, *supra* note 47, at 286–96; SANJEK & SANJEK, *supra* note 38, at 237–38.

82. TOM SHONE, BLOCKBUSTER: HOW HOLLYWOOD LEARNED TO STOP WOR-RYING AND LOVE THE SUMMER 313 (Free Press 2004).

83. Nadel, *supra* note 75, at 801. There is a large literature identifying the need to expend significant amounts in advertising as an entry barrier. *See, e.g.,* A. Michael Spence, *Notes on Advertising, Economies of Scale, and Entry Barriers,* 95 Q. J. ECON. 493 (1980).

84. *See* Lex Borghans & Loek Groot, *Superstardom and Monopolistic Power: Why Media Stars Earn More Than Their Marginal Contribution to Welfare,* 154 J. INSTITUTIONAL & THEORETICAL ECON. 546 (1998); Kee Chung & Raymond Cox, *A Stochastic Model of Superstardom: An Application of the Yule Distribution,* 76 REV. ECON. & STAT. 771 (1994); Moshe Adler, *Stardom and Talent,* 75 AM. ECON. REV. 208 (1985).

85. *See* LANDES & POSNER, *supra* note 39, at 54–55; Ravid, *supra* note 61 *See also* CAVES, *supra* note 47, at 76–78, 109–10. For criticism in the trade press of the high rents paid to stars and celebrities, see D. Cox, *Soaring Star Salaries Induce Labor Pains,* VARIETY, Sept. 11–17, 1995, at 1; R. Welkos, *How to Spend $78 Million,* NEWSDAY, Apr. 11, 1999, at D06. *See also* EPSTEIN, *supra* note 60, at 18–19 (noting that stars are now auctioned off to the highest bidder for each film).

86. *See* LANDES & POSNER, *supra* note 39, at 407; Richard A. Posner, *The Social Costs of Monopoly and Regulation,* 83 J. POL. ECON. 807 (1975) (arguing that firms will dissipate monopoly rents in part by lobbying government to accord or preserve those rents).

87. *See, e.g.,* LANDES & POSNER, *supra* note 39, at 220–21 (describing industry lobbying for copyright term extension); Mark A. Lemley, *Property, Intellectual Property, and Free Riding,* 83 TEX. L. REV. 1031, 1064–64 (2005); JESSICA LITMAN, DIGITAL COPYRIGHT 144–45 (Prometheus Books 2001) (industry lobbying in connection with Digital Millennium Copyright Act); Robert P.

Merges, *One Hundred Years of Solicitude: Intellectual Property Law, 1900–2000,* 88 CAL. L. REV. 2187, 2236–37 (2000) (describing copyright term extension as "a classic instance of almost pure rent-seeking legislation").

88. UNITED STATES COPYRIGHT OFFICE, REPORT ON ORPHAN WORKS (2006), *available at* http://www.copyright.gov/orphan/orphan-report.pdf.

89. *See* Cohen v. Paramount Pictures Corp., 845 F.2d 851 (9th Cir. 1998) (holding that a 1969 synchronization license containing that language did not convey the right to use the plaintiff's composition in videocassette reproductions of the motion picture that was the immediate subject of the license); *see also* Random House, Inc. v. Rosetta Books LLC, 283 F.3d 490 (2d Cir. 2002) (holding that a license to publish novels "in book form" did not extend to "ebook" versions).

90. Michael A. Heller, *The Tragedy of the Anticommons: Property in the Transition from Marx to Markets,* 111 HARV. L. REV. 621 (1998). *See also* James M. Buchanan & Yong J. Yoon, *Symmetric Tragedies: Commons and Anti-Commons,* 43 J.L. & ECON. 1 (2000); Michael A. Heller & Rebecca S. Eisenberg, *Can Patents Deter Innovation? The Anticommons in Biomedical Research,* 280 SCIENCE 698 (1998).

91. The district court presiding over ASCAP's antitrust settlement has recently rejected the performing rights societies' position, holding that digital downloads are not a public performance of the downloaded song. United States v. American Society of Composers, Authors and Publishers, 485 F.Supp.2d 438 (S.D. N.Y. 2007).

92. Mark Lemley was one of the first scholars to highlight this problem. *See* Mark A. Lemley, *Dealing with Overlapping Copyrights on the Internet,* 22 U. DAYTON L. REV. 547 (1997). For helpful explication of the complex matrix of rights implicated in online music, *see* Lydia Pallas Loren, *Untangling the Web of Music Copyrights,* 53 CASE W. RES. L. REV. 673 (2003); R. Anthony Reese, *Copyright and Internet Music Transmissions: Existing Law, Major Controversies, Possible Solutions,* 55 U. MIAMI L. REV. 237 (2001).

93. *See* BENJAMIN M. COMPAINE & DOUGLAS GOMERY, WHO OWNS THE MEDIA? COMPETITION AND CONCENTRATION IN THE MASS MEDIA INDUSTRY 61, 80–100, 382 (Lawrence Erlbaum Associates, 3d ed. 2000); WATERMAN, *supra* note 73, at 20–30. In August 2004, the Federal Trade Commission approved a joint venture of the Bertelsmann and Sony record labels, leaving 85 percent of the market in the hands of four groups: Sony-BMG, Vivendi Universal, EMI, and Warner Music. Federal Trade Commission, Statement of Mozelle W. Thompson, *The Proposed Joint Venture Between Sony Corporation of America and Bertelsmann AG,* File No. 041–0054, July 28, 2004; Noll, *supra* note 45, at 16–17. *See also* VOGEL, *supra* note 67, at 24 (noting that markets for movies, recorded music, and network television are oligopolies and that markets for books, magazines, and radio stations are best described as "monopolistic competition")

94. *See* EPSTEIN, *supra* note 60, at 82–83; COMPAINE & GOMERY, *supra* note 93, at 80–100. Under considerable pressure from shareholders (headed by corporate

raider Carl Icann), following its disastrous merger with AOL, Time Warner spun off Warner Music in 2003. Failed merger attempts between EMI and BMG, Warner and BMG, and EMI and Warner between 2001 and 2003 leave the two smallest of the Big Four record labels unaffiliated with major media conglomerates as of the time this book went to press. Patrick Burkart, *Loose Integration in the Popular Music Industry,* 28 POPULAR MUSIC & SOC'Y 489 (2005). CBS Corporation and Viacom split into two on December 31, 2005. But a single shareholder, Sumner Redstone, still controls 71 percent of the voting stock and serves as chairman of both companies.

95. EPSTEIN, *supra* note 60, at 82–83. Epstein refers to six television networks, but Time Warner and Viacom CBS shut down their respective WB Television and UPN networks and replaced them with their jointly operated CW Television Network in September 2006.

96. *See* MARK COOPER, MEDIA OWNERSHIP AND DEMOCRACY IN THE DIGITAL INFORMATION AGE 146–47 (Center for Internet & Society 2003); Consumer Federation of America, *Testimony of Dr. Mark N. Cooper, Director of Research, on Media Ownership Before the S. Commerce Comm.,* Oct. 2, 2003, at 2, *available at* http://www.consumerfed.org/pdfs/mediatestimony.pdf; Liberty Media Corporation, Investor Relations—Investments, http://www.libertymedia.com/ir/investments.htm (last visited Apr. 4, 2006).

97. EPSTEIN, *supra* note 60, at 82–83. For a description of the distribution of each conglomerate's holdings across media sectors as of 2001, see Sylvia M. Chan-Olmsted & Byeng-Hee Chang, *Diversification Strategy of Global Media Conglomerates: Examining Its Patterns and Determinants,* 16 J. MEDIA ECON. 213, 221–23 (2003).

98. *See* Baker, *supra* note 34, at 878–82; ANDRE SCHIFFRIN, THE BUSINESS OF BOOKS: HOW INTERNATIONAL CONGLOMERATES TOOK OVER PUBLISHING AND CHANGED THE WAY WE READ (Verso 2000); ROBERT W. MCCHESNEY, THE PROBLEM OF THE MEDIA: U.S. COMMUNICATION POLITICS IN THE TWENTY-FIRST CENTURY 138–209 (Monthly Review Press 2004).

99. Media conglomerate conservatism parallels dominant firm reluctance to undertake research and development projects or commercialize innovations when doing so might cannibalize the firm's existing revenue streams. *See* MORTON I. KAMIEN & NANCY L. SCHWARTZ, MARKET STRUCTURE AND INNOVATION 110 (Cambridge University Press 1982) (noting reluctance of firm managers to pursue innovation that conflicts with existing product revenues).

100. *See* Jon M. Garon, *Media and Monopoly in the Information Age: Slowing the Convergence at the Marketplace of Ideas,* 17 CARDOZO ARTS & ENT. L.J. 491, 590–91 (1999) (describing the HarperCollins incident). *See also* Doreen Carvajal, *What Is a Book Publisher to Do When a Parody Hits Home?,* N.Y. TIMES, Feb. 12, 1996, at D1 (reporting that Crown Publishers canceled its contract to publish a book that spoofed the works of another, more popular author, also published by Crown).

101. Scott Collins, *Clamor Outside "South Park" Closet,* L.A. TIMES, Mar. 18, 2006, at E16; Alessandra Stanley, *A "South Park" Character's Return Becomes an Opportunity for Revenge,* N.Y. TIMES, Mar. 24, 2006, at E25.

102. As a general rule, firms without market power cannot use vertical integration to foreclose competitors. *See* RICHARD A. POSNER & FRANK H. EASTERBROOK, ANTITRUST 870 (West Publishing Co. 2d ed. 1982). But this is not the case when the primary (producer) and secondary (distributor) markets are both highly concentrated, as they are in content production and distribution. See United States Department of Justice and Federal Trade Commission, *Nonhorizontal Merger Guidelines,* 57 FED. REG. 41, 552 (1992).

103. *See generally* BENKLER, *supra* note 50, at 401–08. *See also* Jaemin Jung & Sylvia M. Chan-Olmsted, *Impacts of Media Conglomerates' Dual Diversification on Financial Performance,* 18 J. MEDIA ECON. 183, 184–85 (2005) (discussing economic advantages that media conglomerates enjoy over smaller counterparts).

104. *See* CARL SHAPIRO & HAL R. VARIAN, INFORMATION RULES: A STRATEGIC GUIDE TO THE NETWORK ECONOMY 73–78 (1999); Yannis Bakos et al., *Shared Information Goods,* 42 J.L. & ECON. 117, 124–25 (1999).

105. COMPAINE & GOMERY, *supra* note 93, at 378–79.

106. *See* S. C. Ringgenberg, *Bobby London and the Air Pirates Follies,* Comix Art and Graphics Gallery Virtual Museum and Encyclopedia, May 12, 1998, http://www.comic-art.com/intervws/londart.htm.

107. *See* COMPAINE & GOMERY, *supra* note 93, at 326–27 (record labels), 375–80 (motion picture studios). On vertical integration in television, see COOPER, *supra* note 96, at 147–48 (noting that "[o]f the 26 top cable channels in subscribers' and prime time ratings, all but one of them (the Weather Channel) has ownership interest of either a cable company or a broadcast network" and that twenty-one of the top twenty-five cable networks are owned by one of the Big Five media conglomerate television program producers).

108. For considerably more detailed historical accounts, see JOSEPH LOEWENSTEIN, THE AUTHOR'S DUE: PRINTING AND THE PREHISTORY OF COPYRIGHT (University of Chicago Press 2002); MARK ROSE, AUTHORS AND OWNERS: THE INVENTION OF COPYRIGHT 4–100 (Harvard University Press 1993).

109. *See generally* Jane C. Ginsburg, *Copyright and Control over New Technologies of Dissemination,* 101 COLUM. L. REV. 1613 (2001); Randal C. Picker, *Copyright as Entry Policy: The Case of Digital Distribution,* 47 ANTITRUST BULL. 423 (2002).

110. For further description, see SANJEK & SANJEK, *supra* note 38, at 12, 14, 58–78; Timothy Wu, *Copyright's Communications Policy,* MICH. L. REV. 103, 278 (2004). *See also* LAWRENCE LESSIG, FREE CULTURE: HOW BIG MEDIA USES TECHNOLOGY AND THE LAW TO LOCK DOWN CULTURE AND CONTROL CREATIVITY 53–61 (Penguin Press 2004).

111. *See* Michael A. Einhorn, *Intellectual Property and Antitrust: Music Performing Rights in Broadcasting,* 24 COLUM.-VLA J.L. & ARTS 349 (2001) (discussing Rate Court provisions in ASCAP and BMI antitrust consent decrees).

112. Fortnightly Corp. v. United Artists Television, Inc., 392 U.S. 390 (1968); Teleprompter Corp. v. Columbia Broad. Sys., Inc., 415 U.S. 394 (1974).

113. Sony Corp. of Am. v. Universal City Studios, Inc., 464 U.S. 417 (1984).

114. The MPAA sued the manufacturer of the ReplayTV digital video recorder on the grounds that its automatic commercial skipping, thirty-second skip, and Internet-sharing features exceeded the Betamax safe harbor. *See* MPAA v. ReplayTV, Civ. No. 01–09801 (C.D. Cal., filed Nov. 14, 2001). The suit settled when ReplayTV agreed to disable those features.

115. Meg James & Dawn C. Chmielewski, *Media Giants to Compete with YouTube,* L.A. TIMES, Mar. 22, 2007, at A-1.

116. *Id.* (quoting UBS Warburg media analyst Aryeh Bourkoff).

117. *See* SANJEK & SANJEK, *supra* note 38, at 58–60, 65, 165–66, 208–09, 227–28; Orbach, *supra* note 34 But short of collusion, current antitrust doctrine places few limits on incumbents' ability to use copyright as a vertical restraint. For analysis and criticism of antitrust law's current leniency toward the use of intellectual property for vertical foreclosure, see Roger G. Noll, *The Conflict over Vertical Foreclosure in Competition Policy and Intellectual Property Law,* 160 J. INSTITUTIONAL & THEORETICAL ECON. 79 (2004).

118. For a brief summary of compulsory licenses and private copying levies in the United States and Europe, see Neil Weinstock Netanel, *Impose a Noncommercial Use Levy to Allow Free Peer-to-Peer File Sharing,* 17 HARV. J. L. & TECH., 1, 31–35 (2003).

119. *See, e.g.,* A&M Records v. Napster, Inc., 239 F.3d 1004 (9th Cir. 2001) (holding that individuals who distribute copyrighted music files through a peer-to-peer network infringe copyright and that Napster was contributorily liable for its users' infringement); In re Aimster Copyright Litig., 334 F.3d 643 (7th Cir. 2003) (supplier of P2P file-sharing service held contributorily liable for its users' infringement); UMG Recordings, Inc. v. MP3.com, Inc., 92 F. Supp. 2d 349 (S.D.N.Y. 2000) (holding MP3.com liable for enabling its subscribers to access songs on subscriber-owned CDs via the Internet). The current "MP3.com" and "Napster" are successors in name only to the original businesses.

Chapter Seven

1. PAUL GOLDSTEIN, COPYRIGHT'S HIGHWAY: FROM GUTENBERG TO THE CELESTIAL JUKEBOX 216 (Stanford University Press revised ed. 2003).

2. *See id.* at 146, 188–89, 200–01. *See also* STAN LIEBOWITZ, RE-THINKING THE NETWORK ECONOMY 89–91 (Amacon Books 2002); Bell, *supra* note 41, at 589 n.142 (1998); David Friedman, *In Defense of Private Orderings: Comments on*

Julie Cohen's "Copyright and the Jurisprudence of Self-Help," 13 BERKELEY TECH. L.J. 1151, 1168–71 (1998); Trotter Hardy, *Property (and Copyright) in Cyberspace,* 1996 U. CHI. L J. 217, 254–58. *Cf.* Harold Demsetz, *The Private Production of Public Goods,* 13 J.L. & ECON. 293, 295–306 (1970) (favoring use of price discrimination as a means for enabling the private production of public goods generally).

3. *See, e.g.,* LIEBOWITZ, *supra* note 2, at 179–81; Tom Bell, *Fair Use vs. Fared Use: The Impact of Automated Rights Management on Copyright's Fair Use Doctrine,* 76 N.C.L. REV. 557, 587–90 (1998); Friedman, *supra* note 2, at 1169; Trotter Hardy, *Not So Different: Tangible, Intangible, Digital, and Analog Works and Their Comparison for Copyright Purposes,* 26 U. DAYTON L. REV. 211, 237–44 (2001); Christopher D. Kruger, *Passing the Global Test: DMCA §1201 as an International Model for Transitioning Copyright Law into the Digital Age,* 28 HOUS. J. INT'L L. 281, 296–307 (2006).

4. *See* WILLIAM M. LANDES & RICHARD A. POSNER, THE ECONOMIC STRUCTURE OF INTELLECTUAL PROPERTY LAW 40 (Harvard University Press 2003) (noting that there is no firm theoretical or empirical basis for the belief held by many economists that price discrimination is more likely to expand than reduce output or leave it unchanged); Michael J. Meurer, *Copyright Law and Price Discrimination,* 23 CARDOZO L. REV. 55, 98–102 (2001) (discussing costs of implementing price discrimination); Christopher Yoo, *Copyright and Product Differentiation,* 79 N.Y.U. L. REV. 212, 230 (2004) (noting that imperfect price discrimination might exacerbate deadweight loss, not just reduce it).

5. David McGowan, *Why the First Amendment Cannot Dictate Copyright Policy,* 65 U. PITT. L. REV. 281, 318 (2004).

6. Yoo, *supra* note 4; Christopher S. Yoo, *Copyright and Democracy: A Cautionary Note,* 53 VAND. L. REV. 1933 (2000).

7. LANDES & POSNER, *supra* note 4, at 60.

8. For a cogent presentation of these issues, see C. EDWIN BAKER, MEDIA, MARKETS, AND DEMOCRACY 71–94 (Cambridge University Press 2002).

9. *Id.* at 87–94.

10. *See, e.g.,* Cass R. Sunstein, *Television and the Public Interest,* 88 CALIF. L. REV. 499 (2000).

11. *See* Michael Abramowicz, *An Industrial Organization Approach to Copyright Law,* 46 WM. & MARY L. REV. 33, 45-68 (2004); Michael Boldrin & David Levine, *The Case against Intellectual Property,* 92 AM. ECON. REV. 209, 212 (2002). In the context of media generally, see Baker, *supra* note 8, at 30–37.

12. Boldrin & Levine, *supra* note 11, at 212.

13. *See* Abramowicz, *supra* note 11, at 39–43.

14. Christopher Yoo sees the problem of demand diversion as one of promoting excessive entry into the copyright market and thus dividing copyright holder surplus among too many parties. He contends that this problem can be ameliorated by adjusting the degree of similarity that constitutes a copyright

infringement, in other words, broadening copyright holder rights to enable them to prevent more works that are somewhat similar. *See* Yoo, *supra* note 4, at 263–64, 272. *See also* Michael Abramowicz, *A Theory of Copyright's Derivative Right and Related Doctrines,* 90 MINN. L. REV. 317 (2005) (maintaining that reducing rent dissipation arising from the production of redundant works is a primary justification for according copyright owners the exclusive right to make derivative works).

15. *See* Mark A. Lemley, *Ex Ante versus Ex Post Justifications for Intellectual Property,* 71 U. CHI. L. REV. 129, 145–46 (2004) (noting that so long as *Gone with the Wind* retains its appeal, consumer demand for that classic would unlikely be affected by the story's retelling from a slave's viewpoint, and if consumers want the retelling, then so be it).

16. *See, e.g.,* Yoo, *supra* note 4, at 221–22, 250, 253–54.

17. One other reason is that the argument assumes that the new expression induced by broader copyright protection would impose greater market discipline than the new expression and dissemination of existing expression that could take place only if copyright's scope is narrowed. To give an extreme example, it is hard to believe that giving copyright holders the right (and ability) to stop unlicensed peer-to-peer dissemination of copyright-protected sound recordings would cause a reduction in prices for licensed digital distribution of music (which would then no longer have to compete with free), even if that greater right generates the production of a greater number of new sound recordings.

18. Yoo assumes that the "symmetric preferences branch" of Edward Chamberlain's theory of monopolistic competition and Harold Hotelling's spatial competition models, which branch presumes that all available products are in equal competition with one another, applies to copyright markets. *See* Yoo, *supra* note 4, at 242–43. But because of the power-law demand curve, it does not. For further criticism of Yoo's assumption that Hotelling's analysis applies to intellectual property, see Mark A. Lemley, *Property, Intellectual Property, and Free Riding,* 83 TEX. L. REV. 1031, 1056–57 (2005).

19. *See* DOMINICK SALVATORE, MICROECONOMICS 361 (Oxford University Press, 4th ed. 2003) (noting that "[o]ligopoly is the most prevalent form of market organization in the manufacturing section in the United States and other industrial countries").

Chapter Eight

1. *See, e.g.,* Harper & Row, Publishers, Inc. v. Nation Enters., 471 U.S. 539, 560 (1985) (explaining that First Amendment protections are "already embodied in the Copyright Act's distinction between copyrightable expression and uncopyrightable facts and ideas"); Roy Export Co. v. CBS, Inc., 672 F.2d 1095, 1099 (2d Cir. 1982) ("No circuit that has considered the question . . . has

ever held that the First Amendment provides a privilege in the copyright field distinct from the accommodation embodied in the "fair use" doctrine.").

2. *See, e.g.,* trademark: Westchester Media v. PRL USA Holdings, Inc., 214 F.3d 658 (5th Cir. 2000) (trademark involving the polo symbol), L.L. Bean, Inc. v. Drake Publishers, Inc., 811 F.2d 26, 30 n.2 (1st Cir. 1987), and right of publicity: Hoffman v. Capital Cities/ABC, Inc., 255 F.3d 1180, 1183–84 (9th Cir. 2001); Comedy III Prods., Inc. v. Gary Saderup, Inc., 25 Cal. 4th 387, 407 (2001). For extended discussion of case law, see ETW Corp. v. Jireh Pub., Inc., 332 F.3d 915, 924–38 (6th Cir. 2003) (upholding First Amendment defense false endorsement and right of publicity).

3. Restatement (Second) of Torts §§ 566 cmt. a, 581(1) (1977).

4. *See* New York Times Co. v. Sullivan, 376 U.S. 254 (1964) (defamation claims brought by public officials); Gertz v. Robert Welch, Inc., 418 U.S. 323 (1974) (defamation claims brought by private individuals); *but see* Dun & Bradstreet, Inc. v. Greenmoss Builders, Inc., 472 U.S. 749, 759–60 (1985) (holding that *Gertz* does not apply to statements involving matters of purely private concern). For the constitutionalization of privacy law, *see* Virgil v. Time, Inc., 527 F.2d 1122, 1128–29 (9th Cir. 1975); Matthews v. Wozencraft, 15 F.3d 432, 440 (5th Cir. 1994).

5. 537 U.S. 186 (2003).

6. 537 U.S. at 191.

7. *See Eldred,* 74 F. Supp. 2d at 3 (D.D.C. 1999) ("The District of Columbia Circuit has ruled definitively that there are no First Amendment rights to use of the copyrighted works of others."); Eldred v. Reno, 239 F.3d 372, 375 (D.C. Cir. 2001), *rhrg denied,* 255 F.3d 849 (D.C. Cir. 2001).

8. 239 F.3d at 376.

9. Several commentators have argued that copyright law should be subject to strict scrutiny or should otherwise be generally unconstitutional as violative of the First Amendment. Eugene Volokh and Mark Lemley argue that copyright is content-based because whether a person infringes depends on the "content" of his speech. Mark A. Lemley & Eugene Volokh, *Freedom of Speech and Injunctions in Intellectual Property Cases,* 48 DUKE L.J. 147, 186 (1998). Jed Rubenfeld contends that the First Amendment provides absolute protection for "freedom of imagination" and that copyright law unconstitutionally abridges that freedom except as applied to cases of commercial piracy. Jed Rubenfeld, *The Freedom of Imagination: Copyright Constitutionality,* 112 YALE L.J. 1 (2002). Ed Baker insists, similarly, that the First Amendment absolutely protects individuals' speech and countenances no exception for copyright. C. Edwin Baker, *First Amendment Limits on Copyright,* 55 VAND. L. REV. 891 (2002). I have argued, in contrast, that copyright law best fits within the ambit of content-neutral speech regulation, since it does not aim to suppress a message, viewpoint, subject matter, or communicative (as opposed to economic) impact. Neil Weinstock Netanel, *Locating Copyright within the First*

Amendment Skein, 54 STAN. L. REV. 1, 47–54 (2001). In this book, I do not rehearse my argument or detail the arguments of those who would impose strict scrutiny or simply find copyright law unconstitutional (at least as applied to imagination or individual speech). As interesting as this debate is, the Supreme Court sidestepped it by holding in *Eldred* that no First Amendment scrutiny, not even intermediate scrutiny applicable to content-neutral speech regulation, is warranted so long as copyright law remains within its traditional contours.

10. Turner Broadcasting Sys., Inc. v. FCC, 512 U.S. 622 (1994) ("Turner I"), *rhrg denied,* 512 U.S. 1278 (1994), and Turner Broadcasting Sys., Inc. v. FCC, 520 U.S. 180 (1997) ("Turner II").

11. *Turner I,* 512 U.S. at 643.

12. *Turner II,* 520 U.S. at 189.

13. Petitioners' Brief at 22 (in portion arguing that retrospective extension does not "Promote the Progress of Science" as required by the Copyright Clause) *available at* 2002 WL 1041928 (D.C. Cir. 2002).

14. *Eldred,* 537 U.S. at 191.

15. Hurley v. Irish-Am. Gay, Lesbian and Bisexual Group of Boston, 515 U.S. 557, 570 (1995) (holding that parade organizers have a cognizable First Amendment right to determine which organizations may or may not march in the parade).

16. The *Eldred* Court's right-to-make-other-people's-speeches characterization was quoted favorably by Judge Posner in In re Aimster Copyright Litigation, 334 F.3d 643, 656 (7th Cir. 2003).

17. 537 U.S. at 218.

18. In re Verizon Internet Services, 257 F. Supp. 2d 244, 257–58 (D.D.C. 2003), *rev'd,* Recording Industry Ass'n of America, Inc. v. Verizon Internet Services, Inc., 351 F.3d 1229 (D.C. Cir. 2003).

19. The Constitution was ratified in 1789 and the Bill of Rights in 1791. The first copyright statute, the Act of May 31, 1790, ch. 15, § 1, 1 Stat. 124, 124, was enacted in 1790, the same year Congress adopted the Bill of Rights.

20. Regan v. Time, Inc., 468 U.S. 641 (1984).

21. United States v. Grace, 461 U.S. 171 (1983) (Federal District Clause), and Lamont v. Postmaster Gen. of U.S., 381 U.S. 301, 307 (1965) (Post Office Clause).

22. San Francisco Arts & Athletics, Inc. v. United States Olympic Committee, 483 U.S. 522 (1987). *See also* Thompson v. Western States Medical Center, 535 U.S. 357 (2002) (holding that a prohibition on consumer advertising of "compounded drugs," enacted pursuant to Congress's power under the Commerce Clause, is forbidden by the First Amendment). The Supreme Court has also held that the First Amendment restricts Congress's power to enact legislation under its enumerated spending power. Legal Servs. Corp. v. Valazquez, 531 U.S. 533 (2001) (striking down a congressionally mandated

restriction on the use of grants provided under the spending power for certain legal services by recipient organizations under the First Amendment).

23. *See* Lemley & Volokh, *supra* note 9, at 187–88.

24. *See* Turner I, 512 U.S. at 646, 662–64.

25. Turner II, 520 U.S. at 180.

26. Eldred, 537 U.S. at 190.

27. Cohen v. California, 403 U.S. 15, 26 (1971).

28. *See* Frederick Schauer, *Fear, Risk and the First Amendment: Unraveling the "Chilling Effect,"* 58 B.U. L. REV. 685, 688 (1978) (discussing the "chilling effect doctrine").

29. Gertz v. Robert Welch, Inc., 418 U.S. 323, 340–41 (1974).

30. I discuss this point and cite cases in Netanel, *supra* note 9, at 59–67.

31. 512 U.S. at 659.

32. A number of commentators have underscored the First Amendment's concern with pathologies in the political process. *See, e.g.,* Alan E. Brownstein, *Rules of Engagement for Cultural Wars: Regulating Conduct, Unprotected Speech, and Protected Expression in Anti-abortion Protests,* 29 U.C. DAVIS L. REV. 553, 608–09 (1996); Ronald A. Cass, *Commercial Speech, Constitutionalism, Collective Choice,* 56 U. CIN. L. REV. 1317, 1354–60 (1988); Daniel A. Farber, *Free Speech without Romance: Public Choice and the First Amendment,* 105 HARV. L. REV. 554 (1991).

33. For an illuminating account of the history of special interest influence over copyright legislation, *see* JESSICA LITMAN, DIGITAL COPYRIGHT 35–63 (Prometheus Books 2001). Intellectual property industries also exert an inordinate influence over the United States' position in treaty and trade negotiations with other countries. *See* Neil W. Netanel, *Why Has Copyright Expanded? Analysis and Critique, in* 5 NEW DIRECTIONS IN COPYRIGHT LAW 3 (Fiona Macmillan ed., Edward Elgar, forthcoming 2008).

34. William F. Patry, *Copyright and the Legislative Process: A Personal Perspective,* 14 CARDOZO ARTS & ENT. L.J. 139, 141 (1996).

35. *See* 17 U.S.C.§ 1201(a)(1)(A). Shortly before this book went to press, the Tenth Circuit held that another Copyright Act amendment, the Uruguay Round Agreements Act, which restored copyrights for certain public domain works, altered copyright's traditional contours and thus must be subject to First Amendments scrutiny. Golan v. Gonzales, 501 F.3d 1179 (10th Cir. 2007).

36. H.R. Rep. No. 105–551, pt. 2, at 24 (1998) (hereinafter Commerce Comm'n Report) (second quotation quoting a 1997 letter to Congress from sixty-two distinguished law professors).

37. See David S. Nimmer, *A Riff on Fair Use in the Digital Millennium Copyright Act,* 148 U. PA L. Rev. 673, 727–32 (2000).

38. 17 U.S.C. § 1201(c)(1) provides that nothing in the anticircumvention provisions "shall affect rights, remedies, limitations, or defenses to copyright infringement, including fair use, under this title."

39. *See* Universal City Studios, Inc., v. Corley, 273 F.3d 429, 443–44 (2nd Cir. 2001).

40. *See* Commerce Comm'n Report, *supra* note 36, at 26.

41. *Id.* § 1201(c)(4).

42. 17 U.S.C. § 1201(a)(1)(C) (2001).

43. Commerce Comm'n Report, *supra* note 36, at 36.

44. Or one can conclude that the review mechanism is a cruel joke. As one leading commentator has aptly put it: "It is rare for a statute to exhibit a sense of humor." Diane Leenheer Zimmerman, *Adrift in the Digital Millennium Copyright Act: The Sequel,* 26 U. DAYTON L. REV. 279, 279 (2001).

45. The review mechanism in § 1201(a)(1)(B)–(D) applies only to the access prohibition in § 1201(a)(1)(A), not to the device prohibitions in § 1201(a)(2) or in § 1201(b)(1).

46. Copyright Office, Library of Congress, Exemption to Prohibition on Circumvention of Copyright Protection Systems for Access Control Technologies, 37 CFR Part 201, Docket No. RM 2005-11; Federal Register: Nov. 27, 2006 (Vol. 71, No. 227), pp. 68472–68480.

47. *Id.*

48. Turner II, 520 U.S. at 189. Prior to *Eldred,* a couple of lower courts had already applied *Turner* scrutiny in considering First Amendment challenges to the anticircumvention provisions. *See, e.g.,* Universal City Studios, Inc., v. Corley, 273 F.3d 429 (2nd Cir. 2001); United States v. Elcom, Ltd., 203 F. Supp.2d 1111 (N.D. Cal. 2002). The courts upheld the provisions in each case. But especially given those cases' particular postures, they leave the constitutionality of the anticircumvention provisions an open question.

49. Turner I, 512 U.S. at 662 (quoting United States v. O'Brien, 391 U.S. 367, 377 (1968)).

50. *See, e.g.,* Denver Area Educ. Telecomms. Consortium v. FCC, 518 U.S. 727, 758 (1996) ("At this point, we can take Congress' different, and significantly less restrictive, treatment of a highly similar problem at least as *some indication* that more restrictive means are not 'essential' (or will not prove very helpful).")"; Boos v. Barry, 485 U.S. 312, 329 (1988) (stating that the existence of a less restrictive statute suggested that a challenged ordinance, aimed at the same problem, was overly restrictive).

51. As amended by the DMCA, Section 112(a)(2) of the Copyright Act requires copyright owners that have encrypted their works to "make available to the transmitting organization [*i.e.,* broadcasters and webcasters] the necessary means" for making ephemeral and archival copies of transmitted works as permitted pursuant to Section 112(a)(1). 17 U.S.C. § 112(a)(2) (2001). Section 112(a)(2) authorizes transmitting organizations to circumvent on their own if the copyright owner fails to provide the necessary means in a "timely manner in light of the transmitting organization's reasonable business requirements." *Id.* Similarly, the DMCA provides that analog VCRs must conform to copy

control technology, but it generally prohibits the deployment of such technology to "prevent or limit consumer copying." 17 U.S.C. § 1201(k)(2)(2001).

52. *See* Directive 2001/29/EC of the European Parliament and of the Council of 22 May 2001 on the Harmonisation of Certain Aspects of Copyright and Related Rights in the Information Society, 2001 O.J. (L 167) 10, Art. 6(4).

53. 537 U.S. at 221 n.24.

54. *See, e.g.,* Universal City Studios, Inc., 273 F.3d at 458 ("we note that the Supreme Court has never held that fair use is constitutionally required").

55. The Eleventh Circuit initially reversed the district court in a per curiam opinion that applied the First Amendment as an external constraint on copyright. It held that the preliminary injunction was an unconstitutional prior restraint on speech. Suntrust Bank v. Houghton Mifflin Co., 252 F.3d 1165 (11th Cir. 2001). Subsequently, the Eleventh Circuit vacated its per curiam ruling and substituted a more comprehensive opinion that, rather than relying entirely on First Amendment prior restraint doctrine, interprets copyright law in light of the First Amendment. Suntrust Bank v. Houghton Mifflin Co., 268 F.3d 1257 (11th Cir. 2001).

56. Blanch v. Koons, 467 F.3d 244, 253 (2d Cir. 2006) (quoting Pierre N. Leval, *Toward a Fair Use Standard,* 103 HARV. L. REV. 1105, 1111 (1990)).

57. Speiser v. Randall, 357 U.S. 513, 526 (1958). *See also* Eugene Volokh, *Freedom of Speech and Intellectual Property: Some Thoughts after Eldred, 44 Liquormart, and Bartnicki,* 40 HOUS. L. REV. 697 (2003).

58. Campbell v. Acuff-Rose Music, Inc., 510 U.S. 569, 578 n.10 (1994). The Supreme Court reiterated this point in New York Times Co. v. Tasini, 533 U.S. 483, 518–525 (2001) (Stevens, J., dissenting).

59. 17 U.S.C. § 504.

60. *In re Aimster,* 334 F.3d at 656 (internal quotation marks omitted).

Chapter Nine

1. *See* Jed Rubenfeld, *The Freedom of the Imagination: Copyright's Constitutionality,* 112 YALE L.J. 1 (2002).

2. *See* Alex Kozinski & Christopher Newman, *What's So Fair about Fair Use?,* 46 J. COPYRIGHT SOC'Y USA 513, 523 (1999).

3. A multiple taker problem exists when an owner who lacks the right to exclude will not pay a prospective taker to prevent a taking because the owner would subsequently have to pay another prospective taker not to take, and then another and another. *See* Louis Kaplow & Steven Shavell, *Property Rules versus Liability Rules: An Economic Analysis,* 109 Harv. L. Rev. 713, 765–66 (1996) (identifying multiple taker problem as limitation of liability rule regimes in some circumstances).

4. *See* Bernard Weinraub, *Two Films, One Subject. Uh-Oh. In Hollywood, the Race Is On,* N.Y. TIMES, June 23, 1994, at C11 (reporting as highly unusual con-

temporaneous development by two major studios of motion pictures based on same story about threatened escape of deadly virus from medical lab).

5. My thanks to David Nimmer for pressing this point. *See also* Kozinski & Newman, *supra* note 2, at 526 (proposing that a version of the Federal Rules of Civil Procedure Rule 68 offer of judgment be applied to induce parties to agree on licensing terms in the absence of an exclusive derivative right).

6. For further discussion of possible advantages of carefully crafted liability rules, including even to induce bargaining in some circumstances, *see* Mark A. Lemley & Philip J. Weiser, *Should Property or Liability Rules Govern Information?*, 85 TEX. L. REV. 783 (2007); Kaplow & Shavell, *supra* note 3; Ian Ayres & Eric Talley, *Solomonic Bargaining: Dividing Legal Entitlements to Facilitate Coasean Trade*, 104 YALE L. J. 1027 (1995).

7. Brief of Amici Curiae George A. Akerloff et al., Eldred v. Ashcroft, 537 U.S. 186 (2003) (No. 01–618).

8. Quoted in JESSICA LITMAN, DIGITAL COPYRIGHT 77 (Prometheus Books 2001).

9. WILLIAM M. LANDES & RICHARD A. POSNER, THE ECONOMIC STRUCTURE OF INTELLECTUAL PROPERTY LAW 228 (2003).

10. *See* Mark A. Lemley, *Ex Ante versus Ex Post Justifications for Intellectual Property*, 71 U. CHI. L. REV. 129, 136–37 (2004).

11. *Id.* at 138.

12. *See, e.g.,* LAWRENCE LESSIG, THE FUTURE OF IDEAS 251–52 (Random House 2001); Christopher Sprigman, *Reform(aliz)ing Copyright*, 57 STAN. L. REV. 485, 554 (2004).

13. William M. Landes & Richard A. Posner, *Indefinitely Renewable Copyright*, 71 U. CHI. L. REV. 111 (2004).

14. UNITED STATES COPYRIGHT OFFICE, REPORT ON ORPHAN WORKS 127 (Library of Congress 2006).

15. Neil Weinstock Netanel, *Impose a Noncommercial Use Levy to Allow Free Peer-to-Peer File Sharing*, 17 Harv. J. L. & Tech. 1 (2003). For an alternative proposal for a levy, designed ultimately to replace a proprietary copyright, *see* WILLIAM W. FISHER III, PROMISES TO KEEP: TECHNOLOGY, LAW, AND THE FUTURE OF ENTERTAINMENT 199–258 (Stanford University Press 2004).

16. *See* Netanel, *supra* note 15, at 60–67.

17. Bri Holt et al., Analysis of Copyrighted Videos on YouTube.com (Vidmeter Incorporated 2007), *available at* http://www.vidmeter.com.

18. These factors follow those that apply to most compulsory licenses under the Copyright Act. *See* 17 U.S.C. § 801(b)(1).

19. The Copyright Office is currently supporting proposed legislation that would follow a similar compulsory, blanket licensing approach to the digital reproduction and distribution of musical works. Section 115 Reform Act (SIRA) of 2006.

20. Reference books, poetry anthologies, and other collections of discrete, short texts might be an exception, but Google excludes such books.

21. *See* Universal City Studios v. Corley, 273 F.3d 429, 459 (2d Cir. 2001) ("We know of no authority for the proposition that fair use, as protected by the Copyright Act, much less the Constitution, guarantees copying by the optimum method or in the identical format of the original.").

22. For a comparative survey of European moral rights and their U.S. analogues, *see* Neil Weinstock Netanel, *Alienability Restrictions and the Enhancement of Author Autonomy in United States and Continental Copyright Law,* 12 CARDOZO ARTS & ENT. L. J. 1 (1994).

23. LITMAN, *supra* note 8, at 185.

24. 17 U.S.C. § 1202(b).

25. The "Peanuts" case, Trib. de. Gr. Inst. de Paris, Jan. 19, 1977, 92 Revues Int'l de Droit D'auteur 167. *See, also,* the "Tarzoon" case, Trib. de. Gr. Inst. de Paris, Jan. 3, 1978, D. 1979, at 99 (Commentary of Henri Desbois) (holding that a parodic cartoon of Tarzan did not infringe the author's moral right of integrity). France's Author's Rights statute contains a specific exception from the copyright owner's economic rights for "parodies, caricatures and pastiches, within the limits of the Laws of the Art." C. I.P., Art. L. 122-5 4.

26. Marie-Pierre Strowel & Alain Strowel, *La Parodie selon le Droit D'auteur et la Théorie Littéraire,* 1991.26 R.I.E.J. 23, 25.

27. Amicus Brief of Amicus Curiae Creative Commons at 27, MGM Studios, Inc. v. Grokster, Ltd., 545 U.S. 913 (2005) (No. 04–4880).

28. Rebecca Tushnet, *Payment in Credit: Copyright Law and Subcultural Creativity,* 70 L. & CONTEMP. PROBS. 135 (2007).

29. ASSN. OF INDEPENDENT VIDEO AND FILMMAKERS ET AL., DOCUMENTARY FILMMAKERS' STATEMENT OF BEST PRACTICES IN FAIR USE 4–6 (American University Center for Social Media & Washington College of Law 2005).

30. Harper & Row, Publishers, Inc. v. Nation Enters., 471 U.S. 539, 589–90 (1985) (Brennan J., dissenting).

copyright
  as Blackstonian property, 6, 56, 78, 79,
    151–153, 154, 206
  Copyright Clause of Constitution, 5, 11,
    54, 82, 91, 105–106, 174
  derivative right, 60, 196–198
  divisibility of, 142–143
  duration of, 57–58, 199–207
  as "engine of free expression," 3, 4, 6, 37,
    81–84, 180, 217–218
  expansion of copyright holder rights, 6, 7,
    54–80
  and the First Amendment, 169–194
  free speech safeguards, 60, 170, 180–181,
    193
  fundamental goals of, 5, 6, 11, 105–106,
    120, 166–168
  idea/expression dichotomy, 61–62
  as important for our system of free
    expression, 41
  immunity from First Amendment
    scrutiny, 170, 172
  as integral to free speech and
    communications policy, 120
  as needed for "sustained works of
    authorship," 88
  not property, 120
  See also clearance culture and
    self-censorship, copyright
    economics, copyright infringement,
    copyright legislation, copyright
    licensing, copyright's speech
    burdens, copyright's support
    for free speech, fair use,
    paracopyright
copyright economics
  accounting for risk of failure, 126,
    135–141
  "competitive price" for original
    expression, 124–128, 135–141
  congestion externalities, 203–205
  copyright creates artificial scarcity,
    121–141
  copyright as entry barrier, 149–153
  copyright as source of market power,
    128–135
  copyright's contribution to industry
    concentration, 147–153
  expansive copyright leads to clustering,
    162–164

  no justification for longer term, 199
  as necessarily devolving to speech policy,
    11, 128, 166–167
  and price discrimination, 155–158
  pricing system rationale for Blackstonian
    copyright, 160–161
  theory and rational, 84–86
  See also markets for original expression
copyright industries. See commercial mass
    media
copyright infringement
  contributory liability, 78
  de minimis defense to, 61
  fragmented literal similarity as, 60, 62,
    196
  remedies for, 192–193
  as "stealing," 21
  substantial similarity test, 59–60, 61–62,
    196
copyright legislation
  Act of 1790, 54–55, 57, 82–83, 91
  Copyright Act of 1909, 57, 199–200,
    220 n. 8
  Copyright Act of 1976, 55, 57–58, 86,
    205
  Copyright Term Extension Act, 4, 42,
    57–58, 140, 172, 173, 199–200,
    205
  and expansion of copyright holder rights,
    55, 79–80
  Statute of Anne of 1709, 84, 149
  as successful rent-seeking, 182, 184–185
  See also compulsory license, Digital
    Millennium Copyright Act
    (DMCA)
copyright licensing
  and market failure, 21–22, 26–27,
    141–144
  standard, mass-market contracts, 70–71
  and transaction costs, 141–144
  unlikelihood of individualized price
    discrimination in, 157–158
Copyright Office, 142, 205–207
copyright's speech burdens, 6, 13, 109–153
  artistic expression, 19–23
  Blackstonian copyright will not
    ameliorate, 154–168
  biography, 112
  censorial speech burden, 111–116
  copyright as speech regulation, 118–120

fair use (*continued*)
  and parody, 19
  property-centered ruling in *Harper & Row* case, 63–64, 191
  property-centered versus First Amendment approach to, 65–66, 191
  and transformative purpose, 192
  under the DMCA, 69, 186
false endorsement, 51–52
fan fiction, 8, 9, 40, 73, 135
Federal Communications Commission (FCC), 36, 118, 138, 150
Feist Publications v. Rural Telephone, 61
Felton, Edward, 4, 7
file trading, 5, 9
  as falling outside "speech," 44–46, 207
  and free speech policy, 207–210
  instrumental value for free speech, 46–48, 207–208
First Amendment, 4, 6, 169
  compelled speech, 50–51, 176
  content-based speech regulation, 117, 174
  content-neutral speech regulation, 117–118, 174–175
  copyright and, 169–194
  and copyright's free speech benefits, 179–189
  and defamation, 171
  and DMCA anticircumvention provisions, 185–190
  doctrine as distinct from policies, principles, and values, 34–35, 173
  general conduct versus speech regulation, 117
  and government motive, 227–228 n. 34
  immunity of copyright from scrutiny under, 170, 172
  and the inadequacy of copyright's free speech safeguards, 170, 180–181, 193
  and legislation as rent distribution, 182–185
  level of scrutiny applicable to copyright, 262–263 n. 9
  limitations on proprietary and personal rights, 170–171, 181
  protection of artistic expression, 32
  "the right to make other people's speech," 42, 176–177

the right to use particular words, 181
rights of listeners as well as speakers, 47
trumps enumerated powers, 178
values 5–6, 10
See also expressive diversity, freedom of speech
Folsom v. Marsh, 62–63
Forsythe, Tom, 4, 65
Free Republic, 18, 73, 134
freedom of speech, 10
  and author's creative control, 48–53
  "free speech easements," 118–19
  and government media and communications policy, 36–37
  potential dangers of government subsidy and patronage, 89–92, 99–101
  scope of, 31–34, 44–46
  theories of, 31–32, 118–119
  and using others' expression, 42–44, 144
See also expressive diversity, First Amendment, system of free expression

Ginsburg, Jane, 74, 88
Ginsburg, Ruth Bader, 176
Goldstein, Paul, 154
Gomery, Douglas, 148
Gone with the Wind. See Margaret Mitchell
  See also Suntrust Bank v. Houghton Mifflin
Google, 22–23, 56, 115, 150–151
  Google Book Search Project, 5, 23–27, 65, 143, 152, 191, 203, 210–212
  Google News, 27–28, 212–213
Greenawalt, Kent, 45

Hand, Learned, 59, 61, 104
Harper & Row v. The Nation, 63–64, 83, 84, 217
Heller, Michael, 143
hip-hop music, 19–23, 60
Holmes, Oliver Wendell, 72
Houghton Mifflin, 14
Hughes, Justin, 49
Hurley v. Irish-Am Gay, Lesbian and Bisexual Group, 176–177

Internet
  and decentralized communication, 43
  as eroding traditional copyright markets, 56

and personal uses of copyrighted
materials, 73
role in drastically reducing cost of content
distribution, 76, 86, 152
See also: digital technology, peer
communication online

Jefferson, Thomas, 106

Kant, Immanuel, 52–53
King, Martin Luther, Jr., 5, 6, 42, 107

Landes, William, 126, 159, 200–201,
203–205
Lemley, Mark, 180, 201
Lessig, Larry, 66
Litman, Jessica, 107, 215
Los Angeles Times, 18

Madison, James, 54, 91–92
Marclay, Christian, 177
marginal versus average cost pricing,
124–126
market power, 130, 164–165
markets for original expression
concentration of, 131–132, 144–145
demand diversion and clustering,
162–165
and economic rents, 138–140
experience goods, 133
impact of digital technology, 152
marketing costs, 138–139
and need for "normal profits," 127
price discrimination in, 155–158
and risk of failure, 126, 135–137
solidarity and associative goods, 133–134
winner-take-all character of, 132–135,
165
Markie, Biz, 21,109
Mattel Inc., 4, 112, 146
Mattel Inc. v. Walking Mountain Productions,
65
McCullagh, Declan, 17, 69
McGowan, David, 49, 158
Media and communications policy
and cheap access to information, 47
copyright law as integral to, 37–38, 120
"free speech easements," 118–19
as part of our system of free expression,
36–37

Meiklejohn, Alexander, 32
MGM Studios v. Grokster, 78–79
Mitchell, Margaret, 3–4, 6, 7, 8, 41, 48,
50–51
Moore, Michael, 48–49, 50
moral rights, 53, 215–217
multiple taker problem, 198
MySpace, 8, 9–10, 46, 73–74

NBC Universal (and affiliates), 9, 10, 145,
148, 150
new media, 75–80, 150–151
News Corp., 10, 145, 150
New York Times, 4, 5, 17, 71, 98, 103
Nimmer, David, 57, 61
Nimmer, Melville, 4

orphan works, 142, 205–207

Paine, Thomas, 91
paracopyright, 66–71, 156, 186, 213–215
Patry, William, 113, 184
peer discussion online
as contributing to expressive diversity,
40–41, 94–95
not a substitute for the institutional press,
95–99
as undermining copyright's incentive
rationale, 86–88
See also fan fiction, Free Republic
personal uses of copyrighted material,
72–75
Posner, Richard, 113, 126, 159, 193,
200–201, 203–205

Randall, Alice, 3–4, 6, 7, 40, 41, 42, 50–51,
109, 112, 134–135, 158–160, 177,
181
Recording Industry Ass'n of America,
249 n. 38
remix culture, 9, 44
Rubenfeld, Jed, 196–198, 215

sampling, 20–21
Schauer, Frederick, 45, 243 n. 1
Shakespeare, William, 159, 160, 204
Shocklee, Hank, 222 n. 17
Shriffin, Steven, 40
Smith, Adam, 237 n. 7
Sony v. Universal Studios, 78–79, 150